PROJECT MANAGEMENT:
METHODS AND STUDIES

Studies in Management Science and Systems

Editor

Burton V. Dean

Department of Operations Research
Case Western Reserve University
Cleveland

VOLUME 11

NORTH-HOLLAND
AMSTERDAM · NEW YORK · OXFORD

Project Management: Methods and Studies

Edited by

Burton V. DEAN

Department of Operations Research
Weatherhead School of Management
Case Western Reserve University
Cleveland, Ohio, U.S.A.

and

Department of Industrial Engineering and Engineering Management
Stanford University
Stanford, California, U.S.A.

1985

NORTH-HOLLAND
AMSTERDAM · NEW YORK · OXFORD

658.404
P964

ISBN: 0 444 87742 8

Published by:
Elsevier Science Publishers B.V.
P.O. Box 1991
1000 BZ Amsterdam
The Netherlands

Sole distributors for the U.S.A. and Canada:
Elsevier Science Publishing Company, Inc.
52 Vanderbilt Avenue
New York, N.Y. 10017
U.S.A.

Library of Congress Cataloging in Publication Data

Main entry under title:

Project management.

   (Studies in management science and systems ; v. 11)
   1. Industrial project management--Addresses, essays,
lectures. I. Dean, Burton Victor, 1924-
II. Series.
HD69.P75P74 1985   658.4'04   85-4500
ISBN 0-444-87742-8 (U.S.)

Printed in The Netherlands

PREFACE

The subject matter of this book, project management, was developed during World War II and was subsequently extended in the major military and aerospace projects that were undertaken at that time. However, the roots of project management go back thousands of years to the Great Pyramids of Egypt. The Egyptians, with great success, had organized their pyramid-building projects into five different stages:

(1) Planning the building, and surveying the site of the pyramid,

(2) Quarrying the stones,

(3) Shaping and carving the stones,

(4) Transporting the stones by land and water, and

(5) Building the actual pyramid [1].

Although we do not yet understand all of the scientific and engineering principles used by the ancient Egyptians to build the pyramids, we do have some understanding of the management methods and techniques used to manage these large, complex projects that have survived to this day [1].

The bar chart representing a modern method in project management was developed by Gantt in World War I. Subsequently, it was extended by Adamiecke to a network-based planning procedure [2] and rediscovered in the U. S. in the 1950's as CPM [3] and PERT [4], and in Great Britain [5]. Today, network-based planning methods for use in project management exist in a wide variety of forms and details [6].

During the 1960's and subsequently, many project management books and other publications have appeared, addressing a spectrum of topics for managers who need overall concepts to detailed quantitative analyses of individual methods and techniques of interest to management scientists. Increasingly, books have been published for use in colleges and universities as texts in courses for engineers and managers [7].

This book is addressed to three types of readers:

(1) To those functional managers and executives who are required to execute or support projects,

(2) To graduate students who need to understand the contributions of management science and practice to the modern theory of project management, and

(3) To management scientists who wish to contribute to the science of project management.

This book is concerned with both managerial problems and quantitative methods as they affect project management. In those chapters where the primary focus is on the management problem, relevant advances in methods are also included. Correspondingly, where a chapter is concerned with the development or extension of a method in project management, managerial implications are also discussed. For example, an interesting development presented in this book is the use of the network planning method as a project scheduling tool (Chapter 5) and also as a means to build project teams that are oriented toward achieving organizational goals (Chapter 10). In general, extensive mathematical treatments are minimized with sufficient references provided wherever needed.

In the four chapters of Part I, advances in project evaluation and selection methods are presented. Chapters 5 and 8 of Part II deal with recent advances and extensions of the classical network-based planning methods of project scheduling and control. Part III contains Chapters 9 through 12 dealing with a variety of topics in managing human resources associated with project planning and performance. Part IV is concerned with five chapters covering a variety of cases and examples of project management methodology and concludes with a chapter dealing with an extensive survey of recent developments in management science as applied to project management.

Grateful acknowledgement is given to all of the chapter authors and to the many referees who are cited in the book. To my graduate students and advisees I would like to thank them for their valuable comments and suggestions. To my secretary, Rea Flynn, I owe many thanks for her maintaining the necessary organization for completing this project and for typing the final manuscript. I thank my wife, Barbara Dean, for her encouragement and cooperation during the period in which this book project was performed.

Burton V. Dean
Case Western Reserve
University

Cleveland, Ohio U.S.A.
January 1985

[1] Weeks, J., The Pyramids, Cambridge University Press, University of Cambridge, Great Britain, 1971.

[2] Adamiecki, K., "Harmonygraph," Przeglad Organizacji (Polish Journal on Organizational Review), 1931.

[3] Walker, M. R. and J. S. Sayer, "Project Planning and Scheduling," Report 6959, E. I. DuPont de Nemours and Co., Wilmington, Delaware, March 1959.

[4] Malcolm, D. G., J. H. Roseboom, C. E. Clark, and W. Fazar, "Applications of a Technique for R and D Program Evaluation," (PERT) Operations Research, Vol. 7, No. 5, 1959, pp. 646-669.

[5] Lockyer, K. G., Introduction to Critical Path Analysis, Pitman Publishing Company, 3rd Edition, 1969, Chapter 1.

[6] Dean, B. V., "Network Planning Methods," Encyclopedia of Professional Management, McGraw-Hill Book Company, 1978.

[7] Moder, J. J., C. R. Phillips, and E. W. Davis, Project Management With CPM, PERT, and Precedence Diagramming, Van Nostrand Reinhold Company, 3rd Edition, 1983.

TABLE OF CONTENTS

LIST OF CONTRIBUTORS

The Editor is pleased to acknowledge his appreciation to the authors of the papers presented in this volume. Their individual contributions represent a range of interests and viewpoints.

R. Balachandra

College of Business Administration
Northeastern University
Boston, Massachusetts 02115

Joerg Boysen

Consilium Associates
Palo Alto, California

Keith C. Crandall

Department of Civil Engineering
University of California at Berkeley
Berkeley, California 94704

Burton V. Dean

Department of Operations Research
Weatherhead School of Management
Case Western Reserve University
Cleveland, Ohio 44106

James R. Evans

College of Business Administration
University of Cincinnati
Cincinnati, Ohio 45221

Leslie Finkel

35265 Unit B
North Turtle Trail
Willoughby, Ohio 44094

Tony Gear

Trent Polytechnic
Burton Street
Nottingham NG1 4BU
England

Martin E. Ginn

Stuart School of Business
Illinois Institute of Technology
Chicago, Illinois 60616

Robert J. Graham

Management and Behavioral Science Center
The Wharton School
University of Pennsylvania
Philadelphia, Pennsylvania 19104

Sushil K. Gupta

Department of Decision Sciences
Florida International University
Miami, Florida 33199

William R. King

Graduate School of Business
University of Pittsburgh
Pittsburgh, Pennsylvania 15213

Robert C. Leachman

Operations Research Center
University of California, Berkeley
Berkeley, California 94720

Sang M. Lee

Department of Management
University of Nebraska
Lincoln, Nebraska 68588

Matthew J. Liberatore

Department of Management
College of Commerce and Finance
Villanova University
Villanova, Pennsylvania 19085

Geoff Lockett

Manchester Business School
University of Manchester
Manchester M15 6PB England

Gregory R. Madey

Goodyear Aerospace Corporation
Akron, Ohio 44315

Samuel J. Mantel, Jr.

Department of Quantitative Analysis
School of Business Administration
University of Cincinnati
Cincinnati, Ohio 45221

George M. Marko

Gilbane Building Company
2000 East Ninth Street
Cleveland, Ohio 44114

Joseph J. Moder

Department of Management Science and
 Computer Information Systems
University of Miami
Coral Gables, Florida 33124

David L. Olson

College of Business Administration
Texas A&M University
College Station, Texas 77840

John C. Papageorgiou

Department of Management Sciences
University of Massachusetts
Boston, Massachusetts 02125

Albert H. Rubenstein

Department of Industrial Engineering and
 Management Sciences
Northwestern University
Evanston, Illinois 60201

Barry G. Silverman

Engineering Administration and Institute for
 Artificial Intelligence
The George Washington University
Washington, D. C. 20037

Larry R. Taube

Department of Business Administration
University of North Carolina at Greensboro
Greensboro, North Carolina 27412

Vijay A. Tipnis

Tipnis Associates, Inc.
Cincinnati, Ohio

George J. Titus

Department of Management
School of Business Administration
Temple University
Philadelphia, Pennsylvania 19122

Jerome D. Wiest

College of Business
University of Utah
Salt Lake City, Utah 84112

INTRODUCTION

Burton V. Dean
Weatherhead School of Management
Case Western Reserve University
Cleveland, Ohio U.S.A.

Executives will face increasingly complex challenges in the future. Almost all of today's executives agree that the solution to organizational problems involves obtaining better control and use of the existing resources, as well as planning for the acquisition and management of new resources. Project management is one of the techniques now in widespread use in many organizations and countries throughout the world.

Project management has emerged as a specialized area of management to meet the needs of organizations to accomplish specific objectives and goals under conditions of complexity and risk taking.

Projects have been in existence since the earliest times of our society, as for example, the Great Pyramids of Egypt and the Great Wall of China. In current times such projects as the Manhattan Project, and Lunar Project, and the Fifth Generation Computer Project have drawn the attention of both researchers and managers to the importance of project management. However, only recently has project management been recognized as a distinct area of its own, with a methodology and structure susceptible to practice and research.

The project management approach is characterized by newly developed methods and techniques that are continually advancing and evolving as a result of ongoing research. Methods of project management have been investigated by many researchers in such scientific disciplines as operations research, economics, social and behavioral sciences, finance and accounting, and engineering. Project management literature on methodology and applications is scattered in many books and journals. Project management methods and courses are taught in both business and engineering schools in colleges and universities.

In this book, project management consists of those activities associated with the planning, organizing, directing, and controlling of organizational resources for a relatively short-term objective that has been established to complete specific goals and objectives within a specified time period. In this context, the resources to be utilized include one or more of the following categories - monetary, manpower, equipment, facilities, materials, and information/technology. The book is concerned with a careful review and analysis of those methods that have proven to be useful in organizations. The methods and studies illustrated in this book show the power of the project management approach in solving a wide variety of organizational problems.

It is quite clear that project management will be of critical importance in the future. Increasingly, projects are growing more complex, involving multiple resources, organizations, and payoffs. In particular, technology oriented projects are presenting new and diverse management problems, economic opportunities, and risks in both newly formed and established enterprises. Projects are constrained by conflicting objectives of owners, financiers, project executives, federal, state, and local regulations, and ecological and societal environments. Also, project cost and time overruns, economic volatility, and intense competition result in difficult project management problems in many organizations.

Organizations are continually seeking ways to make projects more effective and efficient. In many cases, the survival and growth of these organizations depend on the organization's ability to plan, organize, direct, schedule, and control its projects. In many colleges and universities, project management is an important subject for both education and research activities.

The essential rationale for this book are the following concepts:

(1) A project is a systematic way of accomplishing an organization's objectives,

(2) Project management involves specialized knowledge beyond that normally characterized by functional or general management principles,

(3) The knowledge and understanding associated with project management is not generally available in a single central source, or when such is available, it is usually of a specialized form,

(4) A large range of research approaches and disciplines are involved in project management, and

(5) The methods and technology of project management are changing due to developments in the supporting disciplines and computer applications.

The purpose of this book is to stimulate interest on the part of both managers and management scientists in project management. This is accomplished by presenting the results of recent developments in methods and studies in project management and related areas.

The book was developed on the basis of a call for papers. Over 70 abstracts were received, of which approximately 30 manuscripts were solicited. The 17 revised papers that are published in this volume represent those manuscripts that were accepted by the referees and the editor.

The book is divided into four parts. Part I presents four chapters on project evaluation and selection. Part II presents four chapters on project scheduling and control. Part III presents four chapters on the management of human resources in projects. Part IV presents five specific studies on project management and a state-of-the-art survey of recent research on project management.

It is my hope that the methods and studies presented in this book, along with the references that are described herein, result in future research and findings on project management. It is also anticipated that future improvements will result in the way organizations manage projects.

This book is dedicated to the six other Deans who contributed in many ways to the performance of this project.

Part I
PROJECT EVALUATION AND SELECTION

Project Management: Methods and Studies
Burton V. Dean (editor)
© Elsevier Science Publishers B.V. (North-Holland), 1985

3

THE STRATEGIC EVALUATION OF PROJECTS AND PROGRAMS

William R. King

Graduate School of Business
University of Pittsburgh
Pittsburgh, Pennsylvania
U.S.A.

The void that exists between strategy formulation and strategy implementation, which is the province of strategic program evaluation (SPE), is described. Existing project selection models that might be adopted to the strategy implementation domain do not deal with such complexities as multidimensional strategies, nonquantifiable objectives and heterogeneous programs--all of which are inherent at the level of organizational strategy.

Criteria are developed for prescribing an SPE model that will be appropriate for overcoming the inadequacies and deficiencies that are found to exist when one attempts to apply existing project selection models at the strategic organizational level. Such an SPE model must involve the inherent interdependencies that exist among the various elements of strategic choice--the mission, objectives, strategy, goals and strategic programs of the organization.

An SPE model of this variety is illustrated at both the corporate and business unit levels. While no generic SPE model that is suitable for all organizations can be prescribed, the illustrative example, along with the prescriptive criteria, should provide a basis for selecting and adapting project selection models to the level of organizational strategic programs.

INTRODUCTION

Strategic programs and projects are the vehicles through which an organization's strategy is operationalized. In effect, the development and a prior evaluation of strategic programs represents the link between the organization's strategic management and the resource allocation process that Anthony (1965) termed its "management control" function.

This "linking pin" has not been well developed in the literature or practice of strategic management or of project selection. In strategic management, "strategy implementation" has been given far less attention than that devoted to strategy formulation and strategy evaluation (Grant and King (1979, 1982)). Although the term "strategy implementation" has recently become popular in strategic management, the area is often interpreted to mean little more than a set of skills that need to be developed by the operating manager (Vancil (1983)) rather than a phase of strategic management that can be supported by decision support models and systems.

In its most fulsome context, strategy implementation is viewed as a rather nebulous process involving the consideration of appropriate organizational structure, individual responsibilities, "culture," and controls (Roush and Ball (1980)). The use of formal models and systems for ensuring the appropriate implementation of strategy is only beginning to be developed (Naylor (1983)).

On the other hand, the literature and practice of project selection and evaluation is replete with models and techniques—most of which do not give explicit consideration to <u>strategic organizational issues</u> (Souder (1983), Baker and Freedland (1975)).

For instance, many project screening and evaluation models have focused on efficiency-oriented technical criteria such as reliability, maintainability, safety, etc. (Moore and Baker (1969), Souder (1983)). This use of a set of readily understandable, comprehensive, and presumably orthognal criteria is meaningful when all of the projects and programs to be evaluated are relatively homogeneous, such as might be the case in R&D project selection. However, when the context is at the strategic corporate or business unit level, such homogeneity does not exist. In that context the criteria must be capable of effectively comparing new product options, market opportunities, acquisitions, divestments and a wide range of other programs.

Other project selection models focus on simple financial criteria such as return on investment or some other economic index (Ansoff (1962), Villers (1964), Dean (1970), and Souder (1983)). While such models overcome some of the difficulties associated with those that focus on efficiency measures rather than effectiveness measures (Cleland and King (1983)), they reduce a broad range of organizational objectives to a single economic index. This is an insufficiently rich basis for the effective support of strategic decision making. Most businesses and corporations do not have such a simple strategy that they can effectively use such a single simple measure in decision making, however useful it may be as a "scorekeeping" measure. The typical organization has an array of objectives (Granger (1964)), some of which are readily quantifiable and some of which defy easy quantification. For an evalaution model to be useful at this level, it must take account of this diversity.

Moreover, most existing project selection models of both variety make the implicit or explicit assumption that a good "fit" or "match" between a proposed program and the organization is desired. This may often be true, but a valid <u>strategic</u> evaluation procedure must account for the fact that at the strategy level—as clearly distinct from other levels such as R&D project evaluation—there may be a need to highly value opportunities that may be quite different than those which "fit" well (Grant and King (1982), Schendel and Hofter (1979)).

This latter consideration reflects the essence of strategic management, which may simplistically be thought of as the "mangement of change" or "the management of those elements of the organization that do not currently exist" (King and Cleland (1978)). As such, at this level, as distinct from other levels, there is a pressing need for a model to account for the specific strategy that the organization is proposing to follow—even when it may radically change the organization and those things that are perceived to "fit" it—as well as its possibly diverse set of objectives.

Despite the wide range of available project selection models and techniques, there is therefore clearly a void between the strategic management level of the organization and the implementation level as it relates to strategic projects and programs. Of course, one might superficially argue that this void might be readily filled by using existing models with the appropriate "strategic" criteria inserted in place of the more traditional ones. To some degree this is true—except that the nature of the model that is appropriate for these strategic criteria need first be carefully specified. All models that are appropriate at the tactical level will not be appropriate at the strategic level.

Moreover, the simplistic notion of using existing models that have merely been altered through the insertion of "strategic" criteria in place of the traditional "tactical" criteria does not take account of the richness and interdependence of the elements of strategic management. The organization's mission, objectives, strategies and goals are generally so complex and interdependent as to defy description in the straightforward fashion that is implied by this approach.

This paper is therefore directed toward the description of an appropriate model for strategic program evaluation. This model is described in the context of examples since it cannot be more generally prescribed. However, the descriptions--one at the business unit level and one at the corporate level--are adequate to stimulate the development of analogies that will be appropriate in specific companies and businesses.

However, if these descriptions are to be more than unique examples, they must be supported by a number of elements.   The introductory sections of the chapter therefore deal with:

    (1) Criteria for the Specification of an Appropriate Strategic Evaluation Model
    (2) Organizational Strategic Choice Elements and their Inter-Relationships
    (3) Relationships Among Business Unit and Corporate Strategic Choice Elements

Once these three foundations have been developed, the illustrative strategic program evaluation (SPE) model can be presented. As well, with the understandings that are inherent in these three foundations, the adaptation of the illustrative model to other organizational contexts is straightforward.

CRITERIA FOR THE SPECIFICATION OF AN APPROPRIATE STRATEGIC EVALUATION MODEL

The criteria that are implied by the previously-described void between strategic management and project selection and the deficiencies in existing models are that a strategic program evalaution (SPE) model should:

    (1) explicitly incorporate all levels of an organization's strategic posture--e.g., ranging from its broad mission to specific goals.
    (2) take cognizance of the wide variety of different kinds of measures that are appropriate for these various elements--e.g., some quantitative and some qualitative.
    (3) be capable of integrating multiple objectives and complex multidimensional strategies.
    (4) give appropriate consideration to the interrelationships among various elements of the overall strategic posture.
    (5) be applicable at either the corporate or business unit level—the two levels at which strategy implementation is most meaningful.
    (6) be based on strategic constructs that reflect existing theory so that the multiple project evaluation criteria may be assumed to be "orthogonal."
    (7) be capable of facilitating the comparison of a heterogeneous set of proposed strategic programs.

GENERIC STRATEGIC CHOICE ELEMENTS

Because of the semantics jungle that exists in the area of business strategy,[1] it is necessary to rather precisely define the choice elements of strategy--those specific choices that must be explicitly or implicitly made in the strategic planning process:

    Mission - the "business" that the organization is in.
    Objectives - desired future positions on roles for the organization.
    Strategy - the general direction in which the objectives are to be pursued.
    Goals - specific targets to be sought at specified points in time.
    Programs/Projects - resource-consuming sets of activities through which strategies
                         are implemented and goals are pursued.
    Resource Allocations - allocations of funds, manpower, etc., to various units,
                         objectives, strategies, programs and projects.

These informal definitions are meant to provide a common framework for communication rather than to define the "correct" terminology. Various organizations may use different terminology, but none can escape the need to make choices of each variety (King and Cleland (1978)).

Most organizations conduct strategic planning processes that are aimed at explicitly choosing all or some of these strategic choice elements. However, many do not deal with each of the choice elements explicitly and in detail.

Often, for instance, missions are dealt with implicitly, as in the case of the firm that responds to the mission concept by stating their mission to be, "We make widgets." Such a product-oriented view of the organization's business ignores new market opportunities and strengths which form the most likely areas for future success. Thus, it is these opportunities and strengths, rather than the current product line, that should define the mission.

Strategies are usually chosen more explicitly, but often strategies are thought of in output rather than input, terms. In such instances, strategies may be described in terms of expected sales and profits rather than in terms of strategic directions such as product redesign, new products or new markets.

Thus, the elements of strategic choice are inescapable in the sense that the avoidance of an explicit choice about any of the elements means that it is chosen implicity. However, many firms make poor or inappropriate choices, both explicitly and implicitly, because they do not have a clear awareness of the relationships among the strategic choice elements and their innate interdependence.

RELATIONSHIPS AMONG THE STRATEGIC CHOICE ELEMENTS

One of the most important conditions for the effective operationalizing and implementation of strategy has to do with the relationships among the strategic choice clements. If these relationships are well defined, carefully analyzed and conceived, the strategic plan is likely to be made operational implemented. If they are not, the plan is likely to be a voluminous document that requires substantial time and energy to prepare, but which is filed on the shelf until the next planning cycle commences. Indeed, many plans are so treated precisely because they do not carefully spell out the relationships among various strategic choice elements and therefore do not provide the appropriate information that is necessary to guide the many decisions which must be made to implement the plan and to develop, evaluate and select the projects and programs which will become the operational essence of the strategic plan.

Figure 1 shows the elements of strategic choice in the form of a triangle which illustrates that the mission and objectives are the highest level elements. They are supported by the other elements--the strategies, goals, programs and projects. The strategic resource allocations underlie each of these elements.

Figure 2 shows an illustration of these concepts in terms of a business unit. The mission chosen is that of "supplying system components to a world-wide non-residential air conditioning market." Note that while this mission statement superficially appears to be product-oriented, it identifies the nature of the product (system components), and the market (world-wide non-residential air conditioning) quite specifically. By exclusion, it guides managers in avoiding proposals for the development of overall systems and strategies that would be directed toward residential markets. However, it does identify "the world" as the company's territory and (in an elaboration not shown here) defines air conditioning to include "air heating, cooling, cleaning, humidity control and movement."

The business unit's objectives involve increasing ROI to a 15% level and improving the business' image of being socially conscious. Like most objectives at this level, these are stated in broad and timeless terms.

Supporting the base of the triangle are strategies, goals, and programs. The business unit's strategies are stated in terms of a three-phase approach. First, the company will concentrate on achieving its objectives through existing products and markets while maintaining its existing image. Then, it will given attention to new markets for existing products, foreign and restricted, while improving the company's image. ("Restricted" markets may be thought of as those that require product-safety certification before the product can be sold in that market.) Finally, it will focus on new products in existing markets while significantly improving its image.

Clearly, this is a staged strategy; one that focuses attention first on one thing and then on

Figure 1 Relationship Between Strategic Choice Elements

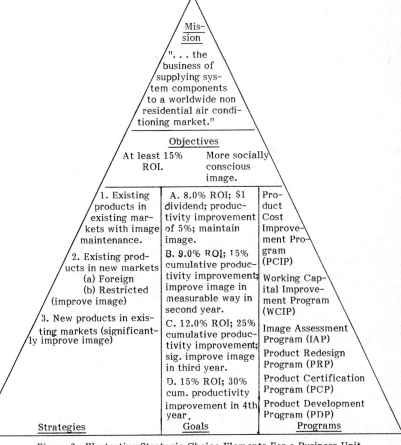

Figure 2 Illustrative Strategic Choice Elements For a Business Unit.

another. This staging does not imply that the first strategy element is carried through completely before the second is begun; it merely means that the first element is given primary
and earliest attention, then the second and third in turn. In effect, the first element of the
strategy has its implementation begun first. This will be made more clear in terms of goals
and programs.

At the right base of the triangle, a number of the firm's programs are identified. Each of
these programs is made up of a variety of projects or activities. Each program serves as a
focus for various activities having a common goal. For instance, in the case of the
Product Cost Improvement Program, the associated projects and activities might be

> Quality Control Project
> Production Planning Improvement Project
> Production Control System Development Project
> Plant Layout Redesign Project
> Employee Relations Project

All of these projects and activities are focused toward the single goal of product cost
improvement.

In the case of the Working Capital Improvement Program, the various projects and activities
might include a "terms and conditions" study aimed at revising the terms and conditions
under which goods are sold, an inventory reduction project, etc. Each of the other programs
would have a similar collection of projects and activities focused on some single well-
defined goal.

The goals are listed in the middle-lower portion of the triangle in Figure 2. Each goal is
stated in specific and timely terms related to the staged strategy and the various programs.
These goals reflect the desire to attain 8.0% ROI (a step along the way to the 15% objective)
next year, along with a 5% productivity improvement while maintaining the business' image.
For subsequent years, the goals reflect a climb to 15% ROI, a continued productivity
improvement and a measurable improved business image.

Figure 3 shows the same elements as does Figure 2, with each being indicated by number,
letter, or acronym. For instance, the block labeled 1 in Figure 3 represents the first stage of
the strategy in Figure 2, the letter A represents next year's goals, etc.

The arrows in Figure 3 represent some illustrative relationships among the various objectives,
programs, strategy elements, and goals. For instance, the arrows a, b, and c reflect direct
relationships between specific timely goals and broad timeless objectives:

(a) A, next year's goals primarily derive from the ROI objective.
(b) B, the second year's goals begin to relate to the "more socially conscious image"
objective as well as to the ROI objective.
(c) D, the quantitative ROI objective is incorporated as a specific goal in the fourth
year.

Similarly, arrow d in Figure 3 relates the first year's goals to the first element of the overall
strategy in that these goals for next year are to be attained primarily through the strategy
element involving "existing products in existing markets." However, arrows e and f show
that the Product Cost Improvement Program (PCIP) and the Working Capital Improvement
Program (WCIP) are also expected to contribute to the achievement of next year's goals.

The second year's goals will begin to reflect the impact of the second strategy element
(existing products in new markets) as indicated by arrow g in Figure 3. The effect of the
Product Redesign Program (PRP) is also expected to contribute to the achievement of these
goals (arrow i), as is the Image Assessment Program (IAP) expected to provide the ability to
measure image by that time.

From Figure 3, various kinds of relationships among the strategic decision elements can be
readily seen:

1. Goals are specific steps along the way to the accomplishment of broad objectives.
2. Goals are established to reflect the expected outputs from strategies.
3. Goals are directly achieved through programs.
4. Strategies are operationalized by programs and projects.

Thus, the picture shown in Figure 3 is that of an interrelated set of strategic factors that demonstrate both <u>what</u> the business wishes to accomplish in the long run, <u>how</u> it will do this in a sequenced and sensible way, and <u>what performance levels</u> it wishes to achieve at various points along the way.

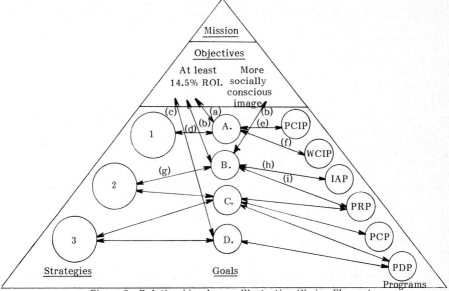

Figure 3   Relationships Among Illustrative Choice Elements.

RELATIONSHIPS AMONG BUSINESS UNIT AND CORPORATE STRATEGIC CHOICE ELEMENTS

In order to develop a model of strategic program evaluation that is appropriate for both the business unit and the corporate level and which, in either instance, is one that gives due consideration to the interdependencies between the two levels, it is useful to delineate the nature of these strategic inter-relationships at the two levels.

Although the generic terms mission, objectives, strategies, goals, programs and resource allocations apply equally well to the business level as to the corporate level, the content of the various choice elements may be quite different. It is easiest to illustrate this by considering the strategic choice elements of a business unit that is defined in product-market terms and those of a diversified corporation that operates many different business units.

In such a case there are a variety of possible relationships between the business units strategic choice elements.

First, some of the business unit's strategic choice elements may represent corporate elements that have been decomposed and allocated to the unit. For instance, a corporate profit objective may be quantitatively apportioned to the various business units, or a unit may simply be directed to follow a "tight ship" strategy during times of economic travail.

Alternately, some of the "real" business unit strategy elements may be in conflict with corporate level strategy. For instance, a business unit's desire for growth may not logically fit into the corporate portfolio of businesses and the corporate-level assessment of the most appropriate role for the unit to play in the corporate portfolio. The uninitiated might believe that while such incongruencies could exist at an initial stage in the planning cycle, they would not exist after business unit strategies have been reviewed and redirected by corporate planning staff. However, in most organizations, the printed plan is not truly a guide to day-to-day or month-to-month actions. Thus, many proposals for capital projects arise from the "real" strategies of the business unit managers rather than from those that are printed in the approved planning documents (Paul, et al. (1978)).

Thus, for example, capital expansion proposals may more reflect the business unit's desire for growth than the role that the business unit is expected to play in the corporate portfolio. This is well-recognized in the case of "cash cow" varieties of business that are run by aggressive growth-oriented managers (Schendel and Hofer (1979)).

The business unit may also have strategy elements that are largely unrelated to the corporate level because the business unit has its own unique situation and stakeholders--suppliers, employee unions, etc.--from which are derived some of its business strategy elements. For instance, a business experiencing product image problems may make this dimension very important, whereas it may be relatively insignificant at the corporate level. As well, many business units have their own constituencies, technologies, regional emphases, etc., that may require strategy elements that are only loosely related to corporate strategy (Emshoff and Freeman (1979)).

The existence of generically distinct varieties of relationships between the corporate-level and business-unit level strategic choice elements dictates the need for formal strategic program evalaution at the corporate level. This may conceptually be done for all proposed programs but can be most practically done for specific classes of programs such as:

(a) those that primarily affect the corporation as an entity (e.g., a corporate "image" program)
(b) those that affect multiple business units (e.g., a joint research program)
(c) those that are "strategic" primarily in the sense of magnitude (e.g., "any program costing over $x")
(d) those that are critical in the sense that they affect elements of the firm that are considered to be critical to its future success (e.g., process technology development program in a firm where low-cost production is seen to be a key to future success) (Bullen and Rockart (1981)).

In a subsequent section, an illustration of such corporate-level strategic program evaluation will be disucssed.

A FRAMEWORK FOR STRATEGIC PROGRAM EVALUATION

Figures 1-3 and the previous section make it clear that the various elements of strategic choice are mutually supportive both within the business unit and the corporation. However, there remains the question of how this high degree of interdependence can be effectively attained.

Certainly, an understanding of the logical relationships that are depicted in these figures should itself lead to better strategic choices. However, while judgement may be appropriately applied at the higher levels of strategic choice, it is an inadequate basis for choice at the lower levels of program/project selection and funding.

In other words, often no formal techniques are needed in choosing among alternative missions and objectives because these choices must inherently be made on a primitive basis of the personal values and goals of management and other stakeholders. At this level, there are only a few viable options from which choices must be made.

At the level of programs, projects and resource allocations, quite the opposite is the case. There are many contenders and combinations of contenders to be considered. Thus, some formal approach may be useful. Indeed, such an approach is not only practically useful, but it forms the integrating factor in the array of strategic choice elements.

The integrating factor is a strategic program evaluation approach which directly utilizes the results of the higher level strategic choices to evaluate alternative programs, projects and funding levels. "Project selection" approaches are well-known and widely used in industry for the selection of engineering projects, R&D projects, and new product development projects. However, if program/project evaluation is to be the key link in unifying the array of organizational strategic choice elements, the evaluation framework must itself be an integral element of the strategic plan.

Figure 4 indicates how an idealized strategic program/project evaluation process can serve as an integrating factor for an array of strategic choices. It shows a wide variety of potential projects and programs being "filtered" through the application of strategic criteria that are based on the higher-level choices that have previously been made—the organization's mission, objectives, and strategies. The ideal output of this filtering process is a set of rank-ordered project and program opportunities that can serve as a basis for the allocation of resources.

Other important strategic criteria must also come into play in implementing this evaluation process. These criteria are those that are implicit in a good specification of the organization's mission, objectives, and strategy. However, they must be specifically addressed if program and projects are to truly reflect corporate strategy. These critiera are:

(1) Does the opportunity take advantage of a strength that the organization possess?
(2) Correspondingly, does it avoid a dependence on something that is a weakness of of the organization?
(3) Does it offer the opportunity to attain a comparative advantage over competitors?
(4) Does it contribute to the internal consistency of the existing projects and programs?
(5) Is the level of risk acceptable?
(6) Is it consistent with established policy guidelines?

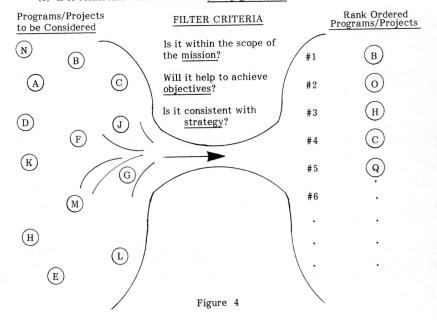

Figure 4

STRATEGIC PROGRAM EVALUATION AT THE BUSINESS UNIT LEVEL

A strategic program/project evaluation approach for business unit application is illustrated in Table 1. In the left-most column of the table is a set of evaluation criteria that directly relates to the example in Figures 2 and 3. The body of the table shows how a proposed new business unit program to begin manufacturing of system components in Europe might be evaluated.

The "criteria weights" in the second column of the table reflect their relative importance and serve to permit the evaluation of complex project characteristics within a simple framework. A base weight of 20 is used here for the major criteria related to mission, objectives, strategy, and goals. Weights of 10 are applied to the other criteria.

Within each major category, the 20 "points" are judgementally distributed to reflect the relative importance of sub-elements or some other characteristic of the criterion. For instance, the three stages of strategy and the four subgoals are weighted to ensure that earlier stages and goals are treated to be more important than later ones. This implicitly reflects the time value of money without requiring a complex discounting calculation.

The first criterion in Table 1 is the "fit with the mission." The proposal is evaluated to be consistent with both the "product" and "market" elements of the mission and is thereby rated to be "very good," as shown in the 1.0 entries in the upper left.

In terms of "consistency with objectives," the proposal is rated to have a 20% chance of being "very good" in contributing to the ROI element of the objectives (see Figure 2), a 60% chance of being "good" and a 20% chance of being only "fair," as indicated by the likelihoods entered into the third row of the table. The proposed project is rated more poorly with respect to "Image" objective.

The proposal is also evaluated in terms of its expected contribution to each of the three stages of the strategy as outlined in Figure 2. In this case, the proposed project is believed to be one which would principally contribute to stage 2 of the strategy. (Note that only certain assessments may be made in this case since the stages are mutually exclusive and exhaustive.)

The proposal is similarly evaluated with respect to the other criteria.

The overall evaluation is obtained as a weighted score that represents the sum of products of the likelihoods (probabilities) and the 8, 6, 4, 2, 0 arbitrary level weights that are displayed at the top of the table. For instance, the "consistency with objectives-ROI" expected level weight is calculated as

$$0.2(8) + 0.6(6) + 0.2(4) = 6.0$$

This is then multiplied by the criterion weight of 10 to obtain a weighted score of 60. The weighted scores are then summed to obtain an overall evaluation of 608.

Of course, this number in isolation is meaningless. However, when various programs and projects are evaluated in terms of the same criteria, their overall scores provide a reasonable basis for developing the ranking shown on the right side of Figure 4.

STRATEGIC PROGRAM EVALUATION AT THE CORPORATE LEVEL

At the corporate level, the primary difference in the SPE approach is in terms of the criteria used. Since there is no need to repeat the mechanics of the procedure demonstrated in Table 1, we shall focus here on illustrations of criteria that might be used at the corporate level. These criteria would be listed down the left side of a matrix such as Table 1 and used in the same fashion as the business unit criteria were used there.

There is usually not a direct corporate analogy to the business unit criterion of "fit with the mission," particularly in the case of a diversified company such as is the best illustration of

Program/Project Evaluation Criteria		Criteria Weights	Very Good (8)	Good (6)	Fair (4)	Poor (2)	Very Poor (0)	Expected Level Score	Weighted Score
"Fit" with Mission	Product	10	1.0					8.0	80
	Market	10	1.0					8.0	80
Consistency with Objectives	ROI	10	0.2	0.6	0.2			6.0	60
	Image	10			0.8	0.2		3.6	36
Consistency with Strategy	Stage 1	10					1.0	0	0
	Stage 2	7	1.0					8.0	56
	Stage 3	3					1.0	0	0
Contribution to Goals	Goal A	8					1.0	0	0
	Goal B	6	0.8	0.2				7.6	45.6
	Goal C	4		0.8	0.2			5.6	22.4
	Goal D	2					1.0	0	0
Corporate Strength Base		10				0.8	0.2	1.6	16
Corporate Weakness Avoidance		10				0.2	0.8	0.4	4
Comparative Advantage Level		10	0.7	0.3				7.4	74
Internal Consistency Level		10	1.0					8.0	80
Risk Level Acceptability		10				0.7	0.3	1.4	14
Policy Guideline Consistency		10			1.0			4.0	40

Total Score　608

Table 1

these ideas. While the corporation has a societal mission, it is generally too broad and general to form a basis for the evaluation of specific programs. Thus, at this level, the issue is generally that of consistency with policy guidelines regarding the corporation's chosen role--e.g., concerning social responsibility. This may be dealt with in a criterion that is analogous to the general "consistency with corporate guidelines" criterion that was used in the business-level analysis.

The notions of consistency with objectives and goals are similar at the two levels. However, at the corporate level, except for those things just discussed, the objectives and goals may be less diverse than at the business-unit level--often having to do primarily with financial measures such as earnings per share.

The "consistency with strategy" criterion at the business unit level has an analogy at the corporate level in terms of the portfolio of businesses that are planned for the corporation. Basically, the issue is whether the proposed program or project will contribute to the overall portfolio plan (e.g., Grant & King (1982)). If the stream of returns over time that the project produce is consistent with the cash flow balance in the overall portfolio, the proposed project will be evaluated positively; if it is not consistent, the evaluation will be relatively more negative.

The business-unit criteria related to strengths, weaknesses, comparative advantages, and internal consistency have direct analogies at the corporate level if the proposed project is one which transcends a single business unit. Otherwise, these criteria will be applied at the business unit level.

The risk level acceptability is also analogous except that the corporation may be better able to tolerate risk than is the single business unit. On the other hand, the corporation will need to assess whether it has the mechanisms for managing a multi-business unit project, since without such mechanisms, the risk level is amplified. Thus, while the risk criterion is the same at the two levels of analysis, the nature of risk is different. At the business unit level, it is largely external market-related risk that is being judged. At the corporate level, it is a combination of external and internal risk considerations that is important.

SUMMARY

The void between strategic management and strategy implementation is the province of strategic program evaluation (SPE). While it is not possible to prescribe a single SPE model that is appropriate for all organizations, criteria may be developed to guide the selection of such a model.

The criteria relate to the model's ability to incorporate all levels of an organization's strategic posture, its ability to utilize both quantitative and qualitative inputs and to deal with complex multidimensional strategies and objectives. They also include its applicability to both the business unit and the corporate level as well as to a heterogeneous set of program options. As well, the model's basic constructs must be theory-based and it must give appropriate consideration to the inter-relationships of the strategic choice elements.

The inter-relationships among strategic choice elements as well as those between corporate and business-unit strategies form the basis for the SPE model that is illustrated. While it is not feasible to prescribe a generic SPE model, this application, together with the criteria for selection of a model form an appropriate basis for choosing a program evaluation model that will be appropriate at the strategic level of an organization.

Of course, the process within which such a model is used is of great importance, but it is beyond the scope of this paper. It is well to remember, however, that the strategic plans themselves do not evolve from a totally rational process. However, this is a rationale' for the utility of an SPE model such as that presented here, since because the SPE model inherently involves judgement, it is capable of handling inputs that may be more psychological and political than they are rational.

REFERENCES

[1]   Abell, D. F., <u>Defining the Business: The Starting Point of Strategic Planning</u>. Englewood Cliffs, N.J.: Prentice-Hall, 1980.

[2]   Ansoff, H. I., <u>Strategic Management</u>, New York: John Wiley 1979.

[3]   Ansoff, H.I., "Evaluation of Applied Research in a Business Firm," <u>Technical Planning on the Corporate Level</u>, J. R. Bright (ed.) Harvard University Press, 1962.

[4]   Anthony, R. N., <u>Planning and Control Systems: A Framework for Analysis</u>, Harvard Business School, Division of Research, 1965.

[5]   Baker, N. R. and Freeland, J., "Recent Advances in R&D Benefit Measurement and Project Selection Methods," <u>Management Science</u>, Vol. 21, No. 10, 1975, pp. 1164-1175.

[6]   Bullen, C. V. and J. F. Rockart, "A Primer on Critical Success Factors," Sloan School of Management, Working Paper #1220-81, Massachusetts Institute of Technology, June 1981.

[7]   Cleland, D. I. and W. R. King (eds.), <u>Project Management Handbook</u>, Van Nostrand Reinhold, 1983.

[8]   Cleland, D. I. and W. R. King, <u>Systems Analysis and Project Management</u> (3rd Edition) McGraw-Hill, 1983.

[9]   Dean, B. V., <u>Project Evaluation: Methods and Procedures</u>, New York American Management Association, 1970.

[10] Emshoff, J. R. and R. E. Freeman, "Who's Butting into Your Business?," <u>The Wharton Magazine</u>, Fall 1979, pp. 44-59.

[11] Granger, C. H., "The Hierarchy of Objectives," <u>Harvard Business Review</u>, May-June 1964.

[12] Grant, J. H. and W. R. King, "Strategy Formulation: Analytical and Normative Models," in Schendel and Hofer (1979), pp. 104-121.

[13] Grant, J. H. and W. R. King, <u>The Logic of Strategic Planning</u>, Little Brown, 1982.

[14] Keeney, R. L. and H. Raiffa, <u>Decisions with Multiple Objectices</u>, John Wiley, New York, 1976.

[15] King, W. R., "Implementing Strategic Plans Through Strategic Program Evaluation," <u>OMEGA</u>, Vol. 8, No. 2, 1980, pp. 173-181.

[16] King, W. R. and D. I. Cleland, <u>Strategic Planning and Policy</u>, Van Nostrand Reinhold, 1978.

[17] Moore, J. R. and N. R. Baker, "An Analytical Approach to Scoring Model Design: Application to Research and Development Project Selection," <u>IEEE Trans. on Eng. Mgt.</u>, EM-16, No. 3, 1969, pp. 90-98.

[18] Naylor, T. H., <u>Corporate Strategy</u>, Volume 8, <u>Studies in Management Sciences and Systems</u>, North-Holland Publishing Company, 1983.

[19] Paul, R. N., N. B. Donavan and J. W. Taylor, "The Reality Gap in Strategic Planning," <u>Harvard Business Review</u>, May-June 1978, pp. 124-130.

[20] Roush, C. H., Jr., and B. C. Ba..., Jr., "Controlling the Implementation of Strategy," <u>Managerial Planning</u>, November-December, 1980.

[21] Saaty, T. L., <u>The Analytic Hierarchy Process</u>, McGraw-Hill, New York, 1980.

[22] Schendel, D. E. and C. W. Hofer (eds.), <u>Strategic Management: A New View of Business Policy and Planning</u>, Little Brown, 1979.

[23] Souder, W. E., "Project Evaluation and Selection," Chapter 10 in Cleland and King (1983a).

[24] Souder, W. E., <u>Management Decision Methods</u>, Van Nostrand Reinhold, New York, 1980.

[25] Vancil, R. F., "Implementing Strategy: The Role of Top Management," Harvard Business School Case Services, #9-983-001, 1983.

[26] Villers, R., <u>Research and Development: Planning and Control</u>, Financial Executives Research Institute, Inc., 1964, pp. 30-38.

[27] Zeleny, M., <u>Multiple Criteria Decision Making</u>, McGraw-Hill, New York, 1982.

-----

[1]The reader should note that some of the terms used here are used in different ways in other literatures. For example, see Zeleny, 1982.

Project Management: Methods and Studies
Burton V. Dean (editor)
© Elsevier Science Publishers B.V. (North-Holland), 1985

A MODEL FOR THE SELECTION OF AN R&D PORTFOLIO WITHIN THE FIRM

Gregory R. Madey

Goodyear Aerospace Corporation
Akron, Ohio
U.S.A.

Burton V. Dean

Case Western Reserve University
Cleveland, Ohio
U.S.A.

This paper describes an R&D portfolio model that was developed and subsequently tested for use within a division of an aerospace firm. The model is used for R&D project evaluation, selection and budgeting. The R&D portfolio model consists of four submodels: (1) a model of the firm's decision makers based on multiattribute utility analysis, (2) a model of the firm's R&D process, (3) a data base model which characterizes prospective R&D projects on multiple economic criteria and (4) an optimization model that selects and budgets a portfolio of R&D projects using multiobjective optimization techniques.

The results in this paper include (1) the application of multiattribute utility theory (MAUT) and multiobjective optimization technique (MOOT) in a complimentary framework and (2) the application of MAUT and MOOT to a real world, moderately large, R&D portfolio selection and budgeting problem (e.g., 40-60 R&D projects).

The model suggests an R&D project portfolio based on the maximization of the expected utility of the portfolio. The model provides a consistent assessment of each project on fifteen strategic planning objectives within the context of the rest of the projects in the portfolio. The suggested R&D portfolio is used by the firm's managers to support the annual strategic planning process and to aid with portfolio revisions throughout the year.

INTRODUCTION

This paper presents a case study on the development and implementation of an R&D portfolio model within a division of an aerospace firm. The R&D portfolio model is used for evaluating, selecting, and budgeting R&D projects for the firm's annual R&D project portfolio and subsequent revisions throughout the year. Multiattribute utility analysis theory (MAUT) and multiobjective optimization techniques (MOOT) are used in a complementary framework.

Background

Prior to the early 1970's, most R&D project selection models described in the literature employed indices, checklists or financial criteria to score projects. The selection process usually involved funding the highest ranked projects in descending order until the R&D budget was completely allocated. R&D portfolio models were developed in the late 1960's that evaluated projects similarly to the scoring models, but made the project selection decision based on the project's contribution to the overall predicted portfolio's performance. Several early approaches are summarized in Gear [11] including (1) linear and integer programming models based on Weingartener's capital budgeting models [39] and (2) decision tree/network models employing linear programming or dynamic programming. Baker and Freeland reviewed the R&D project evaluation and selection literature in the mid-seventies and identified deficiencies, including:

(1)   "inadequate treatment of risk and uncertainty,

(2)   inadequate treatment of multiple, often interrelated criteria,

(3)   no explicit recognition and incorporation of the experience and
       knowledge of the R&D manager,

(4)   the inability to recognize and treat nonmonetary aspects of project
       evaluation and selection, and

(5)   inadequate treatment of the time variant property of data." [1]

Recently, Liberatore and Titus [29], reported the current usage of quantitative techniques for
R&D management. They surveyed 40 respondents from 29 "Fortune 500" industrial firms.
The major findings include a high familiarity and usage of the financial methods of cost/bene-
fit analysis, payback period, and NPV/IRR. Checklists and scoring models rated high in familiarity and relatively high in usage. No mathematical programming based models were being
used. The authors suggest the following possible explanations for the use of simpler approaches but not more sophisticated methods:

(1)   advances in computer technology have not yet been implemented to
       increase the use of quantitative R&D management models,

(2)   many R&D managers are not yet convinced the models offer an
       improvement over their current approaches, and

(3)   many R&D managers feel their R&D management problem is unique
       and not suitable for the application of a general purpose model.

Liberatore and Titus suggest that as the next generation of managers become more computer
literate and as "user friendly" software becomes more available the newer models may gain
wider acceptance.

Several applications of MAUT or MOOT to the problem of R&D and engineering management
have been recently reported. Keefer [19,20,21] used MAUT to address allocating a budget
to several R&D mission areas within a firm. Golabi [13] used decision analysis to support the
development of a solar energy portfolio of 17 projects selected from 77 proposed projects.
Mehrez and Sinuany-Stern [33,34,35] used several variations of a 0-1 interactive integer programming formulation to solve R&D project selection problems based on a MAUT model.

The multiattribute utility approach used in the R&D portfolio model described in this paper
is based on the theory and methods developed and described by Keeney and Raiffa [23],
Fishburn [6,7], Raiffa [37], MacCrimmon [30,31], Keeney [22], Farquhar [4,5], Huber [15],
French [9,10], and Fischer [8]. The multiobjective optimization techniques used in the design
of the model described in this paper are based on the theory and methods described in Zeleny
[43], Goicoechea [12], Chankong and Haimes [3], French [10], Starr and Zeleny [38], Hwang
and Yoon [17], and Hwang and Masud [16]. The integer multiobjective optimization procedures used are based on the theory and methods described in Zionts [44], Koksalan et al.
[24], White [40], and Lee [27,28].

The R&D Decision Problem

The R&D organization for which the R&D portfolio model of this paper was designed partici-
pates in the U. S. aerospace marketplace. The main business includes contract R&D leading
to products and services for transportation, energy and defense. The primary customers are
agencies of the federal government, either directly or indirectly through other aerospace
firms.

The firm usually obtains new R&D contracts by means of competitive bidding. Occasionally
the firm may generate a unique proprietary idea for a product or service and submit an unso-
licited proposal, but usually the customer issues a request for proposal (RFP) for research and

development of a specific product or service and multiple firms respond with a bid and proposal. The contracts the firm competes for are almost exclusively for unique high technology products or services. Typically the RFP defines a functional requirement that must be satisfied. The competing firms propose a technical solution, defend its merits, describe a plan and submit a proposal and bid. The firm with the winning proposal typically receives an R&D contract and often becomes the sole source for that product or service. For a high technology product, the initial contract could be for a design, development, testing and evaluation effort. If the development is successful and the product continues to meet current or anticipated needs, the same firm usually receives contracts for production as well as support of the product after production. Recently, variations of this procurement process have been introduced which maintain competition after the initial contract to control costs, but sole source procurement, after an initial competition, is still the dominant procurement approach.

While the bulk of the firm's sales and profits are derived from production, this work is usually obtained by way of the competition for initial design, development, testing and evaluation. To win on this competition, the firm must have prepositioned an engineering development team capable of providing design ideas, analysis, prototype production and testing of the product. At the time of the issue of the RFP, this development team must have ready the ideas for a proposed solution to the government's requirement and sufficient analysis to support the ideas' merits. Typically the due date for a response to a RFP only leaves time for the proposal writing. The idea generation and supporting analysis must have already been completed. Thus, the firm must identify product technologies it expects to be required for future proposals and allocate R&D resources toward developing those technologies to enhance its chances of winning future R&D contracts. The firm conducts two types of R&D. One type is funded under the government contracts that it has obtained through successful proposals. The other type of R&D helps win the contracts and goes under one of two names, depending on whether it is conducted before or during a proposal writing effort. The respective names are (1) Internal Research and Development (IR&D) and (2) Bid and Proposal (B&P) [32]. The IR&D and B&P resources are internal funds of the corporation that are derived from the profits and overhead of existing contracts. The model developed in this paper is designed to help the firm allocate funds for the second type of R&D, the IR&D and B&P, to the "best" portfolio of R&D projects.

On an annual basis, the firm establishes its overall corporate mission, objectives and strategies. The division of the firm develops an integrated business plan to achieve its expected contribution to the corporate objectives. These objectives include quantitiative and qualitative criteria. The quantitative criteria include:

(1) Achieve an annual minimum sales growth of a given percent in real terms in each of the years of the planning horizon and maximize the growth beyond that minimum in each of the years;

(2) Maintain a given minimum percent ROI in each of the future years of the planning horizon and maximize the ROI beyond that minimum in each of the years; and

(3) Maximize the profit in each year of the planning horizon.

Thus, the division must show how it will contribute a given level of sales growth, a given level ROI and the maximization of sales growth, ROI, and profit in each year of the planning horizon (ten years, five years, and one year). Since the division measures its performance against the corporate objectives at the collective division level, the individual business units within the division can deviate from the objectives as long as the division achieves its overall objectives. In the R&D model, allocation of R&D funds to individual R&D projects is treated as an investment portfolio. The problem that the R&D portfolio model addresses is: "What is the optimum investment portfolio of R&D projects subject to the given R&D resources and other operating and organizational constraints?" The measure of optimality that the R&D portfolio model uses is a multiattribute utility preference function of an idealized corporate decision maker who holds the strategic planning objectives as his own.

These planning objectives conflict with each other over the planning horizon. For example, achieving sales growth in future years may conflict with maximizing profit in the current year. Also, achieving a high ROI may conflict with maximizing profit. The optimal R&D project "investment portfolio" will be one which achieves the best compromise, for the idealized corporate decision maker, between these conflicting objectives.

To implement the model for the firm's R&D portfolio selection and budgeting problem, the firm's existing data bank on R&D projects was used. This data bank contains information on (1) programs under contract, (2) projects currently in the firm's R&D portfolio, and (3) prospective projects that are candidates for inclusion in the division's R&D portfolio. The data bank includes forecasts of (1) future new orders, (2) sales, (3) profits, (4) a subjective probability assessment of the forecasted sales and profits, (5) IR&D and B&P requirements, (6) capital requirements, and (7) the life cycle phase of the program. This data is provided for each future year that it is available, for as many as fifteen years. The forecasts are made for three scenarios: pessimistic, most likely, and optimistic. Each of these forecasts is assumed to correspond to a fractile of a probability function that is dependent on an overall probability of win for the program and the subjective probabilities (in item 4 above) for each of the three scenarios. The forecasts in the data bank are assessed by the business development manager responsible for the project with review by his management. This assessment process is formally imbedded in the firm's planning process and has proven to be reasonably accurate. The information in the data bank is used to (1) prepare annual strategic planning submissions, (2) support bid/no-bid decisions, and (3) support evaluation, selection and funding of R&D projects. The division's managers are intimately familiar with the R&D project information contained in the data bank. Much of the data is collectively generated by their best informed subjective assessments. The R&D project assessments are also subjected to peer and upper level management review.

Two types of uncertainty are included in the model for each R&D project under consideration for the R&D portfolio. The uncertainty of winning the contract and the uncertainty of the value of the contract given that it is won by the firm. These two types of uncertainty were assessed by the firm's managers to be approximately independent of one another and are combined into one probability function as displayed in Figure 1. The discrete probability mass above the zero value in Figure 1 is the probability of losing the contract, i.e., the probability the project value is zero because it is lost. The entire probability mass under the continuous portion of the probability function on the right in Figure 1 is the probability of winning the contract while the distribution of the probability mass represents the density function for the value of the contract given that it is won. The uncertainty of winning the contract is modeled as being dependent on the project's funding level. It was assessed to be a S-shaped

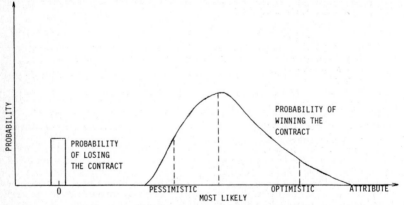

Figure 1: A Combined Probability Function Representing Two Types of Uncertainty:
1: The Probability of Losing the Contract and 2) The Probability of Winning the
Contract Distributed Over the Attribute

function by the firm's managers but because linear programming optimization is used it is approximated in the R&D portfolio model by a piecewise linear concave function as displayed in Figure 2. Thus, when the model selects a project to be included in the portfolio, it must be funded at least at some minimum level.

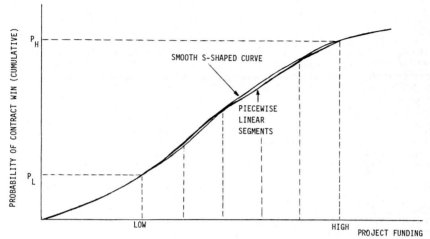

Figure 2: The Piecewise Linear Concave Approximation of the
S-Shaped Probability of Win Function

Within the allowed funding interval for the project, the model allows any R&D funding level on a continuous basis. Details on the manipulation of the data that characterizes the projects' potential contribution to the objectives of sales growth, ROI, and profit and the projects' probability of winning and payback given a win are presented elsewhere [32]. The next section presents the mathematical programming formulation for selecting the firm's R&D portfolio and the multiobjective optimization techniques used to approximately optimize the resultant nonlinear mixed integer programming problem.

The Combined Multiattribute Utility Analysis Theory (MAUT) and Multiobjective Optimization Techniques (MOOT) Solution Approach

Let $A = (A_1, A_2, \ldots, A_n)$ represent the division's set of decision attributes: sales growth, profit, and ROI over some planning horizon with each of these three criterion represented as a different attribute in each different year. Let $a = (a_1, \ldots, a_n)$ represent a specific value of A and let $x = (x_1, \ldots, x_m)$ represent the R&D project funding vector, where each x_i is the funding for project "i." Then $x_i = 0$ if the project is not selected, and x_i is in the interval $[L_i, H_i]$ when the project is selected where $[L_i, H_i]$ is the acceptable funding range (i.e., funding less than L_i is clearly inadequate and funding greater than H_i is clearly excessive). See Figure 3. This interval is also the funding range over which the piecewise linear concave probability of win function is defined.

The decision maker's expected utility for funding vector x is given by

$$\int_A U(a) \, f(a \mid x) \, dA$$

where $f(a \mid x)$ is the joint probability density function over A dependent on funding vector x. The function $F(a \mid x)$ in the R&D management decision problem represents both uncertainty

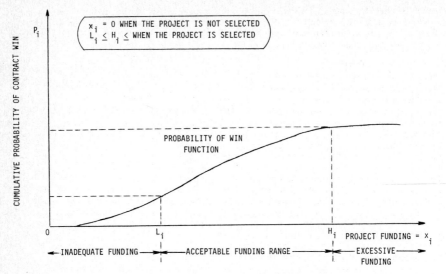

Figure 3: The Probability of Win Function

types--(1) the probability of win and (2) the uncertainty of program benefits, given a win. Based on the assumption of independence between these two types of uncertainty and between the individual projects the Central Limit Theorem allows us to assume that $f(a|x)$ is a jointly normal density function for the decision attributes A because we are taking the sums of independent random variables. This assumption is validated in reference [32]. Although the random variables are independent of the extreme bimodal nature of the probability functions (i.e., the probability "spike" at zero in Figure 1) for the individual projects requires at least 40-50 projects before the hypothesis is satisfied at the 5% confidence level in the Chi-squared test. Since the ROI is measured by the ratio of a project's return over the project's investment, the ROI cannot be obtained by simply summing these ratios. The R&D project's returns and investments are summed separately and the ratio of these two sums results in the ROI for the entire portfolio.

The theory of decision analysis [37], shows that expected utility serves as a normative criterion for selecting the funding vector that best meets the decision maker's preferences. Subject to the accuracy that the utility function represents the decision maker's preferences and attitudes toward risk, the model faithfully determines the project portfolio that is logically consistent with the axioms of rational choice [37]. Put another way, a model which maximizes expected utility serves as an "Expert Management System," consistently using all data and information provided to it through the project's data base to select the "best" R&D portfolio as defined by the decision maker's preference structure.

This results in the following mathematical programming problem:

Model A1 (General Formulation)

$$\text{Max} \int_A U(a) \; f(a|x) \; dA \qquad\qquad A1$$

Subject to:

$$x_{ij} \leq B_j \quad \text{all j resource constraints}$$

and either

$$x_{ij} = 0 \quad \text{i'th project not selected}$$

or $\qquad L_{ij} \leq x_{ij} \leq H_{ij}$ permissible funding ranges

$\qquad\qquad\qquad\qquad\qquad$ for each i,j pair

$\qquad\qquad\qquad\qquad\qquad$ i = 1,2, ... ,m

$\qquad\qquad\qquad\qquad\qquad$ j = 1,2, ... ,p

The j resources are different R&D funding categories (e.g., internal R&D, bid and proposal, etc.), funding in different years, and organization considerations such as minimum or maximum funding to business units or individual projects. For the problem under consideration, the set of attributes are neither strictly statistically nor utility independent. The model of the R&D decision maker developed in this paper assumes that the dependence is weak and that assuming independence will not significantly bias the results. This assumption is validated in reference [32] where it is demonstrated that the R&D portfolio model generates output (sales, profits, and ROI forecasts) equivalent to historic data and forecasts generated by other means within the firm. It is also demonstrated that the R&D portfolio model can find improved R&D portfolios over those developed by the firm without the use of the model. The approximate optimality of the solutions generated using the approximate solution techniques is demonstrated for the case where we assume independence of the attributes. To account for the approximations and the possible biases induced by assuming independence, the model allows for sensitivity analysis on the key parameters, thus providing for successive iterations on the portfolio to generate alternate portfolios for the decision makers to select from. When these iterations are made by varying the weights in the MinSum approach or the MinMax approach we in fact are exploring the nondominated frontier.

The assumption of statistical and utility independence allows the decomposition of the joint density function into a product of the marginal probabilities and the utility function into a simpler additive or multiplicative utility function. The multiobjective programming approaches of goal programming and compromise programming are used to identify a set of compromise solutions for the decision maker to choose from.

Model Approximations Using Multiobjective Optimization Techniques

This section provides various modifications to the formulation of the general optimization model which were made to accommodate the capabilities of various multiobjective optimization techniques. The general Model A1 is a nonlinear mixed integer program which is solvable for small numbers of discrete variables, but the nondecomposed utility function and joint density function for 15 or more attributes would be difficult to assess directly by holistic assessment methods. See references [8, p. 454] and [23, p. 222]. The approximate solutions to Model A1 have been obtained by making assumptions of independence (both statistical and utility).

Model A2 (Nonlinear Formulation)

For Model A2, we assume utility independence between the three attributes of sales, profit, and ROI over a five-year planning horizon. The objective function is treated in both the additive and the multiplicative multiattribute utility function forms. This allowed us to elicit the decision maker's preference structure on each of the fifteen attributes resulting in a simplified assessment procedure. The bias that could be introduced because of the attributes being weakly utility dependent was somewhat mitigated by fixing the complementary set of attributes at their expected levels when the utility function assessment of a given attribute was assessed. Using the methods of reference [23, pp. 188-203], each of the fifteen single attribute utility functions was assessed to be reasonably modeled by a constantly risk averse exponential utility function of the form:

$$\alpha - \beta \exp(-ca)$$

Given that the single attribute utility function modeled by the constantly risk averse exponential form and the attributes have normal uncertainty distributions, the exponential transform [23, p.202] allows us to compute the expected utility for a single attribute as:

$$E[u(a)] = \int_A u(a)f(a)dA = \int_A (\alpha - \beta \exp(-ca))f(a)dA$$

$$= \alpha - \beta \exp(-c\bar{a} + c\sigma^2/2)$$

where $f(a) = \dfrac{1}{\sigma\sqrt{2\pi}} \exp(-(a-\bar{a})^2/2\sigma^2)$, and $\bar{a}$ and σ^2 are the mean and variance of an attribute A.

The constants α, β, and c are shape and location parameters of the utility function that determine (1) the attribute values associated with a utility values of one and zero and (2) the concavity of the utility function and hence the measure of the decision maker's risk aversity.

Thus the linear additive formulation, Model A2.1, is as follows:

$$\text{Max } z = \sum_\ell w_\ell [\alpha_\ell - \beta_\ell \exp(-c\bar{a} + c^2\sigma^2/2)_\ell], \qquad \text{A2.1}$$

subject to the budgetary, funding ranges and (0,1) integer constraints of Model A1. The w_ℓ are the scaling constants of the additive utility function [23, p.295] which can be considered relative measures of importance of the attributes.

The multiplicative utility function formulation, Model A2.2, is as follows:

$$\text{Max } z = \int_A [[\Pi_\ell [k_\ell k \ U_\ell (a_\ell) + 1] - 1]/k] \ f(a)da \qquad \text{A2.2}$$

subject to the budgetary, funding ranges and (0,1) integer constraints of Model A1. The constants k_ℓ and k are the scaling constants of the multiplicative utility function [23, p.289] which can be considered relative measures of importance of the attributes and analogous to the w_ℓ in formulation A2.1. The $U_\ell (a_\ell) = \alpha_\ell - \beta_\ell \exp(-c\bar{a} + c^2\sigma^2/2)_\ell$. The objective function in A2.2 is decomposable and has been optimized using mathematical programming for smaller problems [19,20,21].

The choice between Models A2.1 and A2.2 is influenced by the assessed values of the scaling constants (w_ℓ or k_ℓ). If the scaling constants add to one then the additive form, Model A2.1 is appropriate, and if the sum of the scaling constants is not equal to one then the multiplicative form, Model A2.2, is appropriate. When the scaling constants were assessed by the decision makers of the firm (representative managers from engineering and business development and the division vice president) their sum was close to but not precisely equal to one (the problem of how close to one the sum of the constants should be or how good an approximation are the above decompositions is still an active area of research in decision analysis [41]). The additive form was used in this research and the application of the multiplicative form is identified as an area of future research.

For a small number of (0,1) integer variables (e.g., five to ten projects under selection and funding evaluation with the remaining projects assumed in the portfolio and only evaluated for funding level), Model A2.1 has been solved for a total of 5-10 projects using a barrier penalty nonlinear programming code [25,26]. Solution time on a Univac 1100/80 using an optimized Fortran compiler is under ten minutes of CPU time. Run time (and convergence) is sensitive to the choice of starting point for the algorithm.

Model A3 (Compromise/Goal Programming Formulation)

Model A2 is a nonlinear (0,1) mixed integer program which is not feasible to solve with a large number of variables. Therefore, Model A3 was developed to approximate the multiobjective decision analysis problem with a multiobjective optimization formulation. The separable components of the single objective function of Model A2 are treated as the multiple objectives to be optimized. This step allows us to transform the components into linear expressions resulting in a multiobjective linear programming problem.

For Model A3, we note that the range of each single attribute utility function can be normalized to a range of $(0,1)$ and that the ideal point (i.e., the most preferred value) corresponds to each utility function attaining a value of unity. Model A3 is a compromise or goal programming formulation [18,27,28,43,44] which uses $(0,1)$ mixed integer linear programming to either minimize the sum of the absolute deviations from the ideal point using the L_1 norm or minimizes the maximum deviation from the ideal point using the L_∞ or Chebyshev norm [43, p.315]. To linearize the problem, each of the nonlinear terms in the objective function of Model A2 is set equal to unity, the "ideal" utility value, and solved for the exponent as follows:

$$\text{Let } (\alpha - \beta \exp(-c\bar{a} + c^2\sigma^2/2))_\ell = 1$$

$$\text{then} \quad (c\bar{a} - c^2\sigma^2/2)_\ell = -\ln\frac{\alpha-1}{\beta} = V_\ell, \text{ for all } \ell$$

Setting the solution for the exponent to V_ℓ for the ideal point, then the deviation from the ideal is:

$$d_\ell^- = V_\ell - (c\bar{a} - c^2\sigma^2/2)_\ell$$

where d_ℓ^- is the deviation of a given solution from the ideal solution. In the following three formulations the above equation becomes a constraint for each attribute and the deviation term is minimized in the objective function by three different strategies as follows.

The **Min Sum** formulation is:

$$\text{Min} \quad \sum w_\ell d_\ell^- \qquad\qquad \text{A3.1:}$$

$$\text{Subject to } d_\ell^- + c_\ell \bar{a}_\ell - c_\ell^2 \sigma_\ell^2 /2 = V_\ell$$

and budgetary, funding ranges and 0-1 integer contraints

Formulation A3.1 is based on the approach to forcing the model toward "optimality" by minimizing the weighted sum (i.e., Min Sum formulation) of the deviations from the ideal for each attribute. The w_ℓ is the same scaling constant derived in the multi-attribute utility assessment and is used in A3.1 as a weighting factor for the relative importance of the attributes.

The **Min Max** formulation is:

$$\text{Min} \quad d^- \qquad\qquad \text{A3.2:}$$

$$\text{Subject to } d^- + w_\ell (c_\ell \bar{a}_\ell - c_\ell^2 \sigma_\ell^2 /2) \geq w_\ell V_\ell$$

and budgetary, funding ranges, and 0-1 integer constraints.

Formulation A3.2 is based on the approach to forcing the model toward "optimality" by minimizing the maximum weighted deviation (i.e., the Min Max formulation) from the ideal for all the attributes. The w_ℓ is the same weighting factor used in Model A3.1. The attribute which has the maximum weighted deviation from the ideal will have its respective deviation constraint satisfied as an equality and any minimization of d^- in the objective function will thus reduce the deviation for that attribute.

The **Preemptive Goal Programming** formulation is:

$$\text{Min} \quad W_\ell d_\ell^- \qquad\qquad \text{A3.3:}$$

$$\text{Subject to } d_\ell^- + c_\ell \bar{a} - c_\ell^2 \sigma_\ell^2 /2 = V_\ell$$

and budgetary, funding ranges and 0-1 integer constraints

Formulation A3.3 is based on the approach to forcing the model toward "optimality" by forcing each attribute (one at a time) to its ideal value in order of priority. The W_ℓ are used to preemptively order the minimization of the attribute deviations ordered according to the ranking of the w_ℓ for each attribute. In the actual implementation this can be done by (1) using W_ℓ that are orders of magnitude apart, (2) solving the model successively by adding one deviation constraint at a time, or (3) by using special algorithms developed for goal programming [18,27].

Models A3.1, A3.2, and A3.3 have been solved on the Univac 1100/80 using a Branch and Bound/Primal Dual linear programming package [26] for 50, 0-1 discrete variables (for 50 projects) in under two minutes of CPU time. The solutions from Models A3.1 and A3.2 have been used as starting points in Model A2 resulting in only a slightly differing project funding vector from that suggested by Models A3.1 and A3.2. The suggested portfolios have been considered reasonable by the division management. When forced by additional constraints to resemble historic portfolios, the R&D portfolio model has generated identical forecasts of future sales, profit and ROI performance. When the constraints were relaxed, the model was able to generate a portfolio of projects and funding allocations that was considered reasonable by the firm's managers and suggested an improvement in the firm's R&D portfolio.

The three multiobjective optimization formulations were evaluated on computational efficiency and the attractiveness of their recommended portfolios. All three formulations were approximately equivalent computationally but the MinSum formulation was found to provide the most reasonable portfolios and the best approximations to the original nonlinear optimization problem. Additional results can be found in reference [32].

Results

Some of the more interesting results obtained using the R&D portfolio model are displayed in Figures 4-6. In Figure 4 the results of a sensitivity analysis on the budget show the expected utility of the resulting R&D portfolios. Interestingly, for the current set of candidate projects in the data bank, the firm is already operating near the "knee" in the curve. After a budget equal to 150% of a baseline amount the model refuse to add any additional resources to the remaining unfunded R&D projects. The reason this occurs is that the remaining unfunded projects on the R&D portfolio would cause the expected utility to decline because their

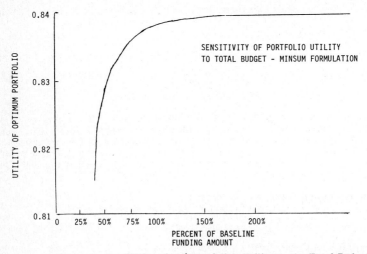

Figure 4: Sensitivity of the Portfolio's Utility to the Total Budget

low ROI overrides their increase in sales. Similarly in Figure 5, the sensitivity of the sales attribute of the R&D portfolio to different budget levels is displayed.

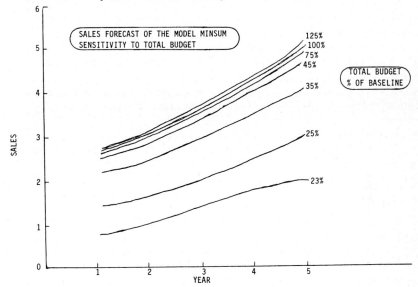

Figure 5: Sensitivity of the R&D Model's Forecast of Sales to the Budget

Figure 6 displays (1) the sales forecasts of the optimum R&D portfolio selected by the model for an actual historic scenario, (2) the sales forecast of the model when it was forced to replicate the same R&D project selections and budgets historically selected by the firm's manager, and (3) the firm's own independent sales forecast for that historic scenario.

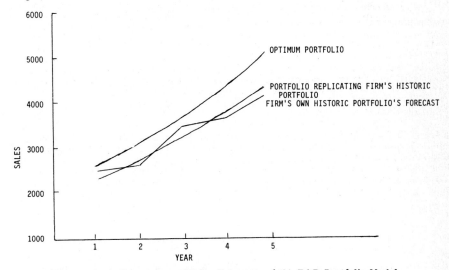

Figure 6: A Comparison of Sales Forecasts of the R&D Portfolio Model

G. Madey, B. V. Dean

From this analysis we conclude that the model offers the potential of suggesting portfolios that may perform better than those generated by the firm's managers unaided by the model.

CONCLUDING COMMENTS

This paper describes an R&D portfolio model based on a combined framework of multiattribute utility theory and multiobjective optimization techniques. Multiattribute utility theory is used to model a decision maker's preference structure over fifteen strategic planning attributes. An optimization model is developed which is designed to maximize the expected utility of the firm's portfolio of R&D projects. To simplify the assessment of the utility function, an additive utility function is assumed and each of the single attribute utility functions is assessed as a constantly risk averse exponential form. Because the resultant optimization problem is still a nonlinear programming problem, the separable terms of the expected utility expression are treated as multiple objectives and the problem is solved by several multiobjective optimization techniques. This allowed the nonlinear terms to be linearized and the maximization of the expected utility of the portfolio of R&D projects is approximately achieved using a standard mixed integer programming package. If an interactive approach is desired (say to explore the nondominated frontier) the weighting on the individual objectives can be varied and the optimization iterated.

The R&D portfolio model has been implemented in the firm and is being used on an ongoing basis (it is estimated that the model could be used on approximately 20 separate occasions per year with approximately 5-10 optimizations conducted on each occasion). For a portfolio design problem that evaluates 100 projects, the current multiobjective linear optimization formulation consists of (1) 100 0-1 integer variables, (2) 645 variables, and (3) 750 constraints. Solutions are obtained in several minutes of computer CPU time.

Multiattribute utility theory was used in the design of the model for several reasons. First, the managers of the firm have been exposed to MAUT on engineering design projects and were familiar and receptive to its use. Second, an interactive system was not considered necessary to most of the managers. A reason for this is the managers have very busy schedules and are interested in one "good" suggested portfolio to which they will add their own personal refinements. A R&D portfolio model that provided suggested R&D portfolios without extensive personal involvement was desired although the ability to iterate on occasion was considered a positive feature. Third, from the methodological research perspective, experimentation with knowledge-based or rule-based R&D portfolio models was desired [14,42]. The multiattribute utility function provided a simple rule-based system and the firm's R&D project data bank provided a simple knowledge base. The model also has approximately 20 rules for setting up the optimization input. The search for a solution is not by an "artificial intelligence" production system but by means of traditional management science branch-and-bound integer programming. Because the R&D portfolio model was designed for ongoing use on a real application, the above reasons contributed to the choice of the MAUT for modeling the firm's decision maker. Multiple objective optimization techniques (MOOT), including compromise programming and goal programming were used to approximate the optimal R&D portfolios as evaluated using MAUT.

It is felt that most limitations of earlier models identified by Baker and Freeland [1] have been addressed by the R&D management model described in this paper. Risk, uncertainty, the use of the manager's knowledge, and the time variant property of project data are addressed by the multiobjective decision analysis methods employed in the model. The suggestions made by Liberatore and Titus [29] were designed into the model, (e.g., use of familiar data and a model tailored to the unique features of the specific firm).

REFERENCES

[1]   Baker, N. R., and J. Freeland, "Recent Advances in R&D Benefit Measurement and Project Selection Methods," Management Science, Vol. 21, June 1975.

[2]   Bischoff, E. E., "Comparing Approaches for Multi-Criterion Optimization," in Multi-Objective Decision Making, French, S., R. Hartley, L. C. Thomas, and D. J. White, editors, Academic Press, London, 1983.

[3]   Chankong, V., and Y. Y. Haimes, Multiobjective Decision Making, North-Holland, New York, 1983.

[4]   Farquhar, P. H., "A Survey of Multiattribute Utility Theory and Decision Making," Multiple Criteria Decision Making, Starr, M. K., and M. Zeleny, editors, North-Holland Publishing Co., Amsterdam, 1977.

[5]   _____, Advances in Multiattribute Utility Theory and Applications," Theory and Decision, Vol. 12, p. 381-394, 1980.

[6]   Fishburn, P. C., Decision and Value Theory, John Wiley, New York, 1964.

[7]   _____, "Value Theory," Handbook of Operations Research, Moder, J. J. and S. E. Elmaghraby, editors, Van Nostrand Reinhold Co., New York, 1978.

[8]   Fischer, G. W., "Utility Models for Multiple Objective Decisions: Do They Accurately Represent Human Preferences?", Decision Sciences, Vol. 10, 1979.

[9]   French, S., "A Survey and Interpretation of Multi-Attribute Utility Theory," Multi-Objective Decision Making, French, S. R., Hartley, L. C. Thomas, D. J. White, editors, Academic Press, London, 1983.

[10] _____, R. Hartley, L. C. Thomas and D. J. White, Multi-Objective Decision Making, Academic Press, London, 1983.

[11] Gear, A. E., "A Review of Some Recent Developments in Portfolio Modeling in Applied Research and Development," IEEE Transactions on Engineering Management, EM-21, November 1974.

[12] Goicoechea, A., D. R. Hansen, L. Duckstein, Multiobjective Decision Analysis with Engineering and Business Applications, John Wiley, New York, 1982.

[13] Golabi, K., C. W. Kirkwood and A. Sicherman, "Selecting a Portfolio of Solar Energy Projects Using Multiattribute Preference Theory," Management Science, Vol. 27, February 1981.

[14] Hayes-Roth, F., D. A. Waterman and D. B. Lenat, Building Expert Systems, Addison-Wesley Publishing Co., Reading, Massachusetts, 1983.

[15] Huber, G. P., "Methods for Quantifying Subjective Probabilities and Multiattributed Utilities," Decision Sciences, Vol. 5, 1974.

[16] Hwang, C-L. and A. S. M. Masud, Multiple Objective Decision Making-Methods and Applications, Springer-Verlag, Berin, 1979.

[17] _____, and K. Yoon, Multiple Attribute Decision Making, Springer-Verlag, Berlin, 1981.

[18] Ignizio, J. P., Goal Programming and Extensions, Lexington Books, Lexington, Massachusetts, 1976.

[19]   Keefer, D. L., "Allocation Planning for R&D with Uncertainty and Multiple Objectives," IEEE Transactions on Engineering Management, EM-25, February 1978.

[20]   _____, and C. W. Kirkwood, "A Multiobjective Decision Analysis: Budget Planning for Product Engineering," Journal of the Operational Research Society, Vol. 29, No. 5, 1978.

[21]   _____, and S. M. Pollack, "Approximations and Sensitivity in Multiobjective Resource Allocation," Operations Research, Vol. 28, January-February 1980.

[22]   Keeney, R. L., "Decision Analysis: An Overview," Operations Research, Vol. 30, September-October 1982.

[23]   _____, and H. Raiffa, Decisions with Multiple Objectives, John Wiley, New York, 1976.

[24]   Koksalan, M. M., Karwan, M. H. and S. Zionts, "An Improved Method for Solving Multiple Criteria Problems Involving Discrete Alternatives," IEEE Transactions on Systems, Man, and Cybernetics, SMC-14, No. 1, January/February 1984.

[25]   Kuester, J. L. and J. H. Mize, Optimization Techniques with Fortran, McGraw-Hill Book Co., New York, 1973.

[26]   Land, A. H., and S. Powell, Fortran Codes for Mathematical Programming, John Wiley & Sons, London, 1973.

[27]   Lee, S. M., Goal Programming for Decision Analysis, Auerbach Publishers, Philadelphia, 1972.

[28]   _____, and R. L. Morris, "Integer Goal Programming Methods," Multiple Criteria Decision Making, Starr, M. K., and M. Zeleny, editors, North-Holland Publishing Co., Amsterdam, 1977.

[29]   Liberatore, M. L., and G. J. Titus, "The Practice of Management Science in R&D Project Management," Management Science, Vol. 29, August 1983.

[30]   MacCrimmon, K. R., Decisionmaking Among Multiple-Attribute Alternatives: A Survey and Consolidated Approach, RM-4823-ARPA, The Rand Corporation, Santa Monica, California, December 1968.

[31]   _____, "An Overview of Multiple Objective Decision Making," Multiple Criteria Decision Making, Cochrane, J. L. and M. Zeleny, editors, University of South Carolina Press, Columbia, South Carolina, 1973.

[32]   Madey, G. R., "A Corporate R&D Strategic Planning and Budgeting Model," Ph.D. thesis, unpublished, Operations Research Department, Case Western Reserve University, Cleveland, Ohio, May 1984.

[33]   Mehrez, A., "A Note of the Comparison of Two Different Formulations of a Risky R&D Model," Operations Research Letters, Vol. 2, No. 5, December 1983.

[34]   _____, and Z. Sinuany-Stern, "An Interactive Approach for Project Selection," Journal of the Operational Research Society, Vol. 34, No. 7, 1983.

[35]   _____, and _____, "Resource Allocation to Interrelated Projects," Water Resources Research, Vol. 18, June 1982.

[36]   Mylander, W. C., R. L. Holmes and G. P. McCormick, <u>A Guide to SUMT-4</u>
        <u>Version 4: The Computer Program Implementing the Sequential Unconstrained</u>
        <u>Minimization Technique for Nonlinear Programming</u>, Paper RAC-P-63, Research
        Analysis Corporation, McLean, Virginia, October 1971, (DTIC-AD731391).

[37]   Raiffa, H., <u>Decision Analysis</u>, Addison-Wesley, Reading, Mass., 1968.

[38]   Starr, M. K., and M. Zeleny, <u>Multiple Criteria Decision Making</u>, North-Holland
        Publishing Co., Amsterdam, 1977.

[39]   Weingartner, H. M., "Capital Budgeting of Interrelated Projects: Survey and
        Synthesis," <u>Management Science</u>, Vol. 12, March 1966.

[40]   White, D. J., "A Branch and Bound Method for Multi-Objective Boolean Problem,"
        <u>Multi-Objective Decision Making</u>, edited by French, S., R. Hartley, L. C. Thomas,
        and D. J. White, Academic Press, London, 1983.

[41]   Winkler, R. L., "Research Discretions in Decision Making Under Uncertainty,"
        <u>Decision Sciences</u>, Vol. 13, pp. 517-533, 1982.

[42]   Winston, P. H., <u>Artificial Intelligence</u>, Addison-Wesley Publishing Co., Reading,
        Massachusetts, 1984.

[43]   Zeleny, M., <u>Multiple Criteria Decision Making</u>, McGraw-Hill Book Co., New York,
        1982.

[44]   Zionts, S., "A Survey of Multiple Criteria Integer Programming Methods," <u>Annals</u>
        <u>of Discrete Mathematics</u>, Vol. 5, pp. 389-398, 1979.

Project Management: Methods and Studies
Burton V. Dean (editor)
© Elsevier Science Publishers B.V. (North-Holland), 1985

DECISION ANALYSIS FOR NEW PROCESS TECHNOLOGY

Samuel J. Mantel, Jr. and James R. Evans

College of Business Administration
University of Cincinnati
Cincinnati, Ohio

Vijay A. Tipnis

Tipnis Associates, Inc. [1]
Cincinnati, Ohio

An important problem in R&D project management is whether or not to invest in the development of process technology which appears to be conceptually feasible but on which little or no preliminary work has been done. The problem of which aspects of a proposed technology should be most heavily researched is a similar problem. These decisions have significant economic and productivity implications. The usual investment decision models do not work very well on these problems because of the high uncertainty about performance parameters for the proposed innovation and, hence, about its probable economic results. This chapter extends the economic model developed earlier[2] to include the effects of uncertainty of performance on the decision to investigate and develop a new process technology. Simulation models are developed, and the managerial use and implications of the results are examined. An example application to process innovations in the production of aircraft parts is used to illustrate these results. The basic model has had a significant effect on laser-assisted machining research.

INTRODUCTION

It is common for firms contemplating a change in production processes to prepare a pro forma financial statement which pictures the system as it would be if the change is made. Such statements are generally flawed. First, they are often cursory before-and-after views of the firm's P and L statement, complete with arbitrary allocation of overhead costs which distort the actual effects of the change. Second, such projections rarely examine the contemplated changes in detail, failing to trace their effects and side effects. Third, these statements almost never reflect the uncertainty inherent in the projected system performance they purport to display.

An approach has been developed to help deal with the first two issues (Mantel, Tipnis, Watwe, and Ravignani (1983) and Mantel and Ravignani (1981)). In this chapter we will extend this approach to include uncertainty about process performance parameters. This extension allows the model to be used to aid the project manager in making two important strategic decisions: 1) the decision about whether or not to invest in research on the proposed innovation given uncertainty about technical success, and 2) the direction in which research should be pursued in order to improve performance.

There are several well established methods for deciding about the advisability of a capital investment (Buck and Tanchoco (1982), Ferguson and Shamblin (1975), Hertz (1975), Hespos (1975), Hillier (1975), Rose (1976), and Weiser (1975)). All these methods require prediction of the cash flows that will result if the investment is made. If the investment is in a piece of real property or equipment, uncertainty about the nature or operation of the physical factors involved causes uncertainty about the size (or timing) or the cash flows. Given that the potential investment has a physical impact on the system, it is helpful to investigate the character of this physical impact in order to understand the nature and sources of the uncertainties in the cash flows.

THE PROCESS MODELING APPROACH

Consider a newly-conceived process technology. Assume that this technology seems to be conceptually feasible, but has not actually been implemented and proven.

In a production process there are only two ways an innovation can be useful: first, it can lower the unit cost of production; and/or second, it can decrease the time required to produce a unit of product. Define ΔC as the cost savings associated with the potential investment, and define ΔT as the time savings.

Time saved has a value; the value of additional outputs produced by the speedier process, if additional identical outputs are desired, or the value of using the system to produce an improved or alternate output. If this value is (oc) per unit of time, then

$$\Delta C + \Delta T(oc) > 0 \tag{1}$$

is a necessary condition for the investment to be economically feasible. Two points should be noted; only costs variant with the change are included and, for simplicity, we assume that the proposed technology does not change costs or revenues at other stages of the production process.

While inequality (1) is necessary for economic feasibility, it is not sufficient. Production will be increased by $p(T/T')$, where p is the current output per period and T and T' are the current and future production time per unit of output, respectively. If ΔI is the estimated present value of the added investment including R&D and other costs of implementing the new technology, then

$$\frac{p(T/T')\{\Delta C + \Delta T(oc)\}\phi}{\Delta I} > DROI \tag{2}$$

is a sufficient condition for investing ΔI, where ϕ is the appropriate discount factor, and DROI is the <u>D</u>esired <u>R</u>eturn <u>O</u>n Investment (or, the "cut off" rate of return). If this condition is met, we will invest in the candidate technology. A fly, however, is imbedded in the analytical ointment. Because the innovation is still in the conceptual stage, we do not know the costs and times associated with the new process and, thus, cannot determine ΔC and ΔT.

Attempts to estimate ΔC and ΔT directly are apt to be the wildest of guesses if the process innovation is even slightly complex. For manufacturing, the estimation process should begin with a manufacturing "operation sequence sheet," detailing each specific job processing step. For each step, one asks, "Is the time and/or cost required for this operation apt to be altered by the candidate technology?"

For example, if the route sheet shows that a piece of metal is to be cut, we try to estimate what, if any, effect the proposed process will have on the time or cost involved in making the cut. Assume that we estimate that the cut can be made faster, and so labor cost is reduced, but no material is saved. If t is the current time required for the cut, then the time required for the new process, t', will be some fraction of the current time, say $t' = at$. Similarly, the new labor cost is $\ell' = b\ell$. Remember, however, that we are uncertain about the exact size of a and b.

Estimates of time and cost changes are gathered by investigating each element of the physical processes. These are substituted for ΔC and ΔT in Equation 2. We can now test to see if the sufficiency condition is met. Further, we can perform parametric sensitivity analysis on Equation 2 seeking values for the several variables required to satisfy it under different assumptions about the desired rate of return and level of required investment.

AN EXAMPLE

Laser assisted machining (LAM) involves the use of a laser to preheat the work material on a machine tool immediately ahead of the cutter as it operates. Heating the workpiece will decrease the cutting forces which, in turn, will increase the rate at which material can be removed. there is a wide range of application for this technology, given that it is economically feasible.

Machining is a fairly complex process, and the addition of a delicate device such as a laser is complicated. Almost any aspect of machine operation might be affected. The proposed change was carefully investigated and the relevant estimations were made (Tipnis, Mantel, and Ravignani (1981)).

Use the following definitions:

T_p = the sum of all processing time per part during the current process that is subject to replacement by the new process

T_s = the sum of all set-up time during the current process that is subject to replacement by the new process

γ = the ratio between the sums of non-cutting time in the new process and in the current process

N = lot size

(LMS) = combined labor, machine, and support cost rate during the current process ($/time)

(cs) = consumable cost per part during the current process

(cm) = material cost per part during the current process

γT_p = the sum of all processing time per part during the new process after replacement of the current process

βT_s = the sum of all set-up time per part during the new process after replacement of the current process

T_c = actual cutting time per part during T_p (with current process)

$\delta T_p = T_c$

ηT_c = actual cutting time per part during T_p (with new process)

$\pi(LMS)$ = combined labor, machine, and support cost rate duirng the new process

$\tau(cs)$ = consumable cost per part during new process

$\varepsilon(cm)$ = material cost per part during new process

From earlier work (Tipnis (1981)), we have

$$\Delta T = \{T_p + (1/N)T_s\} - \{\lambda T_p + (1/N)\beta T_s\} \tag{3}$$

and
$$\Delta C = \{T_p + (1/N)T_s\}\ (LMS) + (cs + cm)$$
$$- \{\lambda T_p + (1/N\beta T_s\}\pi(LMS) - \tau(cs) - \varepsilon(cs) \tag{4}$$

Note also that the following equality must exist for the non-cutting times between the current and the new process,

$$\lambda\ (T_p - T_c) = \lambda\ T_p - \eta\ T_c \tag{5}$$

Rearranging and substituting $\delta = T_c/T_p$, we get

$$\lambda = \eta\delta + \gamma(\delta - 1) \tag{6}$$

Now a physical process representation of the sufficient condition results when Equations (3), (4), and (6) are substituted into Equation (2). Rearranging, we get

$$S = -\eta\delta + \gamma(\delta - 1) - \beta\frac{1}{N}\frac{T_s}{T_p} + \frac{K_1 - \tau(cs) - \varepsilon(cm)}{\{K_2 + \pi(LMS) + oc\}\ T_p} \tag{7}$$

where $S > O$ is the sufficient condition, and where

$$K_1 = \{T_p + (1/N)T_s\}\ (LMS) + oc + cs + cm \tag{8}$$

$$K_2 = (DROI\ \Delta I/\Phi p\{T_p + (1/N)T_s\}. \tag{9}$$

While the cash flows represented by ΔC and $\Delta T(oc)$ no longer are wild guesses, they are still uncertain. To deal with this uncertainty we can use simulation.

MONTE CARLO SIMULATION OF ECONOMIC FEASIBILITY

Monte carlo simulation is often used to evaluate risk and uncertainty in economic decisions [1,4,5]. The value of monte carlo analysis is in its simplicity and effectiveness in computing the convolution of random variables for which no closed form analytical solution is known to exist.

Under conditions of high uncertainty, it is common to assume a Beta probability distribution for stochastic variables. This offers great flexibility for modeling the distribution of stochastic variables, and parameter values can be determined rather easily through expert questioning. In practice, the Beta distribution is often characterized by three parameters, a, m, and b, which correspond to optimistic, most likely, and pessimistic estimates. Given these values, a beta variate over the interval (a,b) can easily be generated [8,10].

Based on the best current available data regarding laser assisted machining, the following parameters were chosen:

LMS = $30		Tc =	16.64 hours/part
oc = $30/hour		Ts =	26 hours/part
cs = $100/part		N =	50 parts/lot
cm = $1000/part		p =	500 parts/year
Tp = 45.8 hours/part		ΔI =	$960,000

Cost of capital = 12%　　　　　　　Inflation rate = 4% per year

Economic life = 6 years

$$\Phi = \sum_{t=1}^{6} 1/(1 + .2 + .4)^t = 3.685$$

Payback period = 6 years, $\therefore$ DROI = 1/6.

Values for the stochastic parameters are given in Table 1, based on the best available information.

	a	m	b
η	.5	.6	.9
β	1.1	1.5	1.8
π	1.1	1.4	1.6
τ	.9	1.5	2.5
γ	.8	1.0	1.2
ϵ	.9	1.0	1.05

Table 1. Values for Stochastic Parameters for LAM

A monte carlo simulation program was written to compute the distribution of S. This is shown in Figure 1. The distribution of S is remarkably normal. This is somewhat surprising in view of the fact that there are no theoretical results about the limiting distribution of combinations of Beta random variables, linear or otherwise. A Chi-square goodness of fit test could not reject normality at a 5% significance level. In fact, further experiments upheld this observation except for extreme cases in which the Beta distributions were all highly skewed in one direction. This enables one to utilize normal distribution theory for further analysis.

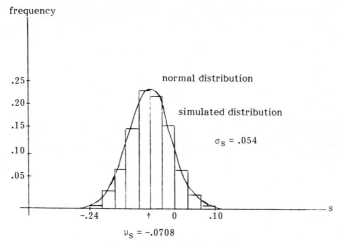

Figure 1. Distribution of S

Analytic study would be considerably simplified if one could appeal to well known results concerning the mean and variance of linear combinations of independent random variables. Unfortunately, S is nonlinear in parameter π. Simulation experiments, however, have found little difference in empirical estimates of the mean and variance of S, from those found by substituting the means and variances of individual parameters into the formulas:

$$\mu_S = -E(\eta)\delta - E(\gamma)(\delta - 1) - E(\beta)\frac{1}{N}\frac{Ts}{Tp} \tag{10}$$
$$+ \frac{K_1 - (cs)E(\tau) - (cm)E(\varepsilon)}{\{K_2 + E(\pi)(LMS) + oc\}Tp}$$

$$\sigma_S^2 = V(\eta)^2 + V(\gamma)(\delta-1)^2 + V(\beta)(\frac{1}{N}\frac{Ts}{Tp})^2$$
$$+ \left[\frac{1}{\{K_1 + \pi(LMS) + oc\}\ Tp}\right]^2 \{(cs)^2\ V(\tau) + (cm)^2\ V(\varepsilon)\}. \tag{11}$$

In other words, we shall assume that π is constant so that S is a linear combination of parameters. It is evident from the above formula for σ_S^2 that the squared term involving π is very small, and thus minor variations in π will have little effect.

SENSITIVITY ANALYSIS AND MANAGERIAL IMPLICATIONS

In this section we apply sensitivity analysis to investigate the risk associated with the economic feasibility of LAM. As we will see, this approach can also be useful for providing direction for future research and development activity. The basic question to be addressed is: given a specified "acceptance level," $1 - \alpha$, for establishing economic feasibility, i.e., $P(S>0)$ $\geq 1 - \alpha$, over what range must parameter values be assured? A related question is the determination of additional investment in R&D to reduce the variance of initial parameter estimates, or to improve the mean estimates of the process parameters, or possibly both.

It is interesting to examine the relationship between $P(S>0)$ and α_S in light of these questions. When $\mu_S < 0$, as σ_S increases, the value of the standardized variable $(S - \mu_S)/\sigma_S$ at $S = 0$ will approach zero, thus increasing $P(S>0)$. Therefore, as long as $\mu_S < 0$, it makes no sense to seek a reduction in the variance of the parameter estimates unless the mean is also improved. On the other hand, when $\mu_S > 0$, a reduction on σ_S will increase the probability.

Consider three cases. First, assume a shift in the mean, independent of the variance. Second, and perhaps more realistic, assume an improvement in the mean along with a reduction in the variance. This is reasonable because experimentation to improve the operation of an emerging technology will also provide better precision of the results. A third approach for improving $P(S>0)$ is to modify the values of managerially specified terms, DROI, and, if possible ΔI. We reduce DROI, lowering the required return on investment. Reduction of ΔI is a cut in the estimated level of investment—if that can be done without jeopardizing the project.

Before proceeding along these lines, we note that $P(S>0) \geq 1 - \alpha$ is equivalent to $\mu_S \leq |Z_\alpha| \sigma_S$. This establishes a range of values that satisfy the sufficient condition for economic feasibility at a given level of risk.

Changes in μ_S can easily be studied by examining the partial derivatives of $E(\cdot)$ in equation (10). These are summarized in Table 2 with numerical values for the example data calculated.

$$\frac{\delta S}{\delta E(\eta)} = -\delta \qquad\qquad = -.3633$$

$$\frac{\delta S}{\delta E(\gamma)} = \delta - 1 \qquad\qquad = -.6367$$

$$\frac{\delta S}{\delta E(\beta)} = -\frac{1}{N}\frac{Ts}{Tp} \qquad\qquad = -.01135$$

$$\frac{\delta S}{\delta E(\tau)} = -cs/(K_2 + E(\pi)LMS + oc)Tp = -.0298$$

$$\frac{\delta S}{\delta E(\epsilon)} = -cm/(K_2 + E(\pi)LMS + oc)Tp = -.2976$$

$$\frac{\delta S}{\delta E(\pi)} = \frac{-[(Tp+\frac{1}{N}Ts)(LMS+oc) + cs(1-\tau)+cm(1-\epsilon)](LMS)}{\frac{(DROI)\Delta I}{\Phi p(Tp+\frac{1}{N}Ts)} + \pi(LMS) + oc^2(Tp)}$$

$$= -.3325$$

Table 2

Clearly γ, the non-cutting time multiplier, has the largest impact, while β and τ have little effect. Figure 2 gives the standard deviation, σ_S, as a function of the proportion of the current range $(b-a)$, of parameter estimates. Variance reduction of β, ϵ, and τ have little effect while increasing precision of η and γ will reduce the variance.

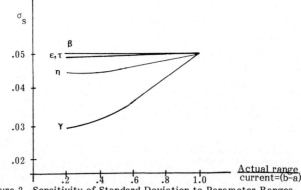

Figure 2. Sensitivity of Standard Deviation to Parameter Ranges

Consider, for example, the reduction of parameter estimates for γ to a = .80, m = .84, and b = .88. Since $E(\gamma)$ = .84, the improvement in μ_s is (1–.84) (.6369) = .102, or μ_s = .0312. From Figure 2, the standard deviation is reduced to σ_s = .0279. Thus,

$$\frac{-\mu_s}{\sigma_s} = \frac{-.0312}{.0279} = -1.12$$

The probability of economic feasibility is .87. In this fashion, various scenarios can easily be studied.

Figure 3 illustrates a contour plot of the probability of a positive sufficient condition as a function of the expected value and variance of γ.

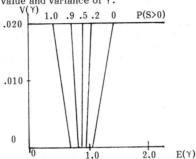

Figure 3. Probability Surface Projection for Parameter γ

Plots such as these provide a simple means for assessing changes in several process parameters as a result of the assumption of independence.

AN OPTIMIZATION MODEL

The optimal allocation of investment in process parameter research and development can be conceptualized as a nonlinear programming problem. Let us assume a functional relationship between ΔI_k, the investment in parameter p_k, and the value of the parameter itself. Typical relationships might be characterized by concave or convex curves. That is, the value of p_k might be expected to decrease with higher investment, either with increasing or decreasing returns. Under these conditions one may write ΔI_k as a function of the parameter mean and possibly the variance, i.e.,

$$\Delta I_k = f(p_k) = f_k(\mu_{p_k}, \sigma^2_{p_k})$$

The optimal allocation of investment would be the solution to the problem

$$\min_k \Sigma \, f_k(\mu_{p_k}, \sigma^2_{p_k})$$
$$\text{s.t. } \mu_s \geq |Z_\alpha| \sigma_s$$

SUMMARY

At base, this paper is concerned with improving the ability to make an investment decision about a potential process innovation. We are particularly interested in a conceptually feasible technology that has not been researched and proven. The decision to invest depends on an estimate of the cash flows expected to result from the unproven technology, a difficult problem at best.

A sufficient condition, S, is satisfied if the present value of the savings is sufficient to generate a desired rate of return on the estimated capital cost required to research, develop, and implement the innovation. The sufficiency condition is met when S > 0. A method for stochastic sensitivity analysis of P(S>0) to all parameters is proposed. Given some acceptable level for P(S>0), it is also possible to consider the impact of additional research expenditures on the expected return on investment. Research funds can be spent to gather information on the innovation (lower the variance of a parameter), and/or on improving the performance of the innovation (improving the expected value of a parameter). This sensitivity analysis not only indicates the specific research targets most apt to yield valuable results, but also provides the information required to establish a stopping rule by generating a cost/effectiveness measure for research spending.

Even when competing technologies are applicable to different production processes they can be examined, and one or more selected for development and implementation. Because the baseline data comes from current technology, the method described here is helpful in deciding when to switch from an existing to a newer production method.

Finally, even when the performance characteristics of a new technology are not so uncertain as the case we have considered, there is considerable value in the detailed process used here to gether information on the expected impact of the new technology, and on the cash expected to flow from it. This method represents a significant improvement over the usual wild guess.

FOOTNOTES

[1]This is part of the Task IV, Economic Modeling, being conducted by Tipnis Associates, Inc., Cincinnati, OH, under a subcontract from GE CR&D Project "Advanced Machining Research Program" DARPA/AFML Project Contract F33615-79-C-5119. Dr. D. G. Flom is the Project Manager at GE CR&D, and Ms. Veronica Blomer, AFWAL, is the Project Manager: Dr. M. Buckley, DARPA, is the Program Manager.

[2]Mantel, S. J., V. J. Tipnis, U. Watwe, and G. L. Ravignani, "Economic Evaluation of Potential Process Innovation," OMEGA, Vol. 11, No. 1, 1983.

[3]The notation of coefficients λ, η, and π, appear as α, μ, and σ, respectively, in the works cited. They were altered here to prevent confusion with standard statistical notation used below.

REFERENCES

[1] Barish, Norman N., and Seymour Kaplan, Economic Analysis for Engineering and Managerial Decision Making, McGraw-Hill, New York, 1978 (2nd ed.).

[2] Buck, James R., and Jose J. S. Tanchoco,"Economic Analysis in an Uncertain Environment," Proceedings, 1982 Fall Industrial Engineering Conference, IIE, Cincinnati, 1982, pp. 510-516.

[3] Ferguson, Earl J., and James E. Shamblin, "Break-Even Analysis," in Risk and Uncertainty, G. A. Fleischer, Ed., EE Monograph Series No. 2, AIIE, Norcross, Ga., 1975, pp. 2-5.

[4] Hertz, David B., "Risk Analysis in Capital Investment," in Fleischer, op. cit. pp. 141-152.

[5] _____, "Investment Policies That Payoff," in Fleischer, op. cit., pp. 153-165.

[6] Hespos, Richard F., and Paul A. Strassmann, "Stochastic Decision Trees for the Analysis of Investment Decisions," in Fleischer, op. cit., pp. 48-55.

[7] Hillier, Frederick S., "A Basic Model for Capital Budgeting of Risky Interrelated Projects," in Fleischer, op. cit., pp. 90-102.

[8] Law, Averill M., and David Kelton, Simulation Modeling and Analysis, McGraw-Hill, New York, 1982.

[9] Mantel, S. J., Jr., V. A. Tipnis, U. Watwe, and G. L. Ravignani, "Economic Evaluation of Potential Process Innovation," Omega, Vol. II, No. 1, 1983.

[10] Pritsker, A. Alan B., The GASP IV Simulation Language, Wiley, New York, 1974.

[11] Rose, I. M., Engineering Investment Decisions, Elsevier, Amsterdam, 1976.

[12] Sullivan, William G., and Gordon R. Orr, "Monte Carlo Risk Analysis of Capital Investments," Proceedings, 1982 Fall Industrial Engineering Conference, IIE, Cincinnati, OH 1982, pp. 521-527.

[13] Tipnis, V. A., G. L. Ravignani, and S. J. Mantel, Jr., "Economic Feasibility of Laser Assisted Machining (LAM)," Transactions of the Society of Manufacturing Engineers, Vol. IX, Dearborn, MI, 1981, pp. 547-552.

[14] _____, S. J. Mantel, Jr., and G. L. Ravignani, "Economic Models for Process Development," in Process Modeling Tools, J. F. Thomas, Jr. (Ed.), American Society for Metals, Metals Park, OH, 1981, pp. 3-21.

[15] _____, "Sensitivity Analysis for Macroeconomid Models of New Manufacturing Processes," Annals of the CIRP, Vol. 30/1, 1981, pp. 401-404.

[16] Weiser, Herbert J., "Break-Even Analysis: A Re-evaluation in Fleischer, op. cit., pp. 6-11.

Project Management: Methods and Studies
Burton V. Dean (editor)
© Elsevier Science Publishers B.V. (North-Holland), 1985

43

AN AGGREGATE MODEL FOR MULTI-PROJECT RESOURCE ALLOCATION

Robert C. Leachman

University of California
Berkeley, California
U.S.A.

Joerg Boysen

Consilium Associates
Palo Alto, California
U.S.A.

An aggregate modeling approach is introduced which accomplishes
multi-project resource allocation without resorting to resource-
contrained scheduling of detailed critical path activity networks.
Aggregate project models are developed by aggregating detailed
activities with similar mixes of resource requirements into aggregate
activities. Using concepts from dynamic production theory and
structural analysis of the underlying detailed networks, input–output
relationships for the aggregate activities are modelled.

Each aggregate project model describes the alternative ways resources
may be loaded on the project. By virtue of some novel modeling
techniques, the aggregate project models restrict resource loads to
patterns which facilitate individual project scheduling, yet the models
consist of relatively few variables governed by linear constraints.

The aggregate project models are combined into a multi-project
resource allocation model which is formulated as a linear program.
The solution of the linear program provides allocations through time
for each project that utilize resource capacities as much as possible
while insuring that projects may be scheduled to meet prespecified
milestone dates. The allocations made to each project are to be
treated as capacities available to each project. The model thus
establishes the basis for a hierarchical approach to resource-constrained
multi-project scheduling, in which resource-constrained scheduling
of detailed activities is performed project by project.

For various choices of milestone dates for the projects, the manager
would interactively compute trial allocations using the model. In this
fashion, the manager may develop resource use plans which lead to
desirable overall levels of resource utilization, and which are consistent
with customer commitments (due dates) for each project.

Application of the aggregate modeling approach to production planning
in a naval shipyard is discussed. An aggregate project model of a naval
ship overhaul is described, and some computational examples using the
allocation model are presented. It is demonstrated that the aggregate
modeling approach is computationally feasible for simultaneously planning
10–20 overhaul projects, each consisting of thousands of detailed activities.

1. Introduction

We consider the problem of production planning and scheduling in project-oriented production systems with inflexible capacities for resources such as labor and equipment.

Traditionally, resource-constrained project scheduling methods based on critical path networks have been the decision aids proposed for such a problem. Heuristic-based computer
programs are commercially available that are capable of simultaneously scheduling dozens

of projects, each consisting of thousands of activities. See Davis (1973) for a review. For more recent efforts, see Kurtulus and Davis (1982), Thesen (1976) and Cooper (1976).

In the authors' experience, there is resistance among large, industrial organizations to such an approach. It is considered impractical to conduct resource allocation using very large models formulated at a scheduling level of detail. Moreover, the level of management that plans the allocation of resources among projects is not responsible for the detailed scheduling and management of individual projects.

The need for a hierarchical approach to project planning has been recognized before. Various authors have investigated multi-level critical path networks, in which each activity of a high-level network decomposes into a network of subactivities. See Harris (1978), Archibald (1976), Vlach (1969), Eardley (1969), Burman (1972) and Parikh and Jewell (1965). These investigations are limited to discussions of the structure and construction of multi-level networks, or in the case of the latter two papers, to techniques for hierarchical scheduling unconstrained by resource capacities.

The most relevant previous work for the problem at hand is by Jones (1979), who proposes an aggregate-disaggregate approach to resource-constrained multi-project scheduling. In Jones' approach, a small number of alternative schedules of detailed activities for each project are developed, and the associated resource load profiles are computed. A binary integer program is then used to identify the most desirable combination of such profiles, and consequently, project schedules.

This approach formalizes a technique the authors have observed in actual industrial practice, whereby a library of alternative load profiles for the resources used in each type of project are maintained (e.g., "fast buildup" curves, "normal buildup" curves, and "late buildup" curves). By trial and error, load profiles and start dates are selected for each project that load resources up to capacity as much as can be achieved. Later, the allocation of slack in each detailed project network is made as consistently as possible with the load profiles selected for the project.

The main shortcoming of this kind of approach is that only relatively few alternatives of project execution can be considered. Consequently, even when optimized in an integer program, one may still wind up with considerable idle resource capacity.

The purpose of this paper is to propose an aggregate method for multi-project resourse use planning in which the flexibility in the execution of each project is modeled <u>directly</u>. Such a model is not concerned <u>explicitly</u> with the alternative ways projects can be scheduled in detail, but rather with the alternative ways each resource can be loaded over the life of each project.

Figure 1 provides a flow diagram of the aggregate method of resource allocation developed in following sections. In Section 2 we develop an <u>aggregate project model</u> from the underlying detailed activity network that describes the alternative distributions of resource use at a level of detail appropriate for multi-project planning. In Section 3 we show how the aggregate models of all on-going and future projects would be combined into a <u>multi-project resource allocation model</u>, formulated as a linear program. Finally, in Section 4 we discuss application of the allocation model.

2. The Aggregate Project Model

2.1 Aggregation of CPM Networks

The decomposition of an industrial project into detailed activities for scheduling purposes is guided by the following criteria: resources utilized, work location, and technical system. An additional criterion used in practice is that activities are defined at a level of detail at which they satisfy the strict precedence relationships of the Critical Path Method (CPM). These criteria lead to detailed scheduling networks for large projects that tend to have many parallel paths involving different work locations or technical systems. Serial activities on each

CONSTRUCTION OF A PROJECT MODEL

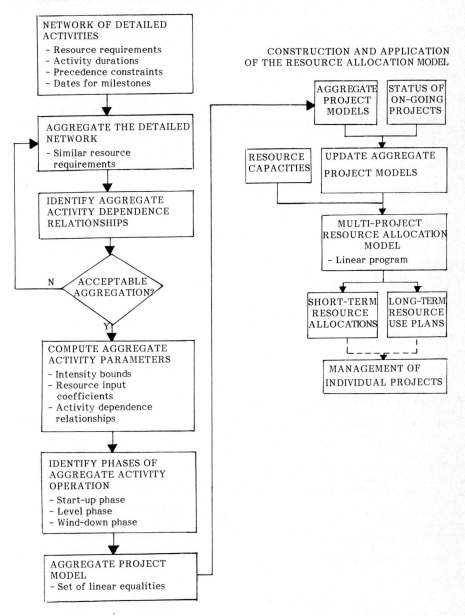

Figure 1. Flow Diagram: Construction and Application
of the Multi-Project Resource Allocation Model

path tend to have different mixes of resource requirements.

Another characteristic of these networks is the presence of <u>restraining events</u> (milestones). Many parallel paths of production activities converge or diverge from such events, whose times are prespecified. The simplest case imaginable is where the only restraining events are the start and completion of the project, but in practice, intermediate restraining events are usually defined as well. The prespecification of occurrence times for the restraining events drives the generation of early and late starting times for all detailed activites.

For the purposes of multi-project resource use planning, only the "resources utilized" criterion is important for project decomposition. The aggregation we shall pursue therefore sacrifices information in detailed networks concerning different technical systems and work locations. This approach also sacrifices strict precedence relationships between activities, contrasting the approach of other authors who have studied the aggregation of CPM networks into higher-level CPM networks. Their approach requires considerable serial aggregation and, as noted above, activities in series frequently utilize different mixes of resources. Consequently, it would be difficult to model accurately the alternatives for resource use if one used a higher-level CPM network.

In order to achieve a reasonable degree of aggregation while still modeling the use of resources well, the aggregation scheme to be presented emphasizes the consolidation of parallel, detailed activities using similar mixes of resources. As will be discussed, the periods of operation of aggregate activities formed in this fashion will overlap. Moreover, each overlap is a function of resource allocation. Strict precedence will still exist in the aggregate network for the instances of restraining events included in the aggregate network.

To demonstrate the development of the aggregate model, suppose a project is characterized by an activity-on-node CPM network of detailed activities $B_1, \ldots, B_L$. The duration of each activity B_l, denoted by D_l, is assumed to be prespecified. It is assumed that each B_l is not interruptable. If S_l is the start time of B_l, then the activity operates (i.e., uses resources) in the half-open interval $(S_l, S_l + D_l]$. We refer to a schedule of start times for detailed activities as a vector $S = (S_1, \ldots, S_L)$. The <u>early start schedule</u> is denoted by $ES = (ES_1, \ldots, ES_L)$, and the <u>late start schedule</u> by $LS = \overline{(LS_1, \ldots, LS_L)}$, as determined from the restraining event dates by well-known techniques. (See, for example, Moder and Phillips (1970).)

We suppose the project requires utilization of nonstorable resources $R_1, \ldots, R_K$. Let b_{kl} represent the total amount of resource R_k that activity B_l requires, $k=1, \ldots, K$, $l=1, \ldots, L$. We assume that resources are loaded on detailed activities at constant rates. We define the <u>operating intensity</u> of detailed activity B_l, denoted by $\bar{z}_l$ as the proportion of each required resource that is used per unit time. That is, $\bar{z}_l = \frac{1}{D_l}$, $l=1, \ldots, L$. Thus B_l uses resource R_k at the rate $b_{kl} \bar{z}_l$ per unit time.

We also represent the project as a network of aggregate activities $A_1, \ldots, A_N$. Each detailed activity B_l is assigned to exactly one aggregate activity A_i, indicated by $B_l \epsilon A_i$. We say an aggregate activity A_i <u>precedes</u> aggregate activity A_j if there is a detailed activity $B_l \epsilon A_i$ which precedes some $B_k \epsilon A_j$.

The aggregate activities are defined in such a way that all detailed activities assigned to an aggregate activity have very similar or identical mixes of required resources. They are also defined so that work flow relationships are preserved, i.e., there are no cycles in the aggregate network. The aggregation should not absorb any restraining events. The only other limitation on aggregation is that activity dependence relationships in the resulting network should not be too complex, as will be discussed later.

2.2 Describing Aggregate Activity Operation

We model the production process of each aggregate activity using the dynamic linear activity analysis model (DLAAM) first proposed by Shephard, Al-Ayat and Leachman (1977), and developed further for continuous flow networks in Leachman (1982) and for critical path networks in Leachman (1983). In this model, it is assumed that resources are applied to an activity in fixed proportions through time. The operation of each aggregate activity A_i is measured in terms of a step function $z_i(.)$ called the <u>operating intensity</u> of A_i. The intensity

$z_i(t)$ expresses the fraction of the total resources required to perform A_i that is applied during the interval $(t-1,t]$. The use of resource R_k by A_i during $(t-1,t]$ is expressed as $a_{ki}z_i(t)$, where the coefficient a_{ki} is the total amount of R_k required by A_i, i.e.

$$a_{ki} = \sum_{B_l \in A_i} b_{ki} .$$

Given an arbitrary schedule S for detailed activities, the use of resource R_k during $(t-1,t]$ by aggregate activity A_i may be directly computed as

$$\sum_{l \in \Lambda(S,t)} b_{kl}\bar{z}_l ,$$

where $\Lambda(S,t)= \{1 \,|\, B_l \in A_i,\ S_l < t \leq S_l + D_l\}$ is the index set of detailed activities which are in operation during the interval $(t-1,t]$, given S. Using DLAAM to represent such resource loading, let $z_i^S(t)$ denote the intensity of A_i induced by the detailed schedule S. For DLAAM to be accurate, we must have

$$a_{ki} z_i^S(t) = \sum_{l \in \Lambda(S,t)} b_{kl}\bar{z}_l , \qquad k = 1, \ldots, K.$$

We see that $z_i^S(t)$ is well-defined if for all k such that $a_{ki} \neq 0$, and for all l such that $B_l \in A_i$, the ratios $\dfrac{b_{kl}}{a_{ki}}$ are independent of k. This condition is equivalent to the requirement that the detailed activities within A_i all utilize the same mix of resources. Choosing some k for which $a_{ki} \neq 0$, we write the common ratio for all $B_l \in A_i$ as

$$\alpha_{il} \equiv \frac{b_{kl}}{a_{ki}} . \tag{1}$$

The induced intensity of A_i may then be expressed as

$$z_i^S(t) = \sum_{l \in \Lambda(S,t)} \alpha_{il}\bar{z}_l .$$

Of course, not all possible intensity functions of A_i are reasonable. From CPM analysis of the underlying detailed activities and the resulting induced aggregate intensity, constraints are developed as follows.

(1) <u>Window</u> <u>of</u> <u>Operation</u> – A_i can only operate (i.e., have positive intensity) in time periods in which the detailed activities within it can. This <u>window</u> <u>of</u> <u>operation</u> is denoted by $(S_i, F_i]$, where

$$S_i = \min_{B_l \in A_i} ES_l \qquad F_i = \max_{B_l \in A_i} LS_l + D_l.$$

Let $Z_i(t) = \sum_{\tau=S_i}^{t} z_i(\tau)$ be the cumulative intensity (i.e., the proportion of work performed by A_i) up to time t. Then $Z_i(S_i)=0$ and $Z_i(F_i)=1$. We shall refer to the time history of cumulative intensity as the <u>operating mode</u> OM_i of A_i, also denoted by $OM_i = \{ Z_i(S_i), Z_i(S_i+1), \ldots, Z_i(F_i)\}$. The operating mode induced by a detailed schedule S is denoted by $OM_i^S = \{Z_i^S(t)\}_t = \{Z_i^S(S_i), Z_i^S(S_i+1), \ldots, Z_i^S(F_i) \}$.

(2) <u>Window Curves</u> – The early and late detailed schedules ES and LS are the extremes for project execution as described by the detailed network. Analogous notions exist in the aggregate network, namely the <u>early and late operating modes</u> $OM_i^E = \{Z_i^E(t)\}_t$ and $OM_i^L = \{Z_i^L(t)\}_t$. Constraints on the operating mode $\{Z_i(t)\}_t$ of A_i are given by

$$Z_i^L(t) \leq Z_i(t) \leq Z_i^E(t) \qquad t = S_i, \ldots, F_i. \tag{2}$$

We refer to OM_i^E and OM_i^L as <u>window curves</u> since all feasible activity operating modes must lie between them, as shown in Figure 2(a).

(3) <u>Intensity Bounds</u> – Considering the range of detailed schedules between the early and late schedules ES and LS, the operating intensity of A_i during a period $(t-1,t]$ that could be realized is bounded above by the following constant:

$$\bar{z}_i(t) \equiv \sum_{l \in \bar{\Gamma}(t)} \alpha_{il} \bar{z}_l,$$

where $\bar{\Gamma}(t) = \{1 \mid B_l \epsilon A_i, ES_l < t \le LS_l + D_l\}$ is the index set of all detailed activities that could possibly operate during (t-1,t]. This bound may overstate the largest possible intensity when detailed activities within A_i are in series. Note that the early and late operating modes satisfy the intensity bound constraints by construction.

Before restricting the shape of operating modes further, it is convenient to turn to dependence relationships between aggregate activities.

2.3 Aggregate Activity Dependence Relationships

Consider an aggregate activity A_i which has a successor A_j, but no other activity succeeds A_i or precedes A_j.[1] Given some operating mode OM_i for A_i, we seek the "earliest" consistent operating mode for A_j, which we denote by $OM_j^* = \{ Z_j^*(t) \}_t$. In other words, an operating mode OM_j for A_j must satisfy $Z_j(t) \le Z_j^*(t)$ for all t to be consistent with OM_i. Without specification of a detailed schedule which generates OM_i, one cannot directly calculate OM_j^*. Experimentation by the authors has shown that OM_j^* cannot reasonably be approximated by applying simple time or load lags to OM_i. (See Leachman and Boysen (1982).) On the other hand, note that if $OM_i = OM_i^E$, it is clear that $OM_j^* = OM_j^E$; similarly, if $OM_i = OM_i^L$, then $OM_j^* = OM_i^L$. If OM_i is between OM_i^E and OM_i^L, then OM_j^* must be approximated. For this purpose, let $p_i(t)$, the _relative_ _earliness_ of A_i at time t, be defined as[2]

$$p_i(t) \equiv \begin{cases} 0 & t = S_i \\[2ex] \dfrac{Z_i(t) - Z_i^L(t)}{Z_i^E(t) - Z_i^L(t)} & t = S_i + 1, \dots, F_i - 1. \\[2ex] 1 & t = F_i \end{cases}$$

We approximate OM_j^* by requiring that its relative earliness be the same as the relative earliness of OM_i, measured at corresponding points of the windows of A_j and A_i.

Figure 2 shows the results of a simple test application of this approximation, excerpted from Leachman and Boysen (1982). A detailed schedule S for a ship overhaul project was developed in which the detailed activities comprising an aggregate activity A_j follow as closely as possible the detailed activities comprising an aggregate activity A_i. (Both A_i and A_j contain more than 70 detailed activities.) Figure 2(a) shows the cumulative intensity curve OM_i^S induced by S, along with A_i's window curves. Figure 2(b) shows the same curves for A_j, plus the curve OM_j developed by equating relative earliness of A_j to the relative earliness of A_i induced by S. For this purpose, the areas between the window curves of both A_i and A_j were partitioned into 8 slices of approximately equal size, with relative earliness equated at the partitioning points. As can be seen, the curve OM_j approximates $OM_j^* = OM_j^S$ reasonably well.

In order to formulate dependence relationships when an aggregate activity has multiple predecessors or successors, one must consider the underlying detailed network structure. For example, suppose aggregate activity A has two successors B and C. (The analysis that follows also applies in the case of more than two successors.) Considering the underlying detailed network, there are two cases.

(a) _Distinct_ _Dependence_ – Suppose each detailed activity in A precedes detailed activities in both B and C, as in Figure 3(a). Since B and C are dependent on the same set of detailed

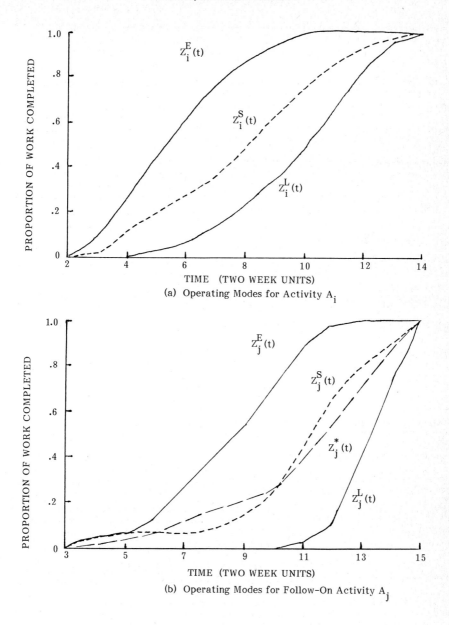

(a) Operating Modes for Activity A_i

(b) Operating Modes for Follow-On Activity A_j

Figure 2. Operating Modes for Aggregate Activities

activities within A, it is appropriate to use separate constraints to constrain the relative earliness of B by the relative earliness of A and to constrain the relative earliness of C by the relative earliness of A. The aggregate network is drawn in Figure 3(b).

(b) <u>Joint Dependence</u> – Now suppose some detailed activities within A precede only detailed activities within B or C but not both, as in Figure 3(c). A given level of progress in the completion of A (in terms of total resource use) could support a variety of combinations of progress in B and C. It is therefore appropriate to use one constraint to constrain a weighted average of the relative earliness of B and C by the relative earliness of A. (Weights for this purpose are presented in Section 2.5.) As shown in Figure 3(d), the aggregate network arcs are consolidated in a dot junction to signify such structure.

For general network structures, fairly complicated joint dependence relationships are possible. Developing dependence constraints becomes increasingly difficult, and in practice, we have found it prudent to limit aggregation so that all joint dependence relationships in the aggregate network involve either a single predecessor or a single successor. (The case in which an aggregate activity has multiple predecessors is analogous to the foregoing example). As noted in Figure 1, this limitation may require the revision of a (trial) aggregation.

2.4 Three Phase Model of Activity Operation

In the previous section, we constrained the operating modes of dependent aggregate activities to be consistent. It is also necessary to constrain each mode to take on only shapes that could reasonably be associated with some schedule for the underlying detailed activities. In this section we restrict the operating modes to reasonable shapes, and at the same time, we represent the modes with fewer variables.

From experience, it is known that resource loading profiles of the aggregate activities are characterized by a start-up phase, during which resource use is increasing, a middle phase, during which resource use is fairly steady, and a wind-down phase, during which resource use decreases. To restrict activity operating modes to such "trapezoidal" shapes, we define one decision variable for each of the three phases of an aggregate activity A_i. In the middle phase, operating intensity is held constant; the phase variable is denoted by $z_i[2]$. In the first and third phases it is relative earliness that is held constant, with variables $p_i[1]$ and $p_i[3]$.

To see that this choice of variables leads to reasonable intensity curves, note that constant relative earliness within a phase implies that the cumulative intensity is a convex combination of the window curves within the phase. Since the window curves meet at the beginning and end of the operating window, initially increasing and terminally decreasing intensities are induced. See Figure 4. However, as seen in Figure 5, constant relative earliness does not guarantee strictly monotone behavior of the intensity curve within each phase. The resulting operating mode is only approximately trapezoidal in shape.

To specify the three phase model, the window $(S_i, F_i]$ of each activity A_i is partitioned into three subintervals:

$$(S_i, F_i] = (S_i, F_i^1] \cup (F_i^1, F_i^2] \cup (F_i^2, F_i].$$

The partitioning points are chosen to divide the window curves into vertical slices of approximately equal size, with a proviso concerning the middle phase.[3] The operating mode $OM_i = \{Z_i(t)\}_t$ in the three phase model is then represented by:

$$Z_i(t) = \begin{cases} Z_i^L(t) + p_i[1](Z_i^E(t) - Z_i^L(t)) & t = S_i, \dots, F_i^1 \\ Z_i(F_i^1) + (t - F_i^1)z_i[2] & t = F_i^1+1, \dots, F_i^2. \\ Z_i^L(t) + p_i[3](Z_i^E(t) - Z_i^L(t)) & t = F_i^2+1, \dots, F_i \end{cases} \qquad (3)$$

To ensure that the curve is continuous, a boundary condition at time $t = F_1^2$ is required, namely

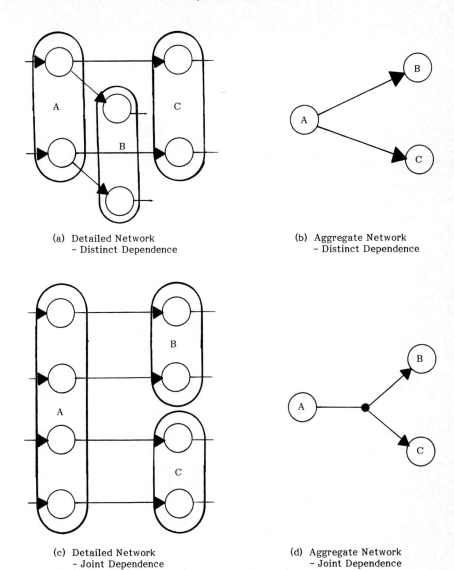

(a) Detailed Network
   – Distinct Dependence

(b) Aggregate Network
   – Distinct Dependence

(c) Detailed Network
   – Joint Dependence

(d) Aggregate Network
   – Joint Dependence

Figure 3. Distinct and Joint Dependence Relationships

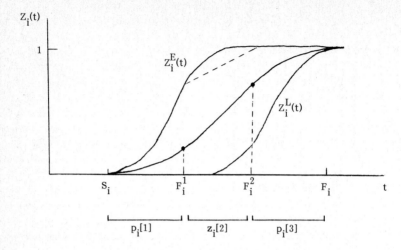

Figure 4. Three Phase Model of Activity Operation

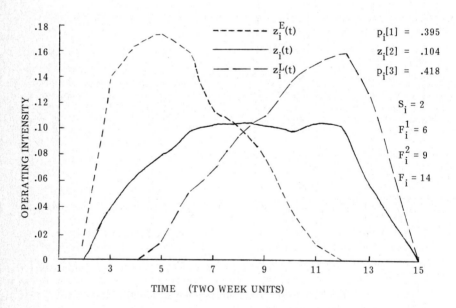

Figure 5. Example Three Phase Operating Mode

$$Z_i(F_i^2) = Z_i^L(F_i^2) + p_i[3] \, (Z_i^E(F_i^2) - Z_i^L(F_i^2) \,). \tag{4}$$

In terms of $z_i(t)$, (3) and (4) can be rewritten as

$$z_i(t) = \begin{cases} z_i^L(t) + p_i[1](z_i^E(t) - z_i^L(t)) & t = S_i, \ldots, F_i^1 \\ z_i[2] & t = F_i^1 + 1, \ldots, F_i^2 \\ z_i^L(t) + p_i[3] \, (z_i^E(t) - z_i^L(t)) & t = F_i^2 + 1, \ldots, F_i \\ 0 & \text{otherwise} \end{cases} \tag{5}$$

and $\ (F_i^2 - F_i^1)z_i[2] = z_i^L(F_i^2) - z_i^L(F_i^1) + p_i[3] \, (z_i^E(F_i^2) - z_i^L(F_i^2)) - p_i[1](z_i^E(F_i^1) - z_i^L(F_i^1)). \tag{6}$

2.5 Formulation of the Aggregate Project Model

In this section we set forth the aggregate project model in terms of the constraints and variables developed in preceding sections.

(1) <u>Intensity Bounds</u> – For all $t = S_i, \ldots, F_i$, the operating intensities of activity A_i, as given by (5) and (6), should satisfy $0 \le z_i(t) \le \bar{z}_i(t)$. These constraints are satisfied by construction in the first and third phases, so that they need to be enforced only in the middle phase, i.e.,

$$0 \le z_i[2] \le \bar{z}_i \, , \text{ where } \bar{z}_i = \min \, \{\bar{z}_i(t) \, | \, t = F_i^1 + 1, \ldots, F_i^2\}. \tag{7}$$

(2) <u>Window Curves</u> – The cumulative intensity $Z_i(t)$ of activity A_i should satisfy (2). In the first and third phases, (2) may be rewritten as

$$0 \le p_i[m] \le 1 \quad m = 1,3. \tag{8}$$

We do not directly enforce (2) during the middle phase, but observe that it is usually satisfied anyway. Referring to Figure 4, note that the cumulative intensity curve for the early operating mode is usually concave in the middle phase, while for the late mode it is convex. If operating intensity is constant in the middle phase, and if the operating mode is within the window curves in the first and third phases, then (2) is automatically satisfied, as the diagonal dashed line in the figure illustrates.

Note that, because of the constant intensity requirement in the second phase, operating modes in the three phase model are so restricted that the early and late modes can only be approximately achieved.

(3) <u>Dependence Constraints</u>[4] – For a distinct dependence relationship between aggregate activities A_i and A_j, the constraint developed in Section 2.3 is applied to the first and last phases as follows:

$$p_j[m] \le p_i[m] \quad m = 1,3. \tag{9}$$

Dependence constraints are not enforced during the middle phase; it is felt that the small loss of accuracy is not worth the additional modeling complexity that would be required. For an aggregate network including both distinct and joint dependence relationships, the dependence constraints are expressed generally as

$$\sum_{j=1}^{N} \bar{a}_{hj} p_j[m] \le \sum_{i=1}^{N} c_{hi} p_i[m] \quad \begin{matrix} h = 1, \ldots, H \\ m = 1,3 \end{matrix}, \tag{10}$$

where there are H dependence constraints in total. By assumption, activity dependencies are limited to relationships involving either a single predecessor or a single successor. In the case of a single predecessor A_i, the right hand side of (10) becomes simply $p_i[m]$, and each coefficient $\bar{a}_{hj}$ expresses the fraction of A_j's resource load on which resource loading of A_j depends, i.e.,

$$\bar{a}_{hj} = \sum_{l \in \Phi(i,j)} \alpha_{il}$$

where $\Phi(i,j) = \{1 \,|B_l \epsilon\, A_i$ and B_l precedes at least one detailed activity within $A_j\}$.

In the case of a single successor A_j, the left hand side of (10) becomes simply $p_j[m]$, and each coefficient c_{hi} expresses the fraction of A_j's resource load that depends on resource loading of A_i, i.e.,

$$c_{hi} = \sum_{l \in \Psi(i,j)} \alpha_{jl}$$

where $\Psi(i,j) = \{1 \,|B_i \epsilon\, A_j$ and B_l succeeds at least one detailed activity within $A_i\}$.

In summary, constraints (6), (7), (8), and (10) define the aggregate project model. As can be seen, a linear constraint set with $(4N+2H)$ constraints in $3N$ variables has been obtained. The following parameters from the detailed network define the constraints:

(i) Resource input coefficients $\{a_{ki}\}$, obtained by summing detailed activity resource coefficients according to the aggregation.

(ii) Activity dependence coefficients $\{\bar{a}_{hi}\}$ and $\{c_{hi}\}$, obtained by summing detailed activity resource coefficients according to the detailed network logic underlying the aggregate network structure.

(iii) Intensity bounds $\{\bar{z}_i\}$, obtained by computing early and late start schedules in the detailed network, and then summing detailed activity resource coefficients according to the schedules and the aggregation.

(iv) Window curves $\{Z_i^E(t)\}_t$ and $\{Z_i^L(t)\}_t$, also obtained by computing early and late start schedules in the detailed network, and then summing detailed activity resource coefficients for each schedule according to the aggregation.

(v) Phase boundaries $\{F_i^1, F_i^2\}$, obtained by dividing the windows according to the shape of the window curves.

During any time interval $(t-1,t]$, the loading of resource R_k on the project for a particular choice of decision variables is given by

$$\sum_{i=1}^{N} a_{ki} z_i(t), \qquad\qquad (11)$$

where the sum may be restricted to only those activities whose windows intersect $(t-1,t]$. Depending on which phase of A_i intersects $(t-1,t]$, the appropriate expression from equation (5) is substituted for $z_i(t)$ in (11).

3. The Multi-Project Resource Allocation Model

We now group aggregate project models into one model for multi-project resource allocation. By combining the models of all on-going and future projects, the total use of resources by the organization is represented. Given this representation, resource allocations to the projects are to be determined that utilize resource capacities most efficiently. The allocations then provide the basis for detailed scheduling at the project level.

Model Formulation

Let the on-going and future projects be denoted by PR_j, $j=1, \ldots, J$. Resource allocations to the projects are to be planned for time periods $(t-1,t]$, $t=1, \ldots, T$. If a project finishes beyond T then activities whose windows extend beyond T will be excluded. If a project is underway at time zero, some activities will be in execution, and others may have been completed;

resource use of such activities is taken as fixed.

Let A_i, i=1, ..., I, denote the aggregate activities under consideration, numbered across all projects. As notation, assume the aggregate project model for project PR_j includes H(j) dependence constraints. An aggregate activity which is part of PR_j will be identified by $A_i \epsilon PR_j$.

We shall discuss variables, constraints and the objective function for the linear programming (LP) allocation model in turn.

(1) Variables

The phase variables $p_i[1]$, $z_i[2]$, $p_i[3]$ for each activity A_i are the actual LP variables. The operating mode $\{z_i(t)\}_t$ of A_i is determined according to (5), and resource use is determined according to (11).

(2) Constraints

(a) Project Execution – The constraints on the execution of a project PR_j, as developed in Section 2, are summarized below:

$$0 \leq z_i[2] \leq \bar{z}_i \qquad\qquad A_i \epsilon PR_j \qquad (a)$$

$$0 \leq p_i[m] \leq 1 \qquad m=1,3; \quad A_i \epsilon PR_j \qquad (b) \qquad (12)$$

$$\sum_i \bar{a}_{hi}p_i[m] \leq \sum_i c_{hi}p_i[m] \quad m=1,3; \quad h=1, \ldots, H(j) \quad (c)$$
$$A_i \epsilon PR_j \qquad\qquad A_i \epsilon PR_j$$

In addition, one has the equality constraints (6) expressing the boundary condition for each $A_i \epsilon PR_j$. These constraints and the middle phase variables can be eliminated by substituting (6) into (12a).

(b) Resource Capacities – Let the capacity through time of resource R_k be denoted by $\bar{x}_k(t)$, t=1, ..., T. These capacities reflect the quantities of exogenous resources available for allocation to A_i, i=1, ..., I. Use of R_k by all projects is then bounded as follows:

$$\sum_{j=1}^{J} \sum_{A_i \epsilon^I PR_j} a_{ki}z_i(t) \leq \bar{x}_k(t) \qquad \begin{array}{l} k=1, \ldots, K, \\ t=1, \ldots, T \end{array} \qquad (13)$$

where the expressions in (5) are substituted for $z_i(t)$ as appropriate.

(c) Size of Constraint Matrix – Suppose that each project contains N aggregate activities using H intermediate products on average, and that, while some projects will not be executed completely within (0,T], the equivalent of J whole projects is incorporated into the LP. Then there are (J)(N+2H)+(K)(T) inequality constraints in (J)(2N) variables with upper bounds.

In developing an aggregate network describing a naval ship overhaul, the authors encountered a value for H on the order of N, the number of activities. For an aggregate planning system in a large shipyard, the following parameter values might arise:

$$J=16 \qquad N=50 \qquad K=20 \qquad T=50,$$

leading to about 3400 inequalities in 1600 upper bounded variables. Such problems are readily handled by existing computer packages.

(3) Objective Function

Since total resource use up to time T is fixed, alternative LP solutions correspond to shifting resource use through time. Unless resource demand saturates capacity for all time periods, resource quantities will be idle at some point. Resources will be utilized most efficiently if occurrences of idle resources are shifted as far into the future as possible. Equivalently, the production system should be "packed" as tightly as possible with project work, thus maximizing productivity.

The objective function which accomplishes efficient resource utilization is the minimization of the total discounted cost of unutilized resources, formulated as follows. Let w_k be the capacity cost of resource R_k, i.e., the cost which would be charged against on-going projects for an unutilized unit of resource R_k. Let β_t be the discount factor; if shifting one unit of idle resource by n time periods has the same value as shifting n units by one period, then β_t may be taken as

$$\beta_k = (T - t+1). \tag{14}$$

For general β_t, the objective function is written as

$$\min \sum_{k=1}^{K} \sum_{t=1}^{T} w_k \beta_t [\bar{x}_k(t) - \sum_{j=1}^{J} \sum_{\substack{i \\ A_i \epsilon PR_j}} a_{ki} z_i(t)]. \tag{15}$$

4. Application of the Model

4.1 Data

The data of each aggregate project model were summarized in Section 2.4. These parameters, taken with the resource capacities in (13), constitute the input data of the multi-project allocation model.

Before each use of the model, variables representing current resource utilization or commitments must be fixed, and input data must be revised according to existing conditions and the latest target dates established for restraining events. The preparation of data for current projects, future projects, and the revision of data are discussed below.

Current Projects

Detailed activity networks are assumed to be available for current projects and those about to start. Restraining event dates will have been fixed for such projects. Aggregate activity parameters are thus obtainable from the detailed activity information using the procedures described in Section 2.

Suppose for the moment that a current project is proceeding well enough that late start dates for detailed activities are still valid, and there have been no major revisions in the project work program. Then no adjustments to the project's activity parameters are required. The status of the project's aggregate activities may be determined by examining their applications of resources so far, and the commitments made for near-term resource use. It is assumed here that if an activity A_i is about to start or just started, then its operation in the first phase, i.e., the value of $p_i[1]$, is predetermined. If it is well underway or complete, then all three phase variables $p_i[1]$, $z_i[2]$, $p_i[3]$ are predetermined. The resource capacities in (13) must be adjusted to reflect such predetermined resource use. Also, the values of the relative earliness phase variables for just-starting, in-progress and completed activities must be fixed in order to properly constrain the progress of succeeding activities. For this purpose, the value of $p_i[m]$, m=1,3, can be approximated as the proportion of the area between the window curves within phase $[m]_i$, m=1,3, that lies below the cumulative intensity curve. Recalling the definition of intensity in Section 2.2, the cumulative intensity $Z_i(t)$ to use in this approximation is simply the fraction of total resources required by A_i that have been applied up to time t.

Future Projects

Detailed data may not be available if a project is still in the planning stage, yet the project may need to be considered in resource use planning. In such a case, development of the aggregate activity network and estimation of aggregate activity parameters must be conducted directly from the planning data that is available. In the process of developing the aggregate data, tentative dates for restraining events must be established. As more refined planning data is developed, aggregate activity parameters would be revised, as discussed below.

Modifying Activity Parameters

Aggregate activity parameters must be modified in case the work content of a project is revised, a restraining event date is changed, or some activity is delayed beyond its late operating mode. If the detailed activity network for the project is kept up to date, then one can simply reapply the procedures in Section 2 to revise aggregate parameters. If the detailed network is not yet available or not kept up to date, then methods to directly update aggregate parameters are required. Some simple, approximate techniques are suggested below in brief.

Suppose an aggregate activity A is delayed beyond its late operating mode. The delay is taken into account by shifting its late window curve into the future. The shift is then repeated (propagated) forward through the network, following the aggregate network arcs up to restraining events. If activity A is only one of several activities on which an activity B depends (and the others are not affected by the delay of A), then a partial shifting of B's late window curve is more appropriate, the amount of shift depending on the particular effect on detailed activities within B that succeed detailed activities within A.

If a restraining event is revised, activity window curves again must be adjusted. Suppose an event is delayed. (A shift to an earlier target date is analogous.) The early window curves of activities succeeding the event are shifted forward in time; the late curves of activities preceding it are shifted backwards in time. These shifts are again propagated through the network.

Suppose an aggregate activity's work content is revised. Then resource input coefficients should be revised according to the change in resource requirements. If the work content revision applies (approximately) uniformly during the activity's operating period, and assuming the resource loading rates of detailed activites are unchanged, then it is appropriate to proportionately rescale (in the time dimension) the activity's window curves. If the change affects only a few, but significant, detailed activities within the aggregate activity, then rescaling only a portion of the window curves may be more appropriate. Once again, there needs to be a propagation through the network of the window curve modifications. For simplicity, it is suggested to shift both early and late window curves of follow-on activites according to the increase in the length of the window of the revised activity. Changes in the shape of the revised activity's window curves are ignored.

4.2. Model Use

The model is used at regular intervals to perform reallocations of each resource on a rolling horizon basis. Only near-term allocations from the model are committed; allocations for more distant time periods are tentative and can be considered as forecasts.

The committed and forecast allocations to each project are to be viewed by the project's manager as resource capacities available to the project. This establishes the basis for the application of resource-constrained scheduling of detailed activities at the project level.

Before each session with the model, the time horizon is rolled forward, data parameters for each project are updated, and resource capacities are revised. A typical session with the model is likely to include several optimizations of the model for various parameters before a desirable resource plan is realized. For instance, experiments with different restraining event dates for future projects may be conducted. Use of the model may indicate an infeasible situation or an unacceptable level of idle resources, in which case event dates will be revised. Activity window curves are then adjusted, as discussed in Section 4.1, for another iteration of the model.

4.3. Application and Computational Examples

An aggregate activity network for an actual ship overhaul was developed by the authors. The original detailed critical path network contained approximately 1150 activities, which were aggregated into 39 aggregate activites. The resources of interest in this case were 12 different types of trade labor in the shipyard. Table 1 lists the labor types and aggregate activity characteristics, including the windows of operation for a particular choice of restraining event dates. The unit of time is two weeks. Figure 6 portrays the aggregate network. Two examples of joint dependence relationships arise.

The aggregate project model consisted of 118 inequalities in 73 upper-bounded variables. (Some variables were predetermined.) The model included 25 activity dependence constraints.

In the case of the shipyard, a limited number of classes of ships are overhauled. It is envisioned that a prototype aggregate network would be developed for each class. It is believed that variations in work content between overhauls of ships in the same class can be adequately reflected through direct adjustment of aggregate parameters, at least to adequately support advance resource use planning.

The multi-project resource allocation model was tested with computer runs on a CDC 6400 utilizing the ALPHAC linear programming package. Various FORTRAN routines were written to generate the aggregate activity parameters from computations using the underlying detailed network. A routine was also programmed to propagate window curve shifts through the aggregate networks. These programs support another routine which generated the constraint matrix for the ALPHAC package.

Figure 5 displays a three phase operating mode obtained from an LP solution. (This is activity A_{27}.) As can be seen, the mode is only approximately trapezoidal.

Figure 7 displays the LP-generated load profiles for labor type 1 for a hypothetical example of three identical ship overhauls (i.e., three copies of the aggregate network shown in Figure 6). In this example, two dry docks are available for the three overhauls, so that overhaul 1 is followed by overhaul 2 in the same drydock, while overhaul 3 is executed in parallel in the other dry dock. Restraining event dates were set so that overhauls 1, 2 and 3 were executed during periods 1-20, 21-40, and 11-30, respectively, subject to arbitrarily defined labor capacities $x^k(t)$, $k=1, \ldots, 12$, $t=1, \ldots, 40$. In Figure 7(b), capacity of labor type 1 (labelled $\bar{x}^1(t)$) is plotted against utilization (labelled $x^1(t)$). Note the "valley" in time periods 19-21, indicating that the undocking event of overhaul 1 and the docking event of overhaul 2 should perhaps be shifted closer together. In Figure 7(a), the load profiles for each overhaul are displayed (labelled $x_1^1(t)$, $x_2^1(t)$, $x_3^1(t)$, for overhauls 1,2,3, respectively). Note how the overhauls are executed very differently, in response to the bulge in available capacity.

For more examples and further details, the reader is referred to Leachman and Boysen (1982) and Boysen (1982).

5. Concluding Remarks

We have considered production planning and scheduling for large-scale, project-oriented systems with inflexible resource capacities. For such systems, it is impractical to perform multi-project resource allocation using detailed activity networks. Instead, a hierarchical approach is required in which a collective plan is prepared for resource use through time by each project. These plans then guide the detailed scheduling of each project.

To implement this approach, the need arises to develop aggregate models of the projects which accurately portray the consequences of alternative resource allocations on project execution. That is, the models must accurately describe the alternatives for resource use by each project.

Table 1
OVERHAUL ACTIVITY DATA

No.	Activity Name	Number of Detailed Activities	Total Work Content (mandays)	Window of Operation (S_i, F_i] S_i	F_i
1	Remove Lagging, Engine & Boiler Rooms	5	500	0	2
2	Remove Structural Components 602-604	11	105	5	9
3	Repair Structural Components 602-604	18	508	6	13
4	Reinstall Structural Components 602-604	13	152	10	14
5	Remove Mechanical Components 602-604	8	127	5	9
6	Repair Mechanical Components 602-604	13	505	7	12
7	Reinstall and Test Mechanical Components 602-604	10	217	9	14
8	Misc. Mechanical Overhals 602-604	18	548	5	14
9	Misc. Electrical Overhals 602-604	32	436	5	14
10	Misc. Structural Overhals 602-604	18	660	5	14
11	Misc. Removals 514-604	10	52	1	6
12	Misc. Repairs 514-604	17	495	2	13
13	Misc. Reinstallations & Test 514-604	19	197	6	14
14	Overhaul Tanks and Voids	40	1668	1	14
15	Overhaul Air Systems	44	885	0	16
16	Misc. Removals 601-609	29	205	0	12
17	Misc. Repairs 601-609	33	764	5	13
18	Misc. Reinstallations 601-609	29	696	8	19
19	Misc. Component Overhauls 601-609	53	1917	0	19
20	Remove Electrical System Components	45	331	0	9
21	Repair Electrical System Components	84	2597	1	15
22	Reinstall Electrical System Components	61	1046	3	16
23	Test Electrical System Components	45	1104	5	20
24	Post Undocking Tests	23	190	14	19
25	In-place Overhaul Engine Room Components	51	1876	1	15
26	Remove Engine Room Components	68	575	1	10
27	Repair Engine Room Components	92	3207	2	14
28	Reinstall Engine Room Components	70	1193	3	15
29	Test Engine Room Components	44	1064	7	16
30	In-place Repair Engine Room Components	14	387	3	15
31	Overhaul Vents & Bilges	11	1385	1	14
32	Repair & Reinstall Lagging	7	1577	5	19
33	Inspect Boiler	8	467	1	4
34	Remove Boiler Room Components	11	624	2	9
35	Repair Boiler Room Components	15	813	3	12
36	Reinstall Boiler Room Components	16	1161	5	15
37	Test Boiler Room Components	21	733	9	16
38	In-place Repair Boiler Room Components	32	1579	3	16
39	System Test Turbine & Boiler	9	114	16	19
	TOTALS	1147	32660		

LIST OF LABOR TYPES

No.	Name	Total Req't (mandays)	No.	Name	Total Req't (mandays)
1	Pipefitting	5913	7	Boilermakers	2309
2	Mechanical Group - Shipboard	5111	8	Weld & Burn	2289
3	Mechanical Group - Shore	4307	9	Structural Group I	1392
4	Electrical	3038	10	Structural Group II	1333
5	Painting	2999	11	Shipwright	638
6	Electronics	2796	12	Rigging	536

60

R. Leachman, J. Boysen

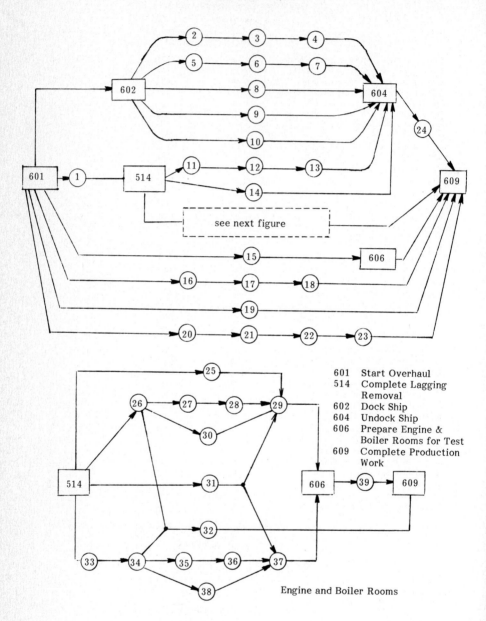

601 Start Overhaul
514 Complete Lagging Removal
602 Dock Ship
604 Undock Ship
606 Prepare Engine & Boiler Rooms for Test
609 Complete Production Work

Engine and Boiler Rooms

Figure 6. Aggregate Overhaul Network

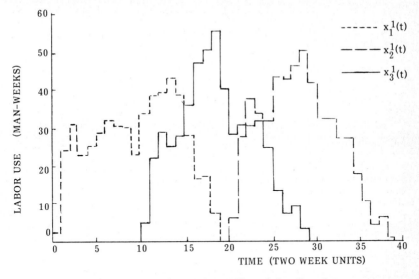

(a) Overhaul Load Profiles – Labor Type 1

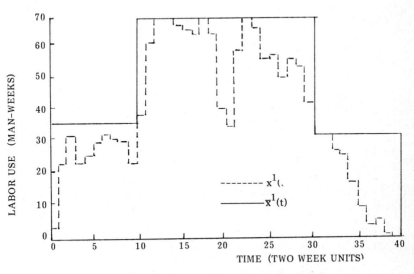

(b) Total Load and Capacity – Labor Type 1

Figure 7. Computational Example

Various authors have studied the aggregation of CPM networks into higher-level CPM net-works. Unfortunately, such aggregation deletes information concerning the alternatives for resource use, and thus is inappropriate for the problem at hand. In this paper, aggregation rules which preserve resource use information have been utilized. The resulting aggregate activities are much more sophisticated in nature than detailed activites. Therefore, the production process of each aggregate activity and dependence relationships between aggregate activites must be <u>modelled</u>.

The key contribution of this paper is the demonstration of simple but accurate methods for this purpose. These methods allow one to model complex relationships using linear inequalities, leading to aggregate project models which are realistic yet computationally tractable.

We have shown how the aggregate project models may be combined into a multi-project resource allocation model, formulated as a linear program. The allocation model is used to establish resource use plans and milestone dates for each project. These plans and due dates then provide the basis for the management of individual projects.

The aggregate modeling approach was developed in the context of production planning in a naval shipyard. Its applicability in such an environment has been illustrated. We have reason to believe the concepts of the approach are applicable in other environments, such as discrete multi-stage manufacturing, and we continue our research efforts toward that end.

Acknowledgements

This research was supported by the Office of Naval Research and the Puget Sound Naval Shipyard under Contract N00014-76-C-0134 with the University of California. The cooperation of various shipyard staff is gratefully acknowledged. Many of the modeling ideas set forth in this paper were inspired by stimulating discussions with the late Ronald W. Shephard. Much of the material in this paper was adapted from Leachman and Boysen (1982) and Dr. Boysen's dissertation, Boysen (1982).

FOOTNOTES

[1] It should be noted that if A_i and A_j are separated by a restraining event, then A_i strictly precedes A_j, i.e., there is no overlap in their operation. The ensuing discussion concerns the case when the operation of A_i and A_j overlap, i.e., there is no restraining event between them.

[2] It is assumed that $Z_i^E(t) > Z_i^L(t)$ for $t=S_i+1, \ldots, F_i-1$.

[3] Referring to (5), note that if for some t in the first or third phases $z_i^E(t)=z_i^L(t) = c$, a constant, then we would be forced to have $z_i(t) = c$ for all alternative operating modes. Usually $z_i^E(t)$ and $z_i^L(t)$ are only equal in the middle phase (see Figure 5), but, for example, both could simultaneously be zero for a number of periods in the first or third phases if A_i was composed of detailed activites with considerable slack, thereby spreading apart the two window curves in Figure 5. To avoid this unrealistic restriction, the middle phase should be widened (if necessary) to include all time periods in the window in which the early and late intensities are equal.

[4] For aggregate activities separated by a restraining event, no dependence constraints are required.

REFERENCES

[1] Archibald, R. D. Managing High-Technology Programs and Projects, John Wiley & Sons, New York, 1976.

[2] Boysen, J., "Aggregate Project Model for Resource Allocation Within Multiproject Construction Systems," Ph.D. Dissertation, College of Engineering, University of California, Berkeley, 1982.

[3] Burman, P. J., Precedence Networks for Project Planning and Control, McGraw-Hill, New York, 1972.

[4] Cooper, D. F., "Heuristics for Scheduling Resource Constrained Projects: An Experimental Investigation," Management Science, 22 (11), 1186-1194, 1976.

[5] Davis, E. W., "Project Scheduling under Resource Constraints - Historical Review and Categorization of Procedures," AIIE Transactions, 5 (4), 297-313, 1973.

[6] Eardley, V. J., "Production of Multi-Level Critical Path Method Networks," Department of Civil Engineering, University of Illinois, Urbana.

[7] Harris, R. B., Precedence and Arrow Networking Techniques for Construction, John Wiley & Sons, New York, 1978.

[8] Jones, C. M., "An Aggregate-Disaggregate Approach to the Large Scale Multiple Project Scheduling Problem," in Disaggregation Problems in Manufacturing and Service Organizations, L. P. Ritzman et al (eds.), Martinus Nijhoff, Boston, 389-401, 1979.

[9] Kurtulus, I. and E. W. Davis, "Multi-Project Scheduling: Categorization of Heuristic Rules Performance," Management Science, 28 (2), 161-172, 1982.

[10] Leachman, R. C., "Production Planning for Multi-Resource Network Systems," Naval Research Logistics Quarterly, 29 (1), 47-54, 1982.

[11] Leachman, R. C., "Multiple Resource Leveling in Construction Systems Through Variation of Activity Intensities," Naval Research Logistics Quarterly, 30 (3), 187–198, 1983.

[12] Leachman, R. C. and J. Boysen, "Aggregate Network Model of Ship Overhaul," Report ORC 82-2, Operations Research Center, University of California, Berkeley, 1982.

[13] Moder, J. J. and C. R. Phillips, Project Management with CPM and PERT, 2d ed., Van Nostrand Reinhold, New York, 1970.

[14] Parikh, S. C. and W. S. Jewell, "Decomposition of Project Networks," Management Science, 11 (3), 444–459, 1965.

[15] Shephard, R. W., R. Al-Ayat, and R. C. Leachman, "Shipbuilding Production Function: An Example of a Dynamic Production Function," in Quantitative Wirschaftsforschung Festschrift Volume (Wilhelm Krelle), J.B.C. Mohr (ed.), Tubingen, 1977.

[16] Thesen, A., "Heuristic Scheduling of Activities Under Resource and Precedence Restrictions," Management Science, 23 (4), 412–422, 1976.

[17] Vlalch, J., "Some Results of Connecting (Aggregating) Networks in Building," Internet 2: Project Planning by Network Analysis, North-Holland, Amsterdam, 418–426, 1969.

Part II
PROJECT SCHEDULING AND CONTROL

Project Management: Methods and Studies
Burton V. Dean (editor)
© Elsevier Science Publishers B.V. (North-Holland), 1985

GENE-SPLICING PERT AND CPM:
THE ENGINEERING OF PROJECT NETWORK MODELS

Jerome D. Wiest

Department of Management
University of Utah
Salt Lake City, Utah
U.S.A.

Since their birth a quarter of a century ago, the original project
network models, PERT and CPM, have followed a roller-coaster
existence: a dizzying ascent, followed by a rapid decline -- at
least among the reluctant clientele of the DOD. Among voluntary
users, however, especially in the construction industry, popularity
has been more enduring--even increasing. While the original models
have been simplified in use, stripped of some of their more interesting
and complex features, researchers and academics continue to modify
and build on the basic models, spinning out newer ones with added
capabilities and wider application.

Thus the original PERT model was expanded early on to merge cost
accounting data with time schedules (PERT/COST). PERT's lack of
resource scheduling led to numerous efforts to incorporate resource
constraints along with precedence constraints in its methodology.
Heuristic models such as RAMPS and SPAR led the way to numerous
other heuristic approaches and a variety of commercial packages for
limited resource project scheduling. Many attempts at developing
true optimizing models have not been as successful in practical terms.
PERT's probabilistic features were criticized and modified (e.g. BPERT)
and ultimately extended to include the network itself, as exemplified by
simulation models such as GERT and VERT with their probabilistic
nodes. Decision CPM (DCPM) introduced the notion of "decision nodes,"
used for network planning purposes.

Alternate representation of the arrow diagram common to PERT and
CPM actually predated these models; known as activity-on arrow
networks, these were later expanded to include additional precedence
relationships, as used in PDM (precedence diagramming method). An
attempt to extend the usefulness of PERT from the development phase
of a new product to the production phase led to PERT/LOB, a marriage
of project networks with line-of-balance techniques. A more recent
amalgam of two distinct models is CPM/MRP, which is intended to
incorporate MRP's focus on lead times and inventory status in the
framework of CPM's activity structure and precedence relationships.

These and many others comprise a large family tree of models engineered
from PERT/CPM genes in the past 25 years. But practitioners are not
easily converted to the use of more complicated models. Gene-spliced
versions such as those mentioned above have had mixed success in actual
applications for a variety of reasons. The subject still attracts the attention of researchers, however, and more genetic engineering is to be expected.

INTRODUCTION

A quarter of a century has now passed since the introduction of the original project network models, PERT and CPM. In that period, their acronyms have become common words in our language and their function well established in use. Hardly a new book on Production Management or Management Sciences can be found that doesn't devote a chapter to them. Like space flights and mirco processors, they have become commonplace; little is remembered of the great hoopla that accompanied their birth. Only those of us old enough to have witnessed the process, and close enough to it by virtue of profession or interest, can appreciate the great stir that was caused. Because PERT (and its many close cousons) enjoyed the patronage of a rich uncle, its ascendancy was swift and overwhelming. Multi-billion dollar government budgets, primarily dispensed through the DOD, brought a lot of converts to this new project management system, and when contract clauses required companies interested in government projects to pert, everyone perted. At least to all appearances.

The Rise and Fall

It was a frenzied period, with everyone trying to jump on the bandwagon at once. There was a great proliferation of training programs, seminars, short courses, briefings and the like to teach contractors, managers, and technicians this new technique. Consultants abounded ("expert" gained a new, double meaning). The body of literature on the subject mushroomed with hundreds of articles, books and recorded speeches. Academic respectability was bestowed by learned papers appearing in professional journals, and many students won masters and doctoral degrees with theses based on project network models. Computer programs grew ever more powerful and capable, until projects with tens of thousands of activities could be accommodated, with endless printouts possible through various permutations of data sorts. Wall-to-wall PERT became a literal reality for project managers.

Not everyone was ecstatic about PERT and CPM, however, and a growing body of criticisms accompanied the wave of testimonial [31]. "Picking on PERT" became a common pastime. As might be expected of any product or concept that becomes over-blown and over-sold, the frenzy of interest could not be maintained. There followed a period of decline, of disillusion, of unwilling converts falling away, especially after the government relaxed its requirements for PERT usage by contractors. It became an embarrassment in some circles to even admit to the use of PERT, which became just another 4-letter word. Its epitaph was well pronounced by a former apostle, Vazsonyi, in his "L'Histoire de Grandeur et de la Decadence de la Methode PERT" [25].

. . . and Reincarnation

Not all users abandoned it, of course. The reluctant clientele of the DOD largely dropped it but PERT and CPM, as generic terms for project network techniques, continue to be widely used, especially in the construction industry [7]. As with the broom of the sorcerer's apprentice, who tried to lay it to rest by chopping it to bits, the pieces of PERT keep arising, in ever-varying garb. The technique has long enjoyed a fascination for both practitioners and academic types, who find in it an ideal model for modifying, building on, and combining with other models to form ingenious hybrids. I can think of no other similar model that has inspired so much genetic engineering and spawned so many related products. It has been so from the beginning, and, interestingly, continues to be so. A search of the literature reveals a more-or-less steady flow of articles on project network models, many dealing with new variants. If PERT is dead (which seems questionable), then sons and daughters of PERT live on; marriages and offspring continue.

Geneology of CPM and PERT

It is a bit of an exaggeration to speak of PERT and CPM as "the original" project network models. Legitimate claims can be made that other similar models preceded it. Fondahl in this country and Roy in France both developed activity-on-node representations of projects about this time, and Andrew in England reported using a "controlling sequence duration method" back in 1955 [27]. There were also many mutants or similar models with different acronyms that vied with PERT for favor, including PEP (the Air Force version), LESS (IBM's model), IMPACT, NASA PERT, PLANET, SKED, SPERT, PERT II, III, and IV, and many others. Whether PERT was better or simply had better PR became moot; its well-publicized success in the Navy's Polaris Missile program gave it an edge the others never overcame. PERT became a generic term for a type of project network model, along with CPM, which benefitted from an acronym that better described the method. (It is more likely for a user to say that he/she used the critical path method than that the program evaluation and review technique was used.)

It wasn't long before modifications of these models began to appear that may best be described as "gene-spliced" models, in which two or more distinct techniques or methodologies were combined in some way. The analogy with genetic engineering may not be precise, but it is close: desirable features of two or more entities are spliced together to yield a product more useful than any of the parents, or so it is hoped. Figure 1 is a graphic representation of the PERT/CPM family, a kind of family group sheet showing some of the many offspring that have resulted from such mergers. To make the geneology a bit more complete, the parentage of PERT and CPM is also shown, along with some of the many mutants. All of the network-based models had their roots in graph theory. Another obvious parent of both PERT and CPM was the Gantt Chart, long used by production managers. Additionally, CPM drew some of its features from network flow theory, and PERT made use of some principles of probability theory.

It should be noted that most of the models shown as spliced versions of CPM or PERT do not make use of the unique features of those two (PERT's probabilistic times and CPM's time-cost tradeoffs) and therefore could be shown connected to either one, considered as a generic model only. The choice of such connections, however, was dictated in most cases by the names of the hybrids.

PERT/COST

The first variations on PERT followed soon after its introduction, to answer the criticism that its time-only orientation was too narrow. PERT/COST was an attempt to include in a common framework both time scheduling and cost accounting, for planning and controlling purposes [11]. In concept, it appeared reasonable: instead of accumulating costs on a functional or departmental basis, identify them by activities in the work structure breakdown, so that managers may more realistically and accurately appraise past and projected costs of a project (see Figures 2 and 3) and identify more precisely the sources of excess costs (Figure 4). In practice, it caused problems. Companies were too used to traditional methods of cost accounting, which were usually not abandoned even when the new system was tried. Dual cost-accounting systems apparently were more bothersome than beneficial. One hardly ever hears about PERT/COST today, except in a historical review.

Figure 2 illustrates a typical PERT/COST chart. Line A, the budgeted cost schedule, is based on a projected work schedule and estimated costs time-phased to that schedule. Line C reflects value of work completed to date. The horizontal distance between this and budget costs is a measure of schedule slippage (line E). Actual costs (line B) relative to value of work complete yields an estimate of cost overrun (line D). Updates of the work schedule with associated completion costs are shown in Figure 3, lines G and F. These in turn lead to projected cost overruns (line H) and schedule slippage (line I). The major sources of cost and schedule overruns can then be traced by examining similar charts for major end items and for departments (Figure 4).

MOST

MOST (for Management Operations System Technique) is one of the simpler modifications of PERT [12]. In essence, it is a late-start Gantt Bar chart with dashed lines connecting bars (activities) to indicate precedence relationships (see Figure 5). The horizontal length of a bar represents its expected time (single estimate), and its left and right ends can be read from the time scale as late start and finish times. The horizontal lengths of dashed lines are a measure of slack of activities connected by the lines. Critical activities are evident as a connected sequence of bars marking the critical path through the MOST network. In a manner similar to Gantt charting, bars are shaded from left to right to indicate the portion of work accomplished, and a vertical reporting line representing the current date indicates graphically

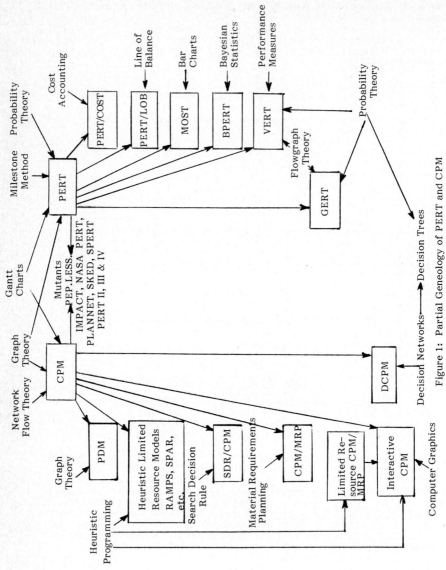

Figure 1: Partial Geneology of PERT and CPM

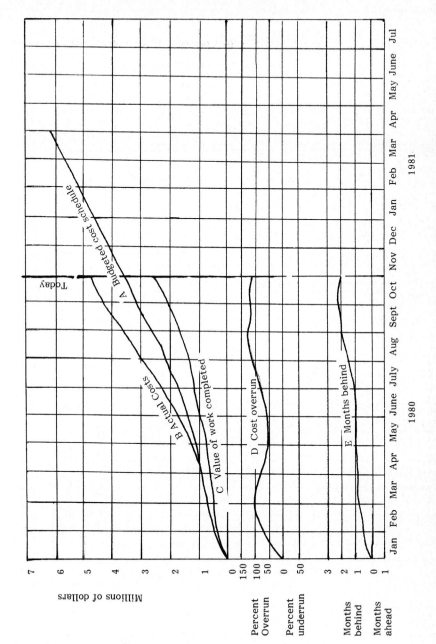

Figure 2. PERT/COST: Cumulative summary to date of actual vs. budgeted costs and work completed.

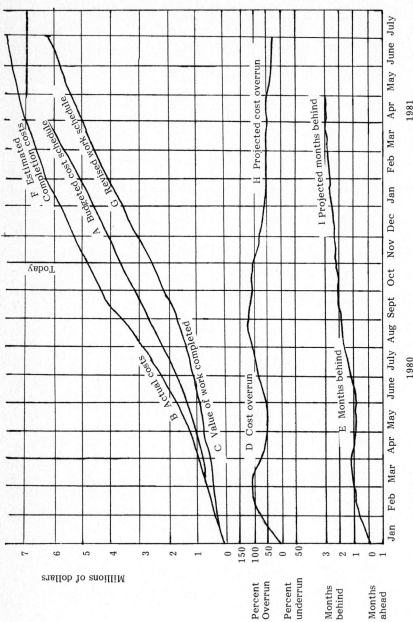

Figure 3. PERT/COST: Projections up to the estimated completion date of actual costs, work completed, cost overrun, and schedule slippage.

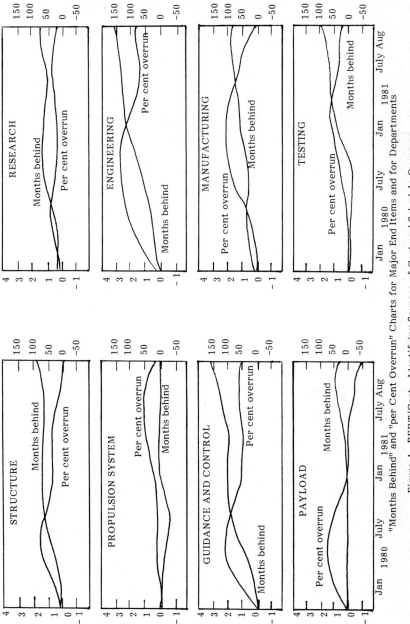

Figure 4. PERT/Cost – Identifying Sources of Cost and Schedule Overruns
"Months Behind" and "per Cent Overrun" Charts for Major End Items and for Departments

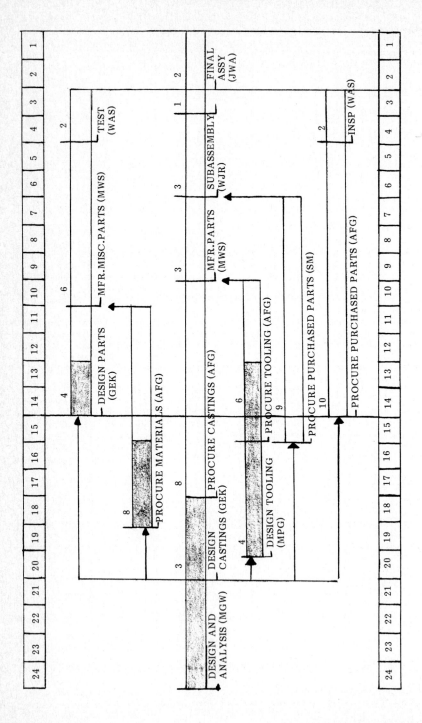

Figure 5. MOST (Management Operation System Technique)

which activities are ahead or behind schedule. Cost and resource analysis may be included on the network. MOST has the advantage of being simple, easily maintained, and clearly interpreted. To keep its size reasonable, activities would have to be kept at a fairly high level of aggregation; thus detailed planning and scheduling of large projects would have to be managed by some other means.

BPERT

Many researchers have addressed the problems of incorporating uncertainty in activity duration times, in order to assess the probabilities of project finishing by various dates. PERT's three-time-estimate approach has been criticized, modified and studied empirically. One suggested revision involves some concepts of Bayesian statistics. BPERT (for Bayesian PERT) suggests that Bayesian point estimates be formulated for beta-distributed activity duration times so as to minimize the potential loss of misestimation. Viewed as certainty equivalents, these time estimates are then aggregated to yield a single project completion date [3]. Conceptually interesting, the system raises questions about managers' ability to deal with Bayesian estimation, when they complained about the complexity of using three time estimates.

PERT/LOB

PERT/LOB was promoted as a management tool that would span from the development phase of a new product (best suited to PERT) to the production period, for which Line of Balance (LOB) had been developed, including the transition period when production first begins (12, 24]. LOB employs a network similar to PERT's which shows the interrelationships and times of activities needed to produce one product (Figure 6). Nodes in the graph, marking the beginning or completion of important events, become control points by which progress is measured. These control points, offset by their lead times, can be projected against a cumulative production schedule to determine the number of parts or components that should be completed by any given progress review date (Figure 7). These quantities, displayed in a characteristic stepped-down pattern (the Line of Balance) on a graph of cumulative quantity vs. control points, can then be compared to actual quantities completed, with problem points showing up clearly (Figure 8).

PERT/LOB modifies the typical project network with one-time activities by including repetitive activities and events to reflect the manufacture of multiple components and end items. Network calculations follow the normal PERT procedures, except that in PERT/LOB repetitive activities have multiple contact points rather than a single point as in the PERT system. Status reports at any point in time portray production information at each control point and show project completion dates for the control point activities.

GERT and VERT

The most ambitious offspring of PERT include GERT [19, 21] and VERT [18], both of which are network-based simulation techniques designed to analyze projects in which there is uncertainty with respect to not only activity durations but to the network itself. Unforeseen circumstances might cause a different path to be taken, failed tests might lead back to "redesign", with looping paths in the network (something prohibited in ordinary networks), or failures might occur that prevent an activity from being completed (PERT networks require that all activities be completed). The flexibility to model such events is obtained through the use of probabilistic nodes, which allow the possibility that existing activities may commence when one or more (but not necessarily all) entering activities are completed. Such nodes also allow for probabilistic exits from the node, in which case only one of several emanating activities is actually taken. Thus, activities themselves may be uncertain, occurring with some stated probability which may be less than 1.

GERT (for Graphical Evaluation and Review Technique) employs eight different types of nodes, with four different input sides controlling the "release" of the node, and two output sides, deterministic and probabilistic (Figure 9). The input logic essentially determines how many incoming activities must be completed before the node is released, which may differ in first and subsequent passes through the node. Figure 10 illustrates some possible combinations. In similar fashion, VERT (for Venture Evaluation and Review Technique) utilizes split

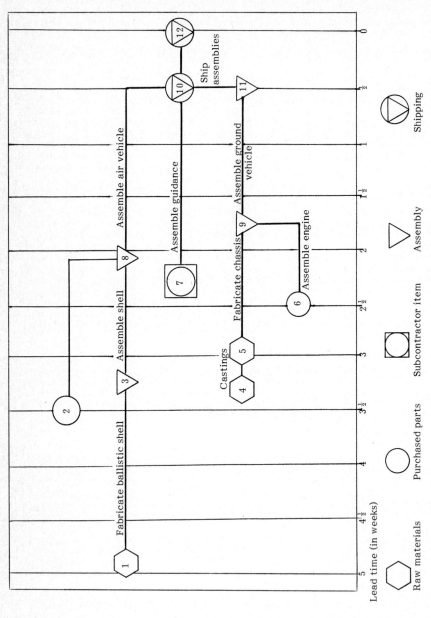

Figure 6.   PERT/LOB – XYZ Corporation: activity interrelationships and time schedules [Numbers denote control points]

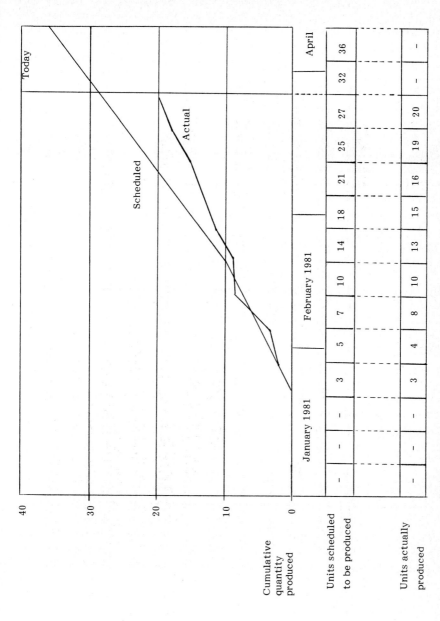

Figure 7. PERT/LOB – XYZ Corporation: mobile missile system schedule objective

J. Wiest

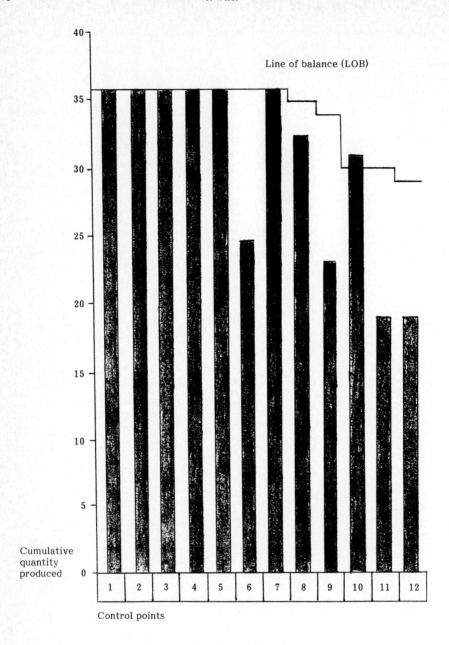

Figure 8. PERT/LOB
Program progress chart as of March 28, 1981

Symbol	Meaning
	The first nodal release will occur when there have been **m** incident activity completions. Subsequent releases require **n** completions.
	The first nodal release requires that **m different** incident activities be completed. Subsequent releases require **n** such completions.
	The first nodal release will occur with **m** incident activity completions. All other on-going incident activities will be halted at that point. Subsequent releases require **n** completions, with the same halting conditions.
	The first nodal release requires **m different** incident activities to be completed. All other on-going incident activities will be halted at that point. Subsequent releases require **n** such completions, with the same halting conditions.
	Deterministic branching node. Upon release of node **j**, all jobs emanating from the node will be initiated.[6]
	Probabilistic branching node. Upon release of node **j**, one of the emanating activities will be initiated, according to the probabilities given.

Figure 9. GERT Symbols

Symbol   Meaning

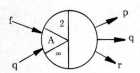

This is the node of conventional arrow diagrams.
Jobs **f** and **g** must both be completed before the node
is released, at which point jobs **p**, **q**, and **r** can begin
(and must ultimately be finished). The ∞ on the input
side indicates that the node cannot be rereleased; it
is not involved in any cycles or feedback loops.

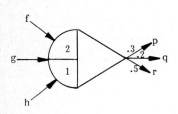

Any two completions among jobs **f**, **g**, and **h** will
release the node the first time. Since the node may be
in a feedback loop, it is possible for the same job to
be completed twice and thus release the node, though
completion of any two from among jobs **f**, **g**, and **h**
would accomplish the same thing. Upon nodal release,
one of the three jobs **p**, **q**, and **r** will start, according
to the probabilities shown. Should the node reoccur
in a feedback loop, only one of the incident jobs need
be completed to release the node.

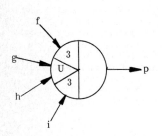

Three different jobs from among **f**, **g**, **h**, and **i**
must be completed to release the node both on
first and subsequent passes. When any three are
completed, work in process on the fourth (if any)
is halted. Upon nodal release, job **p** will begin.

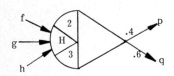

Any two completions of incident jobs will release
the node on the first pass. Three completions are
required on subsequent passes. Completions need
not be for different jobs. After nodal release, on-
going work on any other incident job is halted, and
either job **p** or **q** (but not both) will commence,
according to the probabilities shown.

Figure 10. GERT Symbols

node logic, with four basic input logics and six output logics. Both GERT and VERT have an input node that requires all incoming activities to be completed before the node is released, and other input nodes that 'require some subset of such activities to be completed for the same effect. Both have one output node that initiates all outgoing activities at release, and another node that is probabilistic. VERT additionally has some "filter" output nodes that are activated by certain parameters of project performance. This brief description just begins to suggest the complexity of the models, each with its own special features. Suffice it to say that both of them allow the modeling of a great variety of projects where uncertainty must be addressed.

GERT has been applied to bidding situations, test programs, feasibility studies, research programs with multiple approaches, missile countdown procedures, and so on. It has the most extensive literature of any of the spin-offs from PERT (with the exception of limited resource models), with a bibliography listing over 100 articles and papers plus several books; and it continues to grow [22, 23]. VERT is a more recent effort with as yet a much more limited bibliography. Its authors claim it is more powerful than GERT, in that it examines performance measures as well as cost and time parameters in its analysis of risks involved in new projects or ventures. Its applications have included the analysis of alternative weapon systems, flood control programs, pollution abatement methods, earthquake analysis, rail yard switching operations, production line-balancing, and war gaming. Both GERT and VERT, it should be emphasized, are simulation techniques, and as such are not intended for project scheduling purposes but for analyzing potential outcomes of projects, criticality indexes, and expected values of various project parameters (times, costs, queue lengths, performance measures, etc.). Genetically, they spring from flowgraph theory, simulation techniques, and probability theory, as well as from PERT.

PDM (Precedence Diagramming Method)

On the CPM side of the geneology tree, we note PDM's connection with graph theory. One of the contentions of graph theory is that a network of nodes and arcs always has an alternate representation in which the arcs become nodes. As applied to the usual arrow diagram of CPM and PERT, this means that the activities can be represented as nodes and the precedence relationships denoted by arrows. Activity-On-Arrow (AON) diagrams were apparently developed independently from PERT and CPM, as noted earlier, but their genetic relationship is well founded in graph theory. PDM extended the basic notion of AON networks to include additional precedence relationships [5]. To the traditional "finish-to-start" relationship (which requires that one job be finished before its successor begins) is added "start-to-start," "finish-to-finish," and "start-to-finish" precedence arrows (see Figure 11). And each of these may have a non-zero lead time associated with it, to separate the respective starts and/or finishes by any desired time span.

The expanded set of precedence relationships in PDM increases its flexibility for project networking, but it also increases its complexity, both in terms of interpretation and computation. The PDM algorithm is not nearly so simple as that for ordinary CPM, and the concepts of critical path and slack must be modified [31]. Certain anomalous effects, such as an increase in project length with a decrease in duration of a critical activity, can be experienced when a finish-to-finish relationship is followed by a start-to-start relationship [29]. Thus, the interpretation and use of a precedence diagram must be done with more care than is necessary with the simple arrow diagram. But PDM's particular advantages have proved quite useful in certain specialized applications.

Limited Resource Scheduling: Heuristic Models

The most extensive effort at modifying PERT and CPM started in the early 60's and is still going on. While PERT/COST was a step in the direction of incorporating resource considerations along with time scheduling, it did so in an accounting sense only. It did not schedule resources or consider limitations in their availability; it simply added up the costs of resources implicit in the PERT time schedule. What was needed was a program for scheduling activities under both precedence and limited resource constraints. There were two main tracks taken in these efforts that may be described as an analytical track and a heuristic track. Early researchers briefly considered the daunting problems of the analytical approach

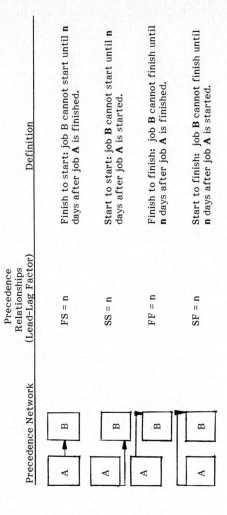

Precedence Network	Precedence Relationships (Lead-Lag Factor)	Definition
A → B	FS = n	Finish to start: job **B** cannot start until **n** days after job **A** is finished.
A → B	SS = n	Start to start: job **B** cannot start until **n** days after job **A** is started.
A → B	FF = n	Finish to finish: job **B** cannot finish until **n** days after job **A** is finished.
A → B	SF = n	Start to finish: job **B** cannot finish until **n** days after job **A** is started.

Figure 11.   PRECEDENCE DIAGRAMMING METHOD

and opted for heuristic models. The earliest models reported in the literature included MS^2 in 1962 [16], and RAMPS [13] and SPAR-1 [28] in 1963. RAMPS was a commercially available product; the other two were research tools (but which eventually led to working models). Many other CPM-based scheduling programs were developed in the years that followed, by both academic researchers and industrial users. U. S. Steel, General Electric, Babcock and Wilcox, and several other firms custom-designed their own proprietary packages; while commercial models were eventually marketed by IBM, McCauto, and many other firms dealing in computer software programs. Today one can acquire highly sophisticated packages (with matching prices) for scheduling projects with limited resources, that will handle an almost unlimited number of activities and resource types. All of these are heuristic-based. The particular heuristics used usually remain proprietary secrets of the marketing firms, but they likely include those that have been evaluated and described in the literature [7,8], or variants thereof.

Figure 12 illustrates the successive application of a simple heuristic ("allocate resources to the most critical jobs first; postpone less critical jobs if necessary") to a small project. The first schedule shown has all jobs scheduled at their early start times, yielding a manpower requirements profile that is much out of balance, with high initial demands trailing off to subsequent periods of low demand. Jobs scheduled first are reexamined, with the most critical ones being allocated the available resources and those with greater slack being delayed to later periods when demand for resources is lower. Repeated re-allocations of resources lead to successively flatter and more economical resource requirements profiles. Not all resource profiles may be leveled so successfully, but more elaborate programs, with well designed heuristics, can often lead to very good resource schedules.

Of all the derivatives from the original PERT and CPM models, the heuristic-based resource scheduling models, as a group, are clearly the most successful and widely used. Part of this may be due to successful marketing efforts; but largely, I believe, it stems from the fact that the models address actual, complex problems that practitioners face and not those simply thought to be of interest by academics.

Optimizing Models

The second approach to limited resource scheduling, via analytical models, has occupied the efforts of many bright researchers. The problems are important in a practical sense and intriguing intellectually; and the prospect of finding an optimal solution to the problem, which heuristic methods cannot promise, is indeed enticing. But the main difficulty is that real-world projects are just too big. Limited resource project scheduling is a combinatorial problem, and the number of variables and the number of possible solutions increases enormously as the project size increases. There is no problem in conceptualizing the problem or of formulating it in clear analytic terms using linear programming or integer programming. But practical-sized problems have too many variables and constraints to be solved, even on today's large computers. One problem I examined had only 55 activities and 4 resources; but the LP formulation required over 1500 variables and 6500 constraints. Other formulations and solution procedures have been examined, including dynamic programming and branch-and-bound methods [8, 10], but none to date are capable of solving problems with more than 50 to 100 activities. So marriages of PERT/CPM with LP, IP, DP or B & B have not been too successful, in a practical sense. Such research efforts are often labeled "promising," but they remind one of the man climbing a tree who claimed he was "making progress" in his efforts to reach the moon. The combinatorics of large project, limited resource scheduling problems are so horrendous that analytic approaches seem hopelessly inadequate for real-world sized problems.

SDR/CPM

A somewhat different approach taken to the limited resource scheduling problem is represented by SDR/CPM, which is an amalgum of search decision rule techniques and critical path scheduling [4]. The scheduling problem is stated in terms of three decision variables for each activity which determine the timing and amount of resource used, plus an objective function which can include regular and overtime labor costs, work force change costs, and penalties

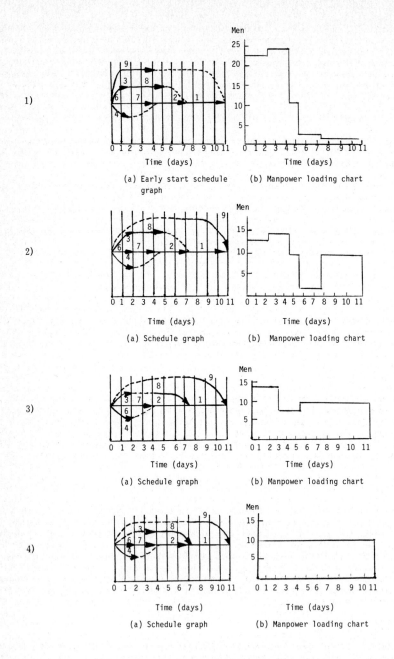

Figure 12. Limited Resource Scheduling

or bonuses for project completion times that are late or early. The number of variables determines the dimensionality of the cost response surface which is explored by an adaptive pattern search program. Hopefully a "good" solution is found after a reasonable number of evaluations of the objective function. One of the advantages of SDR is that it will handle any pre-specified type of cost function; it doesn't have to be linear or quadratic, as in some other solution techniques. In common with other heuristic procedures it cannot guarantee an optimal solution.

Interactive Models of CPM

Another extension of heuristic programming involves the use of computer graphics to create an "Interactive CPM" [14, 31]. The purpose of such a man-machine interactive system is to combine man's heuristic problem-solving skills with a computer's speed and power, interfacing the two by means of computer graphics devices (CRT's, light pen and tablet, joysticks, etc.). By means of a heuristic resource allocation program, the user can quickly generate feasible schedules, graphically display the results on a CRT, and then, perhaps with a light pen, adjust resource levels, change scheduling parameters or modify program heuristics in an effort to improve on the schedule. The ease of entering changes and obtaining results enables the scheduler to try a number of approaches, and hopefully to find a better solution than either the man or the computer alone could find [30].

DCPM

Decision CPM (DCPM), another spin-off of network scheduling, is a second-cousin to GERT, both being related to decision trees, a well known network-based decision technique. Decision trees have both decision nodes and probabilistic event nodes, the latter of which appear in GERT networks. DCPM, on the other hand, makes use of the decision nodes, in an attempt to connect more closely the planning and scheduling phases of project management [6]. During the project planning process, there are usually a number of alternative methods for completing at least some jobs in the project. These are usually sorted through and the "best" ones included in the final network which can then be used for scheduling purposes. DCPM attempts to combine those processes by including in the network not only jobs which must be performed but also subsets of alternative (and mutually exclusive) jobs with their durations and precedence relationships, each subset headed by a decision node (see Figure 13). Selection from among the alternative jobs-sets in effect constitutes the planning phase of project management, and the implications for project scheduling and costs can be performed by usual CPM analysis. Figure 14 shows two possible alternative networks derived from the decision network of Figure 13. If there are very many decision nodes, then there can be a very large number of alternative networks to consider. Heuristic procedures for finding "good" solutions with reasonable computational effort have been developed.

CPM/MRP

One of the most recent gene-spliced versions of CPM makes use of a technique of manufacturing inventory management that has received a lot of attention in the last decade. Material requirements planning (MRP) is a computer-based system for translating a master production schedule into time-phased net requirements for each component needed to implement the schedule [20]. Based on a product structure tree, an MRP schedule resembles a late-start project network schedule. CPM/MRP, a hybrid of the two models, attempts to incorporate some of the features of MRP in a project setting [1]. In particular, it incorporates project activities and technological relationships with resource requirements, acquisition lead times, and inventory records. Thus, activities are scheduled subject to information about the inventory position. An activity may be delayed by either activities which precede it or by resources which must be acquired. An advanced version of CPM/MRP [2] takes into account not only resource lead times but possible limitations on the amounts available, using heuristic scheduling rules found to be most effective in project scheduling. MRP-style output formats yield a project schedule in a form familiar in manufacturing, and the use of MRP suggests that the constrained resource version may be a possible approach to the job shop loading problem.

J. Wiest

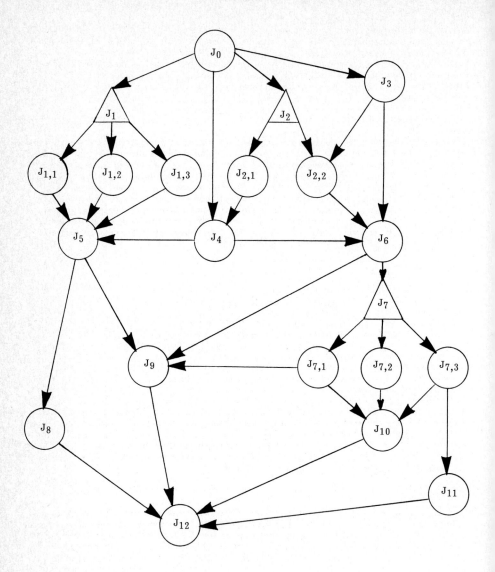

Figure 13. DCPM Decision Networks

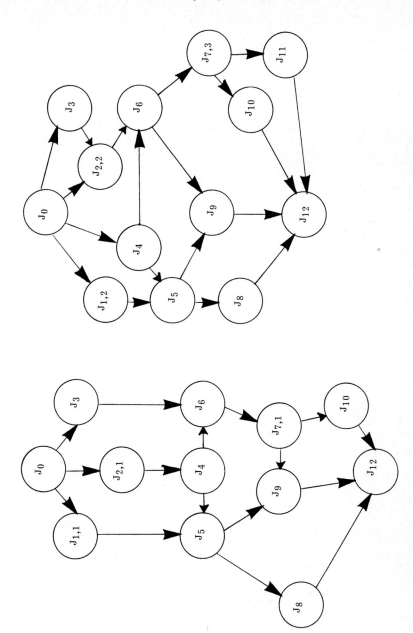

Figure 14. DCPM Alternative Networks Derived from the Decision Network of Figure 13.

Figures 15 through 20 illustrate the application of CPM/MRP to a simple assembly project, showing it in both the traditional network format (CPM) and product structure tree (MRP), elaborated to account for material requirements (bill of material) and inventory levels and ultimately yielding a schedule in MRP format with release dates for labor activities and material orders.

Evaluation of the Hybrids

This enumeration of hybrid CPM/PERT models is not exhaustive, of course. Many others could be mentioned, but these are among the most interesting and best described in the literature. How useful are they, and to what extent have they been employed out in the real world? Unfortunately, relatively little information is available that would enable us to answer those questions. Articles on heuristic resource scheduling models have appeared more frequently in the literature than in any of the others, and the number of commercial programs developed indicates a good deal of interest in the techniques. Also, there is a fairly impressive number of articles describing GERT and its applications. But neither or these begins to compare with the great number of articles that appeared in trade journals and other application-oriented publications that followed the introduction of PERT and CPM (and that continue to do so). One can only speculate about the reasons for the difference.

One possible explanation is that many of the new models are just too complex, too difficult for managers who are supposed to use them to understand. It is interesting to note that PERT and CPM have both been stripped, for the most part, of their original unique features. One hardly ever hears about three-time-estimate versions of PERT being used, or about the cost-optimizing feature of CPM being employed. Most applications today involve the basic, simple network model with a single time estimate. By contrast, all of the hybrid models have moved in the opposite direction--they have added features, enlarged the capabilities of the original models, and in so doing, have made them more complex and probably less comprehensible to those who are expected to use them. One is reminded of the prescriptive acronym, KISS (keep it simple, stupid).

Another criticism that has been leveled at some hybrids is that they are mostly of academic interest. They were developed in relatively asceptic halls of ivy where professorial types sit back with feet on desk and try to imagine the problems of project management, rather than talk with the PM's who are on the firing line or delve into the nitty gritty problems they face daily. Given the reward system in academia, any models developed must be "interesting" to be respectable and (more importantly) publishable, which puts a premium on complexity and obscurity rather than on simplicity and usability. That characterization may be a bit over-drawn and unfair; but it is true that the majority of the models developed came from university settings. In most cases we can assume the developers were sincere in their intent to produce models of value to users; but perhaps there needs to be more communication between the two in the process.

Finally, there is the problem of selling the methods. Businessmen understand this well. Most new products never endure in the market place for more than a year or two, even when highly advertised and promoted by experienced, successful firms. So it is not surprising that most of the models described have not received widespread acclaim. Developers of such models, however skilled at modeling, are often not good promoters; a different temperament is needed. And it helps to have a good sponsor and to get a lot of advertising. That was PERT's good fortune. You can hardly ask for more than to have the DOD standing behind you, to get someone's attention.

Future Prospects

What of the future? It seems fairly safe to bet that those models which have been around for some time and have still not caught on will be regarded with benign neglect. The better commercial resource-allocation models seem to be doing all right, especially when promoted by such firms as IBM and McCauto (though their expense will continue to induce some users to develop their own programs or buy less fancy ones). GERT and VERT seem to have a corner of a small, highly specialized market; but their use requires skilled specialists who understand their complexity. Few managers are likely to do so. CPM/MRP is too new to judge,

a. Assembly Project in Network Format (Activity-on-Node)

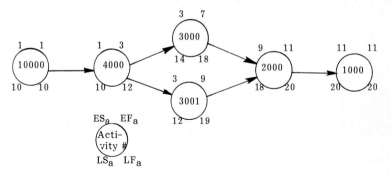

b. Same Project in Product Structure Tree Format

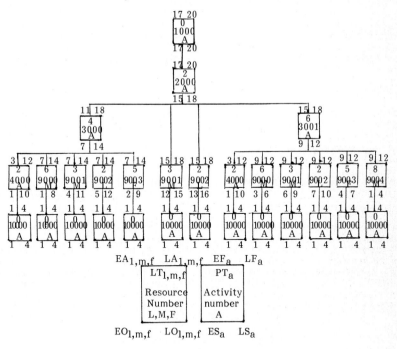

Figure 15. CPM/MRP

Bill of Materials for the Example Project	Assembly (parent)	Part (child)	Quantity	Description
	1000			Complete project
		2000	1	Assemble bench
	2000			Assemble bench
		3000	1	Assemble back
		3001	1	Assemble seat
		9001	1	¼lb., 10¢ nails
		9002	2	Carpenter hours
	3000			Assemble back
		4000	1	Collect tools
		9000	2	2 x 4's
		9001	1	¼ lb., 10¢ nails
		9002	4	Carpenter hours
		9003	2	Handsaw hours
	3001			Assemble seat
		4000	1	Collect tools
		9000	4	2 x 4's
		9001	1	¼ lb., 10¢ nails
		9002	12	Carpenter hours
		9003	4	Handsaw hours
		9004	2	Wrought iron legs
	4000			Collect tools
		10000	1	Start project
	9000			2 x 4's
		10000	1	Start project
	9001			¼ lb., 10¢ nails
		10000	1	Start project
	9002			Carpenter hours
		10000	1	Start project
	9003			Handsaw hours
		10000	1	Start project
	9004			Wrought iron legs
		10000	1	Start project
	10000			Start project

	Type	Number	On hand	Performance time	Lead time	On order
Lead time, quantity on hand, and planned receipts for the activities and resources in the example project	Activity 1000		0	0		0
	Activity 2000		0	2		0
	Activity 3000		0	4		0
	Activity 3001		0	6		0
	Activity 4000		0	2		0
	Material 9000		0		6	0
	Material 9001		0		3	0
	Labor 9002		0		2	0
	Facility and equipment . 9003		0		5	0
	Material 9004		0		8	0
	Activity 10000		0	0		0

Figure 16. CPM/MRP - Material Requirements Data Needed to Generate MRP Schedule

Material Start Project

9000 LT = G	1	2	3	4	5	6	7	8	9	10	11	12	13	14	15	16	17	18	19	20
ROMTS	0	0	0	0	0	0	0	0	0	0	0	4	0	2	0	0	0	0	0	0
PL'ED RECEIPTS	0	0	0	0	0	0	0	0	0	0	0	0	0	0	0	0	0	0	0	0
ENDING INV 0	0	0	0	0	0	0	0	0	0	0	0	-4	-4	-6		-6	-6	-6	-6	-6
ORDER RELEASE	0	0	0	0	0	4	0	2	0	0	0	0	0		0	0	0	0	0

Material 10F. Nails

9001 LT = 3	1	2	3	4	5	6	7	8	9	10	11	12	13	14	15	16	17	18	19	20
ROMTS	0	0	0	0	0	0	0	0	0	0	1	0	1	0	0	0	1	0	0
PL'ED RECEIPTS	0	0	0	0	0	0	0	0	0	0	0	0	0	0	0	0	0	0	0
ENDING INV 0	0	0	0	0	0	0	0	0	0	0	0	-1	-1	-2	-2	-2	-2	-3	-3	-3
ORDER RELEASE	0	0	0	0	0	0	0	0	1	0	1	0	0	0	1	0	0	0	0

Labor Carpenter Hours

9002 LT = 2	1	2	3	4	5	6	7	8	9	10	11	12	13	14	15	16	17	18	19	20
ROMTS	0.0	0.0	0.0	0.0	0.0	0.0	0.0	0.0	0.0	0	.0	0.0	2.0	2.0	3.0	3.0	3.0	3.0	1.0	1.0	1.0
PL'ED RECEIPTS	0	0	0	0	0	0	0	0	0	0	0	0	0	0	0	0	0	0	0
ENDING INV 0	0	0	0	0	0	0	0	0	0	0	0	12	12	16	16	16	16	18	18	18
ORDER RELEASE	0.0	0.0	0.0	0.0	0.0	0.0	0.0	0.0	0.0	2.0	2.0	3.0	3.0	3.0	3.0	1.0	1.0	0.0	0.0	0.0

Fac & Ec Handsaw Hours

9003 LT = 5	1	2	3	4	5	6	7	8	9	10	11	12	13	14	15	16	17	18	19	20
ROMTS																				
PL'ED RECEIPTS	0	0	0	0	0	0	0	0	0	0	0	0	0	0	0	0	0	0	0	0
ENDING INV 0	0	0	0	0	0	0	0	0	0	0	0	-4	-4	-6	-6	-6	-6	-6	-6
ORDER RELEASE	0.0	0.0	0.0	0.0	0.0	0.0	0.7	0.7	1.2	1.2	1.2	1.2	0.0	0.0	0.0	0.0	0.0	0.0	0.0	0.0

Material Wrought Iron Legs

9004 LT = 8	1	2	3	4	5	6	7	8	9	10	11	12	13	14	15	16	17	18	19	20
ROMTS	0	0	0	0	0	0	0	0	0	0	0	2	0	0	0	0	0	0	0	0
PL'ED RECEIPTS	0	0	0	0	0	0	0	0	0	0	0	0	0	0	0	0	0	0	0	0
ENDING INV 0	0	0	0	0	0	0	0	0	0	0	0	-2	-2	-2	-2	-2	-2	-2	-2	-2
ORDER RELEASE	0	0	0	2	0	0	0	0	0	0	0	0	0	0	0	0	0	0	0

Activity Start Project

10000 LT = 0	1	2	3	4	5	6	7	8	9	10	11	12	13	14	15	16	17	18	19	20
ROMTS	0	0	0	2	0	4	4	2	3	13	1	4	0	0	1	2	0	0	0	0
PL'ED RECEIPTS	0	0	0	0	0	0	0	0	0	0	0	0	0	0	0	0	0	0	0	0
ENDING INV 0	0	0	0	-2	-2	-6	-10	-12	-15	-28	-29	-33	-33	-33	-34	-36	-36	-36	-36	-36
ORDER RELEASE	0	0	0	1	0	0	0	0	0	0	0	0	0	0	0	0	0	0	0

Activity Complete Project

1000 LT = 0	1	2	3	4	5	6	7	8	9	10	11	12	13	14	15	16	17	18	19	20
ROMTS	0	0	0	0	0	0	0	0	0	0	0	0	0	0	0	0	0	0	0	1
PL'ED RECEIPTS	0	0	0	0	0	0	0	0	0	0	0	0	0	0	0	0	0	0	0	0
ENDING INV 0	0	0	0	0	0	0	0	0	0	0	0	0	0	0	0	0	0	0	0	-1
ORDER RELEASE	0	0	0	0	0	0	0	0	0	0	0	0	0	0	0	0	0	0	1

Activity Assemble Bench

2000 LT = 2	1	2	3	4	5	6	7	8	9	10	11	12	13	14	15	16	17	18	19	20
ROMTS	0	0	0	0	0	0	0	0	0	0	0	0	0	0	0	0	0	0	0	1
PL'ED RECEIPTS	0	0	0	0	0	0	0	0	0	0	0	0	0	0	0	0	0	0	0	0
ENDING INV 0	0	0	0	0	0	0	0	0	0	0	0	0	0	0	0	0	0	0	0	-1
ORDER RELEASE	0	0	0	0	0	0	0	0	0	0	0	0	0	0	0	0	0	0	0

Figure 17. CPM/MRP Schedule for Assembly Project

but it should benefit from the great amount of publicity and interest generated by MRP in recent years.

As for future developments, I expect that there will continue to be a stream of new models vying for attention. With all the doctoral students looking for a thesis topic, and professors looking for publishable research, and managers looking for ways to ease their management problems, there is a lot of incentive for developing new models. Wherever appropriate genes can be found, someone will design a way to splice them to CPM and PERT. You might call them "designer genes."

REFERENCES

[1] Aquilano, N. J. and D. E. Smith, "A Formal Set of Algorithms for Project Scheduling with Critical Path Scheduling/Material Requirements Planning," Journal of Operations Management, 1 (2), November 1980.

[2] _____, "Resource Constrained Project Scheduling with Critical Path Method-- Material Requirements Planning," Working Paper, Department of Management, University of Arizona (January 1982).

[3] Britney, R. R., "Bayesian Point Estimation and the PERT Scheduling of Stochastic Activities," Management Science, 22 (9), May 1976.

[4] Buffa, E. S. and J. G. Miller, Production-Inventory Systems, Planning and Control, 3rd edition, Richard D. Irwin, Inc., Homewood, Ill. (1978), pp. 650-655.

[5] Crandall, K. S., "Project Planning with Precedence Lead/Lag Factors," Project Management Quarterly, 4 (3), September 1973.

[6] Crowston, W., and G. L. Thompson, "Decision CPM: A Method for Simultaneous Planning, Scheduling and Control of Projects," Operations Research, 15 (3), May-June 1967.

[7] Davis, E. W., "CPM Use in Top 400 Construction Firms," Journal of The Construction Division, ASCE, 100 (CO1), March 1974.

[8] _____, "Project Scheduling Under Resource Constraints--Historical Review and Categorization of Procedures," AIIE Transactions, 5 (4), December 1973.

[9] _____, "Resource-based Project Scheduling: Which Rules Perform Best?", Project Management Quarterly, 6 (4), December 1975.

[10] _____ and J. H. Patterson, "A Comparison of Heuristic and Optimum Solutions in Resource Constrained Project Scheduling," Management Science, 21 (8), April 1975.

[11] DOD and NASA Guide, PERT Cost Systems Design, Washington, D. C., Government Printing Office, June 1962.

[12] Iannone, A. L., Management Program Planning and Control with PERT, MOST, LOB, Prentice-Hall, Englewood Cliffs, N.J. (1967).

[13] Lambourn, S., "Resource Allocation and Multi-Project Scheduling (RAMPS), A New Tool in Planning and Control," Computer Journal, 5 (4), January 1963.

[14] Leahy, J. P., "A Man-Machine CPM System for Decision Making in the Construction Industry," Construction Research Series No. 9, Department of Civil Engineering, University of Illinois (1967).

[15] Lee, Sang M., Gerald L. Moeller, and Lester A. Digman, Network Analysis for Management Decisions, A Stochastic Approach, Kluwer-Nijhoff Publishing, Boston (1982).

[16] Levy, F. K., G. L. Thompson, and J. D. Wiest, "Multi-Ship, Multi-Shop, Workload Smoothing Program," Naval Research Logistics Quarterly, 9 (1), March 1962.

[17] Moder, Joseph J., and Cecil R. Phillips, Project Management with CPM and PERT, 2nd Edition, Van Nostrand Reinhold Company, New York (1970); 1st. Edition (1964).

[18] Moeller, G. L. and L. A. Digman, "Operations Planning with VERT," Operations Research, 29 (4), July-August 1981.

[19] Moore, Laurence J., and Edward R. Clayton, GERT Modeling and Simulation: Fundamentalsl and Applications, Petrocelli/Charter, New York (1976).

[20] Orlicky, J., Material Requirements Planning, McGraw Hill, Inc., New York (1975).

[21] Pritsker, A. A. B. and W. W. Rapp, "GERT: Graphical Evaluation and Review Technique, Part 1: Fundamentals," J. Industrial Engineering, XVII (5), May 1966.

[22] Pritsker, A. Alan B., Modeling and Analysis Using Q-GERT Networks, 2nd. Edition, John Wiley & Sons, New York (1979); 1st. Edition (1977).

[23] Pritsker, A. Alan B., Management Decision Making, A Network Simulation Approach, Prentice-Hall, Inc., Englewood Cliffs, N.J. (1983).

[24] Schoderbek, P. P. and L. A. Digman, "Third Generation, PERT/LOB," Harvard Business Review, 45 (5), September–October 1967.

[25] Vazsonyi, A., "L'Histoire de Grandeur et de la Decadence de la Methode PERT," Management Science, 16 (8), April 1970.

[26] Whitehouse, Gary E., Systems Analysis and Design Using Network Techniques, Prentice-Hall, Inc., Englewood Cliffs, N.J. (1973).

[27] Wiest, J. D., "Project Network Models, Past, Present and Future," Project Management Quarterly, 8 (4), December 1977.

[28] _____, "The Scheduling of Large Projects with Limited Resources," Ph.D. Thesis, Carnegie Institute of Technology, 1963.

[29] _____, "Precedence Diagramming Method: Some Unusual Characteristics and Their Implications for Project Managers," Journal of Operations Management, 1 (3), February 1981.

[30] _____, "Computer Graphics for Project Management," Proceedings of the Seminar-Symposium, Project Management Institute, St. Louis (1970).

[31] _____ and F. K. Levy, A Management Guide to PERT/CPM, 2nd Edition, Prentice-Hall, Englewood Cliffs, N.J. (1977).

Project Management: Methods and Studies
Burton V. Dean (editor)
© Elsevier Science Publishers B.V. (North-Holland), 1985

PRECEDENCE DIAGRAMMING: TIME COMPUTATIONS, ANOMALIES AND REMEDIES

Joseph J. Moder

University of Miami
Coral Gables, Florida
U.S.A.

Keith C. Crandall

University of California
Berkeley, California
U.S.A.

The expanded network logic of precedence diagrams is given along with a discussion of its advantages over arrow or node diagrams in networking a project plan, and controlling project time and cost performance. The complex nature of the criticality of activities in a precedence diagram is illustrated. That is, criticality can be in the normal or reverse manner, and the entire activity or only a portion can be critical. Splitting, or interruption of the progress of an activity is another complication introduced by precedence diagramming. Computational algorithms to compute early/late start/finish times for project activities are developed and illustrated wherein splitting that preserves the continuity of project work flow is allowed. Finally, computer programs that perform this task are discussed. It is shown, through the use of coded bar chart computer printouts, that the complexities of precedence diagramming can be greatly reduced, and that a very effective tool for monitoring progress can be provided.

INTRODUCTION

The development of PERT and CPM in the late 1950's initiated considerable emphasis on the use of Arrow diagrams in project management, where arrows are used to represent each of the activities in a project plan. Since this initial development, there has been a gradual movement away from the Arrow to the Node diagram, where activities are represented by nodes and all connecting arrows merely show dependency relationships. [2,4,5] The latter is of the form predecessor finish must precede successor start, referred to hereafter as a "finish-start" (FS) relationship. The Node diagram has the advantage that it avoids the occasional troublesome nature of the dummy required in Arrow diagramming. This movement to the use of Node diagrams has now reached the point where they are about as widely used as Arrow diagrams. More recently, attention has shifted to the embellishment of the Node diagram logic to include activity constraint relationships of a form other than the simple finish-start type. [3,1]

Since Precedence diagram relationships are expressed between pairs of activities, called predecessor and successor, and since these constraints deal with either the activity start or finish time, there are four possible relationships, as shown in Figure 1. The first type shown means that the start of activity i must lead the start of activity j by at least SS_{ij} time units.

Similarly, the second constraint indicates that the finish of activity j must lag the finish of activity i by at least FF_{ij} time units. The third relationship augments the conventional PERT/CPM logic by indicating that the start of activity j must lag the finish of activity i by at least FS_{ij} time units. For example, if activity i was "pour concrete" and activity j was "strip forms", then FS_{ij} would be equal to the minimum time required for the concrete to strengthen before removal of the forms is allowed. The fourth relationship indicates that the last SF_{ij}'' time units of activity j must follow the completion of the first SF_{ij}' time units of activity i. For example, the completion of the final $SF_{ij}'' = 20$ days of "chasis design" must follow the completion of the first SF'_{ij} = 30 days of "power-train design." Thus, a total lag of at least $SF_{ij}=SF'_{ij} + SF''_{ij}$ =50 days must separate the start of powertrain design (i) and the finish of chasis design (j). (The notation for SF_{ij}, SF'_{ij} and SF''_{ij} is utilized in the computation algorithm; their meaning is clearly shown in Figure 1.) A pair of activities can, of course, be connected by more than one constraint relationship. A common example of this type is a combination of a start–start and a finish–finish constraint.

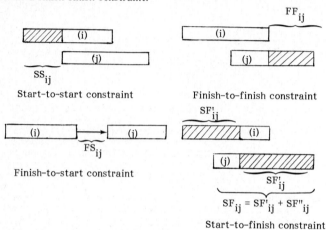

Figure 1. Precedence diagramming constraints with lead/lag times.

Figures 2b and 2c show equivalent logical diagrams using Precedence lead/lag and Arrow networking conventions. This simple example demonstrates one of the principle advantages of utilizing lead/lag logic, which is the significant reduction in the number of activities required to convey the desired plan in Precedence lead/lag conventions. In construction projects, a three fold increase in the number of arrow activities is not uncommon. This increase has several serious disadvantages. First, for many planners and planning situations, the notation used in Precedence diagramming mimics the natural planning thought process quite closely, particularly the combination of the SS and FF relationships in conjunction with the standard FS constraint. As the example demonstrates, the translation of this Precedence diagram logic into an equivalent Arrow or Node diagram that is restricted to the use of the FS relationship only, is very cumbersome and impedes the natural planning process. Field personnel view the activites (work packages) as single entities and are confused when these packages are subdivided to achieve proper concurrent logic in Arrow networks. In reviewing computational results from Arrow networks, field managers have been known to assume the first segment of a segmented activity (e.g. segment 1-2 of framing in Figure 2) actually represented the entire activity, thereby making major errors in field execution.

The second disadvantage of the increase in the number of activities is that it complicates cost/resource planning and control. When activities are arbitrarily split into two or more portions to permit activity concurrency, costs and resources must also be split. This aggravates the allocation problem, which is already considered by many as being an excessive burden.

PRECEDENCE DIAGRAMMING ANOMALIES

The computation and interpretation of early/late start/finish times for Precedence diagram activities are considerably more complex than those for the basic finish–to–finish constraint logic of Arrow or Node diagrams. For the latter, the computation and interpretation of these times is both simple and unique. This is an important advantage of the PERT/CPM system. Unfortunately, this does not usually hold for Precedence diagrams; a number of complications can arise, as will subsequently be shown.

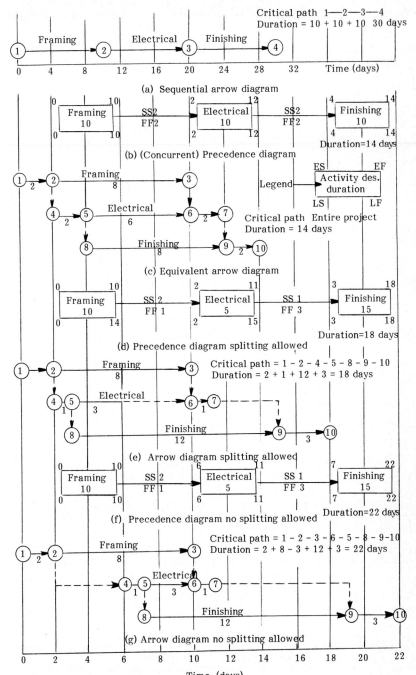

Time (days)

Figure 2. Arrow and precedence networks to illustrate splitting vs. no splitting; activities are shown at their early start times.

The basic computational approach described during the remainder of the paper is a procedure recommended by Crandall[1], and developed in detail in Moder[3], that will lead to activity early/late start/finish times for a Precedence diagram network, that are <u>identical</u> to those that would be obtained for the <u>equivalent</u> Arrow or Node diagram and the conventional forward and backward pass computations.

Consider a construction subcontract consisting of <u>framing</u> walls, placing <u>electrical</u> conduits, and <u>finishing</u> walls, with the duration of each task estimated to be 10 days, using standard size crews. If the plan is to perform each of these tasks sequentially, the equivalent Arrow diagram in Figure 2a shows that a project duration of 30 days will result.

To reduce this time, these tasks could be carried out concurrently with a convenient lag of say 2 days between the start and finish of each activity. This plan is shown in Figure 2b in Precedence diagram notation. The equivalent Arrow diagram shown in Figure 2c indicates a 14 day project schedule. Note how the SS = 2 and FF = 2 lags of Figure 2b are built into the equivalent arrow diagram in Figure 2c. Thus, the 10 day electrical task must be broken up into 3 sub-activities of 2, 6 and 2 days duration, respectively.

So far, precedence diagramming is easy to follow and is parsimonious with activites. But let us see what happens if the duration of the 3 tasks in this project are unbalanced by changing from 10, 10, 10 to 10, 5, and 15 days, respectively. These changes are incorporated in Figures 2d and e, along with appropriate new lag times. Note that SS = 2 was chosen between framing and electrical to insure that a full days work is ready for electrical before this task is allowed to start. Similarly, FF = 3 was chosen between electrical and finishing because the last day of electrical work will require 3 days of finishing work to complete the project. The other lags of 1 day each were chosen as minimal or convenience values needed in each case. These lags define the activity breakdown shown in Figure 2e where we see the critical path is the <u>start</u> of framing (1-2), then the <u>start</u> of electrical (4-5), and finally the <u>totality</u> of finishing (8-9-10). This is also shown in the Precedence diagram, Figure 2d, where ES = LS = 0 for the <u>start</u> of framing, ES = LS = 2 for the start of electrical, and finally ES = LS = 3 <u>and</u> EF = LF = 18 for the totality of finishing. Since the Precedence diagram shows each of these tasks in their totality, EF ≠ LF even though ES = LS for the framing and electrical tasks. For framing in Figure 2d, LF - EF = 14 - 10 = 4 days of float, which corresponds to the 4 days of float depicted by activity 7-9 in Figure 2e. Similarly, for electrical in Figure 2d, LF - EF = 15 - 11 = 4 days of float which is also depicted by activity 7-9 in Figure 2e. The middle electrical activity 5-6 in Figure 2e <u>appears</u> to have an additional path float of 4 days, or a total of 8 days. This attribute is not shown at all in Figure 2d because it depicts only the beginning and end points of each activity, but not intermediate sub-activites such as 5-6. The discussion provided in this paper allows for evaluation of these intermediate sub-activities if necessary; results of such evaluations can be displayed graphically in computer generated bar-charts as will be shown in Figure 7. Closer examination of Figure 2e will show that the interaction between electrical and finishing (arrow nodes 5 through 9) is not completely and uniquely defined. Continued work on finishing may require continuing work on electrical as a prerequisite. This problem is shared by both arrow and precedence diagrams, and the user should understand this. It does not, however, present a real problem in the applications since the job foreman generally has no difficulty in the day-to-day management of this type of interrelationship among concurrent activities. It is generally felt that it is not worthwhile to further complicate the networking and the computational scheme to show all interdependencies among activity segments, since these tasks can be routinely managed in the field. As mentioned earlier, it is this simplification of detail that enhances the use of Precedence diagramming as the planning tool at the field level. Field managers are concerned with the efficient utilization of their manpower and equipment resources and use network generated information only as one of many inputs to their daily assignment of these resources. If the network information is complex and confusing, it is accorded less significance during this allocation process. In the extreme, confusing information will be totally ignored.

A very important difference between Figures 2c and e, other than the 4 day difference in the project durations, lies in the electrical task which is represented by 3 sub-activities in both diagrams. In Figure 2c these 3 sub-activities are expected to be conducted without interruption. However, in Figure 2e this is not possible. Here, the last day of the electrical task 6-7 must follow a 4 day interruption because of the combined effect of successor constraint SS = 1 (hereafter called SS1) depicted by activity 5-8, and predecessor constraint FF1 depicted by activity 3-6. This forced interruption will henceforth be referred to as splitting of the electrical task.

It should be noted that this splitting occurs naturally in the equivalent Arrow diagrams. It was recognized as an interesting phenomenon when Precedence computational methods were derived to produce equivalent results with these equivalent Arrow diagrams. Early Precedence computational methods prevented this splitting by producing solutions equivalent to Figure 2g. Managers were often unaware of the impact of the Arrow diagramming "splitting" and the early Precedence "non-splitting", accepting the computational results at face value. Once the phenomenon was recognized, managers realized that some activites cannot "split" (e.g. placement of concrete) and the diagramming model should allow individual activites to be designated as "non-splitting."

If it is desired, splitting of the aforementioned electrical task can be avoided in several ways. First, the duration of the electrical task could be increased from 5 to 9 days. But this is frequently not desirable in projects such as maintenance or construction because it implies a decrease in productivity. The second way to avoid splitting would be to delay the start of the electrical task for 4 days, as shown in Figure 2g where it is assumed that activity splitting is not allowed. At first, it may seem that there is no difference between these two alternatives, but this is not so. Reflection on Figure 2g shows that delaying the start of the electrical task to avoid splitting will delay the start of the finish work, and hence the completion of the project is delayed by 4 days. But increasing the duration of the electrical task will not have this effect. Actually, we have described an anomalous situation where an increase of 4 days in the duration of an activity on the critical path (starting 4 days earlier and thus running 4 days longer), will decrease the duration of the project by 4 days, from 22 to 18. If you are used to dealing with basic Arrow diagram logic (FSO logic only), this anomaly will take some getting used to. It results from the fact that the critical path in Figure 2g goes "backwards" through activity 5-6, and thus subtracts from the total duration of this path. As a result, the project duration shifts in the reverse direction of shift in the duration of such an activity. That is, the project duration decreases when the activity duration increases, and increases when the activity duration decreases. The anomalous situation occurs whenever the critical path enters the completion of an activity through a finish type of constraint (FF or SF), goes backwards through the activity, and leaves through a start type constraint (SS or SF.) It should be noted that any Precedence computational method that utilizes "non-splitting" without changes in duration is subject to this anomaly.

The Precedence diagram in Figure 2f shows that the entire project is critical, since ES = LS and EF = LF for each task. While it appears that the electrical task has float in Figure 2g, this is not true since splitting is not allowed. As noted earlier, non-splitting is a constraint not explcitly incorporated in the Arrow diagram logic.

Critical Path Characteristics

Wiest[6] was first to describe the anomalous behavior of activity 5-6 in Figure 2g picturesquely by stating that this activity is reverse critical. Similarly, in Figures 2d and e both framing and electrical are called neutral critical. They are critical because their LS = ES, but they are called neutral because their LF > EF, and the project duration is independent of these task durations. A task is neutral critical when a pair of start time constraints result in the critical path entering and exiting from the starting point of the task, or a pair of finish time constraints enter and exit from the finish point of a task. These situations could also be referred to as start or finish critical. In Figures 2d and e, the framing and electrical tasks are both start critical, while finishing is normal critical. That is, a shift in the duration of the Finishing task will have a normal effect on the project duration, causing it to shift in the same direction. Wiest suggests that Precedence diagram computer outputs would be more useful if they identified the way in which tasks are critical. The authors suggest that the following nomenclature be considered for this purpose:

NC -- denotes an activity that is Normal Critical; the project duration shifts in the same direction as the shift in the duration of a NC-activity.

RC -- denotes an activity that is Reverse Critical; the project duration shifts in the reverse direction as the shift in the duration of a RC-activity.

BC -- denotes an activity that is Bi-Critical; the project duration increases as a result of any shift in the duration of a BC-activity.

SC -- denotes an activity that is Start Critical; the project duration shifts in the direction of the shift in the start time of a SC-activity, but is neutral (unaffected) by a shift in the overall duration of the activity.

FC -- denotes an activity that is Finish Critical; the project duration shifts in the direction of the shift in the finish time of a FC-activity, but is neutral (unaffected) by a shift in the overall duration of the activity.

MNC — denotes an activity whose Mid portion is Normal Critical.

MRC — denotes an activity whose Mid portion is Reverse Critical.

MBC -- denotes an activity whose Mid portion is Bi Critical.

To conclude this discussion, it should be noted that the critical path always starts with a job (or a job start), it ends with a job (or a job finish), and in between it consists of an alternating sequence of jobs and precedence arrows. Although the critical path may pass through a job in any one of the several ways listed above, it always moves forward through precedence constraint arrows. Hence, any increase (decrease) in the lead-lag times associated with SS, SF, FF, or FS constraints on the critical path, will always result in a corresponding increase (decrease) in the project duration.

Following the suggestion of stating the nature of the criticality of activities on the critical path, for Figure 2d this would consist of the following alternating activites and precedence constraints: framing (Start Critical - SC); SS2; electrical (Start Critical - SC); SS1; finishing (Normal Critical - NC). Similarly, for Figure 2f it would be: framing (NC); FF1, electrical (RC); SS1; finishing (NC). It should be noted here that electrical is labeled reverse critical (RC), which puts the manager on notice that any shift in the duration of this activity will shift the duration of the project in the reverse direction. As stated above, it is reverse critical because its predecessor constraint is a finish type (FF1), and its successor constraint is a start type (SS1).

Computational Procedures

Obviously the forward and backward pass computational problem becomes more complex with Precedence diagramming, and it calls for establishment of several ground rules which were unnecessary with the unique nature of basic Arrow or Node diagram logic. In the generalized computational procedures to follow, we will assume that the specified activity durations are fixed, e.g., because of the productivity argument cited above. This assumption can be relaxed, of course, by varying the activity durations of interest, and repeating the calculations. Regarding task splitting, three basic cases will be treated.

Case 1:   Activity splitting is not allowed on any activities.

Case 2:   Activity splitting is allowed on all activites.

Case 3:   Combination of 1 and 2; activity splitting is permitted only on designated activities.

Figure 2g and e represent Cases 1 and 2, respectively. The effect of not allowing splitting (of the electrical task) is a 4 day increase in the project duration. Here, the choice must be made between the extra cost of splitting the electrical task, and the cost of a 4 day increase in project duration. Case 3 is provided to allow the project manager to take the possible time (project duration) advantage concomitant with splitting on those activities where it can be tolerated, and to avoid splitting on those activities where it cannot be accomodated and is the recommended procedure.

Computational Assumptions

The computational procedure for Case 1-No-Splitting Allowed, is analogous to the Arrow diagram procedure. The use of lead/lag constraints can create situations where activities are logically connected to the remainder of the diagram solely by "finish" constraints such as activity D in Figure 3. For this reason all computational cases will assume the minimum early start (ES) for all activities is a default value of zero (0), hereafter called Initial Time. In making the forward pass calculations, one must consider all constraints leading into the activity (j) in question, i.e., the start time constraints (SS_{ij} and FS_{ij}) as well as the finish time constraints (SF_{ij} and FF_{ij}), to determine which one(s) is binding. Considering all such constraints a tentative ES_j is determined by the maximum value when considering all start related constraints, and the Initial Time. (These are FS_{ij} and SS_{ij} constraints). Then, the EF_j is determined by the maximum value when considering all finish related constraints as well as the tentative ES_j plus the duration. (These are SF_{ij} and FF_{ij} constraints or tentative ES_j + duration.) The final ES_j will always be set equal to the EF_j minus the duration, thereby preventing activity splitting.

The backward pass computations follow a similar procedure to find the late start and finish times for each activity. In this case, an additional time, called Terminal Time, is required to prevent the occurrence of a late finish time (LF_i) exceeding the project duration, or the scheduled project completion time. This can occur for activities logically connected solely by start constraints such as activity G in Figure 3. As usual, the project duration is taken as the maximum (latest) of the early finish times computed for each activity in the forward pass computations. For example, this is equal to 42 units in Figure 3, which is the largest of all activity early finish times and is also the default Terminal Time. Working backwards along each constraint leaving the activity (i) in question, determine a tentative LF_i as the minimum value when considering all finish related constraints and the Terminal Time. (These are FS_{ij} and FF_{ij} constraints.) Similarly, determine the LS_i as the minimum value when considering all start related constraints as well as the tentative LF_i minus the activity (i) duration. (These are SS_{ij} and SF_{ij} constraints or tentative LF_i minus the duration of activity i.) The final LF_i will always be set equal to the LS_i plus the duration, and activity splitting will have been prevented.

To illustrate the use of computers for these computations, the completed basic scheduling computations for this network are shown in Figure 4, using a program written by K. C. Crandall. The upper portion of this figure gives the early-start activity schedule, while the lower portion gives the late-start schedule. A study of this figure will reveal that the information given is identical to Figure 3, but in graphical rather than numerical form.

Case 2 - Forward Pass Computations - Splitting Allowed

This procedure assumes that activities can be split whenever the combination of constraints associated with the activity in question result in early start/finish (or late start/finish) times whose difference exceeds the activity duration. When this occurs, the activity is assumed to split so that it preserves the continuity of project work flow from the predecessor activity in the forward pass, and the successor activity in the backward pass. Examples of splitting have been described for Figure 2 and can be seen when comparing Figure 5 with its corresponding time scale bar-chart, Figure 6. Once an activity has split, the first segment can have float associated with it if it is not entirely critical. For example, activity 5-6 in Figure 2e and activity B in Figure 6. Since float exists, the non-critical portion can be scheduled by field management within the available associated float period. The computational method outlined

102   *J. Moder, K.C. Crandell*

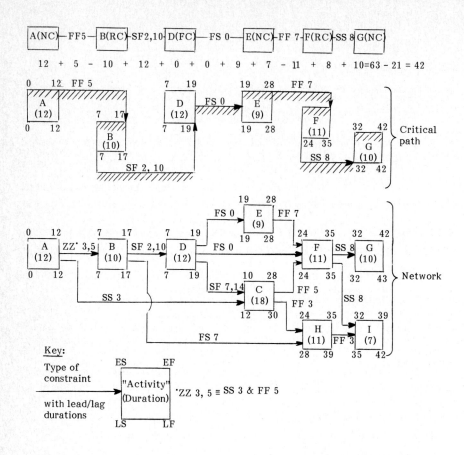

Figure 3. Example network with forward and backward pass times shown,
and the notation of the critical path -no splitting allowed.

OWNER: MODER TEXT – THIRD EDITION   CONTRACTOR: I AM AN EXCELLENT CONTRACTOR

COMPUTER SOLUTION SHOWING THE 'NON SPLITTING OPTION CALCULATION   UPDATE
FOR THE THIRD EDITION OF THE MODER TEXT ON 'CPM & PERT'   CALENDAR   3AUG81 16:55:11 Net Mod 1
TEST CALCULATED ON PACKAGE BY K C CRANDALL   MODIFICATION   3AUG81 17:04:38 Run No. 1
                                                                    CALCULATION   3AUG81 17:17:11

                               * * * CPM EARLY START ACTIVITY BARCHART * * *
                                                                                                      Page 1–1
SYMBOLS USED ARE: <*> CRITICAL PATH; <0> WORK DAY; <-> TOTAL FLOAT; <-> HOLIDAY–WEEKEND; <-> UPDATE DATE

                                          AUG 81   SEP 81
                                       1   2   3   1
                       3456789012345678901234567890112345678901234567890123
                       mtwtfssmtwtf ssmtwtf ssmtwtfssmtwtf ssmtwtfss
LABL DESCRIPTION   CALNDR DAYS ->   10   20   30   40   50   60   70   80
AAAA This is Activity 'A'   ************
BBBB This is Activity 'B'   ************
CCCC This is Activity 'C'   0000000000000000000--
DDDD This is Activity 'D'   ************
EEEE This is Activity 'E'   ************
FFFF This is Activity 'F'   ************
GGGG This is Activity 'G'   ***********
HHHH This is Activity 'H'   000000000---
ITII This is Activity 'I'   0000000---

                               * * * CPM LATE START ACTIVITY BARCHART * * *
                                                                                                      Page 1– 1
SYMBOLS USED ARE: <*> CRITICAL PATH; <0> WORK DAY; <-> TOTAL FLOAT; <-> HOLIDAY–WEEKEND; <-> UPDATE DATE
                                          AUG81   SEP 81
                                       1   2   3   4
                       3456789012345678901234567890112345678901234567890123
                       mtwtf ssmtwtfssmtwtfssmtwtfssmtwtf ssmtwtf ss
LABL DESCRIPTION   CALNDR DAYS ->   10   20   30   40   50   60   70   80
AAAA This is Activity 'A'   ************
BBBB This is Activity 'B'   ************
CCCC This is Activity 'C'   *********************
DDDD This is Activity 'D'   ************
EEEE This is Activity 'E'   ************

Figure 4. Bar-chart computer outputs for the basic scheduling computations on the network shown in Figure 3 –no splitting allowed.

in this paper maintains the non-critical portion of this segment at its early start to demon-strate the entire available float.

The forward pass computations are very similar to those already defined for the non-splitting case. The major difference is that the previously defined tentative ES_j is the final ES_j in the splitting case. When an activities EF is determined by finish constraints and not be ES plus duration, the activity splits and the number of days in the first segment must be noted. If an activity which has been split has start constraints (SS_{ij} or SF'_{ij}) to other successor activities, care must be taken to recognize those cases when these start constraints have durations ex-ceeding the duration of the first split segment. (Details of this consideration are presented in Moder[5], and occur in the bar-chart Figure 6 for the SS8 constraint between activity F and its follower activities G and I.) The program that creates the bar-charts shown in Figure 6 uses the duration of this first segment, the starting time of the second segment and the num-ber of critical days at the beginning of either the first or second segment as additional data to the normal early/late start/finish values. A first segment occurs only when an activity splits, and its length is the difference between the activity duration and the value of the con-trolling finish time constraint (FF_{ij} or SF''_{ij}). For example, on activity B in Figure 5, the early finish of 17 is set by the $FF_{AB}=5$ constraint between activities A and B. Hence, the duration of the first segment is $\alpha_B = D_B - FF_{AB} = 10-5=5$. The start time of the second segment is merely the early finish time of the activity minus the duration of the second segment. For activity B, we obtain $EF_B - (D_B - \alpha_B)=17-(10-5)=12$. Thus, the second segment starts at the end of day 12, or on day 13 as shown in Figure 6. Also, the critical days at the beginning of either the first or second segment is determined by successor constraints. Again, in the case of activity B, the critical length pertains to the first segment because activity B is start cri-tical, and is equal to 2 because of the successor constraint SF=2, 10. For activity F, $\alpha_F = D_F - FF_{EF}=11-7=4$ and the critical length is set by SS=8. Since this activity is neither start or finish critical, a mid-portion is critical and its length = $SS_{FG} - _F = 8-4=4$, as shown in Figure 6. Note also in this figure that the float time for the first segment is 5 days, which agrees with $LS_F - ES_F=20-15=5$, and float time on the second segment is 7 days which agrees with $LF_F - EF_F=38-31=7$. Thus, the only information required to develop the barchart in addi-tion to the normal early and late start values are: first segment length, critical length and starting point of the second segment. It should be noted that only activities B and F had "critical length" values while activities B, C, D, F and I all had first segment length and second segment starting values.

The backward pass computation is also similar to that defined in the non-splitting case. Once again the tentative LF becomes the final late finish. The number of days in the second seg-ment are noted for those activities that have an LS less than LF minus duration. As in the forward pass care must be taken when an activity with a split during the backward pass has finish constraints to predecessors with values greater than the duration of the split segment. This can be seen on the Figure 6 late start bar-chart between activity F and its predecessor E.

The above computational results are shown in Figure 5. The two critical paths through this network are shown at the top of this figure. To show that these results are identical to those obtained for the equivalent Arrow diagram, Figure 7 is given with early/late start/finish times and total path float times noted. To compare these two figures, recall that the Precedence diagram treats each task (activity) in totality. For example, activity F is broken into 4 sub-activities in Figure 7. The early start time of the first subactivity is 15, and the early finish time of the last one is 31. These are the only two times shown for activity F in Figure 5. Similarly, the latest start/finish times are 20 and 38, respectively. A special situation occurs here in that activity F is on the critical path, yet its start time has 5 units (20-15) of float, and its finish time has 7 units (38-31) of float. The critical nature of activity F lies in the fact that its mid subactivities (8-10 and 10-15 in Figure 7) are critical. This fact is noted at the top of Figure 6, where the critical path is shown to contain F(MRC), i.e., activity F has a mid portion that is reverse critical. The latter occurs because its predecessor constrains its

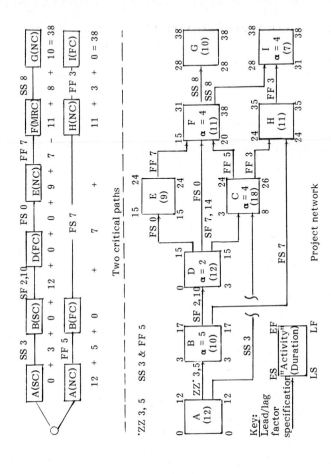

Figure 5. Example network with forward and backward pass times shown –splitting allowed.

OWNER: MODER TEXT – THIRD EDITION   CONTRACTOR: I AM AN EXCELLENT CONTRACTOR

COMPUTER SOLUTION SHOWING THE 'SPLITTING' OPTION CALCULATION   UPDATE   Net Mod 1
FOR THE THIRD EDITION OF THE MODER TEXT ON 'CPM & PERT'.   CALENDAR   3Aug81 16:55:11   Run No 1
TEST CALCULATED ON PACKAGE BY K C CRANDALL   MODIFICATION 3Aug81 17:04:38
                                                       CALCULATION 3Aug81 17:42:38
                                                      Page: 1-1

*** CPM EARLY START ACTIVITY BARCHART ***

SYMBOLS USED ARE: <*> CRITICAL PATH; <0> WORK DAY; <-> TOTAL FLOAT; <.> HOLIDAY-WEEKEND; <> UPDATE DATE

```
                     AUG 81          1           2           3       SEP 81
                     3456789012345678901234567890123456789
                     mtwtfssmtwtfssmtwtfssmtwtfssmtw
LABL DESCRIPTION     CALNDR DAYS ->   10        20        30        40        50        60        70        80
---- -------------   --------------------------------------------------------------------------------------------
AAAA  This is Activity 'A'           **********
BBBB  This is Activity 'B'           **000--*****
CCCC  This is Activity 'C'           0000--0000000000000--
DDDD  This is Activity 'D'           00--**********
EEEE  This is Activity 'E'                **********
FFFF  This is Activity 'F'                      0000--------****000------
GGGG  This is Activity 'G'                                    **********
HHHH  This is Activity 'H'                                    **********
IIII  This is Activity 'I'                                        0000--***
```

*** CPM LATE START ACTIVITY BARCHART ***
                                          Page: 1-1

SYMBOLS USED ARE: <*> CRITICAL PATH; <0> WORK DAY; <-> TOTAL FLOAT; <.> HOLIDAY-WEEKEND; <> UPDATE DATE

```
                     AUG 81       1           2           3       SEP 81
                     3456789012345678901234567890123456789
                     mtwtfssmtwtfssmtwtfssmtwtfssmtw
LABL DESCRIPTION     CALNDR DAYS ->   10        20        30        40        50        60        70        80
---- -------------   --------------------------------------------------------------------------------------------
AAAA  This is Activity 'A'           **********
BBBB  This is Activity 'B'           **--***********
CCCC  This is Activity 'C'           ****************
DDDD  This is Activity 'D'           **************
EEEE  This is Activity 'E'                **********
FFFF  This is Activity 'F'                          **********----***
GGGG  This is Activity 'G'                                    **********
HHHH  This is Activity 'H'                                    **********
IIII  This is Activity 'I'                                        ********
```

Figure 6. Bar-chart computer outputs for the basic scheduling computations on the network shown in Figure 5 –splitting allowed.

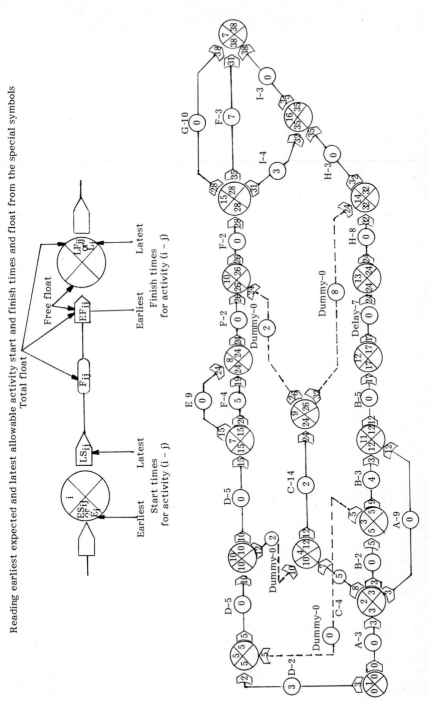

Reading earliest expected and latest allowable activity start and finish times and float from the special symbols

Figure 7. Arrow diagram equivalent to the precedence diagram shown in Figure 5 -splitting allowed.

finish time (FF7) and its successor constrains its start time (SS8).

Comparing Figures 3 and 5, we note that the project duration is 4 units less (42-38) when splitting is allowed. This results from the fact that activity B is <u>required</u> to split, because its <u>late start time plus its duration is less (earlier) than its early finish time</u>. That is,

$$LS_B + D_B < EF_B \text{ or } 3 + 10 < 17.$$

Thus, there must be a 4 unit idle time between the two segments of activity B, and this results in a 4 unit reduction in the project duration. This reduction occurs because the splitting of activity B allows it to start 4 units earlier, and hence its successor D can finish 4 units earlier, since these two activities are connected by a critical start-finish constraint (SF2,10).

Another difference in Figures 3 and 5 is found in their critical paths. In Figure 3, it is a single path, with a duration of 42 units. In Figure 5, there are two critical paths, each having a duration of 38 units. These paths are shown at the top of Figure 5.

The computer generated bar-charts, Figures 4 and 6 graphically display these points. A review of Figure 6 will show three effective segments for activity F. Namely a four day non-critical first segment followed by four critical days at the beginning of the second segment and finally three more non-critical day prior to completion. A review of Figure 7 will verify that the two center segments are consecutive and critical as shown in Figure 6. The bar-charts also show the identical critical paths identified on Figures 3 and 5.

Case 3 - Combination of Case 1 and Case 2

This option requires that the individual activities be identified as to their ability to be split. Given this identification the appropriate computational method can be applied to each activity.

Current Implementation

The use of the splitting/non-splitting computational methods normally require that they be incorporated in computer programs. Many early programs including those developed by IBM[3], incorporated the non-splitting methodology. After the publication of the splitting method by Crandall[1], several firms incorporated the computation into their scheduling programs. Among these were the Gary F. Atkinson Company of South San Francisco and Impell of San Francisco. The output shown in the paper was produced by a program written by Crandall for Construction Management Consultants in Alaska.

The actual implementation is straightforward and readers are advised to review the detailed algorithms presented in Crandall[1] and Moder[5]. The bar-charts that result from the implementation contain a significant amount of information with the important advantage of having subactivities shown by a single bar (line).

SUMMARY

Managers of large projects are once again directing their attention to network scheduling tools to assist in minimizing delays and resulting cost overruns. Although the Arrow diagram was widely heralded in this role, it failed to gain complete acceptance because of its networking complexity. The development of Precedence diagrams with lead/lag times should eliminate this complexity and allow managers to define relations between work packages (activities) in a logical manner, much closer to their standard planning methodology.

The algorithm referred to in this paper allows for an evaluation between the Precedence diagram with lead/lag times and its equivalent Arrow diagram. More significantly, the discussion of the algorithm raised the issue of an activities ability to be physically "split" during execution. This concern is not addressed at all in the standard Arrow network evaluation algorithm. It is relatively easy for a manager to define the lead/lag logical relations between activities and further to indicate which activities cannot be interrupted during their conduct in the field. Thus the joint use of "splitting" and "non-splitting" algorithms will yield a model that is much more realistic and have fewer activities than the Arrow diagram with proper equivalent concurrent logic.

The use of Precedence diagramming allows the use of work packages which are not separated into artificial smaller segments just to show their relationship to other work packages, as required to develop an equivalent Arrow diagram. Since the evaluation algorithm applied to Precedence diagrams created pseudo segments similar to the approrpiate arrow definition of concurrent logic, it is necessary to redefine the significance of float. The authors have demonstrated the level of information available from the evaluation process and recommend that the suggested critical path nomenclature be adopted for "split" activities to allow managers to make more meaningful use of the results. Although not yet implemented, this nomenclature would be utilized only on tabular listings as representative computer generated bar-charts would display the information graphically. Once the nomenclature for explaining the nature of an activity's critical segments is more universally understood, managers will more completely grasp the interactions between field work packages. The use of the computer generated bar-charts has already proven to be superior by the referenced firms. This bar-chart graphical representation is especially valuable for first line field managers as it requires little formal training and is useful to display the short interval schedule. The volume of output required to display a large project prevents its sole use defining the critical nature of activities.

Precedence diagramming with its flexible logic coupled with algorithms that provide the "splitting" and "non-splitting" evaluation has created an environment whereby managers can monitor a project without the network diagramming complexity previously required by concurrent Arrow diagrams.

REFERENCES

[1]   Crandall, K. C., "Project Planning with Precedence Lead/Lag Factors," Project
       Management Quarterly, Vol. 4, No. 3, Sept. 1973, pp. 18-27.

[2]   Fondahl, J. W., A Noncomputer Approach to the Critical Path Method for the
       Construction Industry, Dept. of Civil Eng., Stanford University, Stanford, Calif.,
       1st Ed. 1961, 1nd Ed. 1962.

[3]   IBM, Project Management System, Application Description Manual (H20-0210).
       IBM, 1968.

[4]   Moder, J. J., "How to Do CPM Scheduling Without a Computer," Engineering News-
       Record, March 14 (1963) pp. 30-34.

[5]   Moder, J. J., C. R. Phillips and E. W. Davis, "Project Management with CPM, PERT
       & Precedence Diagramming," Van-Nostrand Reinshold Company, New York, 3rd
       Ed., 1983.

[6]   Wiest, J. D., "Precedence Diagramming Methods: Some Unusual Characteristics and
       Their Implications for Project Managers," Journal of Operations Management, Vol. 1,
       No. 3, Feb. 1981, pp. 121-130.

[7]   Wiest, J. D., F. K. Levy, "A Management Guide to PERT/CPM with GERT/PDM/DCPM
       and Other Networks," Prentice-Hall, Inc., Englewood Cliffs, NJ, 2nd Ed., 1977, p. 145.

Project Management: Methods and Studies
Burton V. Dean (editor)
© Elsevier Science Publishers B.V. (North-Holland), 1985

A TRACKING MODEL FOR R&D PROJECTS

R. Balachandra

Northeastern University
Boston, Massachusetts
U.S.A.

At the time of approving an R&D project for development there is
much uncertainty about such key project parameters as the potential
for success, investment required, compatibility with the product
line, and resource availability. As the project progresses better
parameter estimates are usually available, which may either enhance
or detract from the project's worth. A study of over 50 R&D projects
in the electronics, communication, data processing and other high
technology based industries identified four critical factors and a set
of 12 significant variables which help in deciding whether to terminate
or continue the project in development. The factors were derived
from extensive discussions with R&D managers and from a review of
projects unilaterally terminated. The variables were extracted from
a larger set through stepwise discriminant analysis.

The variables reflect the changes taking place in the project during
the development stage, as for example, changes in probability of
commercial success, top management support, and internal competition. This paper also describes a monitoring scheme incorporating
these variables and factors i) in tracking the progress of R&D projects
and ii) for helping in the decision to terminate or continue them.
The results of such monitoring could lead to a better reallocation of
resources for better returns from the R&D portfolio.

INTRODUCTION

Much uncertainty exists in evaluating an R&D project at the time of approval for its funding.
Decisions regarding budgets have to be made on the basis of estimates of many critical
pieces of information such as expected benefits, investment required, probabilities of achieving techical and commercial success within the desired time frame, etc. These estimates
have to be made at a time when not much is known, and the available information is generally of low quality. Additionally these estimates are mostly subjective.

As the project progresses usually more and better information becomes available, which may
either enhance the estimate of the project's worth or detract from it. Such information
usually consists of evaluations of some important variables describing the progress of the
project and changes in the economic, technical, and socio-political environment. These types
of information are generally monitored on an informal basis, unless there is a system for
formal reviews of the project's progress [9].

The evaluation and monitoring of a portfolio of projects is an involved and complex exercise,
especially when the number of active projects in the portfolio is large. The effort on some
projects may have to be reduced because of unfavorable evaluations, leading to their termination (or as it is euphemistically called 'putting them on the back burner'); the resources
released from these terminated or deemphasized projects could then be transferred to other
more promising projects thereby enhancing their probabilities of success or advancing their
completion times; or made available to new R&D projects.

This paper describes a set of key variables which indicate the potential for a R&D project's successful completion. These variables have been derived from a study of over 50 R&D projects from a sample of high tech industries such as dataprocessing, communications and electronics. The key variables are incorporated into a scheme for monitoring the progress of projects in the R&D portfolio. The scheme produces a desirability index for each project at important milestones. This index can then be used to develop a viable portfolio of on-going R&D projects by terminating projects achieving a desirability index less than a certain threshold value.

R&D Project Management

Increasing competition from abroad in even the traditional strongholds of U. S. industry is forcing managers to place greater emphasis on managing and controlling industrial R&D projects. Firms are interested in successfully completing a larger percent of R&D projects in the development stage. Increasing the prospects of completing an on-going R&D project requires an understanding of how it moves from the stage of conception to its final stage of successful commercialization. It also requires a knowledge of how to monitor an on-going R&D project through its developmental stage so that potential failures can be identified sufficiently early to prevent unnecessary expenditure of scarce resources.

Industrial R&D projects are usually started after a thorough investigation into their merits and anticipated pay-offs. An R&D project starts out as an idea. It is then explored for its commercial potential. An informal review at this stage may lead to a further study to estimate the technical and economic feasibility. The project is then subjected to a comprehensive review as there are a number of competing projects within the company needing resources to embark on the development phase.

Many models have been developed to help in selecting the ideal set of projects. These models range from simple ranking of the competing projects to complex mathematical programming models. (For a good discussion of these models see Baker and Freeland [2]).

After an R&D project has been approved for inclusion in the development portfolio, adequate resources will be allocated in the form of technical personnel, equipment and other physical resources according to the project proposal. These allocations are made on the basis of evaluations of the attrativeness of the project in comparison with others approved for development.

In the development stage the project is pursued according to plans and schedules laid out earlier. The team of technical personnel is assembled and equipment and materials are procured. The schedules may be modified if the funds allocated are different from the originally requested amount.

As the project progresses during this phase a better understanding of the technical problems will be developed. There would be still a number of technical and design issues to be resolved and the probability of resolving them may change over the course of time, depending on a number of factors: the type of communication the technical personnel receive during this phase and the interaction they have with other individuals (see Allen [1] for a comprehensive discussion of the perceived change in the probability of technical success during the life of a project). Some projects may proceed at a rapid rate, while others may languish depending on the nature of communication.

A number of external factors exert a great deal of influence on how the project proceeds during this phase. Some of these are critical resulting in the project's termination if there is a large unfavorable change in one of these factors. If the change is not large, these factors may contribute to the postponement or slowing down of the project. For example, if one were working during the early 70's on the development of a new base for a cosmetic derived from a petroleum compound, the oil embargo of 1973 would have forced a reevaluation of the project for the availability of raw materials. Such a critical factor may strongly influence the management to decide to either terminate the project or, at least, to postpone it until conditions improve. Another example is the introduction of a competing product much earlier than originally anticipated. Depending on an appraisal of how the new product impacts on the market, the R&D project may be speeded up or even terminated.

From a review of project termination decisions and discussions with several R&D managers a set of four critical factors have been identified, which can lead to certain termination of the R&D project if there is a large unfavorable change in any one. These are:

1. Probability of technical success
2. Continued existence of the anticipated market
3. Government regulations
4. Raw material availability

If none of the critical factors show large unfavorable changes the project may not appear to be completely hopeless; however, it may not be as much of an attractive proposition as it was earlier. With the passage of time, other factors (though not critical) may show adverse changes, leading to a decision to postpone, slow down, or even terminate the project.

More and better information usually becomes available during the development phase of the R&D project. Revisions in the estimates of important variables are fairly common in a number of areas such as time and cost estimates, projected return on investment, market share, enthusiasm shown by the project team and its leader towards the project etc. Informal mechanisms are more common for monitoring such information; some companies, though, have established elaborate R&D project review procedures.

In a pioneering study, Dean [9] examined 40 companies and described the existing practices in industry with regard to a number of criteria used in terminating R&D projects in these firms. In a similar study, Rubinstein and others [13] identified a large number of factors influencing success at the project level. These studies, however, did not attempt to identify the weights assigned by the decision makers in arriving at the decision to terminate or continue the project. Another attempt to identify the factors responsible for the rejection of projects in the U.K. (project Sappho) produced a list of ten factors [14]. Based on personal experiences, Buell [7] and Holzman [10] give more lists of factors for help in deciding whether an R&D project should be terminated or not. Murphy and others [12] developed a large list of determinants of project success based on a survey of a larger class of projects which included construction, equipment building, research studies, etc. in addition to R&D projects. In a similar vein, Cooper [8] reported 19 factors for identifying new product winners.

These and other similar studies provide a great deal of insight into the complex task of project management and project termination. They provide a qualitative basis and guidelines for the termination decision. The multiplicity of factors and a lack of uniformity in their definition, however, make it difficult to operationalize the results of these studies.

Balachandra and Raelin [5] suggest that an intuitive discriminant function operates for deciding whether to terminate a project or not and list a number of factors which could probably be included in this discriminant function. They further suggest that the absolute values of these factors are not important, but only changes in the variables between successive review periods.

This hypothesis was tested in a recent study by Balachandra and Raelin [6]. Over 100 R&D projects were studied from different industries in the U.S. Half of these were terminated before their introduction into market and the other half were successfully introduced. Data were collected on a number of important variables at two distinct points in time – one at the time of the most recent decision when it was decided to terminate or continue the project, and the other at the time of the preceding decision when it was decided to continue the project. It was expected that by analyzing the variables at these two points in time, the variables which underwent unfavorable changes could be identified leading to the termination decision.

The final data set from this study comprised of 114 projects, of which 57 were successfully completed and the rest were terminated, abandoned or left on the back burner. A total of 66 variables were identified as relevant for this decision. This set of 66 variables excluded the critical factors already discussed, as their presence would confound the effects of the discriminating variables. This data set was analyzed using stepwise discriminant analysis to identify the significant variables for classifying the projects into successful and terminated ones. In this procedure variables are selected one at a time in order of their contribution towards discriminating between the two groups of projects. This selection terminates when additional variables do not add significantly to the discriminating power. (The results of this analysis are described fully in [3], [6]).

This data set was broken up into two groups – the high tech industries and the non high tech industries. The high tech industry group comprised of companies in the electronic, communication and data processing industry. There were a total of 51 projects belonging to this group. This smaller data set was subjected to a similar analysis as the total data set. The results of this analysis are shown in Table 1. There is a good deal of commonality between this set of discriminating variables and the set of variables from the full sample which included non high tech firms.

Table 1

Discriminating Variables for High Tech R&D Projects

No.	Discriminating Variable	Discriminant Function Coefficient	Significant Level
1	Probability of Commercial Success	1.414	0.01
2	Top Management Support and Commitment	0.765	0.01
3	Effectiveness of Project Leader	0.732	0.01
4	Commitment of Project Staff	1.505	0.01
5	Project Leader is Project Champion	0.532	0.05
6	Life cycle of the Product/Process	1.17	0.01
7	Meeting Time Schedules	0.32	0.05
8	Rate of New Product Introduction	0.837	0.01
9	Alliance with Corporate Goals	0.255	0.05
10	Internal Competition	0.628	0.01
11	Number of End Uses	0.278	0.01
12	Chance Events	0.693	0.05

Note: The discriminant analysis was performed using the SPSS package with the default values for tolerance (0.001) and the F value for entering and removing variables (1.000).

The discriminant scores are for the variable values as measured by the study. Some of them were dichotomous, some were on a five point scale, and some others were actual numbers. Accordingly, the application of the model using the actual discriminant scores would not be very meaningful if the variables were not measured in an identical fashion. Additionally many of these variables are measured as the difference in their values at two points in time.

The discriminant function was able to correctly classify 89.5% of the class. Jackknifing and split sample analysis were not attempted as the sample size was small and the number of variables was large. Validation of the model was however done using Montgomery's V3 method [11].

The canonical correlation of this discriminant function was 0.83; the function was able to classify correctly 89.5% of the cases.

Discriminating Variables in R&D Project Management

Even though there are no significant adverse changes in the critical factors described earlier, the project may still have to be terminated because of changes in a number of other circumstances, resulting in an increased potential for failure. There is usually a slow deterioration in some factors as the project progresses. It is important to identify these changes and detect them in time so that the termination decision could be made early. The discriminating variables listed in Table 1 above can help in identifying projects headed for possible termination. In the following paragraphs these discriminating variables and their impact on project success will be described briefly.

1. Probability of Commercial Success: For successful completion of the project, it is necessary that, not only the technological problems should be solved, but the market should also be ready for the outcome of the project so that the firm could make a reasonable return on its investment. This implies an evaluation of the market potential, both in terms of the size and the price that could be charged as well as an evaluation of the feasibility of accomplishing the technological task of completing the project within the planned time frame. Initially, this probability would have been estimated at reasonably high levels for the project to get funded, but may get downgraded as unforeseen problems are discovered. If the decrease in this probability is significantly large then, of course, the project is doomed. On the other hand, if the decrease is marginal, it could be of some concern; in due course, it may even be significant.

2. Top Management Support and Commitment: The support of top management is very important, as discussed by both Dean [9] and Rubenstein and others [13]. Without it, the project may not receive the necessary encouragement and the release of funds may not be forthcoming quickly. This will affect the project's progress and the motivation of project workers. If the support of top management is perceived to have decreased in the course of time, it may produce an adverse effect on the project leader and the project team. On the other hand, if it is perceived by the project personnel that the interest and support of top management has increased, then there is likely to be a greater degree of motivation leading to a successful completion of the project.

3. Project Leader's Effectiveness: This is similar to top management's support in its effect on the project's progress. The commitment and dedication of the project leader and the effectiveness with which he handles the problems encountered usually gets communicated to the project team, resulting in a greater degree of effort being put into the project and making it more likely to result in a success. Any decrease or perceived decrease in the project leader's commitment can adversely affect the progress of the project.

4. Commitment of Project Staff: A number of factors contribute to increased commitment of project staff toward the project, chief among them being a sense of loyalty to the project leader. Additionally, a liking for the project and the resulting product will greatly enhance the commitment. A higher level commitment on the part of the project workers contributes to a greater degree of success of the project.

5. Project Leader in the Project Champion: It has been demonstrated that the presence of a project champion is very critical to the success of a project [12], [13]. However, if the project leader himself happens to be the project champion, there is a greater likelihood of pushing the project through to success.

6. <u>Life Cycle of the Product/Process</u>: The life cycle of the product or process under development is very important in the decision to continue or terminate the project. If the product under development is in its infancy stage, there are many uncertainties with the technology and the probability of not achieving a successful product is very high. On the other hand, if the product is in a growth phase, most of the initial hurdles in the technology would have been overcome. Therefore, if the product class enters the growth phase during its development, there is a much greater likelihood of its being successfully completed.

7. <u>Meeting Time Schedules</u>: Meeting time schedules is a major indicator of the progress of an R&D project in development. If the time schedules have to be frequently revised, it is a clear indication that there is trouble and unforeseen problems with the project. This constitutes a signal that there are technical or management problems making it less likely that the project will be completed according to the planned schedule in terms of both time and cost.

8. <u>Rate of New Product Introduction</u>: If new products or significant adaptations of existing products are introduced in the field fairly regularly, say once in six months or so, it is an indication that there is a great deal of innovation taking place and that the market is still in the growth phase and has not reached maturity yet. In such an environment, any reasonable new product with even marginal improvements over the available products has a good chance of being successful.

9. <u>Alliance with Corporate Goals</u>: The project should be consistent with the corporate goals. If not, it may dilute the efforts of the organization in directions where the corporation is strong. Although this aspect would have been examined carefully at the time of starting the project, later developments in the life of the project may distract it from the original concept. With such changes there is a great danger that the project will not be commercially successful.

10. <u>Internal Competition</u>: Competition for similar resources from another project, in many cases, can act as a catalyst for successful completion of the project. The demand for resources can force the project leader and the workers to put in extra effort to complete the project successfully. This is analogous to parallel research strategy. Increasing competition can, therefore, be a motivating factor for successful completion.

11. <u>Number of End Uses</u>: The originators of an idea often think that their idea can solve a large number of problems and it has a wide range of applications. If the project attempts to meet a great many of these applications, which may be completely unrelated, much effort will be spent developing a general product, leading to a possible failure. On the other hand, a focused development, where the end uses are very clearly established, can lead to a greater degree of success. The danger is greater when new applications are thought of during the development leading to ambiguity in the basic specifications for the product.

12. <u>Chance Events</u>: The occurrence of chance events cannot be foreseen. Some of them may be favorable to the project, while others may be detrimental. Some may be of such significance that the decision on the project is clear cut (as in the case of the oil embargo), while in others, it may not have such a significant impact. In any case, the occurrence of a chance event which may influence the outcome of the project should be considered in the decision to continue or terminate the project.

It is important to note that the termination decision is based on the extent of progress made by the project in the interval between an earlier review and the current review. The key variables monitored for such a decision have to be evaluated at these two points in time and only the changes that have occurred in the interim are important. With this premise, the following scheme is proposed for monitoring R&D projects in the portfolio. This procedure utilizes the discriminant variables listed in Table 1 and described above. It is possible to identify at a sufficiently early date those projects which have a greater likelihood of failing, leading to appropriate termination decisions. The portfolio of R&D projects can be chosen and pruned so that the success probability of projects is considerably enhanced.

Monitoring R&D Projects

It is normal practice to review the progress of on going R&D projects at frequent intervals. These reviews are usually informal, where the R&D manager has discussions with the project leader to determine whether the project is progressing according to the original time and cost schedule or if there have been any unforeseen delays or problems. If there are some problems with regard to personnel and budgets, new allocations may be made at this time if it is felt that the progress is satisfactory and the technological problems are not unsolvable. On the other hand, if it is felt that the progress is less than expected, the R&D manager may decide either to postpone the project or abandon it completely. In some larger organizations, the reviews are more formal, where an evaluation report is prepared based on the assessment of the R&D manager on a number of dimensions, chief among which is the probability of technical success. This report is studied and a decision is made regarding terminating or continuing the projects.

As discussed earlier, the decision to terminate a project is difficult to make in either the formal or informal reviews. It becomes very difficult when the factors have not significantly deteriorated. In such cases, a formal review of the critical factors described in the foregoing paragraphs in combination with a decision rule proposed below helps in clarifying the situation so that better decisions can be made.

At these reviews, in addition to whatever formal reviews exist, the project is evaluated for the critical factors: technology, market, government regulations, and raw material availability. If there are significant shortcomings in any one of these factors, the project is a good candidate for termination. If there are no serious problems with these factors, then the project is reviewed for changes in the twelve discriminating factors (Table 1).

These variables are examined with a view to elicit information only on whether there were any changes in the desired direction. Evaluation of the discriminating variables cannot be very precise, as most of them are subjective in nature and even the rest are only estimates. What is really important is not their absolute values, but the direction of change since they were last reviewed. For example, one needs to know whether the commitment of the project leader to the project has increased, remained the same, or decreased since the last review. As long as it has remained the same or increased, the factor can be assumed to be positively contributing to the success of the project. If it has, this factor is scored a '1'; if it has decreased, this factor is scored a '0'. Other factors are evaluated similarly. The Desirability Index (D.I.) of the project is the sum of the scores received by it.

Ideally each of the discriminating variables should be evaluated and multiplied by the appropriate discriminant function coefficient (Table 1), and these scores should be added to get the discriminant score. If the variables have been standardized, a positive discriminant score would imply a case for continuing, and a negative score a likely termination. However, this is infeasible in most cases because the evaluation of the variables is very imprecise. One way out of this problem is to assume that the discriminating variables are equally important for this decision. This is a practical measure as the result of this review is to obtain an indication of how desirable the project is and whether the project should be continued rather than to decide to terminate the project. Therefore, if a majority of these variables have a favorable change the project has a high probability of successful completion.

If the Desirability Index (D.I.) of a project is 12 i.e., all twelve variables scored '1's (favorable changes) the project has a very high probability of success. Similarly, if the D.I. is six or less (six or less showed favorable changes) there is a good chance that the project will fail. Because of the poor precision of measurement of the variables it is more practical to have a threshold value for the D.I. set at nine for continuing the project (i.e., nine factors with favorable chances can imply that the project has a high likelihood of being successful).

Projects with a D.I. of less than nine need to be examined more closely as they are likely candidates for termination. This examination may reveal that either nothing could be done to salvage the project, in which case it should be terminated, or some factors are only marginally unsatisfactory. In the latter case, those factors which showed an unfavorable change could be looked at more carefully to determine if additional resources can make the factors show a favorable changes. For example, if time schedules were not being met because of lack of coordination, employing a person to bring about the necessary coordination may help improve performance with regard to meeting time schedules, thus bringing a favorable change in a critical factor. This monitoring scheme is shown graphically in Figure 1.

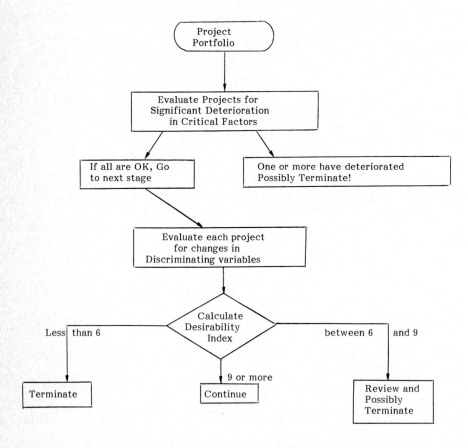

Figure 1. A Tracking Model for High Tech R&D Projects

The information gathered from detailed examination of the factors can suggest whether it is possible to improve the evaluation of the project by providing additional resources. With such evaluations, it will be possible to determine which of the projects headed for termination should be provided with additional resources so that they could be completed successfully. If none of these projects could be selected for allocating additional resources, the portfolio of projects should be curtailed and new projects could be brought in or the released could be applied to the other successful projects so that they can be completed sooner.

An Illustrative Example

Consider an actual case from an electronics company where the R&D portfolio consists of four projects at various stages in the development stage. Some important facts about these projects are shown in Table 2.

Table 2

Characters of Four Sample Projects

Item	Project # 1	2	3	4
Budget	$7.2 M	$3.5 M	$18 M	$25 M
Size of Project Team	45	35	110	70
Life Cycle Stage	Maturity	Maturity	Infancy	Maturity
Expected Profit Margin	30%	50%	10%	2%
Estimated Time	36 Months	72 Months	96 Months	36 Months
Time at Review	30 Months	60 Months	80 Months	29 Months
Amount Spent at Review	$6.7 M	$3.6 M	$16 M	$20 M

As there were no major changes in the four critical factors, the decision to terminate any of these projects has to be based on the next set of twelve discriminating factors. The evaluation of these factors are shown in the table below:

Table 3

Scoring of the Sample Projects Using Discriminating Variables

# Factor	Project # 1		2		3		4	
1 Probability of Commercial Success	D	0	I	1	D	0	S	1
2 Top Management Support and Commitment	D	0	I	1	S	1	S	1
3 Effectiveness of Project Leader	D	0	I	1	I	1	I	1
4 Commitment of Project Staff	D	0	I	1	S	1	S	1
5 Project Leader is Project Champion	NO	0	Y	1	Y	1	NO	0
6 Life Cycle of the Product/Process	M	1	M	1	IN	0	M	1
7 Meeting Time Schedules	S	1	D	0	D	0	S	1
8 Rate of New Product Introduction	S	1	S	1	D	0	S	1
9 Alliance with Corporate Goals	S	1	S	1	S	1	S	1
10 Internal Competition	I	1	S	1	S	1	S	1
11 Number of End Uses	D	1	I	0	S	1	S	1
12 Chance Events	NO	1	NO	1	NO	1	NO	1
DESIRABILITY INDEX	7		10		8		11	

120   R. Balachandra

Key

D	Decreased
I	Increased
IN	Infancy
M	Maturity
NO	No
S	Remained Same
Y	Yes

From this table, it is seen that projects #2 and #4 score D.I.'s of 10 and 11. The threshold value of D.I. for intensive review is nine; therefore, these two projects could be continued. On the other hand, projects #1 and #3 have scored less than the required nine and, therefore, are possible candidates for termination, and an intensive review should be performed for these two projects. It is by no means suggested that the termination decision should be based on the evaluation of the D.I. alone.

The D.I. evaluation, however, discloses the areas which are contributing to the possible failure of the project. For example, in project #3, the probability of commercial success has decreased between two consecutive reviews. Similarly, it has not been meeting time schedules. It is possible that additional resources may help in improving the probability of commercial success as well as improving its performance in meeting time schedules.

In the actual case, projects #1 and #3 were terminated; the other two projects were successfully completed.

CONCLUSION

The termination decision of an on going R&D project in the development stage is very difficult to make. Which projects to terminate from a portfolio of projects is a question that has to be considered very carefully so that one does not terminate a project that could prove to be successful later on.

This paper identifies a set of discriminating factors and variables based on a study of over 50 R&D projects in the electronics, data processing and communications (high tech) industries. These have been grouped into two types: critical factors (four) and discriminating variables (twelve). Any significant deterioration in the critical factors can lead to termination of the project. Deterioration in the discriminating variables needs to be evaluated more carefully. Actual measurement of these variables it not necessary, but only an assessment of the direction of change. The number of discriminating variables which did not show an unfavorable change in called the Desirability Index (D.I.) of the project. If the D.I. of a project is below a threshold value (nine), the project is a serious candidate for termination.

In the illustrative example described in the paper, four actual projects from an R&D portfolio of an electronics firm were evaluated using this methodology. Two of them obtained D.I.'s of 10 and 11, and the other two received seven and eight. After a careful review of the projects receiving D.I. of less than nine, they were terminated; the two other projects (with D.I.'s of 10 and 11) were successfully completed.

With such evaluations of the discriminating factors and an understanding of the effect of additional resources on these factors, one could reallocate funds released from terminated projects to other continuing projects so that the completion probabilities are enhanced, or applied to new candidate projects.

It should however be emphasized that the termination decision of a project should not be based on this scheme alone. This scheme should be used only as an indicator of potential failures. Projects identified by this scheme as likely candidates for termination should be more closely reviewed and evaluated before the decision is made to terminate them.

REFERENCES

[1]   Allen, Thomas J., Managing the Flow of Technology, Cambridge, MA, The MIT Press, 1977.

[2]   Baker, Norman and Freeland, James, "Recent Advances in R&D Benefit and Project Selection," Management Science, June, 1965.

[3]   Balachandra, R., "GO/NOGO Signals for New Product Development," Journal of Product Innovation Management, Vol. 1, No. 2, April, 1984.

[4]   Balachandra, R., "Effective Control of R&D Projects," Paper presented at the TIMS/ORSA National Meeting, San Francisco, May 1984.

[5]   Balachandra, R., and Raelin, Joseph A., "How to Decide When to Abandon a Project," Research Management, July, 1980.

[6]   Balachandra, R., and Raelin, Joseph A., "Factors Explaining Decisions to Terminate or Continue R&D Projects," Report to the National Science Foundation under Grant No. ISI-8105585, May 1983.

[7]   Buell, C. D., "When to Terminate a R&D Project," Research Management, July 1967.

[8]   Cooper, Robert G., "How to Identify Potential New Product Winners," Research Management, September 1980.

[9]   Dean, Burton V., "Evaluating, Selecting, and Controlling R&D Projects," Research Study #89, American Management Association, New York, 1969.

[10] Holzmann, R. T., "To Stop or Not: The Big Research Decision," Chemical Technology, February, 1972.

[11] Montgomery, D. B., "New Product Distribution: An Analysis of Supermarket Buyer Decisions," Journal of Marketing Research, 1975, 12, pp. 255-264.

[12] Murphy, David C., Baker, Bruce, N., and Fisher, Dalmar, "Determinants of Project Success," Boston College, 1974.

[13] Rubenstein, A. H., Chakrabarty, A. K., O'Keafe, R. D., Souder, "Factors Influencing Innovation Success at the Project Level," Research Management, May 1976.

[14] "Success and Failure in Industrial Innovation," Centre for the Study of Industrial Innovations, London, 1972.

Project Management: Methods and Studies
Burton V. Dean (editor)
© Elsevier Science Publishers B.V. (North-Holland), 1985

PROJECT SCHEDULING FOR MULTIPLE OBJECTIVES

Sang M. Lee

University of Nebraska
Lincoln, Nebraska
U.S.A.

David L. Olson

Texas A&M University
College Station, Texas
U.S.A.

The typical scheduling problem involves multiple time periods, multiple projects, multiple resources and multiple management objectives. This paper presents a means of formulating the resource constrained scheduling problem in a goal programming model. The technique used to solve this zero-one model is the branch and bound goal programming algorithm. For larger models, zero-one linear programming packages can be used to solve a sequence of linear programming models equivalent to the goal programming formulation presented. This approach gives managers the means of modifying unconstrained time minimization schedules to reflect other important objectives, such as resource limitation. The results of the study indicate that this approach gives managers the capability of analyzing delicate tradeoffs in time, cost, resource limitations, and other important objectives.

Project scheduling is a major topic in operations management. PERT, CPM, and other variations are widely discussed because of their practical importance [3,4,5,6]. Another reason why approaches to project scheduling are important in the literature is because of the limitations of existing methods. PERT and CPM, at least in their widely known forms, require the assumption of unlimited resource availability. The output of such models are schedules that minimize project completion time, without consideration of resource limits.

In practice, minimization of project completion time is not the only desired feature of a schedule. Managerial objectives in addition to time might involve the use of critical resources. If a work force and equipment fleet are of a given size, it generally would be beneficial to schedule only those quantities of resources. A project schedule generated on the basis of predecessor activities and durations alone would likely result in overscheduling of some critical resource.

A number of approaches have been developed to answer the problem of limited resources. Bowman [2] presented a zero-one formulation that would, if soluble, allow for limited resource schedules. Pritsker, et al. [16] presented a simplification of this technique, and demonstrated how such a model could be formulated with a single objective of time minimization. However, Pritsker noted that practical solution of real problems with this approach is not attainable with present zero-one programming algorithms [9].

Past algorithms and techniques have treated all requirements beyond time minimization as constraints, if at all. For example, an efficient integer programming algorithm for solving resource-constrained scheduling problems has been proposed by Talbot and Patterson [18]. Also, Weglarz [19] has presented an approach for project scheduling with continuously-divisible, doubly constrained resources. The objective of these approaches is minimization of project duration. It is proposed that time minimization is a valuable feature of a schedule, but that there often are more important elements to a problem. We would stress the need for a technique allowing flexibility and focus upon the decision maker's goals.

The Pritsker, et al. formulation to a project scheduling problem has the flexibility mandatory for multiple objective approaches such as goal programming, where the decision maker requires the latitude to change relative ranking of time or resource limit targets. While we have been able to solve the models presented here with branch and bound techniques (on a slow minicomputer), it is expected that more efficient means of solution than have been proposed in the literature for resource constrained scheduling will be required. Network flow algorithms have recently been proposed as more efficient means of solving zero-one formulations [10] for the mixed zero-one models goal programming would entail. By reformulating models into network form, application of the flexible Pritsker, et al. formulation would be practical for much larger problems.

In many scheduling problems, deadlines are given. If the expected completion time is later than the deadline, high importance may be given to minimization of time. However, in those more desirable cases where expected completion time is earlier than the deadline, less emphasis may be placed upon time minimization, and other goals may become more important. The technique we propose presently is an iterative zero-one goal programming approach. This approach allows not only the resource leveling method of Bowman [2] and Pritsker, et al. [16], but also accommodates the analysis of multiple objectives in terms of priorities and the solution method by integer programming.

This paper presents an example project scheduling problem for demonstration, which is solved in a series of four steps. The first step, assuming the single objective of time minimization, could be solved using a critical path algorithm. Other goals placing emphasis upon limiting overscheduling of critical resources are added in later steps of the procedure. This additional type of constraint requires solution through a zero-one goal programming algorithm [11].

The Goal Programming Approach

Today, a considerable body of knowledge exists concerning the normative and descriptive approaches to decision making. A growing number of studies have appeared which attempt to describe the decision making behavior in organizations. Thus, the "satisfying" approach based on the concept of bounded rationality has emerged as a pragmatic, descriptive methodology of decision making [17]. In this approach, a set of tangible, multiple aspiration criteria replaces an abstract, global optimization criterion.

Goal programming (GP) is a powerful tool of multiple objective decision making (MODM) with satisficing operational assumptions. The decision maker's multiple aspirational goals are expressed in either ordinal (lexicographic) or numerical (cardinal) terms so that multiple goals can be analyzed on the basis of their importance. Thus, GP is capable of analyzing MODM problems without burdening the decision maker to define cost or utility involved with the various goals. Furthermore, GP allows the decision maker to incorporate his or her personal judgment about the unique aspects of the decision environment.

Although the original development of GP was based on an extension of linear programming, the basic philosophy and conceptual framework of GP are much broader than linear programming. GP is a pragmatic approach that reflects the actual decision making process in real-world situations. With the recent advances in GP, in terms of refined algorithms, interactive decision support systems and new extensions, GP has become a powerful, self-contained MODM technique.

The general GP model with $\underline{q}$ priority levels, m_0 goal constraints, m_1 system constraints, and $\underline{n}$ decision variables can be expressed as follows:

$$\text{Minimize } z_0 = \sum_{k=1}^{q} \sum_{i=1}^{m_0} P_k(w_{ki}^- d_i^- + w_{ki}^+ d_i^+)$$

subject to $\sum_{j=1}^{n} a_{ij}x_j + d_i^- - d_i^+ = b_i, \quad i=1,2,...,m_0$

$\sum_{j=1}^{n} a_{ij}x_j = b_i, \quad i=m_0+1, m_0+2,...,m_0+m_1$

$x_j, d_i^-, d_i^+ > 0, j=1,2,...,n, \quad i=1,2,...,m_0$

where

P_k : the $\underline{k}$th priority level, $P_k \ggg M_{Pk+1}, \quad k=1,2...q-1$

w_{ki}^-, w_{ki}^+ : numerical weights attached to deviational variables of the $\underline{i}$th goal at a given priority level p_k,

d_i^-, d_i^+ : negative and positive deviational variables about the $\underline{i}$th goal,

a_{ij} : the technological coefficient of the $\underline{j}$th activity for the $\underline{i}$th goal or system constraint,

b_i : the $\underline{i}$th goal or resource level,

x_j : the $\underline{j}$th decision variable.

The zero-one GP technique applied in this paper was developed by Lee and Morris [12]. The technique utilizes Balas' additive algorithm [1] and Glover's backtracking procedure [8]. The solution combinations are evaluated by introducing one decision variable at a time through the branching operation. When no further variables can be added to improve the solution beyond the current optimal solution, the solution is "fathomed." Then, a backtracking technique is instituted to evaluate other combinations in a systematic fashion. The optimal zero-one solution is the upper bound solution when all possible combinations are evaluated. The complete computer program is presented in reference [11].

Objectives in Scheduling

The resource scheduling problem arises from the interdependence of time and resource availability. If two project elements both call for a scarce item of equipment, a conflict would result if these elements were scheduled simultaneously.

The basis for decision in scheduling problems may rest upon time, cost, resource levels, as well as other criteria. Rarely will decision makers have a single criterion upon which to select a schedule. Lee, et al. [13] developed a project scheduling method which considered critical resources, such as highly expensive equipment, in addition to minimization of time. Quite frequently, project managers are faced with local short run scarcity of critical equipment or personnel. Additional resources could possibly be obtained, but often at a premium. Managers of construction proejcts may often establish the accomplishment of required tasks with existing equipment or skilled personnel as objectives. Such situations involve a tradeoff in goals [14]. It would be useful if a model capable of reflecting these tradeoffs were developed.

Development of a GP model requires specific determination of priorities for the goals and aspiration levels. This process is sometimes complex. Nevertheless, determination of project goals and their priorities has always been the most important responsibility of the project manager. Furthermore, a number of interactive GP approaches have been developed to alleviate much of the decision maker's burden for specifying priorities and aspiration levels [7,15].

A Scheduling Problem

The following construction scenario is presented to demonstrate application of the proposed technique. The project is to construct a building, with 22 activities involving different equipment and crew requirements. Table 1 presents project data.

TABLE 1

PROJECT DATA

	Activity	Duration	Predecessors	Cranes	Carpenters	Laborers
A	Excavate & Footers	4	–	1	2	2
B	Pour Concrete Foundation	2	A	1	2	4
C	Frame & Roof	4	B	1	4	–
D	Brickwork	6	C	1	–	2
E	Basement Plumbing	1	B	–	–	–
F	Pour Basement Concrete	2	E	1	–	4
G	Rough Plumbing	3	E	–	–	2
H	Initial Wiring	2	C	–	–	–
J	Heat & Ventilation	4	C,F	1	–	–
K	Plaster	10	G,J	–	–	–
L	Finish Flooring	3	H,K	–	4	–
M	Kitchen Fixtures	1	L	–	–	–
N	Finish Plumbing	2	L	–	–	–
P	Finish Carpentry	3	L	–	4	–
Q	Finish Roof	2	C	1	3	–
R	Gutters & Downspouts	1	Q	1	–	–
S	Storm Drains	1	B	1	2	2
T	Varnish Floor	2	U	–	–	3
U	Paint	3	P	–	–	–
V	Finish Electrical	1	M	–	–	–
W	Finish Grading	2	D,R	–	–	2
X	Walks & Landscape	5	S,W	1	2	2

It is likely that management will seek a schedule with a number of desired features. It is generally useful to complete work as quickly as possible, as resources can be diverted to other revenue generating projects. While finishing as quickly as possible is desirable, it is even more critical to complete projects before deadlines, as penalties are often involved. In this problem, a deadline of 40 working days is assumed.

In addition to time, other factors may be extremely important as well. In this problem, it is assumed that the existing operation has one crane, which is shared by a number of specialty activities. The critical path solution will assume that additional crane resources can be obtained should more than one crane be required. However, this may be expensive, if possible at all.

A similar limitation involves skilled labor. It is assumed in this problem that there are five carpenters available to work on the project. In many areas, additional carpenters could easily be obtained. In other areas, carpenters are a scarce resource that may not be possible to expand. Other classes of labor, involving less skill, may be readily available, although for reasons of training and reliability, it may be desirable to remain within existing crew sizes.

The model is built from a critical path analysis of the problem, including the deadline time of 40 time periods. This critical path analysis provides available slack for all activities.

Variable Definition

A zero-one variable x_j is required for each time frame an activity can be assigned. The number of variables necessary to define a specific activity is 1 + (allowable slack). Activity A has an allowable slack of 5 time periods, as do activities B and C. Activity D has allowable slack of 17 time periods. Variables are assigned as follows:

Activity A (duration 4)		Activity B (duration 2)	
variable	time frame	variable	time frame
x_1	periods 1 through 4	x_7	periods 5 through 6
x_2	2 through 5	x_8	6 through 7
x_3	3 through 6	x_9	7 through 8
x_4	4 through 7	x_{10}	8 through 9
x_5	5 through 8	x_{11}	9 through 10
x_6	6 through 9	x_{12}	10 through 11

In like manner, variables x_j (j=13,18) represent activity C, and x_j (j=19,35) represent activity D.

Membership Constraints

Only one time frame can be selected for each activity. Therefore for activity A,

$$\sum_{j=1}^{6} x_j = 1$$

There are twenty two of these constraints for the twenty two activities. There are no deviational variables included, because these structural constraints must be satisfied.

Precedence Constraints

For each precedence relationship, a constraint is required to guarantee maintenance of that relationship. Precedence constraints are of the form:

$$\sum_j a_{ij}x_j - \sum_{j'} a_{ij'}x_{j'} \geq 0$$

where j includes all variables representing the preceding activity and j' includes all variables representing the following activity. The preceding activity is given positive coefficients and the following activity negative coefficients. Maintenance of precedence requires the function have a positive value. The coefficients are assigned so that early preceding activity assignments release later time period assignments for the following activity, but not the reverse. For example, to model activity A preceding activity B:

$$6x_1 + 5x_2 + 4x_3 + 3x_4 + 2x_5 + 1x_6 \qquad\qquad \text{(preceding activity A)}$$

$$- 6x_7 - 5x_8 - 4x_9 - 3x_{10} - 2x_{11} - 1x_{12} \geq 0 \qquad\qquad \text{(following activity B)}$$

If x_1 is selected for Activity A, any assignment for B is valid. On the other hand, if activity A is delayed to time frame 2-5 (x_2), x_7 is prohibited. There are 26 such precedence relationships in the model.

Resource Limitation Constraints

A constraint is required for each limited resource in each time period. Every variable representing an activity scheduled during the modeled time period is included in that constraint. The form of this type of constraint is:

$$\sum a_{ij}x_j + d_i^- - d_i^+ = b_i.$$ The deviational variable d_i^+ is minimized at the selected priority $\forall\, x_j$ included in that time period.

The quantity of resource required for activity j is included as a_{ij}. The right hand side b_i is the target resource limit desired. If d_i^+ is zero, the goal is met for that time period. As an example, there is a desired target level of 1 for the crane resource. In time period 1 through 6, there are no possible conflicts in crane usage. In time period 7, activities C (x_{18}) and S (x_{197}) could be scheduled, requiring one crane each. The constraint for crane usage in time period 7 is:

$$x_{18} + x_{197} + d_i^- - d_i^+ = 1$$

and d_i^+ would be minimized at the selected priority level, along with the other crane limitation deviational variables. This goal would be met if the sum of these positive deviational variables were 0. For time period 8, two variables representing activity C $(x_{18}$ and $x_{19})$ and one each for activity F (x_{50}) and activity S (x_{198}) could be scheduled.

$$x_{18} + x_{19} + x_{50} + x_{198} + d_i^- - d_i^+ = 1.$$

For the carpenter and laborer constraints, the coefficients for resource usage could be different than 1. In time period 7, activities C (x_{18}) and S (x_{197}) could be scheduled requiring carpenters. There is a desired limit of 5 carpenters. Activity C requires 4 carpenters and activity S requires 2 carpenters. The constraint is:

$$4x_{18} + 2x_{197} + d_i^- - d_i^+ = 5$$

These two activities could not be scheduled at the same time if the goal of using no more than five carpenters were to be met.

Minimization of Time

A goal constraint minimizing time can be developed by minimizing a function which gives heavier weights to later time frames for each activity. One scheme would be to give a weight of one to the earliest time frame for each activity, two for the next variable, and so on. The overall project time would be minimized by minimizing this function including all variables for all activities in the model. The goal constraint for this function is:

$$\sum a_{ij}x_j + d_i^- - d_i^+ = 0 \qquad \text{minimize } d_i^+$$

Model Notes

The model formulation process is complex. LINDO allows descriptive variable names, vastly improving the ability to sort out model complexity. For MPSC, a code could be written to generate the input file given the critical path input data found in Table 1. The authors have successfully written a code to generate input for a network flow algorithm.

In addition, there is a great deal of potential for variable and constraint elimination. Activities A and B begin the project in series. All other activities follow B. The early start time frames for these activities will be in all solutions. Therefore, variables x_1 through x_{12} could be eliminated from the model, along with the membership constraints for activities A and B. In addition, resource constraints involving no nonzero coefficients, or only one variable, could be eliminated, such as resource constraints for time periods one through six.

Goal Consideration

To demonstrate the impact of various goal rankings by decision makers, a series of models were solved utilizing a zero-one goal programming package. Each model had 263 decision variables and 48 system constraints (22 activity and 26 precedence constraints). As additional goals are introduced, a number of goal constraints are added to the model. Thus, model 4 involved 263 decision variables, 170 constraints, and 5 priority levels. The objectives and priorities placed upon these objectives were:

        Model 1 - Priority 1 Minimize completion time

        Model 2 - Priority 1 Schedule only one crane

                (40 goal constraints)

                2 Minimize completion time

        Model 3 - Priority 1 Schedule only one crane

                (40 goal constraints)

                2 Schedule no more than five carpenters

                (40 goal constraints)

                3 Minimize completion time

                (1 goal constraint)

        Model 4 - Priority 1 Schedule only one crane

                (40 goal constraints)

                2 Schedule no more than five carpenters

(40 goal constraints)

3   Complete project with 40 day time limit

(1 goal constraint)

4   Schedule no more than five laborers

(40 goal constraints)

5   Minimize completion time

(1 goal constraint)

A well known and easily coded critical path algorithm would yield the solution to Model 1. The resulting schedule for this Model is given in Figure 1. The project could be completed in 35 working days, although three cranes would be required in days 11 through 13. In addition, six carpenters would be required on working day 7, and six laborers in days 8 and 9.

Model 2 would restrict the number of cranes to one. The critical path algorithm would not be able to include this restriction, despite the possible importance of such a constraint. In practice, the schedule could be adjusted around crane availability, although in complex projects, such adjustments could result in suboptimal schedules. Figure 2 presents the solution to this model.

Model 3 would place priority upon limiting the number of carpenters to five over minimizing completion time. The zero-one formulation for this model required 263 variables and 129 constraints. The zero-one solution, as shown in Figure 3. The resulting schedule limits carpenters to five maximum. The cost in terms of working days is that 37 days would be required for project completion. Figure 3 presents this schedule.

Model 4 places an additional limitation upon laborers (no more than four). The priority given to this objective would not totally preempt time. Priority three was given to completion of the project within 40 working days. The resulting solution (given in Figure 4) required 129 working days.

Limitations of the Model

The primary limitation of the proposed method is the use of the zero-one formulation. This formulation provides the flexibility required due to consideration of multiple objectives, as well as the capability of introducing mutually exclusive constraints, either/or constraints, and other scheduling formulation features [11]. However, use of a zero-one model introduces a problem in required solution time. All zero-one models are restricted by the number of variables modeled, given existing computer technology. The proposed formulation generates a zero-one variable for each time frame each activity is allowed.

Because more slack in a schedule yields a larger model, more restricted scheduling problems are easier to solve (they are smaller models). Therefore, one way to lower required solution time is to use variable reduction techniques presented by Pritsker, et al. [16]. The approach can be extended by modeling only those activities which are users of critical resources, and conducting a feasibility check for those activities not modeled.

It is a simple task to solve relatively small zero-one GP models by the existing algorithms [11]. However, if a project scheduling problem results in a large-scale model, other existing software such as LINDO can be utilized. Solution of the goal programming model does not always require a goal programming package. Existing single objective packages can be used to solve a sequence of linear programming models reflecting the preemptive structure of the goal programming model. Model 4 presented in this paper required 6 minutes and 34 seconds of solution time using LINDO on a Prime 750 minicomputer. Our computational experience indicates that a Prime 750 is roughly ten times as slow as an IBM 370 in solving linear

Figure 1. Schedule for Model 1

PRIORITY

1 MINIMIZE COMPLETION TIME

```
ACTIVITY            DUR PRED    DAY
                                    1 1111111112 2222222223 3333333334
                            1234567890 1234567890 1234567890 1234567890

A  FOOTERS          4   -    XXXX00000
B  FOUNDATION       2   A      XX0000 0
C  FRAME & ROOF     4   B        XXXX 00000
D  BRICKWORK        6   C             XXXXXX0000 0000000000 000
E  BASE PLUMB       1   B      X000 000
F  BASE FLOOR       2   E       XX0 00000
G  ROUGH PLUMB      3   E       XXX 000000000
H  WIRING           2   C             XX00000000 000000000
J  HEAR & VENT      4   C,F    XXXX00000
K  PLASTER          10  G,J         XXXXXX XXXX00000
L  FINISH FLOOR     3   H,K                     XXX000 00
M  KITCHEN FIXT     1   L                          X00 000000000
N  FINISH PLUMB     2   L                          XX0 0000000000
P  FINISH CARP      3   L                          XXX 00000
Q  ROOF             2   C             XX00000000 0000000000 00
R  GUTTERS          1   Q              X0000000 0000000000 000
S  STORM DRAIN      1   B       X000 0000000000 0000000000 00000
T  SAND & VARN      2   U                                   XX00000
U  PAINT            3   P                                  XXX00000
V  FINISH ELECT     1   M                           X0 0000000000
W  GRADING          2   D,R                  XX00 0000000000 00000
X  LANDSCAPE        5   S,W                    XX XXX0000000 0000000000

   CRANES                    1111112221 3332110011 1110000000 0000000000

   CARPENTERS                2222226444 3300000022 2220444444 0000000000

   LABORERS                  2222442662 2222222222 2220000000 0003300000
```

Figure 2. Schedule for Model 2

PRIORITY

1   CRANE <= 1
2   MINIMIZE COMPLETION TIME

```
ACTIVITY              DUR  PRED  DAY
                                           1 1111111112 2222222223 3333333334
                                  1234567890 1234567890 1234567890 1234567890

A  FOOTERS             4    -     XXXX00000
B  FOUNDATION          2    A     XX0000     0
C  FRAME & ROOF        4    B     XXXX       0000
D  BRICKWORK           6    C                000000XXXX XX00000000 000
E  BASE PLUMB          1    B     X000       000
F  BASE FLOOR          2    E     000        XX000
G  ROUGH PLUMB         3    E     XXX        000000000
H  WIRING              2    C                XX00000000 000000000
J  HEAR & VENT         4    C,F              00XXXX000
K  PLASTER            10    G,J              00XXXX     XXXXXX000
L  FINISH FLOOR        3    H,K                         00XXX0     00
M  KITCHEN FIXT        1    L                           00X        000000000
N  FINISH PLUMB        2    L                           00X        X000000000
P  FINISH CARP         3    L                           00X        XX000
Q  ROOF                2    C                0000000000 00XX000000 00
R  GUTTERS             1    Q                00000000   0000X00000 000
S  STORM DRAIN         1    B     0000       0000000000 00000X0000 00000
T  SAND & VARN         2    U                                      00XX000
U  PAINT               3    P                                      00XXX000
V  FINISH ELECT        1    M                           00         X000000000
W  GRADING             2    D,R              0000       00000XX000 00000
X  LANDSCAPE           5    S,W                      00 0000000XXX XX00000000


   CRANES                         1111111111 1111111111 1111110111 1100000000

   CARPENTERS                     2222224444 0000000000 0033024666 6600000000

   LABORERS                       2222440222 4400002222 2200042222 2200033000
```

Figure 3. Schedule for Model 3

PRIORITY

1   CRANE <= 1
2   CARPENTERS <= 5
3   MINIMIZE COMPLETION TIME

ACTIVITY DUR PRED   DAY

```
                                    1 1111111112 2222222223 3333333334
                            1234567890 1234567890 1234567890 1234567890

A  FOOTERS        4   -     XXXX00000
B  FOUNDATION     2   A     XX0000 0
C  FRAME & ROOF   4   B     XXXX 00000
D  BRICKWORK      6   C         000000XXXX XX00000000 000
E  BASE PLUMB     1   B     X000 000
F  BASE FLOOR     2   E     000 XX000
G  ROUGH PLUMB    3   E     XXX 000000000
H  WIRING         2   C         XX00000000 000000000
J  HEAR & VENT    4   C,F       00XXXX000
K  PLASTER       10   G,J        00XXXX XXXXXX000
L  FINISH FLOOR   3   H,K              00XXX0 00
M  KITCHEN FIXT   1   L               00X 000000000
N  FINISH PLUMB   2   L               00X X000000000
P  FINISH CARP    3   L               00X XX000
Q  ROOF           2   C         0000000000 00XX000000 00
R  GUTTERS        1   Q          00000000 0000X00000 000
S  STORM DRAIN    1   B     0000 0000000000 00000X0000 00000
T  SAND & VARN    2   U                           00XX000
U  PAINT          3   P                          00XXX000
V  FINISH ELECT   1   M                    00 X000000000
W  GRADING        2   D,R       0000 00000XX000 00000
X  LANDSCAPE      5   S,W            00 0000000000 00XXXXX000


   CRANES           1111111111 1111111111 1111101000 0011111000

   CARPENTERS       2222224444 0000000000 0033024444 4422222000

   LABORERS         2222440222 4400002222 2200042000 0022255000
```

Figure 4. Schedule for Model 4

PRIORITY

```
1   CRANE <= 1
2   CARPENTERS <= 5
3   TIME <= 40
4   LABORERS <= 4
5   MINIMIZE COMPLETION TIME
```

```
ACTIVITY DUR  PRED      DAY
                                    1 1111111112 2222222223 3333333334
                              1234567890 1234567890 1234567890 1234567890

A  FOOTERS        4   -    XXXX00000
B  FOUNDATION     2   A      XX0000 0
C  FRAME & ROOF   4   B      XXXX 00000
D  BRICKWORK      6   C           000000XXXX XX00000000 000
E  BASE PLUMB     1   B    X000 000
F  BASE FLOOR     2   E     000 XX000
G  ROUGH PLUMB    3   E     XXX 000000000
H  WIRING         2   C          XX00000000 000000000
J  HEAR & VENT    4   C,F        00XXXX000
K  PLASTER       10   G,J          00XXXX XXXXXX000
L  FINISH FLOOR   3   H,K                   00XXX0 00
M  KITCHEN FIXT   1   L                       00X 000000000
N  FINISH PLUMB   2   L                       00X X000000000
P  FINISH CARP    3   L                       00X XX000
Q  ROOF           2   C        0000000000 00XX000000 00
R  GUTTERS        1   Q          00000000 0000X00000 000
S  STORM DRAIN    1   B       0000 0000000000 00000X0000 00000
T  SAND & VARN    2   U                                 0000XX0
U  PAINT          3   P                            00XXX000
V  FINISH ELECT   1   M                         00 X000000000
W  GRADING        2   D,R         0000 00000XX000 00000
X  LANDSCAPE      5   S,W          00 0000000000 00XXXXX000

   CRANES         1111111111 1111111111 1111101000 0011111000

   CARPENTERS     2222224444 0000000000 0033024444 4422222000

   LABORERS       2222440222 4400002222 2200042000 0022222330
```

programs. Thus, our model can be applied to many moderate size real-world project scheduling problems without computational difficulties.

CONCLUSIONS

The proposed technique provides a means of obtaining a project schedule subject to resource limitations. In practice, it is doubtful that the currently available zero-one goal programming algorithm would have sufficient capacity for all scheduling problems. Small models, such as that given in this paper, could probably be scheduled in a satisfactory manner without the aid of a large-scale software. Larger models, which would benefit by the application of the zero-one GP approach proposed in this paper, can be solved by such available software as LINDO.

It is expected that solution of this model with a network flow algorithm will yield much more attractive computation times. The network nature of the problem should allow dramatic increase in model size for practical solution. We are continuing our research in this area.

Viewing model limitations as objectives rather than rigid constraints allows decision makers the flexibility of listing desired schedule features. Emphasis upon objectives as flexible goals rather than as rigid constraints allows the decision maker to state the tradeoffs that would be necessary to reconcile conflicting objectives. Ordering these goals can provide a means of obtaining a solution with the features of the best possible schedule subject to desired requirements as much as is possible. Thus, the applicability of our approach to real-world project scheduling problems is very promising indeed.

REFERENCES

[1]   Balas, E., "An Additive Algorithm for Solving Linear Programs with Zero-One Variable," Operations Research, Vol. 13, No. 4 (1965), pp. 517-545.

[2]   Bowman, E. H., "The Schedule-Sequencing Problem," Operations Research, Vol. 7, No. 5, (1959), pp. 621-624.

[3]   Davis, E. W., "Resource Allocation in Project Network Models - A Survey," Journal of Industrial Engineering, Vol. 17, No. 4 (1966), pp. 177-188.

[4]   Davis, E. W., "Project Scheduling under Resource Constraints - Historical Review and Categorization of Procedures," AIIE Transactions, Vol. 5, No. 4, (1973), pp. 297-313.

[5]   Davis, E. W. and Heidorn, G. E., "An Algorithm for Optimal Project Scheduling under Multiple Resource Constraints," Management Science, Vol. 23, No. 12, (1971), pp. B803-816.

[6]   Elmagharby, S. E., Activity Networks: Project Planning and Control by Network Models, John Wiley & Sons, New York, 1977.

[7]   Franz, L. S.; Lee, S. M.; and Van Horn, J. C., "An Adaptive Decision Support System for Academic Resource Planning," Decision Sciences, Vol. 12, No. 2 (1981), pp. 110-115.

[8]   Glover, F., "Multi-phase Dual Algorithm for the Zero-One Integer Programming Problems," Operations Research, Vol. 13, No. 6 (1965), pp. 879-919.

[9]   Hall, J. R., "Management Science Update Column: Multiproject Scheduling through Zero-One Programming," Management Science, Vol. 16, No. 2 (1980), pp. 228-229.

[10]   Kochenberger, G. A. and Richard V. H., "A Simple All Primal Branch and Bound Approach to Pure and Mixed Integer Binary Programs," Operations Research Letters, Vol. 1, No. 5, 1982, pp. 182-185.

[11]   Lee, S. M., Goal Programming Methods for Multiple Objective Integer Programs, Atlanta: American Institute of Industrial Engineers, 1979.

[12]   Lee, S. M., and Morris, R. L., "Integer Goal Programming Methods," in M. K. Starr and M. Zeleney, eds., Multiple Criteria Decision Making, TIMS Studies in the Management Science, Vol. 6, Amsterdam: North-Holland (1977), pp. 273-289.

[13]   Lee, S. M., Park, O.E.; and Economides, S. C., "Resource Planning for Multiple Projects," Decision Sciences, Vol. 9, No. 1 (1978), pp. 49-67.

[14]   Moore, L. J.; Taylor, B. W.; Clayton, E. R.; and Lee, S. M., "Analysis of a Multi-Criteria Project Crashing Model," AIIE Transactions, Vol. 10, No. 2 (1978), pp. 163-169.

[15]   Nijkamp, P. and Spronk, J., "Interactive Multiple Goal Programming: An Evaluation and Some Results," in G. Fandel and T. Gal, eds., Multiple Criteria Decision Making: Theory and Application, New York: Springer-Verlag, 1980, pp. 278-293.

[16]   Pritsker, A. A. B.; Watters, L. J.; & Wolfe, P. M., "Multiproject Scheduling with Limited Resources: A Zero-One Programming Approach," Management Science, Vol. 16, No. 1 (1969), pp. 93-107.

[17]   Simon, H. A., "Rational Decision Making in Business Organizations," The American Economic Review, Vol. 69, No. 4 (1979), pp. 493-513.

[18]   Talbot, B. and Patterson, J. H., "An Efficient Integer Programming Algorithm with Network Cuts for Solving Resource-Constrained Sequencing Problems," Management Science, Vol. 24, No. 11 (1978), pp. 1163-1174.

[19]   Weglarz, J., "Project Scheduling with Continuously-Divisible, Doubly Constrained Resources," Management Science, Vol. 27, No. 9 (1981), pp. 1040-1053.

Part III
HUMAN RESOURCES MANAGEMENT

Project Management: Methods and Studies
Burton V. Dean (editor)
© Elsevier Science Publishers B.V. (North-Holland), 1985   141

A BEHAVIORAL APPROACH TO MULTIGOAL DECISION MAKING

AND ITS IMPLICATIONS FOR USE IN PROJECT APPRAISAL

Barry G. Silverman

The George Washington University
Washington, D. C.
U.S.A.

This paper describes an approach to Research and Development
(R and D) project selection/evaluation models called PAM that
has been successfully implemented and at times institutionalized
at five separate organizations including the U.S. Navy, the
Department of Energy, the Gas Research Institute, the National
Academy of Science, and Los Alamos Scientific Labs. While each
of these applications is unique, they all stem from a common
approach to the design of planning support systems as described
in this chapter.

The central device explained here (which is also employed at each
of the five using organizations) is the "script", a behavioral construct
used to account for the players' roles, the rules of the "game", and
the conduct of play. This chapter describes how the approach is
tailored to each new application (Section 1), the theoretical underpinnings (Section 2), and an example of an application (Section 3).
The contribution of these concepts (and hence of this Chapter) to
project management and to management scientists is an approach
that is tried, tested, and working at a variety of organizations.

"All the world's a stage,
And all the men and women merely players."

- William Shakespeare

1. INTRODUCTION

A number of recent reviews and analyses have confirmed that few quantitative models of
the R and D (research and development) project selection and resource allocation decision
have been implemented and used by R and D managers [1-6]. This despite the fact that
hundreds of such models are documented in the literature. Furthermore, even where such
models were adopted and used, once their developers and/or a sympathetic sponsor left
the organization many such models have fallen into disuse [1, 2, 3, 6]. A Booz, Allen &
Hamilton study [6] found only three R&D models or approaches that have out-lasted their
developers and/or that appear to be institutionalized: Texas Instruments' OST, General
Electric's method, and the Gas Research Institute's PAM.

The purpose of this paper is to examine an approach, called Project Appraisal Methodology
(PAM) which is extensively used. As one of the designers of this approach, the author will
also provide insight into the theoretical underpinnings of PAM (Section 2) and how those
underpinnings can be operationalized (successfully) not just at the Gas Research Institute
(GRI) but at other organizations as well (Section 3). This latter point is not an idle claim.
To date the PAM approach has been tailored to five separate organizations as follows:

1) Naval Ordinance Systems Command's PAM (1972) -- This was a procedure for establishing relative priorities among competing programs so that benefits to the fleet could be maximized given limited funds [7].

2) Department of Energy's PAM (1974-present) — The approach was adopted by the Division of Conservation Research and Technology (ERDA) and subsequently by three divisions of the Department of Energy, DOE [8-9].

3) Gas Research Institute's PAM (1978-present) -- In its first private sector application, PAM is used organization-wide for the once-a-year development of the annual budget and 5-year plan [6,10].

4) National Academy of Science's PAM (1979/80) -- PAM was adapted to the Ship R&D Committee for its long range research prioritization and benefits appraisal exercises [11].

5) Los Alamos Scientific Laboratories' PAM (1981-present) -- PAM is being used for the evaluation of research and technology programs [12].

There is no universal project evaluation scheme; it must be customized to each organization. Hence PAM is a concept and a process, not a model, that has been uniquely tailored to each of these cases. The reasons for such a long and spreading "run" of PAM are difficult to establish in their entirety, however, some of the more obvious reasons include:

(a) support of top management: PAM is always "sold" at the top.

(b) focus on participation, expert opinion, and managerial judgment: PAM depends on participatory involvement and consensus-taking at all levels of the organization, it requires expert opinion as well as technical information for input, and it permits managerial control of the results (where "control" is used in the formal sense).

(c) script as a methodology: The script or plot is clearly defined including all the human roles to be played for the duration of the exercise.

(d) other: There are a number of other desirable attributes including self-documentation, generation of the audit trail, traceability, simplicity, and the attributes of "good" decision making as discussed in Section 2 of this paper.

The analogy of the "script" is not meant in a trivial sense. For a play to be successful, it must attract and hold the interest of directors, sponsors, stage hands, actors, critics, and audiences. Similarly, for PAM to be successful it must have roles defined for and appealing to planners, managers, system integrators, project personnel, review teams, and advisory bodies, respectively. Thus the script is a formula for the interaction and activity of the various parties upon whom project funding decisions will have an impact. It is work breakdown structure, milestone/CPM chart, rules of interaction, and considerably more. "Playing" PAM is like playing a game such as baseball, football, etc. The script has been used by other researchers in the field of artificial intelligence to explain behaviors in social processes (causal chains) [13].

A planning support system for project appraisal must be custom tailored to each organization desiring to use it. The process by which this tailoring occurs is a social evolutionary one in which (1) a prototype is developed that is attuned to the specific project selection/evaluation problems and decision making information needs of the organization, and that is in keeping with the relevant theoretical prescriptions; (2) the prototype is verified (tested) to ensure it does what its designers claim it will do and validated to ensure that those claims are appropriate with respect to the best available intelligence of the organization's needs; (3) it is implemented in the organizational selection/evaluation process; (4) the reactions of the organizational users and participants to the prototype are collected in terms of its strengths and weaknesses; and (5) the next generation version of the support system is prepared (i.e., repeat these 5 steps). Early versions of the system may be complete "throwaways" (i.e., a prototype that is altogether inadequate) whereas later versions will involve only small incremental refinements. This evolution process never entirely stops but after the first relatively good version is evolved (generally on the second or third try) responsibility for the refinement process is transferred from the designers (outside consultants) to the planning staff of the organization itself.

This tailoring procedure is summarized in Figure 1 which also indicates the organization of this chapter. Specifically, since the scripts are generated from a body of theoretical concepts the chapter begins by examining the underlying theory in Section 2 (the "why"). The script, roles, and "props" of a typical version are then presented in Section 3 (the "how") along with a discussion and some user reactions. Due to space limitations the reader will on occasion be referred to the author's earlier [8,9,23] published writings on this subject.

2. THORETICAL UNDERPINNINGS: WHY PAM WORKS

The approach described in this paper draws its principal theoretical underpinnings from five topic areas: decision making frameworks, theories of the group, theories of the individual, measurement theory, and decision rules. Each of these topic areas is represented in Figure 2 by a closed circle within which are depicted several of the most relevant factors that must be considered in designing a project appraisal technique (e.g., participative-nonparticipative theories of the group). Each of these factors involves a continuum of alternatives with the labels ("participative", "nonparticipative", etc.) representing extremes or critical concepts along the continuum. The approach described in this paper offers an integration of the concepts at that end of the continuum of each of the factors in each of the five topic areas that is enclosed by the dashed line of Figure 1.

The literature relating to these five topics is enormous--e.g., see Hammond, McClelland and Mumpower [17], Sage [18], and Zmud [19].but there is a need for efforts to integrate it from the perspective of systematic design of systems for project selection/evaluation decision support. There are a number of recent surveys available that discuss one or a limited number of the topics important for the design of project selection/evaluation support systems--e.g., Freeland and Baker [1], Odjanda and Weyant [2], Pohler [3], Souder [4], Keen and Morton [14], Snapper [15], Mason and Swanson [16]. This chapter, however, attempts a selective integration of this voluminous literature and extensions and interpretations of it from the perspective of the ultimate potential usefulness for the design of project selection/evaluation or planning support systems.

The proliferation of concepts across so diverse a set of topics constitutes a threat to the cumulative nature of the scientific study of judgment and decision making. It is therefore a purpose of this part of this paper to attempt to organize and integrate contemporary topics, factors, and concepts in order to assist in the continuance of what may in the future become a unified field of endeavor. The intent of this section is to introduce the reader to the content of each topic area from an integrated view and to cite specific references that address the key topics in more detail.

2.1 Decision Making Frameworks

As Snapper [15] points out, attempts to answer the question "what is a good decision" have generated not one but hundreds of "Answers". Snapper goes on to quote Wildavsky: "certain key items appear over and over again: planning is good because it is systematic rather than random, efficient rather than wasteful, coordinated rather than helter skelter, consistent

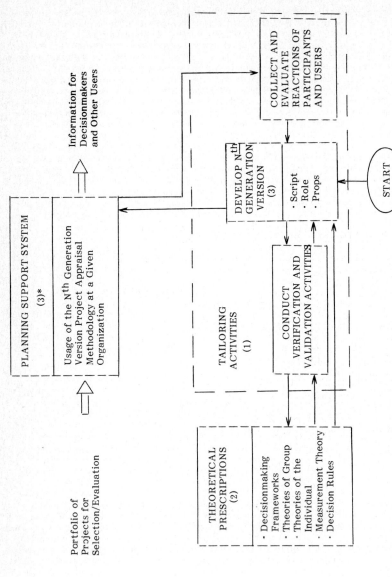

*Numbers in parenthese refer to section of this paper.

Figure 1. OVERVIEW OF THE PROCEDURE BY WHICH THE PLANNING SUPPORT SYSTEM IS TAILORED

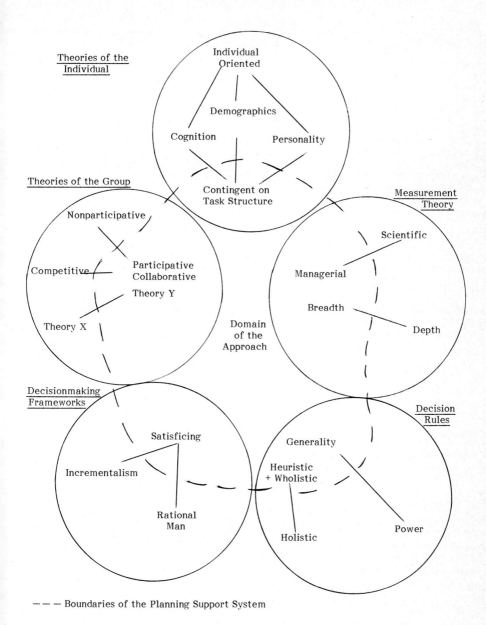

– – – Boundaries of the Planning Support System

Figure 2. AN INTEGRATED VIEW OF THE BEHAVIORAL APPROACH

rather than contradictory, and, above all, rational rather than unreasonable." In short good decisions are those that give rise to more therapeutic effect than iatrogenic effect. The controversy over good decision making has generated answers which, at the risk of some imprecision, can be characterized as varying between two extremes.

At the one extreme, there is reliance upon "rational man" approaches or frameworks. Here the decisions are assumed to be based on perfect knowledge, i.e., where the decision maker knows exactly all the probabilities of each of the potential outcomes as well as their values to him/her. One starts with the recognition and analysis of the (long-range) problem, and then through a series of sequential and progressive steps and thorough review of all feasible alternatives and the possible consequences of these alternatives, the "optimal" solution is eventually chosen. This process is highly quantitative and supposedly comprehensive in relation to problem solving and maximization of goals. However, it often disregards irrationalities of political processes, idiosyncracies of human behavior, and the vagaries of ideas and preferences of individual decisionmakers. It generally fails to recognize the subjective nexus between decisions and world views of decision makers and decision executors. Consequently, solutions are often unacceptable to the policy makers, and if accepted, sometimes difficult to implement for socio-political reasons.

At the other extreme is the incrementalism, bureaucratic approach, or "muddlin' through". Advances are made in small steps (disjointed marginal adjustments) and there is rarely any drastic change. It assumes that there is no one right decision, but a continuous stream of minor decisions. It eschews absolute solutions, is frequently a short-term approach, and rarely are the short term objectives linked to the long term goals. However, it is politically pluralistic, practical in real settings, permits tradeoff/revisions of views, tolerates ambiguity, and is sensitive to power struggles and the concerns of interest groups: it is sometimes called "the art of the possible." However, it implicitly assumes that the shorter the projected effect term and the smaller the effect scope, the easier it is to nullify or compensate for iatrogenic effect. Incrementalism may be a good approach when the original decisions were good to begin with. If the original decisions were bad to begin with (or if conditions have substantially changed) then they will still be bad after muddling. This mode of decision making is common to many governments and political institutions.

The pursuit of the second approach does not mean that a decision maker is innately irrational. The inherent complexities and inter-connectedness of present-day society dictates that rationality in most circumstances, is neither clearcut nor automatically determinable, particularly when multidimensionality is considered. And as C. J. Hitch has stated: "First it is wrong to look upon intuition and analysis or minds and machines as rivals or alternatives. Properly used they complement each other. We have seen that every systems analysis is shot through with intuition and judgment. Every decision that seems to be based on intuition is probably shot through with species of analysis." [16]

Clearly the middle ground between these two framework extremes is well tread. Indeed, Herbert Simon, has charted this interior region in a series of monographs for which he was awarded the 1978 Nobel prize in economics [44]. He argued that it was impractical to think of generating all of the relevant alternatives. Furthermore, even if this were to be done, the "bounded rationality" of the human decision maker makes the information unassimilable. Simon concludes that the rational conception is completely lacking in descriptive reality and suggests a definition of satisficing man, who does the best he can but does not even attempt optimization. A similar assertion may be found in Etzioni's "mixed scanning" approach [45].

As Pohler points out [3], an underlying assumption of many past efforts to improve the project selection/evaluation process has been that, given sufficient information and analysis, decisions could be made under conditions of certainty (or at least under minimal risk). However, economic reality dictates that formal analysis stop prior to this point. When information and analysis have yielded their insights, authority must take over and make the decision. McDonough defines authority as "the license to use intuition" [3]. Thus the middle ground of decision making involves a simplification of effort, realization of socio-political and cognitive realities, and some linkage of short term solutions to long term goals: such an approach can be systematic, efficient, coordinated, consistent, and rational.

Other decisionmaking frameworks exist such as Cyert and March's Organizational Process Model [45] which is a variant of incrementalism; Etzioni's Mixed Scanning [43] approach which is a variant of satisficing; and Cohen et al's Garbage Can Model [46]. However, the range of possibilities has been sufficiently established for the purpose of this paper.

1.2 Theories of the Group

Several of the review studies cited in Section 1 concluded, among other things, that two reasons for failure of R and D models are: (1) the naive assumption that project selection/evaluation decisions can be both fully simulated and programmed, and (2) the lack of adequate User participation in the conception and development of the models, and in the interpretation and application of the results obtained from models. Or as Twiss argues [20]:

> "As much attention needs to be paid to the process of project evaluation
> as to the particular techniques to be used. This process must encourage
> information cooperation of all those managers who can contribute infor-
> mation necessary for an evaluation to the depth appropriate to the decision
> or who will later be responsible for implementation of a stage of the
> innovation chain." [20] p. 143.

Due to the concerns expressed by Twiss as well as the concern for user desires, safety, environment and the like, the process of deciding the merits of a particular project may be likened to the making of social choice decisions. In that field the concern is to measure each new policy alternative against some absolute indicator of social value- e.g., a social value function. Surprisingly often, one encounters the argument that social value functions (or frameworks other than the Incrementalism) are impossible, and one is sometimes even advised the "proof" is supplied by Arrow's Impossibility Theorem [25]. This misunderstanding has formed the basis for the arguments for some critics. As Keeney and Raiffa [21] discuss in some detail, however, Arrow's theorem does not imply that social value functions are impossible, only that their development requires some interpersonal comparisons of preference. The problem is not one of theoretical impossibility, but rather the reasonableness of modeling assumptions and the practicality of obtaining requisite comparisons of preference. Three common ways to solve the problem are: (a) enlist the aid of a powerful or "supra Decision Maker" [21] who specifies the necessary preferences or weights; (b) when faced with competing sets of values but these values are not attributable to distinct individuals (groups) use standard multidimensional techniques; and (c) when distinct interest groups pose conflicting values/preferences use negotiation or methods of discussion. In the absence of (a) either (b) or (c) will apply.

The wisdom of these various arguments appears to have found root in a number of methods which do use group processes--in the formulation of overall objectives, identification of relevance of potential projects to these objectives, assignment of relevance ratings, and determination (by computerized routine) of the best allocation of funds--to provide management with estimates of the relative merits of competing projects. Perhaps the most widely known industry variants of this approach for research and development project appraisal are PATTERN and OST [6]. TORQUE, an Air Force technique, uses the same reasoning as PATTERN except that PATTERN incorporates a funding level analyzer [2]. In part because of common authors, TORQUE closely resembles a set of other allocation techniques including BRAILLE, QUEST and MACRO R&D [3]. QUEST in turn has much in common with the Naval Ordinance laboratory predecessor of PAM which was mentioned in Section 1.[1]

Having established the importance of group processes, a brief review of some of the more important influences on these processes is in order. For example, two of the principal arguments for group discussion in the innovation process are: (1) the almost parasitic relationship between innovation success and user community felt need for the innovation as widely demonstrated (yet commonly ignored) [22] and (2) the role of participation upon ultimate implementation as concerns the attitudinal aspects.

According to the popularized tenets of participative management, people tend to carry out the decisions they help to make. For example, Coch and French [28] and others [29] found in

American industry that generally speaking when managers and employees discussed proposed technological changes, productivity increased and resistance to change decreased once these procedures were initiated. Of course this is the well known philosophy of Japanese participative management as documented in Ouchi's Theory Z [30]. While examination of such studies shows the benefits of participation appears to grow with the level of task-relevant maturity, some individuals tend to resist engagement in "group think". Instead they prefer decisions to be made by highly qualified experts [31]--a conclusion of some interest to managers of technological innovation.

Two additional aspects of the process are also often misjudged or entirely overlooked: the diverse roles which must be filled in participative activities and the techniques of discussion. While the author had originally thought these concepts to be "obvious", the experience discussed in the latter half of this chapter has indicated the need to alert other (systems) practitioners to the fundamental requirement for "planned spontaneity." That is, stimulation, extraction, and/or representation of ideas/knowledge from the minds of a group of people --i.e. of spontaneous discussion--can only be guaranteed to offer a positive impact on the organization if they are carefully staged. The reader is referred to an earlier paper by Silverman [23] for a more thorough treatment of this subject.

In summary, despite many of the disadvantages of discussion--(1) it takes time and money, (2) it requires skill, (3) it dilutes individual responsibility, (4) it doesn't work in emergencies, and (5) it embraces several potentially limiting factors such as status differences, majority pressure, prior commitments, and certain personalities which perform poorly under "group think" --it is an essential ingredient in the success of an R and D model. Further, the way the group process is handled is as critical as its inclusion.

2.3 Expert Judgment

The discussion in this section represents a paraphrase (without quotation marks) of a more detailed review and analysis contained in "Expert Intuition and Ill-Structured Problem Solving" [24] and in a forthcoming book [25] both by Silverman. A more complete set of references to the related literature may also be found in those same two references: due to space restrictions no other references are cited here. Also, "proof" of these concepts is deferred to the original two studies. In brief these two works explain how the thought processes associated with expertise work and how in ill-structured problem settings they are deleteriously affected by formalisms such as analytic performance aids (e.g., computer models, decision theory, etc.). The very nature of expert human thought leads to the rejection of R&D models.

It is useful to start by defining ill-structured problems as those which are neither routine and well-defined with standard conditions, nor easily solved by immediate application of well-known procedures or decision rules. Examples of ill-structured problems include innovation, executive decision making, and diagnostic evaluations by project managers. One could use any other situation where neither the goal nor the procedure for accomplishing the goal are well-understood at the outset.

A cognitive view of the expert and his problem solving thought processes provides even more evidence concerning the "poor fit" of decision theory with R and D problem solving situations. For example, the recent work of several authors [24, 32-34] has indicated that expertise arises not from mental analytic power but from perceptual abilities: from the paradigm of the Gestalt tradition of instant recognition.

The highest level of skilled performance depends on (right-brained) intuitive abilities: abilities to rapidly and accurately perceive a current situation as similar to a certain one which past experience has caused to be stored in the brain [25, 35-37]. These past experiences (situational states or brain patterns) constitute concrete examples of untroubled, stable, and proper environments. If a new situation does not match a past situation within some tolerance level, the manager's sense that action is required to resolve the differences is aroused (note that experience has not necessarily taught the manager why this intuitive resolution is necessary, only that in the past it has worked).

Many practicing managers, planners, and engineers demonstrate a keen appreciation or intuitive understanding, for what some in the so-called "rational" disciplines tend to overlook: that intuitive (concrete, right-brained) thought is an essential component of effective engineering management. For example, there is a falacious assumption in some circles today that science, the spread of formal scientific education, and the large, well-organized research laboratory have transformed the methods of invention (7). Yet a 20 year-old Harvard student (Land) produced the first practical light-polarising material; one of the inventors of the pneumatic tire (Dunlop) was a veterinary surgeon; and a patent lawyer (Carlson) invented xerography.

In short, combining the nature of ill-structured problems, on the one hand, with the nature of expert thought, on the other hand, leads to a relatively clear picture of the reason(s) for the non-use of so many of the "rational" R and D models. Or as Ouchi, the author of <u>Theory Z</u> points out: "Managers are often heard to complain that they feel powerless to exercise their judgment in the fact of quantitative analysis, computer models, and numbers, numbers, numbers" [38]. People are used to dealing with ambiguous poorly-defined situations and with "growing" a decision. The use of prescriptive decision analysis methods can have the potential of "freezing" the situation and eliminating flexibility. Creativity may be stiffled, options not in the "recipe" overlooked, and the value of seeking information in terms of reflective time eliminated. Many "formal" (mathematical <u>or</u> organizational) procedures can be correlated positively with such deleterious effects beyond some minimal threshold.

Thus many, experts feel quite rightly that decision rules, analytical methods, etc. are for novices: i.e., those who have few analogues to draw on in assessing a situation. The expert's internal situational conditioning does indeed surpass the naive assumptions and contextual insensitivities of the rule in most cases.

This is not to suggest, however, that intuition, alone will suffice. Psychologists have studied the validity of judgments or expert intuition and have established a fairly lengthy list of biases experts tend to make [24, 39]. For example, several of these biases have entered our everyday language such as conservatism, fact-value confusion, gamblers fallacy, habit, and wishful thinking. The general trend of many of these biases is that people tend to be too confident and they tend to see correlation and non-randomness where there is only chance variation.

As a second set of reasons to introduce a planning support system, it should be noted that at least in technology management the problem facing the expert is that (a) due to the increasing size of systems, the fewer systems a manager will handle, resulting in lowered knowledge from which to draw from his own memory banks; (b) experts who could help provide the necessary knowledge are themselves a scarce resource; (c) there has been found to be a major deficiency in the education of managers (this is the well-documented human capital formation problem).

To summarize, a planning support system, to be successful, must address the case of expert decision makers confronted by moderately ill-structured problems where (1) their thought processes are largely non-verbalizable and intuitive, (2) their intuition is based on large numbers of concrete experiences, (3) their productivity and performance can be enhanced by the strength of judgment-debiasing/assisting (rather than judgement-forming) performance aids. The specifics of such a planning support system in terms of a decision rule for the R and D domain is treated in the following two sections. This view of the expert is also further argument in favor of the group process component of the planning support system as discussed in Section 2.2.

2.4   Measurement Theory

Quantification is frequently attempted in project selection/evaluation due to the complexity, number of projects, temporal aspects, and sectoral pluralisms of criteria. It is clear, however, that any "scheme" of measurement holds the potential to do violence both to reality and the perceived meaning. Thus every measure must be concerned with the following four choices, each of which requires the judgmental act of distinction.

(1) <u>Choice of Managerial vs. Scientific Measurement:</u>
As Mason and Swanson indicate, "it has generally been assumed that managerial measurement is a form of scientific measurement and, hence, as an ideal managerial measurement should seek to satisfy the principles of scientific measurement" [16]. No one would quarrel with drawing on the vast history of scientific measurement in order to improve measurement for management decision. However, this smacks of the incrementalism-rational man dichotomy. Measurement must be likened to a lens through which a manager sees organizational reality: the lens is fit to the manager, not the reverse. The lens is the manager's worldview.

(2) <u>Choice of Language:</u> Depth vs. Breadth Criteria: A major aim of measurement particularly for managerial decision, is to communicate to as many potential users as possible: measurement is a language. The choice of which language to use frequently rests on the depth vs. breadth criteria. That is, a language which is broadly understandable is frequently preferable in decisionmaking (not science) to a language that is capable of fine distinction (depth). (The more precise a language, the less broadly it is understood and the aim of minimizing effort to adjust data usually conflicts with the aim of precision). Such an example is preference between two objects which is a simple (numerial) language that is widely understandable rather than the language of utilities.

(3) <u>Choice of Dimensions:</u> Of fundamental concern in multi-goal decision measurement is that the decision criteria (dimensions along which projects are compared) selected provide a structurally valid analytical framework. To this end, each criterion must be designed to shed light on a project's desireability from a different angle (mutually exclusive-or-orthogonality). All significant angles must be covered (collectively exhaustive) and no single criterion can by itself provide sufficient information for judging the merit of a project. A single value that summarizes all the various criteria scores (measures) into a single grand total obscures use.

(4) <u>Choice of Scale:</u> If measurement is the language of preserving empirical information, then scales are the vocabulary (adjectives) used to describe aspects of the objects or events in the problem space. Of the variety of scales that may be selected from (e.g., nominal, ordinal, interval, and/or ratio), the principle selection criterion is the:

<u>Principle of Invariance:</u>

"Once an isomorphism has been mapped out between aspects of objects
or events, on the one hand, and some one or more features of the number system, on the other hand, the isomorphism can be upset by whatever
transformations fail to preserve it." S.S. Stevens [6]

Accordingly, if a scale preserves the empirical information, the scale form is said to remain invariant. There are several drawbacks to so ill-defined a criterion for storing empirical information, for example: (a) an empirical observation is always attended by error. As Lebesque said, a scale "never enables us to discriminate between one number and all the numbers that are extremely close to it" [40]. However, this issue may be more appropriate to scientific measurements where fine tuning is a serious concern (and where statistics serve to damp bias down to the least possible) and (b) specification of what empirical information is to be preserved is often a difficult task and care must be taken neither to obscure relevant dimensions nor to transform the scale so as to distort the desired information. Therein lies the primacy of measurement (over statistics): it sets bounds on the appropriateness of statistical operations.

To summarize, the point of these four choices is to indicate that relatively simple measurements may possess disproportionately high degrees of validity. Preservation of meaning for the sake of communication does not require (and in fact tends to be damaged by) sophistication.

2.5 Decision Rules/Scoring Theory

Decision rules are those formalisms that enable the user to compare, prioritize and evaluate/ select projects in terms of their relative merits. The choice of decision rules will depend in large measure upon the decision framework, contingency task structure, and group demographics. With such factors in mind Schoemaker attempts a two level classification scheme which Sage [18] then extends to a three level scheme consisting of: wholistic judgment, heuristic elimination, and holistic evaluation. The holistic decision rules correspond to rational actor models and techniques such as utility theory and operations research methods. The heuristic decision rules include the bounded rationality type approaches. The wholistic decision rule is the unquantified use of expert judgement (e.g., via reasoning by analogy, intuition, and/or standard operating procedures).

While many of the more successful project evaluation schemes devised to date (e.g., see Booz Allen [6]) do not use quantitative techniques, the wholistic judgement question has already been addressed and this section will focus on holistic and heuristic rules. In addition only a sampling of the more familiar forms of these rules will be discussed. The alternative decision rules considered here are: potential pareto improvement, decision theoretic approach, risk assessment, optimization, graph-oriented approach, and scoring theory.

The single unambiguous measure with which economists provide us is the Pareto criterion. While Potential Pareto Improvement produces a unified set of measures (dollars) it provides several significant disadvantages, the most prominent of which is precisely the forced aggregation of different individuals' benefits and costs into monetary terms. While some might object to any attempts to include nonmoney benefits and to discourage elaborate procedures that generate implicit money magnitudes from tenuous money-nonmoney tradeoffs, such arguments suggest a considerable misunderstanding of how seriously differences in the incomes of individuals impacts upon their marginal utility of money. A multidimensional decision rule is based on measures which do not have such obvious biases: the benefits are expressed in terms more equally valued by everyone.

Decision theory is defined here as the expected utility concepts that as described by Hammond et. al. [17] restricts its theoretical interest to the case which involves a person making decisions without full knowledge of the task situation and without feedback about the effect of the decision. The resulting probability and utility estimates are produced by decision makers in response to special circumstances (e.g., lotteries) presented by the decision analyst. Concerning the latter, even Raiffa alludes to the reproducibility problem [21]. Secondly, decision theory is logic-oriented but the behavior people manifest is of the "bounded-rationality" type. Finally, even former students of utility theory, upon reaching executive-level positions, have commonly been observed to not employ it. Decision theory is not an empirically-oriented approach and there has been no response by decision theorists to critisms such as those mentioned above.

The next two methods assessed--risk assessments and optimization--which are commonly combined (see for example Cetron[5]) are found to suffer from some of the same problems. Both techniques are generally of great power and depth but lack breadth and generality (particularly so in the eyes of the unitiated). As Little [41] indicates, optimization further suffers from its perceived potential to coerce the decision makers' control over the results. The fifth method, the graphical or structural-modeling approach is appealing in terms of breadth/generality but provides no mechanisms for measurement of project success criteria (multidimension) achievement.

The (multidimensional) scoring theory therefore is appealing for lack of acceptable alternative. It is true that such techniques are not as powerful in the consideration of tradeoffs across different value dimensions (with the possible exception of Saaty's method [42]). When there are a large number of choice options, however, decisionmakers tend to select heuristics such as scoring models which quickly eliminate some options albeit by approximate methods. Further, scoring theory satisfies many of the guidelines such as, (a) fitting the current decision making process, (b) permitting avoidance of structural invalidities at minimal cost, (c) allowing robust measurement capability (breadth), (d) being viewed by management as potentially noncoersive, (e) providing a useful visual and structural aid for focusing discussion. The term "scoring theory" is defined here as various combinations of additive and multiplicative forms of the figure of merit or weighting-scaling multidimensional benefit-cost model with simplified subjective probability measures. While scoring theory is often connoted with ordinal scales, it is used here in a cardinal sense to insure distinction from cardinal utility theory which is also interval in nature. The use of scoring theory is meant here to also encompass such techniques as the Analytic Hierarchy Process [42], mixed scanning [43], or bounded rationality [44].

2.5.1   Design of The Decision Rule

Whatever rule ultimately chosen, if quantitative, its design should be based not on the modeler's preference but on three touchstones of good practice:

(a)   <u>Automation of Repetitive Tasks</u> -- A number of authors (see, for example, Keen and Scott Morton [14]) have indicated the primacy of identifying the current decisionmaking process and restricting the automation to those steps which are menial, repetitive, and amenable to artificial intelligence. Thus not only is change in the current decisionmaking process minimized, but the implementation and ultimate usefulness of the algorithm is more nearly assured.

(b)   <u>Avoidance of Structural Invalidities</u> -- Often a problem which on the surface may appear to be one of measurement is actually linked to underlying problems or invalidities in structuring the analysis. An example of a structural invalidity is a grossly defective strategy upon which an incrementalist attempts to make minor changes in direction. Dror's criticism of muddlin' seems especially appropriate:"If the policy and implementation strategy were bad to begin with they will still be bad after muddling...". A vital goal of analysis is thus to avoid structural invalidities by selecting alternatives that are not 'dominated'. The marginal gain in expected utility of avoiding invalidites is for more than that of moving from nondominated alternatives to optimal alternatives.

(c)   <u>Robust Measurements</u> -- The implication of the previous point is that no amount of fine tuning optimal of data can compensate for the structural invalidity. By the same token, the entire measurement discussion up to this point has stressed the simple approach (i.e., the tradeoff between understandability and precision) to measurement. Lindblom has observed that "every administrator faced with a sufficiently complex problem must find ways to drastically simplify." This in turn translate into a recognition that planning reaches a point of "diminishing returns." Thus modest amounts of planning (i.e., avoiding structural invalidites but simplifying the measurements) may yield relatively large gains in strategy effectiveness while additional fine-tuning yields small ones. This conception is in concert with Herbert Simon's satisficing and bounded rationality ideas [44].

3.   A Typical Version of the Behavioral Approach

Section 1 of this paper has dealt with the integration of theoretical underpinnings. In this section an attempt is made to demonstrate to the practitioner how the various threads of that integration may be woven into a smoothly functioning process. This will be done by describing a typical version of the behavioral approach in the form of a case study. The case used here is an early version of the Gas Research Institute's (GRI) PAM. The case study is used here rather than a theoretical study for two reasons: (a) IT WORKS! The case described here is a successful process, and (b) the failure of "rational" disciplines (economics, management science, etc.) to recognize the necessity of simple <u>descriptions</u> of processes that permit adaptive application of analytical aids. It should also be noted that the process described here conforms with much that has been published on the theory of implementation of change as viewed in a social and evolutionary context [27].

A script is a structure which explains how a sequence of causally related social actions will occur; what roles are to be filled by the requisite "actors"; and what "props" will facilitate the conduct of the sequence and roles. In PAM, as indicated by Figure 3, 5 categories of roles are to be filled; 3 acts (10 scenes) must be "played"; and 5 sets of props have to be prepared. These roles, acts, and props are described more fully in what follows. While PAM is usually "played" (Act I and Act II (2-5)) for only a few days each year, as can be imagined from the complexity and level of detail implied by Figure 3, the setting up of the first version of a script for a given organization involves several months of effort as does the refinement and tailoring effort for the second generation version. Once the set up and tailoring is finished, however, there is a minimal need (less than 1 staffer) for stage hand effort except during actual "playings."

Properly articulated and hierarchical objectives are fundamental to the success of any technology research or innovation program and are a first step in the evaluation process. These objectives communicate R&D goals to senior management personnel as well as to scientists and engineers. For example, when PAM was first adapted to the Gas Research Institute (i.e., at the time of the founding of GRI), three sets of objectives--overall, strategic, and tactical--were defined and/or initiated (Act I, Scene 1 and 2). The Overall Objectives describe the basic "business" the Institute is in and do not concern us here. The Strategic Objectives translate these Overall Objectives into three time frames into which GRI divides its research program. The intersection of the Overall and Strategic Objectives summarize the 9 major technical thrusts of GRI's program (Figure 4).

After formulating the top two levels of goals in this fashion they were seen to be too broad to allow critical appraisal of individual projects or project areas. Therefore, Tactical Objectives were designed to set forth specific results required to accomplish higher level objectives (Act I, Scene 2). Originally seven such Tactical Objectives were devised (Figure 5); the list has since been expanded to over 50. Again the specific meaning of the objectives is unimportant for the purpose of this paper.

As the non-profit research arm of the U.S. gaseous fuels and utilities industry, GRI has an extensive superstructure of advisory bodies. The four principal advisory bodies which report directly to the Board of Directors are:

- Advisory Council: Eminent scientific, consumer, industrial and other interest groups as well as seven state regulatory commissioners--all members are from outside the gas industry. Their goal is to assure the public interest is represented.

- Research Coordination Panel: Also from outside the gas industry, its membership consists of technical experts who can assure coordination of GRI's program with those conducted elsewhere.

- Industrial Technical Advisory Committee: Gas industry experts who advise GRI on research needs and priorities.

- Municipal Gas System Advisory Committee: Representatives who advise GRI on the customer needs of publically owned gas systems.

In addition (a) the Federal Energy Regulatory Commission (FERC) monitors all GRI goals, activities, and budgets; and (b) fourteen project advisory groups now exist consisting of about 200 technical experts who also advise the R&D staff directly. The values in the cells of the matrices in Figures 4 and 5 represent early versions of the aggregated preferences of the members of many of these advisory committees. These preference values were obtained during interactive sessions in which the three sets of objectives were discussed, refined, and then voted on. In a series of meetings each year the members also discuss and vote on various elements of the PAM scoring model and, later, on the ranking results of the PAM exercise

B.G. Silverman

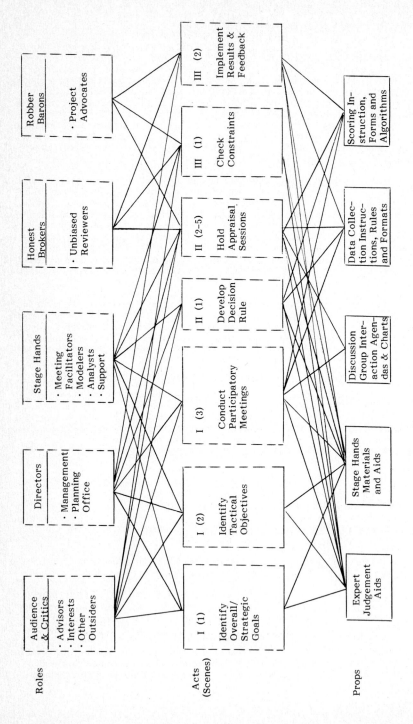

Figure 3. OVERVIEW OF A TYPICAL SCRIPT FOR A "PLAYING" OF PAM

Figure 4

GAS RESEARCH INSTITUTE'S

RELATIVE EMPHASIS ON NINE STRATEGIC OBJECTIVES (1979)

OVERALL OBJECTIVES	TIME PERIODS			TOTALS (%)
	NEAR-TERM	MID-TERM	LONG-TERM	
SUPPLY OPTIONS	15 %	15 %	10 %	40
EFFICIENT UTILIZATION	15 %	11 %	10 %	36
ENHANCED SERVICE	11 %	7 %	6 %	24
TOTALS (%)	41	33	26	100

Figure 5

GAS RESEARCH INSTITUTE'S

RELATIVE IMPORTANCE OF TACTICAL OBJECTIVES (1979)*

TACTICAL OBJECTIVES	SUPPLY OPTIONS	EFFICIENT UTILIZATION	ENHANCED SERVICE
GAS PROVIDED	33	17	8
GAS SAVINGS	17	33	8
GAS OPTIONS ENHANCED	13	13	13
CONSUMER SAVINGS	13	13	20
SAFETY AND RELIABILITY OF SERVICE	8	8	17
ENVIRONMENTAL IMPACTS	8	8	17
LEGAL, SOCIAL, AND INSTITUTIONAL EFFECTS	8	8	17
TOTALS	100	100	100

*The number of ties between importance levels is due to discussion amongst voters after the first round of votes and their deliberate decision to equalize several of the importance numbers.

and on the budget itself. Thus PAM serves both as a communication device and as a way to organize meetings and discussion (Act I, Scene 3). A variety of props facilitate these meetings such as expert judgment aids (brainstorming, consensus taking, etc.). These are standard items that are prepared once and reused year after year.

Using the Tactical Objectives as 7 dimensions or benefit vectors, (j) with which to compute scores (S_j) for the relative merits of each alternative project (i); the preferences as priority multipliers or weights (W_j); and the project budget as its discounted life cycle cost (C_i), a standard figure of merit type of scoring function was evolved such as,

$$R_{ik} = \frac{1}{(C_{ik})} (P_{ik}) \sum_{j=1}^{7} W_{ijk} \; S_{ijk} \qquad (1)$$

Here P_{ik} is the probability of success of the technical effort and R_{ik} is the aggregate rating of the ith project. The subscript k denotes the funding level being considered (as in a Zero Based Budgeting [8] type exercise). The scores, S_{ijk}, are measured on an interval scale such as

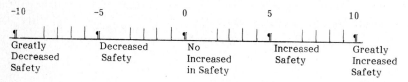

	-10	-5	0	5	10
	Greatly Decreased Safety	Decreased Safety	No Increased in Safety	Increased Safety	Greatly Increased Safety

At GRI, a variant quite similar to this is still used (Act II, Scene 1). Standard instructions and data sheets are issued for the collection of information concerning the 7 scores for each of the four funding levels. These data sheets are completed each year by the project area managers with reference to the previous year's data as updated by recent progress and analyses. Scoring instructions are similarly distributed for a self-scoring exercise.

The major activity for PAM at GRI (scoring, weighting, ranking, reviewing, and adjusting) transpires within a several week period each year, leading to the submission of a final plan and budget. The process begins with the presentation of the data sheets and resulting scores by the project managers to the PAM Review Panel (Act II, Scene 2). This panel is composed of "unbiased" experts both internal (e.g., from the Planning Office, the CEO, etc.) and external to the organization. The PAM Review Panel evaluates the validity of the data submission by sampling randomly from each project's data and conducting ad hoc studies/literature checks as time and resources permit. Both quantitative and qualitative (judgmental) information are reviewed and "Honesty Factors" are derived and applied that express the degree of overoptimism contained in the original submissions (Act II, Scene 3): hence the name of "Honest Brokers" for this Panel honesty factors may take the form of additions (subtractions) or multiplication (division) to any of the variables of equation (1).

The revised data is presented to the project staffs who are offered the opportunity for rebuttal (Act II, Scene 4). This is generally an important step that takes a number of judgemental factors into consideration--e.g., mix of projects in terms of various subjective aspects such as risk or likelihood of others to fund them, and various rules for converting scores to budgets. The finalized results are converted to a prioritized list of projects under each Strategic Objective in terms of Tactical Objectives for each of several funding levels (Act II, Scene 5). Act II (Scenes 2-5) is thus an intensive period of activity which, to run smoothly, relies heavily on preparation of adequate and errorfree "props" ranging across all of those displayed in Figure 3. Smooth functioning and professionalism throughout these Acts and Scenes is vital due to the large number of participants needing to be coordinated, scheduled, monitored, and supported.

The Act II results are transmitted to various upper management and Advisory Bodies for deliberation and constraint checking (Act III, Scene 1). Constraint checking covers activities ranging from assessing political and bureaucratic realism to conducting computer based sensitivity analyses of the rankings (e.g., how sensitive is each project's score to small, moderate, and large shifts in the critical variables?). The final step involves the feedback of results into an improved design of PAM for use in the next iteration (Act III, Scene 2). This includes the second verification, validation, and evaluation activities shown in Figure 1. This Scene concludes with the development of an implementation plan for any improvements deemed necessary.

The preceding two paragraphs are general to PAM and not specific to GRI, however, they are highly representative of the process followed in all PAM applications. The PAM is thus seen to represent a compromise between a rigorous, decision-theoretic model and the subjective judgements of experienced, highly trained, and broadly representative personnel. A recent Booz-Allen-Hamilton study surveyed a number of the GRI participants and found [6]:

- FERC (Opinion 96): "PAM plays a dominant role . . . in GRI's overall planning process. Absent any compelling reason, we are unwilling to involve ourselves in . . . refinements to this system."

- DOE Energy Research Advisory Board: ". . . the more familiarity one has with PAM, the more one is impressed with its attempt to rationalize . . . a subjective process. Some attempt should be made to keep the system simple, even if it means relying on the frailties of human judgement."

- GRI Director of Planning States: "R&D staff personnel tolerate PAM, recognizing they will be required to use it or a similar system. They would, however, prefer a more bottom-up planning system.

  GRI's top management and its officers are strongly supportive of PAM, believing it fulfills necessary planning requirements in a pragmatic and effective manner.

  GRI's advisory bodies differ somewhat on their attitude toward PAM. Generalists and non-technical personnel appear to be very favorably disposed toward the process. Technical people range from warm to lukewarm. Those among them who personally manage R&D programs tend to be the most skeptical, preferring greater reliance on expert judgement."

This last quote reveals that "all is not roses" with PAM and there is no attempt to claim otherwise in this Chapter: e.g., some of the R&D staff personnel and technical people at GRI prefer even less formalism. There is, however, no technique that is univerally acceptable to all parties. In the absence of such a universal solution, a technique such as PAM appears to be a viable compromise.

3. SUMMARY AND CONCLUSIONS

This chapter has presented a brief description of a behavioral approach to selection/evaluation of the project portfolio that has been successfully applied to five separate organizations, and institutionalized at three of these (DOE, GRI, LASL), and which is now well into its second decade of "life." The approach relies upon the "script" as its principal methodological technique, where a script is defined as a structure that explains how a casually related sequence of social actions will occur. It also accounts for roles to be "played" and "props" required throughout the sequence.

The features of such an approach include (see Section 1): (1) a systematic and complete procedure for conducting an inherently subjective planning process; (2) preparation of all the planning and executing minutia required by each of the dozens (and at times hundreds) of participants through each "Act and Scene" of the script; (3) the minimization of "gamesmanship" by project advocates ("Robber Barons") attempting to optimize their inputs so as to maximize their share of the budgetary pie. The approach permits application of "honesty factors" and (4) all the other features commonly suggested for "good" project appraisal techniques (e.g., self-documentation, traceability, reproducibility, consistency, rationality, etc.).

Achieving these types of features in so successful a fashion (nearly a two decade "run") does not happen without a substantial amount of forethought and effort. The overall procedure by which the approach is tailored to each new organization was explained in Section 1 (Figure 1) to include a social evolutionary prototyping in which a version is generated and used. This is followed by the creation of a next generation version that is sensitive to the concerns encountered in the earlier version such as verification, validation, and user evaluation.

To be successful a planning support system must recognize and integrate the human as well as the computational processes. The various versions or generations of the script are developed on the basis of theoretical considerations drawn from five topic areas (see Figure 2 and Section 2): decisionmaking frameworks, theories of the group, theories of the individual, measurement theory, and decision rules. Factors, concepts, techniques, and principles from each of these five topic areas were discussed from an integrating viewpoint. A summary of that integration is perhaps best stated by noticing that in topic after topic the argument was seen to be not whether to simplify the decision making process but <u>how</u> to do it <u>and to what degree</u>: even the most rigorous of decision analyses involve some degree of simplification and incompleteness. "Classic" or "pure" rational approaches are now regarded as rather quaint and are rarely used as a touchstone of good decision making. Further, the traditional view of the mathematical model--as a stand alone system--ignores the requirements of the process and the people in that process. On the other hand, although often regarded as the archetypical intuitive-complex problem, project portfolio decisions are in fact amenable to a reasonable degree of structuring.

Section 3 describes briefly a case study so as to illustrate how the script provides such a structure by integrating behavioral with computational elements. The roles, acts and scenes, and props of a typical version of a script (i.e., the first generation version of GRI) were described and the innumerable details of setting up a smoothly running process encompassing, in this case, over a hundred participants in a several week period were addressed. Robber Barons, Honest Brokers, Stage Hands, Directors, Audience & Critics, 3 Acts (straddling 10 scenes), and 5 sets of props were explained. The reactions of a variety of participants and observers lead to the conclusion that substantial improvement can occur by attention to detail and <u>interactive processes</u> aided by simplified decision rules that help the decision maker avoid gross errors.

ACKNOWLEDGEMENT

The author would like to express his appreciation to D. J. Monetta for initially encouraging him to work on PAM, to H. B. Sewell for his careful review of this chapter, and to D. Hunter for so patiently typing all the redrafts.

FOOTNOTES

[1]RAND found PATTERN, TORQUE, and QUEST have fallen into disuse, while Booz-Allen found that OST and PAM have succeeded in achieving continuous use. Hence, one can only conclude that group processes do not lead to failure. There must be other reasons for the "failure" of PATTERN, TORQUE, and QUEST.

REFERENCES

[1]   Baker, N., Freeland, J., "Recent Advances in R&D Benefit Measurement and Project Selection Methods," Management Science, Vol. 21, No. 10, June 1975, pp. 1164-1175.

[2]   Ojdana, E. S., Weyant, J. P., An Assessment of Selected Models Used for Evaluating Military R*D Projects, RAND Report R-1847-PR, Santa Monica: The RAND Corporation, September 1976.

[3]   Pohler, C. H., Project Management of the Technology Base: Concepts and Practices for Selecting Projects and Allocating Resources, Washington, D. C., Naval Sea Systems Comm.and (unpublished manuscript, 1978).

[4]   Souder, W. E., "Analytical Effectiveness of Mathematical Models for R&D Project Selection," Management Science, Vol. 19, No. 8, pp. 907-923, April 1973.

[5]   Cetron, M. J., Martino, J. and Roepcke, L., "The Selection of R&D Program Content-Survey of Quantitative Methods," IEEE Trans. Engineering Management, Vol. EM-14, No. 1, pp. 4-13.

[6]   Rust, C. L., McCambridge, J. J., Case Studies of Innovation in R&D Planning, prepared by Booz-Allen-Hamilton, Inc., Palo Alto: Electric Power Research Institute (EA-2154), 1981.

[7]   Staff, Advanced Planning and Appraisal of NAVORD Research and Technology, Washington, D. C.: Naval Ordinance Systems Command, 1974.

[8]   Silverman, B. G., "Project Appraisal Methodology: A Multidimensional R&D Project Benefit-Cost Assessment Tool," Management Science, Vol. 27, No. 7, July 1981, pp. 802-821.

[9]   _____, "Project Appraisal Methodology: Market Penetration Elements," Management Science, Vol. 29, No. 2, Feb. 1983, pp. 210-224.

[10]   Staff, 1980-1984 Five Year Research and Development Plan and 1980 Research and Development Program, Chicago: Gas Research Institute, 1979.

[11]   Staff, "Benefits and Priorities Appraisal Methodology," prepared by Santa Fe Corporation, for Ship Structures Committee (an Interagency Group), National Academy of Science, 1979 (draft).

[12]   Monetta, D. J., PAM: An R&D Project Appraisal Methodology, Ph.D. Dissertation, University of Southern California, 1981, available through University Microfilms.

[13]   Bobrow, D. G., Collins, A., Representation and Understanding, New York: Academic Press, 1975.

[14]   Keen, P. G. W., Morton, M. S. S. Decision Support Systems: An Organizational Perspective, Reading: Addison-Wesley, 1978.

[15] Snapper, K. J., "Public Policy Decisions: How to Simplify When you Must," research paper, prepared for Department of Justice, 1978, unpublished.

[16] Mason, R. O., Swanson, E. B. (ed.), Measurement for Management Decision, Reading: Addison-Wesley, 1981.

[17] Hammond, K. R., McClelland, G. H., Mumpower, J., Human Judgement and Decisionmaking: Theories, Methods, and Procedures, New York, Praeger, 1980.

[18] Sage, A. P., "Behavioral and Organizational Considerations in the Design of Information Systems and Processes for Planning and Decision Support," IEEE Trans. on Systems, Man, and Cybernetics, Vol. SMC-11, No. 9, Sept. 1981 (pp. 640-678).

[19] Zmud, R. W., "Individual Differences and MIS Success: A Review of the Empirical Literature," Management Science, Vol. 25, No. 10, pp. 966-979, Oct. 1979.

[20] Twiss, B., Managing Technological Innovation, London: Longman Group Limited, 1974, p. 64.

[21] Keeney, R. L. and Raiffa, H., Decisions with Multiple Objectives: Preferences and Value Tradeoff: New York: Wiley, 1976.

[22] Baer, W. S., Johnson, L. L., Merrow, E. W., "Government-Sponsored Demonstrations of New Technologies," Science, May 27, 1977, pp. 950-957.

[23] Silverman, B. G., "On the Utility of Participatory Workshops to R&D Management," 11th Annual Modeling and Simulation Conference Proceedings, Pittsburgh: Instrument Society of America, 1980.

[24] _____, "Expert Intuition and Ill-Structured Problem Solving," in D. Lee (ed.) Management of Technological Innovations, Washington, D. C., NSF, May 1983. Available as an Institute for Artificial Intelligence Technical Report, Washington, D.C.: GWU, 1983.

[25] _____, "Expert Systems and Aids for Managers: Organizational Improvements and the Analogical Paradigm," (unpublished manuscript: book), Available as an Institute for Artificial Intelligence Technical Report, Washington, D.C., GWU Summer 1984.

[26] Moore, J. R., Baker, N. R., "Computational Analysis of Scoring Models for R&D Project Selection," Management Science, Vol. 16, No. ____, Dec. 1969, p. B213.

[27] Silverman, B. G., Liebowitz, J., Moustakis, V., "Ad Hoc Modeling, Expert Problem Solving, and R&D Program Evaluation," IEEE Transactions on Engineering Management, August 1983.

[28] Coch, L., French, J.R.P., "Overcoming Resistance to Change," in Group Dynamics: Research and Theory, 2nd ed., D. Cartwright, Cartwright, Zander, A., (eds.), Evanston: Row, Peterson, 1960, pp. 319-41.

[29] Arensberg, C. M., "Behavior and Organization: Industrial Studies," in Social Psychology at the Crossroads, Rohrer, J. H., Sherif, M. (eds.), New York: Harper & Row, 1951, pt. V.

[30] Ouchi, W. G., Theory Z, New York: Addison-Wesley, 1981.

[31] Hersey, P., Blanchard, K., Management of Organizational Behavior, Englewood Cliffs: Prentice-Hall, 1981.

[32] Klein, G. A., "Automated Aids for the Proficient Decisionmaker," in Proceedings of the International Conference on Cybernetics and Society, pp. 301-304, New York: IEEE Society, 1981.

[33] Degroot, A., Thought and Choice in Chess, The Hague: Mouton, 1965.

[34] Larkin, J., McDermott, J., Simon, D. P., Simon, H. A., "Expert and Novice Performance in Solving Physics Problem," Science, Vol. 208, No. 20, pp. 1335-1342, 1980.

[35] Silverman, B. G., "Cost and Productivity Improvements for Software Managers," Computer Magazine, IEEE, 1985.

[36] Leavitt, H. J., "Beyond the Analytic Manager: Part II", California Management Review, Vol. 17, pp. 11-21, Summer, 1975.

[37] Oppenheimer, J. R., "Analogy in Science," American Psychologist, Vol. II, pp. 127-135, 1956.

[38] Dreyfus, S. E., "Formal Models vs. Situational Understanding: Inherent Limitations on the Modeling of Business Expertise," Office: Technology and People, Vol. 1, pp. 133-165, 1982.

[39] Tversky, A., Kahneman, D., "Judgment Under Uncertainty: Heuristics and Biases," Science, Vol. 185, pp. 1124-1131, 1974.

[40] Lebesque, H., Measurement and the Integral, San Francisco: Holden Day, 1966.

[41] Little, J. D. C., "Models and Managers: The Concept of a Decision Calculus," Management Science, Vol. 16, No. 8, pp. B466-485, April 1970.

[42] Saaty, T. L., The Analytical Hierarchy Process: Planning, Priority Setting, and Resource Allocation, New York: McGraw-Hill, 1980.

[43] Etzioni, A., "Mixed Scanning: A Third Approach to Decision Making," Public Admin. Review, Dec. 1967, pp. 385-392.

[44] Simon, H. A., "A Behavioral Model of Rational Choice," in H. A. Simon, Models of Man, pp. 241-260, New York: Wiley, 1957.

[45] Cyert, R. M., March, J. G., Behavioral Theory for the Firm, Englewood Cliffs: Prentice-Hall, 1963.

[46] Cohen, M. D., March, J. G., Olsen, J. P., "A Garbage Can Model of Organizational Choice," Admin. Sci. Quart., Vol. 19, No. 3, pp. 1-25.

Project Management: Methods and Studies
Burton V. Dean (editor)
© Elsevier Science Publishers B.V. (North-Holland), 1985

THE ROLE OF NETWORK TECHNIQUES IN TEAM BUILDING
FOR PROJECT MANAGEMENT

Robert J. Graham

Management and Behavioral Science Center
University of Pennsylvania
Philadelphia, Pennsylvania
U.S.A.

Many people view network techniques (such as PERT and CPM) as
merely mathematical tools for planning and controlling the schedule
for special projects. Such a view misses much of the potential value
of such methods for team building and development. This paper
examines the broader implications of using network techniques as an
integral part of the total process of team building and functioning
in project management. To do this a process is outlined involving
team members participating in the network design by first creating
the ideal network chart, and then iterating towards a feasible solution
that becomes the initial project plan. It is argued that through such
a process, people from divergent fields can begin to develop the routine
necessary for a smoothly functioning team. In addition, the iterative
negotiation process also helps to establish behavioral norms and levels
of trust that are needed for effective groups. Finally, building an
ideal network and then reviewing the feasible network are shown to
be aids to increasing creativity in project design as well as commitment
to implementing the initial project plan.

INTRODUCTION

Network techniques such as PERT and CPM are often viewed only as mathematical techniques
potentially useful to managers during the planning and controlling of the timing of activities
needed to complete a special project. As a result, much emphasis has been placed on methods for estimating time, discovering critical activities, trading time for money, keeping on
schedule and budget, and other such schemes useful during the execution of a project. However, in discussion network techniques with practicing managers, many state that the most
useful result of using a network technique is not in the execution of the project but rather
with the initial project plan.

At first glance this may seem somewhat paradoxical as it is well known that projects rarely
proceed according to the initial plan. The thesis presented here is that such statements are
not as strange as they initially seem because the proper management of the network building
process can be seen to be a technique for team building and development. The project team
is usually a new, temporary group without previous experience of working together. However, it is the well formed team that yields the benefits that the project managers sense. Typically, management scientists spend most of their concern on the details of a technique
such as PERT, with little concern for the group processes that are taking place as people
work with the technique. This paper aims to remedy a part of that problem. Thus, the purpose of this paper is to explore the roles of a network building process in terms of the part
the process plays in the development of behavioral patterns and expectations that can result
in a well functioning team.

It should be stressed here that the life of any project can be divided into three somewhat fuzzy and overlapping stages: (1) the decision to do a particular project, (2) the planning of the
project, and (3) the execution of the project. This paper is not concerned with stage one ex-

cept to note that this stage sets the "givens" of the project - such as the final goal, total assets available and a general time schedule. Nor is there concern for the third stage, except to note that it may be necessary to adopt a different leadership style to execute rather than plan a project and that replanning occurs often as the project proceeds. We are concerned here with the planning of the project and the management of the collaborative, creative and iterative process which produces the initial network diagram with which the project begins. The emphasis is on building a project team and not the content of any particular project.

The general argument of the paper is outlined below. The content of the argument has been distilled from discussions with over 250 project managers during the past three years. Once the argument is stated, literature from various sources is cited in an attempt to validate the argument and show the benefits of the project management process developed. The paper closes with a discussion of leadership styles appropriate for the various stages of the project management process suggested.

A Project Management Process

Complex projects require complex teams which subsequently require their own set of work rules and norms. Most of the early examples of project management came from the construction industry, where the activities were fairly autonomous and could be carried out relatively independently. For more complex projects such as the development of new expertise or new products, there is a great deal of learning involved and the performance of the current activity becomes dependent on what was learned during the completion of the last activity. Such a high degree of interdependency requires a very well functioning and cohesive team.

Complex projects also require a variety of people with a wide range of skills from throughout the organization. These people will normally not be accustomed to working with each other. They have become accustomed to working according to the norm for behavior used in their home department. A mixed collection of such behavioral patterns and expectations could be counterproductive. Thus developing a cohesive team requires developing a set of norms for behavior that may be different than the norms the team members are accustomed to using. It is felt that developing behavioral patterns and expectations should be attended to before the project work commences, and that this process can be enhanced by having all of the members of the project team work together to build the initial project plan.

A process which many project managers have used instinctively, and which agrees with many management principles (as discussed later) is given as:

    I.   Once the end product of the project has been specified, an initial project team should be assembled, have the goal explained to them, be given a 'rough' network diagram as drawn by the project manager and asked:

        (a)   who else should be on the team, and
        (b)   without concern of budget restrictions, what would each member contribute to the project if they could do whatever they wanted.

    II.   From the answers to the above, the team and the project manager then construct an idealized network, the project network that they would implement if there were no restrictions.

    III. If the idealized network is within budget, the ideal becomes the initial project plan and implementation can begin. If the ideal is not within budget, and the budget cannot be increased, then the team members must develop ways to negotiate with one another and the project manager to take aspects away from the ideal design. Each aspect taken away becomes another iteration towards a realistic plan.

    IV. The process of negotiation continues to iterate until a feasible solution is found: a network that is operationally viable and within budget. This network becomes the initial project plan--that is, the plan with which the project execution begins.

Some Aspects of Team Development

The above process is itself an idealization and need not, and perhaps cannot, be followed exactly. After many years of dealing with project managers I have found that a number of successful projects have used this method almost by default. This is due to the fact that at the beginning of the project either the budget was not known, or the means for achieving the end result were not clearly specified, or both. Without these guidelines it was required that the project team first idealize what they would do and then interate towards a more feasible solution. These are two important aspects of the process, and the reasons for their importance are discussed in subsequent sections.

Project managers often say that they could accomplish any task if only they had the "right" people. One common characteristic of these "right" people is that they can operate with a minimum of instructions and supervision. They seem to know what to do without being told. The ability to operate in this manner if often the result of an individual's enculturation to a clear set of goals and norms for behavior. In a stable situation such as a standing department, the norms are taught through a system of customs which have been developed over many years in the presence of the stable situation. When people from different departments are assembled for a project they form a temporary social system and as it is new, there is no system of customs that indicate proper behavior while working on that project. Each person brings his/her own set of customs, beliefs, and perceptions to the project and these may not form a coherent team culture. Without such a culture people will behave as if they were "back home" and such behavior could be in conflict with the smooth operation of the project. For example, one of the main functions of military indoctrination programs is to eliminate "back home" behavior while the person is acting in a military capacity. The development of a team culture, to be used while people are working on a project, should also be one of the prime management considerations during the project planning stage.

To clarify the idea of developing a group culture, I will use some of the concepts of culture as developed in the field of anthropology. Many older theories of culture ([5], [14]) assumed the concept of the "group mind", a common set of objectives and motives which were shared by a group of people and which fostered the cohesiveness and solidarity of that group. It was assumed that most behavior was done for the good of the whole and that this was so because of a commonality of motives shared by the members of the society.

For most recurring purposes, people develop standards for behavior which then become routine within that group. Goodenough[7, p.22] thus defines the operating culture of a group to be the set of standards attributed to a group which the individual uses when he is operating with or within that group. It thus seems important for a project manager to develop an operating culture for the project team.

But how is this to be done in a heterogeneous group where one cannot assume a commonality of motives? Wallace [17] concludes that it is not necessary that all members of a group have the same set of beliefs and motives in order to select the correct behavior under various circumstances. All they need to do is to be able to predict the others' behavior. Wallace sees the unifying mechanism as the perception of partial equivalence structures, the recognition that the behavior of other people under various circumstances is predictable, regardless of knowledge of their motivation, and is thus capable of being predictably related to one's own actions. Such a system of equivalent mutual expectancies is termed an implicit contract. As an example, Wallace [17, p.34] points out that:

> The relationship between the driver of a bus and the riders is a contractual one, involving specific and detailed mutual expectancies. The motives of drivers and riders may be as diverse as one wishes; the contract establishes the system.

Wallace goes further by stating that many human endeavors often require nonsharing of certain motivations and cognitions among participants in a variety of institutional arrangements. This nonsharing serves two important functions. First, it permits a more complex system to arise than most, or any, of its participants can comprehend. Second, it alleviates the participants in a system from the heavy burden of learning and knowing each other's motivations and cognitions.

Given the above discussions, the stance taken here is that a participatory process of developing the project network is an important step in creating a project culture. The initial project plan is the explicit contract for the team. Working towards building that network helps to develop the implicit contracts which are necessary for a smoothly working team. That is, it helps to set up the routines. Since most projects are quite complex, some nonsharing will be necessary. Thus it is not necessary for participants to explain exactly how each activity will be completed. It is only necessary to negotiate for the definition of the end product of each activity along with the assets and time that will be allotted to each activity.

During the process of negotiation, people's assumptions and propositions concerning various aspects of the project will be tested. Some of these will be assumed to be true. This will give rise to a set of beliefs concerning the goal of the project and the goals of the other people who will be working on the project team. These beliefs will give rise to a system of customs that will be used to indicate proper behavior while working on the project. That is, the interaction of members of the project team will become routine. This is the way that the project culture is created.

Attributes of Effective Groups

Many attributes of groups have been defined in the literature. Three attributes, however, seem to be common to all definitions. These are:

(1)   Members perceive themselves as in a group and they know who is in the group and who is not in the group.

(2)   There is at least one objective that all members agree upon, although each individual member may have a multitude of other objectives.

(3)   There is a need for interaction because of the interdependeices of the people in the group as they work towards the agreed-upon objective.

A project team working collaboratively on a network plan should certainly fit this definition. It is assumed here that there is initially some idea of the activities that need to be completed during the project and that the people who are going to manage these activities are brought together for an initial meeting of the project team. In this way it is revealed who is on the team and who is not. As the planning continues some people may be added or deleted, but this should be done with the full knowledge of all members of the team. It is rare that any complex project finishes with the same team members with which it began. In order to keep true to the concept that the members perceive themselves as a group, it is important that all members are aware of any changes in group membership as the project planning proceeds.

A comment should be made here concerning group size. It has been suggested that the first stage of the participation process should include idealized design, where team members consider the project plan without regard to constraints on assets. This could lead to an initial project team that is quite large in size. Lewenstein [11] notes that the larger the group, the greater the diversity of talent, skills and knowledge, the riskier the decisions the group is willing to make. The tradeoff, however, is that in larger groups there is less chance of individual participation. "The 'neglected resource' is a common feature of large groups; the retiring expert whose views are never heard or never noticed because his participation level is so low." [8, p.152] Studies indicate that heterogeneous groups tend to be more productive than homogeneous groups [15].

However, using the network diagram as the focal point of the group's activities may help alleviate the non-participation problem and thus obviate the problem of size. At the initial meeting of the team, each person should discuss how he/she could help the team towards its objectives. As the network begins to take shape, each person begins to negotiate for activities and assets. When the network is complete, each person should review and explain to the others what it is he/she has contributed to the project. In this way participation becomes one of the behavioral expectations of the group and pressure will be brought to bear on the "retiring expert" to contribute as much as possible.

The second attribute of the effective group is the common objective. As the members of the group start to perceive themselves as a group there needs to be some agreement on the common objective. The completed project that defines the end of the network should be the stated common objective of all members of the team. If all team members have a very clear understanding of the final result and agree that this is an objective to be reached, the group will tend to be more effective.

It is well known, however, that most people also bring hidden agendas to groups. Hidden agendas are a set of personal objectives which often may have nothing to do with the declared objectives of the group. In most project situations it is not possible to satisfy all of the individual and group objectives simultaneously. To reach the best combined result each individual on the team, including the project manager, has to be willing to make a trade-off of one objective to reach another. Each individual has to be willing to take a risk and to be ready to accept a less-than-optimum outcome for himself. Handy [8, p.158] states that this will happen only if the participants can agree on a common objective and if they trust each other. He further states that these conditions will normally only happen if the individuals are given a chance to communicate about objectives and they are allowed to prove that trust is justified by putting it to test in some other instance. An exception noted is when there are clear group norms or rules. But since one of the features of a project team is the initial lack of such norms, the exception does not apply in this case. Thus there is a need to build trust.

The trust needed during project execution can be formed during the negotiation for assets. The negotiation phase is seen as the "other instance" where people can put each other to the test. By proposing a contribution to a project without constraints of budget, people will be inadvertently revealing their objectives and hidden agendas. When the constraints are applied all will have to make some trade-offs. The ability to make the trade-offs, and to stay true to them, will establish the level of trust that each person has in one another during the execution of the project. If this process is well managed, and if the project manager insures that all trade-offs are strictly adhered to, the level of trust can be quite high. The negotiation process is also important for establishing the implicit contracts that are a central part of the project culture. It is during negotiation for assets that each person finds out what makes the others tick, and this sets up behavioral patterns that will last for the duration of the project.

The third attribute listed for effective groups is the recognition of the interdependencies of people for the completion of both the individual activities and the project as a whole. The vivid, graphic display of interdependencies has long been known as one of the main advantages of using network techniques. When an activity is placed in a network it becomes immediately clear exactly who is dependent on whom in order to begin their activity. In addition, network techniques identify critical activities which are, in essence, those activities that everyone is dependent upon. Thus focusing on the network is certainly an aid for this aspect of an effective group.

The collaborative procedure of iterating towards an initial project network is supported by Tuckman's [16] review of group process studies. In this article group maturation is categorized as having four successive stages:

1. <u>Forming</u> At this stage the group is not yet a group but a set of individuals. This stage is characterized by talk about the purpose of thr group, the definition and title of the group, its composition, leadership pattern and life-span. In the case of project management, this stage should be completed by the first or second meeting of the project team, where the objective and participants of the team are introduced and discussed.

2. Storming   This is the conflict stage where the preliminary consensus on purposes, on leadership and other roles, on norms of work and behavior, is challenged and re-established. At this stage a lot of personal agendas are revealed and a certain amount of inter-personal hostility is generated. This stage is particularly important for testing the norms of the group. In the case of project management, this stage is analogous to the stage where team members negotiate for assets and iterate towards the initial project plan.

3. Norming   At this stage the group establishes norms and practices. Norms of functioning of the group are determined such as when and how it should work, how it should take decisions, what type of behavior, what level of work and what degree of openness, trust and confidence is appropriate. Group members will also determine their level of commitment. In the case of project management, this stage occurs when the initial project plan is completed, each person reviews their part in the plan and commits to the completion of their activities at the level of assets negotiated.

4. Performing   This is the stage where the plan is executed. Only when the three previous stages have been successfully completed will the group be at full maturity and be able to be fully and sensibly productive. It is assumed that there will be changes to the initial project plan during this phase. However, because of the level of trust and the explicit contracts built up during the iteration towards the initial project plan, changes should be implemented much more smoothly than if the group were just handed the network chart and told to get to work.

Two other concepts seem to indicate the benefits of participatory iteration. The first is the interactive planning paradigm given by Ackoff [1]. This paradigm is based on the belief that the principal benefit of planning comes from engaging in it. With this principle, the process is the most important product in planning. A major consequence of participation is seen as a reduction of problems associated with implementing plans. This is based on the feeling that most people would rather be asked than told.

The key to interactive planning is the way that ends and means are selected in it [2]. This selection is based on the preparation of an idealized design. An idealized network chart consists of what the team members would contribute to a project without regard to budget or other resource constraints. An idealized design is subject to only two constraints. First it should be technologically feasible, otherwise it could turn out to be science fiction. Secondly, the entire network should be operationally viable, that is, capable of survial if it were brought into existence. The remainder of the planning process is directed at approximating this ideal as closely as possible given the resource constraints and the combination of the objectives of the people on the project team.

The advantages of basing the planning process on such a design have been listed in [2]. Another benefit of using network techniques is to incorporate the difference in thought processes between the left and right hemispheres of the human brain. Recent brain research [3], [4], [12] has concluded that the left side of the brain is most adept at language, mathematics and the general analytic and logical type of thinking that is used in constructing the elements of a network diagram. To complement this, the right side of the brain is more synthetically perceptual, realizing the whole, being able to process many different inputs at once and recognizing relations and simultaneous dependencies. By concentrating on the details of constructing a network and then standing back to study the entire network, team members exercise both sides of their brain and construct a more complete image of the entire project.

The use of network diagrams seems unique among operations research techniques for stimulating this type of whole-brain synthesis and subsequent creativity. The network diagram with its indicators of interdependencies shows the entire picture, the gestalt of the situation, in a way that the output of other techniques, such as linear programming, cannot begin to match. But in order to get the full benefit it seems important that team members take the time to look at the network as a whole. It is thus re-emphasized that once the initial project plan is realized, each member of the team should reiterate his/her part in the plan in the presence of all other team members. In this way each person can realize how each other activity relates to his/her own activity, which is a left brain process, while simultaneously realizing how each activity relates to the whole, and thus completing the right-brain synthesis.

Project Management and Leadership Style

Up to this point we have been concentrating on the behavior of the individual team members. I would now like to shift emphasis to the behavior of the project manager. The shift is motivated by a comment by Pearson and Davies [13] concurring the value of network techniques. They claim that

> It can be argued that some of these techniques are very valuable aids
> to project managers and to individual team members if seen as compo-
> nents of leadership style.

The basic assumption is that project management is more the management of the team than the management of the tasks. It has been argued that the team goes through various stages in its development and maturity. Pearson and Davies argue that there is a different leadership style appropriate for different levels of group maturity. Their study, however, was concerned with static levels of maturity. That is, if a project manager finds a group with a given level of maturity then they should exhibit a particular management style. The results can also be used in a process context, saying that as the group matures the project manager should shift styles from one level to the next. It will be argued that this process framework indicates that a different management style may be appropriate for the four different steps of the team development process given in Section 2.

The Pearson and Davies studies draw heavily on the leadership styles framework developed by Hersey and Blanchard [10]. This framework posits four levels of task-relevant maturity of any group, going from level M1, the lowest level of task-relevant maturity, to M4, the highest. At level M1 the group cannot accomplish the task without direct supervision. At level M4, the group has matured to accomplish the task with a minimum of supervision.

Four corresponding leadership styles are outlined. These are given as:

S1 - Structuring

Organize and direct the work of others, make each person accountable for specific activities and motivate by demonstrating what needs to be done. With this leadership style the network chart is "handed down" to the team.

S2 - Coaching

Set high but realistic standards of performance, explain what needs to be done and motivate by giving feedback and being personally involved. With this leadership style the network is "jointly drawn" by the team and the manager.

S3 - Encouraging

Recognize and praise good work, be open and supportive and motivate by letting others structure work. With this leadership style the network is "follower drawn" by the team itself.

S4 - Delegating

Assign task responsibility and let others carry them out. Motivate by giving control and showing respect. This leadership style is most appropriate for the execution of the project where emphasis is on meeting scheduled milestones.

These four categories correspond with the four steps of the project management process given in Section 2. The first step suggests that the project manager provide a "rough" network diagram in order to introduce the task to the team members. At this point the team will have very low task maturity so the network is essentially "handed down". The next step suggests that the team and the project manager construct an idealized design, allowing the group to mature some by working on a network that is jointly drawn. In step three, the responsibility shifts more to the team as they negotiate for assets. At the end they all review, with the project manager and with each other, their part in the project. With such agreement the initial project network has been essentially drawn by the team. With step four the project commences with a high degree of task maturity in the group. The project can now proceed with a minimum of direct supervision by the project manager.

CONCLUSION

Throughout this paper it has been argued that the process used for designing a project network may often be more important than the network itself. A process was presented where all project team members work together to build the initial project plan. The plan is devised by first building the ideal plan, without regard to budget or other resource constraints, and then having team members negotiate towards a feasible project plan. It was argued that such a scheme will (1) help build a project culture while team members become accustomed to working together; (2) help to build a more effective team as members begin to trust one another; and (3) help to release large amounts of creativity as team members idealize and use both the left and right brain activities. With these arguments, it seems important that project managers pay more attention to the team building aspects of network planning techniques in the future.

REFERENCES

[1]   Ackoff, R. L., <u>Redesigning the Future</u>, Wiley, New York, 1974.

[2]   _____ , "Resurrecting the Future of Operational Research," <u>J. Op. Res. Soc.</u>, <u>30 (1979)</u>, pp. 189-199.

[3]   Bogen, J. E., "The Other Side of the Brain: An Appositional Mind," <u>Bulletin of the Los Angeles Neurological Societies</u>, 34 (July 1969), pp. 135-162.

[4]   Carrington, P., <u>Freedom in Meditation</u>, Doubleday, New York, 1978.

[5]   Durkheim, E.,<u>The Rules of Sociological Method</u> (orig. 1895), Free Press, New York, 1938.

[6]   Foster, G. M., <u>Traditional Cultures and the Impact of Technological Change</u>, Harper, New York, 1962.

[7]   Goodenough, W. H., <u>Culture, Language and Society</u>, Addison-Wesley Modular Publications, No. 7, 1971.

[8]   Handy, C. B., <u>Understanding Organizations</u>, Penguin Books Ltd, Harmondsworth, England, 1982.

[9]   Harrison, R., "How to Describe Your Organization," <u>Harvard Business Review</u>, Sept-Oct 1972.

[10]   Hersey, P. and Blanchard, K., <u>Management of Organizational Behavior</u>, (3rd ed), Prentice Hall, Englewood Cliffs, 1977.

[11]   Lewenstein, E. R., "Group Size and Decision Making Committees," <u>Applied Soc. Studies</u>, 1971.

[12]   Ornstein, R., <u>Psychology of Consciousness</u>, W. H. Freeman and Co., San Francisco, 1972.

[13]   Pearson, A. W. and Davies, G. B., "Leadership Styles and Planning and Monetary Techniques," <u>R & D Management</u>, 11, July 1981.

[14]   Radcliffe-Brown, A. R. <u>Structure and Function in Primitive Society</u>, Oxford University Press, London, 1952.

[15]   Schutz, U. C., <u>FIRO: A Three Dimensional Theory of Interpersonal Behavior</u>, Rinehart, New York, 1958.

[16]   Tuckman, B. W., "Developmental Sequence in Small Groups," <u>Psych. Bulletin</u>, 1965.

[17]   Wallace, A. F. C., <u>Culture and Personality</u> (2nd Edition), Random House, New York, 1970.

Project Management: Methods and Studies
Burton V. Dean (editor)
© Elsevier Science Publishers B.V. (North-Holland), 1985

PROJECT MANAGEMENT AT SIGNIFICANT INTERFACES IN THE R&D/INNOVATION PROCESS [1]

Albert H. Rubenstein

Northwestern University
Evanston, Illinois
U.S.A.

Martin E. Ginn

Illinois Institute of Technology
Chicago, Illinois
U.S.A.

In the R&D/Innovation process, project management is perceived to occur within two main contexts: (1) within functional areas and (2) across functional areas, i.e. in technology transfer. In the second case--which may involve interfaces between R&D, Production, and Marketing--situations are generally more ambiguous and difficult for project managers. Members of Northwestern's Program of Research on the Management of R&D/Innovation (POMRAD) have undertaken various theory-based empirical studies to address these problems. Included in the studies are: examination of the R&D/Production interface and pilot plant operations; conflict at interfaces when technology is introduced; transfer of new technology from R&D to Marketing; the role of key communicators; and the role of "imbedded technology" in the R&D/Production interface. Conceptual models and related propositions are given to illustrate the perspectives of various POMRAD participants. An integrated model is presented which suggests general guildelines for project managers. Also explored are implications for the management of R&D/Innovation projects and for the study and design of project management systems by both academic researchers and management scientists. Emphasis is placed on barriers to successful project management and on facilitators for overcoming such barriers. Managers need to appropriately have "in place" management commitment, intra-organizational factors (such as imbedded technology capability), and inter-organizational support to achieve project success.

INTRODUCTION

Project management occurs in two significantly different contexts in the overall R&D/Innovation process. The first is the routine management of projects within a functional area such as research, development, engineering, production, or marketing. Lines of responsibility, territories, power relationships, reporting channels, and other management aspects are relatively clear in the first case. The second case occurs when project management is carried on (or attempted) across functional areas--e.g., transfer of technology from R&D through the R&D/Marketing interface. In the second case, the situation is generally ambiguous and difficult for project managers. In a series of recent studies of "Interface Relations in the R&D/Innovation Process," members of Northwestern's Program of Research on the Management of R&D/Innovation (POMRAD) have undertaken a series of theory-based, empirical studies of multi-faceted aspects of this general phenomenon. The studies included examination of R&D/Production relations revolving around pilot plant operations, conflict at the R&D/Production interface when new production technology is introduced, new channels for "arms-length" transfer of new products between independent firms, the role of key communicators in cross-functional or cross-divisional relations, the role of R&D in adapting and adopting purchased technology and the role of "imbedded technology" [2] in the R&D/

Production interface. All of these interface aspects have implications for project management in the R&D/Innovation process. This paper presents theoretical background on this set
of topics as they relate to project management and a set of propositions derived from the
work of the POMRAD group and other research groups in the field of "Research-on-Research."
Implications for both the actual management of R&D/Innovation projects and the study and
design of project management systems by both academic researchers and in-house management scientists are explored. Particular emphasis is placed on barriers to successful project
management across the interfaces in the R&D/Innovation process and to potential means for
overcoming such barriers, i.e., via facilitators.

Some Potentially Researchable Questions and Some Definitions

Project management is often portrayed as a manifestation of personal skill and experience
in dealing with people, technology, organization and the environment. There is an abundant
literature on "how to do it," "how we do (or did) it," and "how you should do it." The literature is much less bountiful, however, in reports of basic research into the phenomenon of
project management--the "whys" of the process in terms of explanations of the observed behaviors of project managers and members of project teams. In focusing our series of studies
on the R&D/Production interface, we started out with a series of general questions which
arise continually during attempts to design for, actually do, and systematically study the process by which projects "flow" or "transit" through the R&D/Production interface. Some of
these questions arise in a repetitive manner during the transition process in a wide range of
contexts--very large companies and not so large ones, highly complex technologies and not so
complex ones, hard-driving organizations and those that are less so, urgent project transitions
and less urgent ones. Certainly, particular circumstances--size, complexity, urgency, and
the particular individuals who happen to be involved in a given interface situation--strongly
influence the process itself and its outcomes. However, there are also a number of generic
aspects of the process which seem to be present across the range of particular circumstances
and which form grist for the mill of organization theorists and other behavioral and management scientists. In connection with an NSF-supported study which began in September 1982
we attempted to integrate the experience of Northwestern's R&D/Production interface team
(nine people with a total of over 100 years of experience in managing and doing research on
R&D, production, and the interface between them). From the dozens of potentially researchable questions which might have formed the impetus for the study, the following were selected as an initial take-off platform for designing the study. Many of them arose from the dis-
tillation of literature and personal experience of five members of the team who have been
conducting dissertation research in this general area.

(1)   How can productivity of the R&D/Production interface be assessed (employing appro-
       priate indicators and quantitative measures), and how do intergroup relationships
       engineering design changes, barriers and facilitators, and other factors influence
       interface effectiveness?

(2)   What roles do imbedded technology capabilities (including unique facilities) play in
       the R&D/Production interface and in related stages of the R&D/Innovation process?

(3)   What organizational design features (structural, procedural, and coordinating mech-
       anisms) and management practices(staffing, supporting, skill identification and
       development, resource allocation, etc.) are especially relevant and identifiable as
       guides to effective and ineffective ways of functioning at the interface?

(4)   What are the sources of conflict which arise at the interface and which of these
       are task-related as compared with person-, specialty-, or organization-related?

(5)   How do interactive involvements by R&D and production at various stages of the
       project life cycle influence the quality of the transition and the ultimate success
       of the project?

(6)   How do <u>marketing factors</u> affect the economics and overall feasibility of transferring new products from R&D through production?

(7)   How can the factors and indicators, which significantly influence the interface, be built into a monitoring and evaluation system for <u>improving performance</u>?

(8)   What <u>policy implications</u> are there in connection with the R&D/Production interface which impact on: R&D management, production management, new product planning, general management, the federal government, engineering schools, and on other educational and training institutions?

Some pertinent definitions for this line of research are:

(a)   <u>Industrial R&D</u> - those formal, primarily "laboratory"-based activities in an industrial firm which are aimed at developing new and improved products and processes, as well as building and maintaining the technology base on which the company depends. The overwhelming percentage of industrial R&D is mission-oriented toward the products and activities in which the firm is currently or is likely to be engaged within a fairly short time horizon. In many firms, the "laboratories" are called engineering departments, product development groups, or similar names.

(b)   <u>R&D/Innovation</u> - the overall process, including the laboratory or R&D phases, which encompasses the many steps required to introduce a new or improved product, process, or service to the factory and/or the market place. The exact boundaries and specific components of this process vary according to different authors and practitioners, but the major components and stages are readily recognizable in the industrial firm.

(c)   <u>The R&D/Production Interface</u> - a temporal, spatial, and functional concept which represents the organizational and interpersonal (managerial and professional) exchange of information and know-how. It also is a part of the R&D/Innovation spectrum which can be: an arena for cooperation or conflict; a generator or repository for ambiguity about locus of responsibility; and a source of high costs, delays, and technical difficulties. When the interface works smoothly and quickly, products and processes seem to "slide" effortlessly through the R&D/Innovation process. When it does not, the process falters and often breaks down. In many cases, production people serve as "receivers" of technology from R&D.

(d)   <u>The Organizational Setting of the R&D/Interface</u> - includes both the formal organizational structure and the "way the system really works." The latter involves: the decision and communication processes; distribution and use of personal and organizational power; credibility and trust; actual resource allocation (how the people, facilities, and funds are actually allocated and used vs. the formal budgets); and many other factors which can influence R&D/Innovation productivity and effectiveness. In this series of studies, we are looking at a variety of organizational settings for the R&D/Production interface, including: highly centralized and highly decentralized organizations, large and small organizations, and various levels of technological sophistication.

(e)   <u>Productivity of the Interface</u> - the way in which product and process innovations are transferred between R&D and production. Productivity is considered in terms of: speed and cost of transfer; effect on the technical features of the innovation (e.g., quality, usability, reliability, maintainability); impacts on the organization (conflict, reduction or enhancement of organizational effectiveness); and impact on individual managers and technical people (stress, skill-development, etc.).

(f) <u>Imbedded Technology Capabilities</u> – those informal individual skills and organizational capabilities which can significantly affect the success of the R&D/Innova-
tion process, but which are not necessarily represented in formal laboratories or
functional groups in the organization. They represent the accumulated experience
on "how to do things", what works and does not work, and clever approaches which
are not part of the formal bag of tricks of a particular discipline. In some sense,
imbedded technology (IT) is a residual when the formal R&D components of the
overall R&D/Innovation process are removed. One test for "stand alone" IT is
the appearance of innovation and technological capability in the absence of formal
R&D organizations and roles. An elegant or rigorous definition of IT is not yet
available and it is not clear that one would satisfy all interested parties. Imbedded
Technology, as we use the term in this chapter, involves several kinds of things,
loosely defined for the present:

(1) Specific <u>knowledge</u> which is (a) embodied in materials, products, processes,
procedures, and systems and which (b) accrued or occurred in a gradual, non-
break-through manner.

(2) <u>Ideas</u> for or knowledge of how to make improvements in materials, products,
processes, procedures, and systems which may not have been specifically
incorporated, but which may be available "on the shelf."

(3) The variety of <u>individual</u> technical <u>skills</u> which are not readily classified
or even described, but which involve accumulated experience on: how to
do things, what works and what doesn't work, etc.

(4) The aggregate clusters of individual skills which make up an <u>organizational</u>
<u>capability</u>--"a first rate design group," "a savvy start-up crew," "a clever
and innovative methods department."

CONCEPTUAL MODELS, PERTINENT LITERATURE, AND EMERGING PROPOSITIONS[3]

1.   A Simplified, Integrated Model

Based on various field studies and experience of researchers, an illustrative <u>case study com-</u>
<u>posite</u> is given, as follows, to introduce the integrated model presented in this section:

> At the insistence of Sales and Marketing in a consumer products company, R&D
> developed a new product to meet a specific customer's needs. The product turned
> out to be limited in potential volume but, according to Sales, it was critical in
> importance to retain the good will of one key customer. There was substantial
> pressure on R&D to develop the product within a very tight time frame. The
> product was of such a character that it required a substantial change in processing
> procedures within the production facility, if this new product was to be commercially
> produced. Manufacturing management was involved late in the project and just
> prior to going into a scale-up stage. The V.P. of Manufacturing balked vigorously
> and refused to implement the new process without assurances that the market size
> was sufficient to warrant large capital expenditures and a substantial reduction
> of plant volume (productivity). Sales and Marketing tried to push through the new
> product, but a new development by a competitor changed their priorities and they
> began to move in different directions. Top management has been somewhat aloof
> during this, waiting to see how things "would come out." R&D and Manufacturing
> were left in disarray and with feelings of frustration and substantial doubts about
> the criteria used in decision making.

This case study composite incorporates and reflects some of the notions/problems cited in
the various conceptual models and propositions which were employed in deriving the integrated model. The case notes problems arising from lack of corporate commitment, from differing goal orientations (goal incompatibility), from an imbalance in demand-pull in the market-

place and from lack of coupling with manufacturing. There were pressures to act prematurely with inappropriate production capabilities. Substantial conflict resulted which had negative impacts on productivity and project success.

Figure 1 gives the coordinated model integrating the various theories posited in this research. The model indicates that three primary elements may be considered to serve as independent variables, i.e., conceptually, as the "driving factors" which determine the success and behavioral dimensions of various projects (dependent variables). The driving factors include level of commitment, intra-organizational interactions, and inter-organizational factors. Interface facilitators are constrained by barriers which impede the technology transfer during the innovation process. Overriding challenges to the project manager are: to ensure a high level of corporate/divisional commitment to the process of innovation; to make certain there is appropriate support in the environment to "pull" the innovations; to have proper facilitators in-place within the organization such as key communicators, product champions, imbedded technology capabilities, and adequate coupling of manufacturing; and to be able to deal effectively with such barriers to transfer as complexity, uncertainty, and goal incompatability.

Inter-Organizational Interactions

External and inter-organizational factors represent an important component of the independent (or input) variables developed in the integrated model (Figure 1). These factors and the resulting model of Figure 2 were deduced from considerations of organizational structure and process, power dynamics, intergroup climate, communications problems, performance evaluation and goal compatibility.

Both the "wisdom" and theory-based literature suggest numerous "arrangements" which are pertinent to the topic of organizational interfaces. Examples of arrangements range from the use of proper procedures for effecting technology transfer, to the use of individuals, dyads, teams and departments for improving success ratios in developing and introducing new products within corporations (Johnson and Jones, 1957; and Quinn and Mueller, 1963). Gerstenfeld (1977) proposed five basic mechanisms (or arrangements for transferring technology from R&D to manufacturing, namely: product specifications or drawings, manufacturing participation in R&D, R&D participation in manufacturing, use of a corporate coordinator or use of transfer teams.) Various methods of coordinating activities (coordinating mechanisms) may be applied depending on the organization's design parameters (cf. Mintzberg, 1983). The alternative mechanisms encompass the pre-programmed or the impersonal mode, the personal mode involving mutual task adjustments among individuals, and the group coordination mode involving mutual task adjustments among groups (Van de Ven, et al, 1976). Further differentiation of personal and group coordination modes can be distinguished by considering the relative permanence of the new products work unit, the commitment of time, and the extent to which the work unit services the entire firm (corporate), a division, a product group, or a product line (Bensen and Chasen, 1976). Van de Ven, et al (1976) showed that as the level of uncertainty increases for various tasks, there is correspondingly greater frequency of mutual work adjustments to facilitate the work process. The mutual work adjustments operate through horizontal communications channels. Group meetings are employed to effect coordination when hierarchical and impersonal programming are inadequate (Van de Ven, et al 1976, p. 332), and when work interdependence necessitates facilitative arrangements to maintain work flow (Thompson (1967)).

The power structure within the company can be systematically analyzed using the strategic-contingencies theory of interdepartmental power proposed by Hickson, et al, (1971). Using Emerson's (1962) concept of power arising out of dependency in a social relationship, Hickson et al (1971) identified three variables contributing to intra-organizational dependence: (1) the degree to which a sub-unit copes with uncertainty, (2) the extent to which the sub-units' coping activities are substitutable; and (3) centrality, referring to the varying degree, above a minimum, with which the activities of a sub-unit are linked with those of other sub-units. At the R&D-Manufacturing interface, power is, perhaps, most strongly based on a department's ability to cope with the uncertainty faced by other departments.

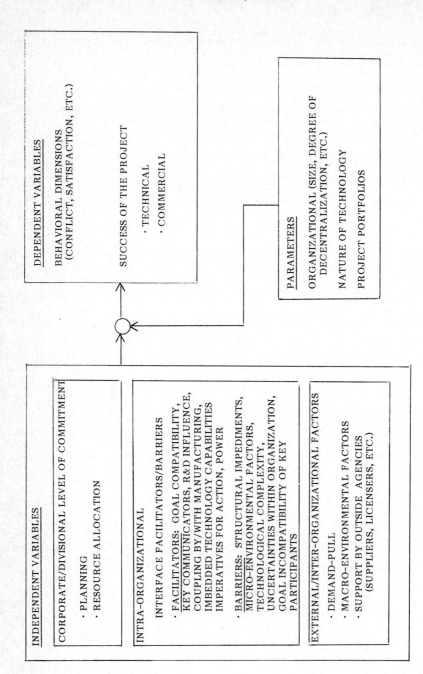

FIGURE 1.　INTEGRATED MODEL FOR FACTORS OF IMPORTANCE AT INTERFACES IN THE R&D/INNOVATION PROCESS

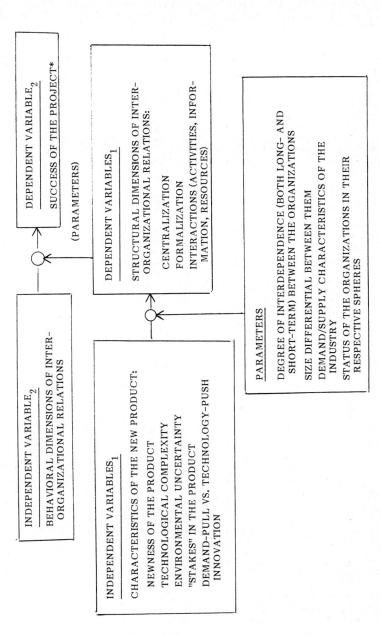

INDEPENDENT VARIABLE$_2$

BEHAVIORAL DIMENSIONS OF INTER-ORGANIZATIONAL RELATIONS

DEPENDENT VARIABLE$_2$

SUCCESS OF THE PROJECT*

(PARAMETERS)

DEPENDENT VARIABLES$_1$

STRUCTURAL DIMENSIONS OF INTER-ORGANIZATIONAL RELATIONS:

CENTRALIZATION
FORMALIZATION
INTERACTIONS (ACTIVITIES, INFOR-MATION, RESOURCES)

INDEPENDENT VARIABLES$_1$

CHARACTERISTICS OF THE NEW PRODUCT:

NEWNESS OF THE PRODUCT
TECHNOLOGICAL COMPLEXITY
ENVIRONMENTAL UNCERTAINTY
"STAKES" IN THE PRODUCT
DEMAND-PULL vs. TECHNOLOGY-PUSH INNOVATION

PARAMETERS

DEGREE OF INTERDEPENDENCE (BOTH LONG- AND SHORT-TERM) BETWEEN THE ORGANIZATIONS
SIZE DIFFERENTIAL BETWEEN THEM
DEMAND/SUPPLY CHARACTERISTICS OF THE INDUSTRY
STATUS OF THE ORGANIZATIONS IN THEIR RESPECTIVE SPHERES

*NON-ECONOMIC INDICATORS

FIGURE 2: TECHNICAL COOPERATION BETWEEN MANUFACTURERS AND DISTRIBUTORS OF NEW PRODUCTS (PRASAD)

A review of the organizational (Barth, 1970; Douds 1970) and interrorganizational literature (Benson, 1975; Reve 1980) helped identify various behavioral dimensions that are important for effective intergroup functioning. These behavioral dimensions are defined as follows:

Intergroup Climate: The relatively enduring quality of the intergroup socio-technical system which (a) is experienced by members of two task interdependent groups and (b) influences their interpersonal and task interactions...(Barth, 1970).

Communication Problems: A measure of the proper ties and adequacy (as perceived by the respondent) of the task-relevant information exchange between the focal group and its reference group (Barth, 1970).

Performance Evaluation: The judgment by members of one group of the value to them of the work by the other (Benson, 1975). Positive evaluation will be reflected in increasingly cooperative arrangements, while negative evaluation may be an obstacle (Reve, 1980).

Goal Compatibility: The extent to which both groups perceive they can simultaneously attain their goals given the actions and/or goal of the other (Reve, 1980).

An inter-organizational model was developed by applying the above concepts to understand the nature of technical cooperative between manufacturers and distributers of new products (Figure 2, Prasad). This two-tier model separates independent variables into those comprising characteristics of the new product and those involving behavioral dimensions of inter-organizational relations. The first tier is operated upon by certain parameters which relate to the nature of the organizations involved, e.g., to the size differential, degree of interdependence, etc. Structural dimensions of inter-organizational relations (dependent variables-1) are related to the characteristics of the new product (independent variables-1), i.e., its newness, the technological complexity, the environmental uncertainty, "stakes" for the new products and the dynamics involving demand vs. technology-push for the innovation. This evolving subsystem then is perceived to interact as parameters in the second tier process. In that subsystem, the behavioral dimensions of inter-organizational relations are related to the success of the project (the second level of dependent variables).

The first five propositions of this chapter evolved from the inter-organization model of Figure 1, as follows:

Proposition 1. Greater Productivity at the R&D/Manufacturing interface is positively related to use of personal/group coordination modes and reciprocal work arrangements to facilitate work flow.

Proposition 2. For Technology-push or means-stimulated innovation, the greater the power of R&D, the greater the productivity of the R&D/Manufacturing interface.

Proposition 3. For demand-pull or needs-stimulated innovations, the greater the power of R&D, the lower the productivity of the R&D/Manufacturing interface. (This trend is offset by the presence of marketing orientations within R&D).

Proposition 4. The productivity of the R&D/Manufacturing interface is positively related to:

(a)   greater power for R&D at the Research phase;
(b)   balanced power between R&D and Manufacturing in the Development phase;
(c)   greater power for Manufacturing in the Engineering/Pilot Plant phase.

Proposition 5. The productivity of the R&D/Manufacturing interface is positively related to favorably promoting the behavioral dimensions, by fostering:

(a) high levels of warmth/interteam spirit as evidenced by a harmonious intergroup climate;
(b) lower levels of communication problems as perceived by members of the two groups;
(c) mutually positive performance evaluation;
(d) a high degree of intergroup goal compatibility.

Certain salient implications may be derived from the inter-organization model of <u>Figure 2</u> and the derived propositions 1-5. First, it is suggested that the nature of structural dimensions of centralized and formalized activities, and the frequency and quality of interactions between groups, will be influenced by the characteristics of each new product, i.e., its newness, complexity, etc. These structural dimensions in turn influence the behavioral dimensions of inter-organizational relations. The emerging challenge to the project manager is appropriately focused on managing behavioral dimensions, in the inter-organizational context, to achieve: a favorable intergroup climate, proper communications, positive performance evaluation and a high level of goal compatibility between groups. Appropriate behavioral patterns would also be expected to promote the productivity of the R&D/Manufacturing interface.

The inter-organization model of Prasad leads logically to a consideration of the technology acquisition model by Sen (<u>Figure 3</u>). In this model, the role of R&D in acquiring and implementing new technology is developed. The model applies to situations where organizations must go "outside" to acquire new technology. As such, the model has a strong emphasis on inter-organizational factors which include: the degree of R&D contact with outside groups, the urgency perceived in relation to competitive organizations, and the extent to which the needed technology exists in the desired form.

Sen extends the focus to include intra-organizational factors, since these relate to the adapting organizations' ability to <u>implement</u> the new technology. The intra-organizational factors include: R&D's influence over other interfacial entities (such as production, marketing, etc.); its credibility; and its capabilities.

Personality and attitude factors are also included, such as those relating to the specific nature of R&D management and the attitude of top management towards R&D. These notions suggest that there should be an appropriate congruence of various factors which are favorable to the technology acquisition/implementation process. These inter-organizational, intra-organizational, and personality/attitude factors of Sen constituted his portfolio of independent variables.

The dependent variables of greater relevance to Sen were the extent to which R&D groups played a role during acquisition/implementation stages and the nature of such roles. Thus, the R&D involvement in the acquisition/implementation of innovations is perceived to be related to the aforementioned inter-organizational, intra-organizational, and personality/attitude factors which are most strongly directed to the character and strength of the R&D component of an organization.

The acquisition/implementation of the new technology is impacted by certain parameters, according to Sen, which include: the nature of the technology, the contractual arrangements involved, and the economic resources available.

Propositions 6-14 are related to the Sen model and are given as follows:

Proposition 6. The greater the extent to which a research lab is <u>exclusively</u> chartered on any development in a given product/process, the fewer are the problems it is likely to encounter with production. (A non-exclusive charter would be where, e.g., in printed circuits a Research center draws up the circuit but a division lab has the basic charter for "printed circuit research" and Quality Control has the charter for material specs that would go into making such circuits).

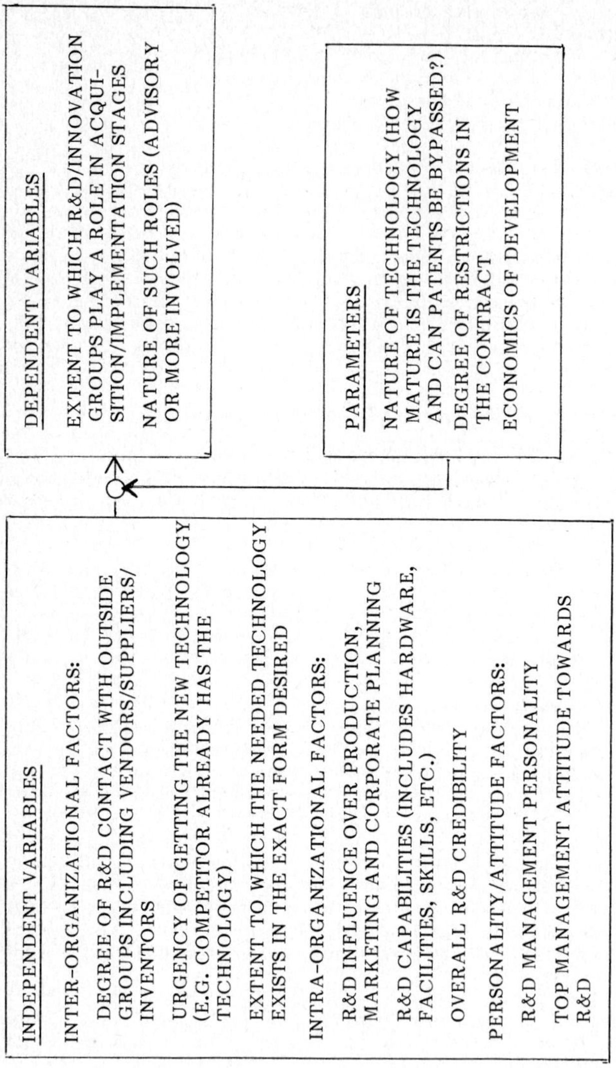

A. Rubenstein, M. Ginn

INDEPENDENT VARIABLES

INTER-ORGANIZATIONAL FACTORS:

DEGREE OF R&D CONTACT WITH OUTSIDE
GROUPS INCLUDING VENDORS/SUPPLIERS/
INVENTORS

URGENCY OF GETTING THE NEW TECHNOLOGY
(E.G. COMPETITOR ALREADY HAS THE
TECHNOLOGY)

EXTENT TO WHICH THE NEEDED TECHNOLOGY
EXISTS IN THE EXACT FORM DESIRED

INTRA-ORGANIZATIONAL FACTORS:

R&D INFLUENCE OVER PRODUCTION,
MARKETING AND CORPORATE PLANNING

R&D CAPABILITIES (INCLUDES HARDWARE,
FACILITIES, SKILLS, ETC.)

OVERALL R&D CREDIBILITY

PERSONALITY/ATTITUDE FACTORS:

R&D MANAGEMENT PERSONALITY

TOP MANAGEMENT ATTITUDE TOWARDS
R&D

DEPENDENT VARIABLES

EXTENT TO WHICH R&D/INNOVATION
GROUPS PLAY A ROLE IN ACQUI-
SITION/IMPLEMENTATION STAGES

NATURE OF SUCH ROLES (ADVISORY
OR MORE INVOLVED)

PARAMETERS

NATURE OF TECHNOLOGY (HOW
MATURE IS THE TECHNOLOGY
AND CAN PATENTS BE BYPASSED?)

DEGREE OF RESTRICTIONS IN
THE CONTRACT

ECONOMICS OF DEVELOPMENT

FIGURE 3: THE ROLE OF R&D IN ACQUIRING AND IMPLEMENTING NEW TECHNOLOGY (SEN)

Proposition 7. Where the Research labs are not part of the division but more autonomous (corporate), an aggressive marketing strategy may be required to convince production of the usefulness of the new product/process.

Proposition 8. In corporate labs where the lab enters a new area more at the behest of top management rather than the production units and given that the lab has little influence directly on the production units, then besides aggressive marketing of their ideas, the lab needs to work out a cooperative development strategy with the manufacturing units at an early stage.

Proposition 9. At an early stage such cooperation need not have any personnel commitment on the part of the manufacturing unit but should result in a realistic view of manufacturing constraints and an evaluation of the impact of the innovation on manufacturing. If this is done, there will be fewer problems later on.

Proposition 10. At later stages, there should be more manufacturing commitments to the development of the product/process. Where this is done there is a greater likelihood of a smooth interface with production.

Proposition 11. Where the research lab has relative autonomy vis a vis the production unit, e.g., a corporate research lab, the existence of some kind of "warranty" from the lab will facilitate the transfer to production. Such warranty will ensure the lab's involvement in the case of "bugs."

Proposition 12. The greater the number of people with "factory savvy" and personal contacts in production, the fewer will be the problems encountered in the transfer process (this is related to the "IT" concept).

Proposition 13. Rotational programs where people from factories come to the lab are useful in the R&D-Production interface if such rotations occur in the context of specific development projects.

Proposition 14. An internship program where scientists work under a factory manager, facilitates the R&D-Production interface if the intern learns the formal routines of factory life and gains an increased understanding and respect for the pressures on and the goals of the production people and if the intern increases the credibility of the lab.

Propositions 6-14 suggest that the activities and character of the R&D component are central in importance to the innovation process, and extend from acquisition of technology through implementation with manufacturing. Implications are that a strong R&D component, combined with early manufacturing involvement and commitment, would facilitate technology transfer across organizational interfaces. Personnel interchange and manpower rotational programs between R&D and production provide effective means for promoting understanding and cooperation.

In a sense, the conceptual model and perspectives of Sen have provided a bridging from the strong inter-organizational focus of Prasad to a greater emphasis on the intra-organizational elements of the R&D/Innovation process.

Intra-Organizational Factors

The R&D/Production Interface and the Type of Innovation Involved. Although a growing literature has appeared on the R&D-Marketing interface in organizations (Souder, 1978; Ginn, 1981; Mansfield, 1975), little empirical research has been done on the R&D-Production interface. Wisdom and informed opinion suggests the latter may be equally important. Twiss (1980, p. 111) observes that when a technology strategy is being developed, a major consideration is both the capability of production to manufacture the new product and the ability to manufacture it at a cost that leaves adequate profit. R&D project evaluation criteria often do not include such considerations, and it is up to the generalist, i.e. the top manager, to make such considerations explicit. The earlier in the product/project planning cycle these problems are considered, the smoother the transition from R&D to production. Yet the creative process of R&D might be inhibited by introducing manufacturing cost criteria prematurely (related to Prop. 15, below).

It is also noted that the optimal time to incorporate manufacturing capability and cost information into R&D project selection may vary with the type of innovation. New products that are radical technological departures from existing offerings in the industry usually require process changes in production (Hage, 1980). Valid manufacturing cost estimates and capability statements may be extremely difficult to obtain under these conditions (also related to Prop. 15). Propositions 15-17 were contributed to the POMRAD R&D/Production interface project by J. Ettlie (cf. 1973).

> Proposition 15. Successful introduction of manufacturing capability and cost information criteria into the project selection process of R&D depends on appropriate timing. The optimum time allows the creativity of R&D to generate a secure enough idea to work with in engineering but is not so late as to allow projects that will produce technically feasible but too costly manufacturing plans. Top management, or the role of the organizational generalist, will be crucial in insuring a higher number of successful products through optimal timing of this manufacturing information for the R&D selection process.

Organization Strategy. It has often been asserted that operations problems in organizations stem primarily from the shortsighted planning horizon of production management. If this is true, it may be with good reason, or is justifiable from the production perspective in any organization. Miller and Graham (1981, p. 567) observe that as marketing has become the dominant force in strategic decision making or long-range planning sessions, production concerns are not taken into account. Although the training and attitudes of production people often contribute to this problem, projecting an image of apparent aversion to long-range planning methodologies and orientations, the imbalance of contributions to strategy by marketing, R&D and production has probably contributed significantly to many productivity problems and lack of competitive effectiveness of many American firms. Given that new plant and new process decisions are perhaps two of the most significant strategic issues of any organization, operations personnel have been unwisely excluded or poorly prepared to participate in strategic decision making. The number of start-up surprises that most organizations experience with especially new process technology is one of the symptoms of this problem. The interface between R&D and production would benefit greatly by the integration that would be forced by a balanced participation of the key functional areas in strategic planning (Prop. 16).

> Proposition 16. The degree to which R&D, production and marketing participate equally and influence organization strategy will influence the effectiveness of the R&D, production and marketing interfaces. If production or operations does not participate and influence organization strategy, significant new product implementation problems will result, ultimately having a significant negative impact on organization effectiveness.

CAD/CAM and the R&D/Production Interface. Computer aided design and manufacturing systems have had a significant impact on companies world-wide, and the computer has obviously made the transition from the office to the shop floor. However, there are significant problems that accompany the introduction of these systems. The startup periods are often very long and stressful for participants (Ettlie and Rubenstein, 1980). Implementation often uses more resources than intended by the organization (Gerwin, 1981). Most firms do not realize the full productivity potential benefits of new discrete parts manufacturing technology (Stecke, 1981). One estimate has been calculated that suggests that CAD/CAM systems have the potential to enhance productivity by five to 20 times, but seldom is this potential realized (Donlan, 1980). It seems apparent that the production-R&D interface contributes to the underutilization of CAD/CAM systems.

One of the basic decisions that an organization has to make when adopting new discrete parts manufacturing technology is the degree of centralization of the system. Does the firm go with a centralized CAD/CAM or a decentralized, programmable microprocessor-controlled machine tool (Miller and Graham, 1981, p. 565)? Clearly, the degree of centralization will depend upon many factors, including the organization's commitment to the philosophy of technological change in discrete parts manufacturing (Ettlie, 1973), the strategy of the firm, including its implementation strategy and manufacturing policy, and R&D policy (Prop. 17).

> Proposition 17. The degree of fit between an organization's strategy for and commitment to process innovation in discrete parts manufacturing will determine the success of implementing this technology. The firm's strategy and structure should be consistent or congruent in order to be successful. The type of commitment and structure for effective CAD/CAM utilization will probably not be the same as for effective numerical control or computer numerical control (CNC) utilization.

Key Communicators. The notion that communications are important in intergroup relations has been extended to the intra-organizational area by Knapp in considering the role of key communicators. Throughout the organization, key communicators serve as facilitators of the R&D/Innovation process.

The literature suggests that key communicators differ from their colleagues in several important respects: (Allen, 1977; Tushman, 1977; Rubenstein, et al, 1976):

(1) They read a great deal more of the scientific and technical literature.
(2) They maintain broader, more diverse and longer term relationships with experts in the field located outside of their immediate working environment.
(3) They understand how the perspective of outside experts differs from that of their colleagues within the organization.
(4) They are able to translate information into terms that can be understood and are relevant to their colleagues within the organization.
(5) They are effective filters of information, channeling information appropriate to the current needs of colleagues within the work environment.

As technology gets defined in terms of the interests, goals, and the culture of particular organizations, it becomes difficult to translate across organization boundaries through sole reliance on formal mechanisms. Informal "linking" persons are needed to promote innovation.

The macro-organizational literature (i.e. Lawrence and Lorsch, 1967) differentiates the functional specialties within the organization (e.g. marketing, manufacturing, R&D) on such dimensions as time frame, goals, language, and structure. This suggests a parallel difficulty of translating technological information across internal organizational boundaries into terms that are understandable, relevant, and appreciated by individuals in other functional specialties--in this case within manufacturing.

In our study of key communicator effectiveness in a decentralized industrial organization, we have noted the apparent importance that effective key communicators and their clients, who are in the manufacturing operation, attribute to such factors as the ability of the key communicator to respond in a short time frame. Manufacturing prefers to deal with R&D people who understand the particular constraints, demands, responsibilities and concerns of the manufacturing function. Another characteristic that appears to be important is the willingness of the key communicator to initiate contact with relevant individuals in the manufacturing operation, "to wander down to the shop floor with relative frequency" and give some indication that they know and appreciate the culture (e.g. hard hat and safety glasses if a key communicator visits a site where that is appropriate dress protocol)(Proposition 18).

<u>Proposition 18.</u> The effectiveness with which a key communicator manages the
R&D-Manufacturing interface = f (1. the ability to respond quickly.)
(2. an understanding of the concerns and
constraints of the manufacturing function.)
(3. the willingness to initiate contact with the
manufacturing function and act in accordance
with the dictates of their culture.)

Intra-organizational dynamics relating to the R&D/Production interface were studied in
depth by Ginn using the model described in <u>Figure 4</u>. The Ginn model was based on the
following theoretical concepts:

<u>Imperatives for Action and Success</u>. Imperatives for action are literally commands to per-
form or accomplish certain tasks. The "command" may emanate from an individual or agen-
cy or it may arise from perceptions of a chain of events (stimuli) or from changes in a micro-
or macro-environment. Kahn (1956) notes in quoting Bertrand Russell that "mankind" decided
that it would submit to monotony and tedium in order to diminish the risk of starvation.
The perceived need of individuals to diminish such risk is an example of an imperative for
action. Rubenstein et al (1976) studied products in nine field sites which had various levels
of performance in the innovation of different product types. The examination of the impetus
for innovation for over 100 projects revealed that certain factors were important for technical and/or for commercial success. These significant success factors relating to impetus
were summarized under the heading of "recognition of needs" and included: "level of explicit-
ness of need," "maintenance of rate of growth," "responses to changes in government actions
or tariffs," "degree of urgency," and the "relative advantage of the innovation" (Rubenstein
et al, 1976, p. 17). Included among significant factors related to outcomes was the "level of
profitability."

The degree to which there exists a powerful impetus (or imperative) to develop, scale-up, and
commercially produce specific new products is postulated as a key independent variable
which determines the degree of overall success of the R&D-Production interface. The basis
for this postulate derives from the researches of Rubenstein and coworkers (1976), and from
certain landmark, enormously successful projects, e.g., the atomic bomb (Bernstein, 1976),
Polaris (Sapolsky, 1972) and Apollo (Fortune Magazine, 1974). Based on this literature,
"imperatives for action" constitutes a key independent variable which positively correlates
with interface success. The importance of the concept of imperatives for action particularly
arises when there is a gap between expected performance and actual performance, and when
pressures for successful project completion are substantial.

<u>Goal Compatibility, Power, and Conflict</u>. Schmidt and Kochan (1972) examined conflict from
a conceptual point of view, based on a comprehensive literature survey. They defined <u>conflict</u>
as being dysfunctional (compared to <u>competition</u> which could be functional). Conflict was
held to occur when two organization members hold divergent goals and one member is motivated to behave such that goal attainment by the other is impeded. Accordingly, divergent or
<u>incompatible</u> goals among organizational subsystems such as for R&D and production would
be expected to yield conflict when performance of the goals results in outcome (products)
having characteristics which impede one or the other's (in this case production's) goal attainment. For production, the assumed goal of special interest would be to maximize productivity
(output or profit per manhour), subject to certain constraints.

Hunger and Stern (1976) examined the effects of <u>superordinate</u> goals on conflict. Superordinate goals were considered to be goals which would be highly appealing to conflicting groups.
The attainment of superordinate goals is beyond the abilities of any one group, and requires
concerted action, so that a means of reducing dysfunctional conflict was postulated. Application of superordinate goals are considered to afford elements not only of conflict reduction
but of power exercises and motivation as well (Props. 21-24).

According to the "strategic contingencies" theory of Hickson et al (1971), uncertainties of
inputs, throughputs, and outputs must be dealt with if organizations are to be effective. The

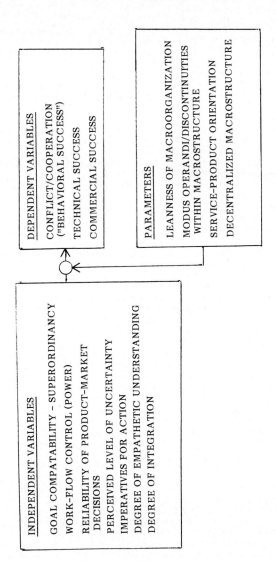

FIGURE 4: KEY FACTORS AFFECTING THE R&D-PRODUCTION INTERFACE (GINN)

ability of individuals and organizations to effectively cope with uncertainty gives power and is an exercise of power; and this represents one of Hickson et al's hypotheses. Power also derives from the inability of an organizational subunit to be substituted by another. The occurrence of substitutions imposed by one subunit over another, or by a higher authority, therefore, represents the application of power. These exercises of power are reflected in the number and frequency with which interventions are made. Resistance to such incursions is postulated to represent "territoriality," which may have positive as well as negative consequences. The incidence of territorial behavior by R&D or production or other pertinent subsystems is evidence that power is being exercised.

In the project SAPPHO at the University of Sussex, where success and failure in industrial innovations were studied, attempts were made to quantify the product champion function (Maidique, 1980). It was concluded that responsible individuals (product champions) operating in successful innovations have more power and authority than those individuals operating in unsuccessful attempts. Key roles of product champions are indicated in the development and implementation of innovations. During implementation (or commercialization), the role frequently involves that of an "executive champion," who has direct or indirect influence over allocation of resources, and can direct this power to a new technological innovation. Because there is uncertainty, there are also risks which must be assumed by the product champion.

According to Lawrence and Lorsch (1967, a,b), patterns leading to a conflict are called into play when mechanistically and organically oriented subsystems are called upon to assume the others' character to some substantial degree. This situation arises at the R&D-Production interface during scale-up and explains some of the conflict which occurs. Lawrence and Lorsch (1967a) established that the degree of differentiation of behavior and orientation between the various subsystems was inversely related to the degree of integration obtained between these subsystems. Integrative roles and devices were positively linked with success in achieving goals. It is also postulated that organizations can institutionalize integration so that it occurs essentially in the absence of explicit integrator roles; and, in such cases, the positive correlation of ad hoc integrating structures with project success will be weak (Selznick, p. 99 in Rubenstein and Haberstroh, 1966). Task related asymmetries, mutual dependency, differing reward criteria, sharing of common resources, and ambiguities of role and expectations affect the degree to which conflict is prevalent between organizations subsystems (Souder and Chakrabarti, 1978). Technical and marketing uncertainty were proposed to be positively related to the degree of conflict present between marketing and R&D (based on Lawrence and Lorsch, 1967b). It is postulated that this relationship between uncertainty (of outcome) and conflict is particularly strong and positive for the R&D and production interface. Such uncertainties may arise from inappropriate product design, or from faulty processes in production. Negative consequences from product defects have an immediate impact on productivity and, therefore, are expected to result in severe issues of conflict.

The above theoretical development led to the following propositions (19-24) of Ginn:

> Proposition 19. The degree of overall success of a project will depend strongly
> and positively on the extent to which imperatives exist in the environment
> (micro- and macro-) to impel successful completion of projects. Examples of
> such postulated imperatives include the necessity to fulfill a technological or
> marketing opportunity, the necessity to respond to a directive from a highly-
> placed product champion, and so on.

> Proposition 20. When imperatives for action impel premature introduction of
> products into production prior to the total control of technical uncertainties,
> conflicts of serious proportions will arise, and the level of conflict will be
> higher in those projects which have imperatives for action than those which do
> not. At the same time that conflict exists, because imperatives for favorable
> actions also exist, there may be the apparent anomaly that the degree of
> cooperation among subsystems be high when conflict is high.

Proposition 21. Interdepartmental conflict among key organizational subsystems (R&D and Production) will increase as the degree of uncertainty increases for acceptability of product outcomes in micro- and macro-environments. Uncertainty will tend to increase with the complexity of the production process.

Proposition 22. If the process employed during production and the product's overall performance following production are consistent or compatible with the goals of key organizational subsystems, then interdepartmental conflict is likely to be lower than when the performance results are not compatible with production expectations. Interdepartmental conflict will be particularly severe when goals of the production subsystems are incompatible with the attributes of the process used to derive the finished product.

Proposition 23. Superordinate goals will tend to be positively correlated: with conflict (between R&D and production); with uncertainty of product outcome acceptability; and with imperatives for action which impel the project forward, --aiming for successful completion.

Proposition 24. Integration may tend to increase with uncertainty and when imperatives for action are present. The relationship is predicted to be somewhat weak because, in many innovating industrial organizations, integration has already been formalized or "institutionalized" by the organizational power structure.

The importance attributed by Ginn to the actions of highly placed product champions, to the applications of power, and to imperatives for action, suggests that top management would play a key role in the R&D/Innovation process. This line of thinking leads naturally to the conceptual model of B. Fischer (Figure 5) which emphasizes the importance of top manage-ment's commitment as a driving force in implementing a new process into production. A further thrust of B. Fischer's focus is the recognition that technology transfer across the R&D/Production interface is a change process. To a substantial degree, this change process emanates from the corporate level or from the commitment of top management.

The area of particular interest to B. Fischer involves corporate-divisional relations in intro-ducing new production technology (Figure 5). The dependent variables of time required, costs, and effectiveness in implementation of a new process technology are related to the commit-ment of top and divisional management and to adaptation of production personnel to the attendant change required. In this model, the parameters are: organization size, degree of decentralization and market share, and the scope of the project.

Resistance to Change. Hage and Aiken (1970) noted that change in complex organizations is a multi-staged process, as is the process of technological innovation. These authors argued this since production often emphasizes high volume of production as one of its salient goals. This led Hage and Aiken to hypothesize that: -when volume of production is high there will be a correspondingly low rate of program change -- assuming that production's concurrence is needed for the change. Thus, organizations with high volumes of production would be more inclined to resist the development and introduction of new products or services. Hage and Aiken suggest that the "elite" (or top management) of an organization, through their policies and levels of commitment to change, determine to a great extent the nature and degree of change that takes place. Levy and Zaltman (1975, p.46) note that pressure for change may originate among the top managers of an organization who direct change activities downward or they may arise at a "grass-roots level." Citing Rogers (1973), Levy and Zaltman suggest that changes which are initiated by "elites," i.e. are "top-down," may be more likely to suc-ceed than are bottom-up changes.

A change will usually be opposed by the affected employees unless they have requested the change. This is particularly true in the case of supervisory personnel since they may be stak-ing their status, prestige, or job on the change (Huse, 1980). When a change is requested by an individual or group, there will be a commitment to the execution of the change. There will be ego-involvement (Allport, 1954) and, therefore, a commitment to the successful im-plementation of the change. Ego-involvement is a deep level of commitment and will result

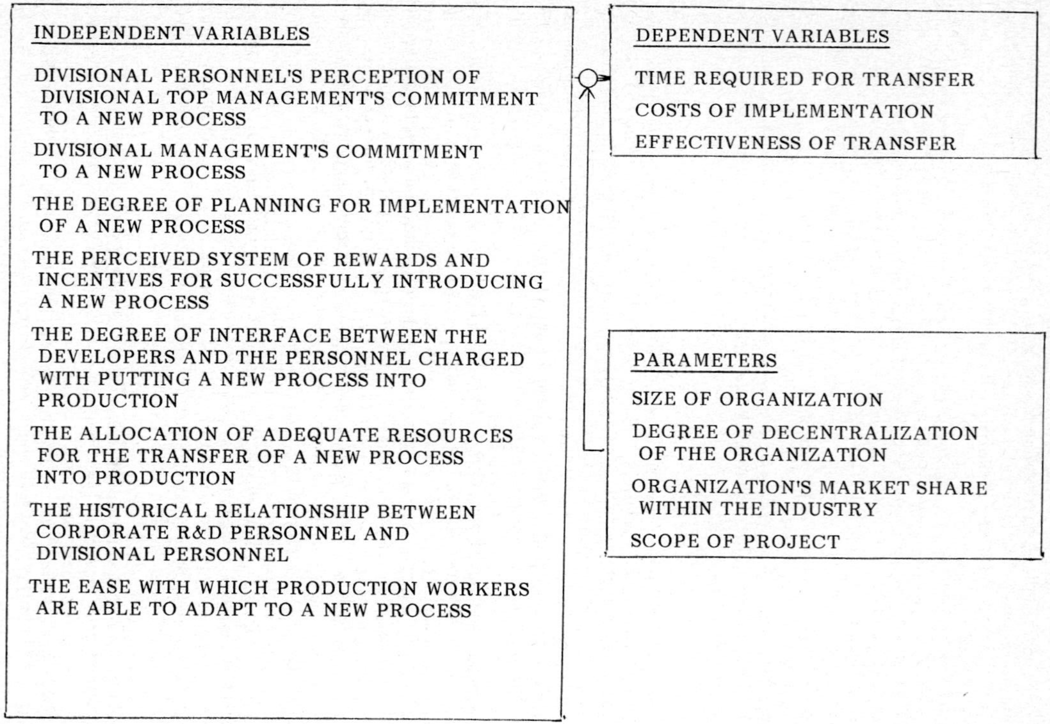

DEPENDENT VARIABLES

TIME REQUIRED FOR TRANSFER
COSTS OF IMPLEMENTATION
EFFECTIVENESS OF TRANSFER

PARAMETERS

SIZE OF ORGANIZATION
DEGREE OF DECENTRALIZATION OF THE ORGANIZATION
ORGANIZATION'S MARKET SHARE WITHIN THE INDUSTRY
SCOPE OF PROJECT

INDEPENDENT VARIABLES

DIVISIONAL PERSONNEL'S PERCEPTION OF DIVISIONAL TOP MANAGEMENT'S COMMITMENT TO A NEW PROCESS

DIVISIONAL MANAGEMENT'S COMMITMENT TO A NEW PROCESS

THE DEGREE OF PLANNING FOR IMPLEMENTATION OF A NEW PROCESS

THE PERCEIVED SYSTEM OF REWARDS AND INCENTIVES FOR SUCCESSFULLY INTRODUCING A NEW PROCESS

THE DEGREE OF INTERFACE BETWEEN THE DEVELOPERS AND THE PERSONNEL CHARGED WITH PUTTING A NEW PROCESS INTO PRODUCTION

THE ALLOCATION OF ADEQUATE RESOURCES FOR THE TRANSFER OF A NEW PROCESS INTO PRODUCTION

THE HISTORICAL RELATIONSHIP BETWEEN CORPORATE R&D PERSONNEL AND DIVISIONAL PERSONNEL

THE EASE WITH WHICH PRODUCTION WORKERS ARE ABLE TO ADAPT TO A NEW PROCESS

FIGURE 5: CORPORATE-DIVISIONAL RELATIONS IN INTRODUCING NEW PRODUCTION TECHNOLOGY (B. FISCHER)

when the proposed change is in response to a perceived need. When a change is the result of a request by production personnel and the new manufacturing methods are responsive to the request, the degree of resistance to change will be low and will be correlated with the degree of responsiveness of the change to the request for change by production personnel.

Fear of the unknown is a chief cause of resistance to change (Duncan, 1981). If concerns over the possible effects of a change can be decreased, resistance to change may be reduced. In the absence of information concerning the effects of a change, there will be a tendency to expect the worst of possible outcomes from a change. Communication concerning a proposed change should involve an explanation of the goals of the change and, also, should provide for feedback from those affected by the change (Reitz, 1981). The information provided should explain not only what is to happen but also why (Sayles and Strauss, 1966). The avoidance of a complete explanation of a change that is about to be implemented will foster feelings of suspicion and powerlessness among those who will be affected. The sense of being manipulated may result in frustration and resentment may be vented through a dogged resistance to the change.

The success of communication in promoting change depends upon many factors (Newman, Summer, and Warren, 1976). Differences in perceptions, persuasiveness, personal biases, type of medium chosen, and various other elements of communication influence the effectiveness of communication and therefore, the degree of resistance to change by production personnel.

The not-invented-here syndrome is an often mentioned barrier in intergroup relations in organizations. Without a sense of ownership, there is significantly less desire to cooperate in implementing a change.

Participation must be real and not contrived (Davis, 1977; Miller, 1977). Real participation is based on respect and is acquired when a staff member recognizes the reality that he or she needs the contributions of the operating people (Von Fange, 1959). Certain conditions must be present for real participation. The atmosphere of the organization must be conducive to participation. Production personnel must see the relevance of the problem and be capable of becoming contributors to the research effort (Longenecker, 1977). Participation may have certain unexpected negative consequences (Leavitt, 1972). Production personnel involved in the research effort may question decisions made by the research team and may disagree with the ultimate results.

The above qualifications do not, by any means, diminish the significance of participation by production personnel in research efforts as a means of reducing resistance to change. There should be a strong negative correlation between production personnel involvement in a research project and their subsequent resistance to changes in manufacturing methods brought about by the research (Props. 25-26).

Proposition 25. The success of the R&D-Production interface will be negatively correlated with the degree of resistance to a change by production personnel.

Proposition 26. The degree of resistance to a change by production personnel will be negatively correlated with:

(a) the extent to which production personnel request the change;
(b) the success of the communication concerning the proposed change;
(c) the degree of involvement of production personnel in the initiation and progression of R&D effort on the technological innovation requiring the change in manufacturing methods;
(d) the perceived support for the change by production management;
(e) the perceived rewards for the successful transfer and operation of the new methods of production;
(f) the merits and value of the change as perceived by production personnel;
(g) the ability of the managers involved to manage conflict between production personnel and researchers;

(h) the amount of retraining done to adjust to the change in manufacturing
     methods; and
(i) the extent that individual work methods are favorably altered by the
     change in manufacturing methods.

Proposition 27. The likelihood that appropriate change will occur, promoting
successful technology transfer, will be positively correlated with the level of
commitment by corporate and divisional executives to project success.

Imbedded Technology. The last approach described in this research review deals with the
introduction of imbedded technology capabilities (ITCs) into a model involving the R&D/
Production interface. The notion of the importance of strong and capable technological support in technology transfer flows logically from the models of Prasad, Sen, and Ginn which
include technology components as independent or dependent variables.

Rubenstein's model (Figure 6) relates the character of ITGs (imbedded technology groups), as
independent variables to the effectiveness of transfer of technology (represented by several
dependent variables). This influence process is also acted upon by certain parameters which
include: organization size and structure, nature of the technology, and the project portfolio
existing in the organization.

According to Rubenstein (1980), imbedded technology includes clusters of special knowledge,
ideas and skills which give groups a highly effective capability for solving problems in the innovation process. Utilizing this concept, the extent of barrier reduction in technology transfer, the level of conflict, the degrees of technical and commercial success, the existence of
problems, and other dependent variables, are influenced by the degree of existence of ITCs
and the level of effectiveness and power in the organization (Figure 6).

IMPLICATIONS FOR MANAGERS AND MANAGEMENT SCIENTISTS

Even without the final results of the specific Northwestern/POMRAD studies described in this
chapter, the mere identification of key variables affecting project management at the R&D/
Production interface and their formulation into research questions and potentially testable
propositions can be of service to operating managers and management scientists in the following ways:

(1) Implications for Managers

     (a) Helping managers who are having or anticipating problems with projects
          at the R&D/Production interface to focus on common or frequently-
          encountered problems which occur relatively independently of the specific
          nature of the project, technology, or people involved.

     (b) Shifting the focus from exclusive attention to the personalities and
          behavior of individuals which may be difficult to change in the short
          run (the life of that particular project) to more general organizational
          behavior (e.g., communication and decision-making patterns) which may
          be more amenable to change by managers.

     (c) Changing the style of management of some projects from "blaming" and
          "yelling" to consideration of why things are going wrong and what changes
          in the organization and conduct of the project might prevent or ameliorate
          problems.

     (d) Providing a basis for more participative management by members of
          project teams from both sides of the interface in cooperating to improve
          the design and operations of the interface.

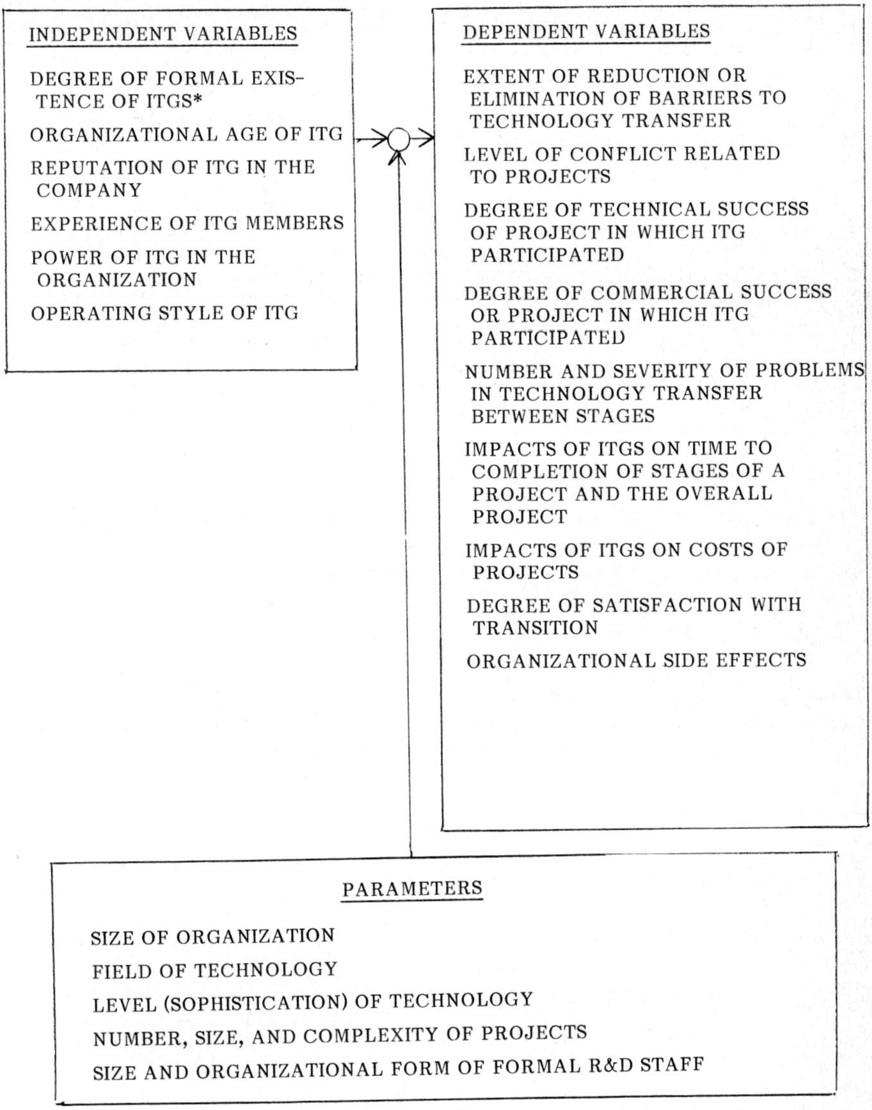

INDEPENDENT VARIABLES

DEGREE OF FORMAL EXIS-
TENCE OF ITGS*

ORGANIZATIONAL AGE OF ITG

REPUTATION OF ITG IN THE
COMPANY

EXPERIENCE OF ITG MEMBERS

POWER OF ITG IN THE
ORGANIZATION

OPERATING STYLE OF ITG

DEPENDENT VARIABLES

EXTENT OF REDUCTION OR
ELIMINATION OF BARRIERS TO
TECHNOLOGY TRANSFER

LEVEL OF CONFLICT RELATED
TO PROJECTS

DEGREE OF TECHNICAL SUCCESS
OF PROJECT IN WHICH ITG
PARTICIPATED

DEGREE OF COMMERCIAL SUCCESS
OR PROJECT IN WHICH ITG
PARTICIPATED

NUMBER AND SEVERITY OF PROBLEMS
IN TECHNOLOGY TRANSFER
BETWEEN STAGES

IMPACTS OF ITGS ON TIME TO
COMPLETION OF STAGES OF A
PROJECT AND THE OVERALL
PROJECT

IMPACTS OF ITGS ON COSTS OF
PROJECTS

DEGREE OF SATISFACTION WITH
TRANSITION

ORGANIZATIONAL SIDE EFFECTS

PARAMETERS

SIZE OF ORGANIZATION

FIELD OF TECHNOLOGY

LEVEL (SOPHISTICATION) OF TECHNOLOGY

NUMBER, SIZE, AND COMPLEXITY OF PROJECTS

SIZE AND ORGANIZATIONAL FORM OF FORMAL R&D STAFF

*IMBEDDED TECHNOLOGY GROUPS, SOME EXAMPLES ARE: PROCESS ENGINEER-
ING, PILOT PLANT, DESIGN REVIEW, COST ANALYSIS, MANUFACTURING
SYSTEMS, MATERIALS REVIEW, HEAT TREATING, FACILITIES ENGINEERING,
UNIT OPERATIONS, LUBRICATION, WELDING, COATING.

FIGURE 6: FLOW MODEL OF THE ROLE OF IMBEDDED TECHNOLOGY (IT)
IN THE R&D–PRODUCTION INTERFACE (RUBENSTEIN)

(e) Pointing up important skills and capabilities which have a low profile before, during, and after transition through the interface but which may be critical to transition and, eventually, project success.

(f) Providing lessons on "how to do the next one better," based on more careful attention to the organizational and interpersonal processes which go on during a project.

(g) De-emphasizing the bad or disruptive aspects of intergroup conflict that are influenced or caused by the characteristics of the project itself as well as value and style differences, and guiding the reduction of non-functional conflict without trying to achieve "zero conflict" --a condition which might lead to "zero progress" on the project.

(2) Implications for Management Scientists

(a) Opening up a new "product line" for management scientists (OR/MS people) in terms of studies they could do for their in-house clients.

(b) Guiding non-behaviorally-oriented OR/MS people to and through the relevant behavioral literature and converging ideas in this field.

(c) Suggesting that "measurements" are feasible in this field, even though they may be less quantitative and the "models" may be less mathematical than the OR/MS professional is used to in areas such as inventory, scheduling, or financial planning.

(d) Providing an "over-the-shoulder" look at project management from analysts who are not directly involved in the interface or transition and who may be able to objectively observe and interpret behavior that is detrimental to the success of the project.

(e) Providing a basis for "organizational design" exercises, aimed at increasing the chances of project success, by combining systematically-observed past experience in their own organizations with the general state of the art of project management.

FOOTNOTES

1 Work on this subject has been supported by a grant from the Production Research
Program, National Science Foundation and Northwestern University funds. This
chapter draws upon the dissertation research of Bruce Fischer, Martin Ginn, Connie
Knapp, Lakshmanan Prasad, and Falguni Sen, as well as the ideas of the other members
of the Northwestern R&D/Production interface team: Bruce Buchowicz, John Ettlie,
Elizer Geisler, Milton Glaser, and A. H. Rubenstein.

2 Imbedded technology is defined in item (f).

3 The 27 propositions in this chapter come from current research by several members of
POMRAD at Northwestern, as do the literature reviews in Section 3. Specifically, these
propositions were suggested by these people: 1-5, Lakshmanan Prasad; 6-14, Falguni Sen;
15-17, John Ettlie; 18, Connie Knapp; 19-24, 27, Martin Ginn; 25-26, Bruce Fischer.

REFERENCES

The references below constitute a sample of the open literature on the R&D/Production
interface and related topics. At the end of the reference list is a set of interim citations to
the work of the five dissertation students who contributed to this chapter and who are
members of Northwestern/POMRAD's "R&D/Production Interface" team.

[1]   Allport, Gordon, W., "The Psychology of Participation," The Psychological Review,
        May 1945.

[2]   Barth, Richard T., The Relationship of Intergroup Organizational Climate with
        Communication and Joint Decision Making Between Task-Interdependent and R&D
        Groups, Ph.D. Dissertation, Northwestern University, 1970.

[3]   Benson, George, and Chasen, Joseph, "The Structure of New Product Organization,"
        New York, American Management Association, 1976.

[4]   Benson, J. Kenneth, "The Interrorganizational Network as a Political Economy,"
        Administrative Science Quarterly, 20(3):229-249.

[5]   Bernstein, B. J., The Atomic Bomb, Little, Brown and Company, Boston, 1976.

[6]   Berty, J. M., "The Changing Role of the Pilot Plant," Chemical Engineering Progress,
        Vol. 75, No. 9, September 1979.

[7]   Biller, A. D. and Shanley, E. S., "Understanding the Conflicts Between R&D and
        Other Groups," Research Management, September 1975, 16-21.

[8]   Davis, Keith, Human Behavior at Work: Organizational Behavior, New York:
        McGraw-Hill Book Company, Fifth Edition, 1977.

[9]   Donlon, Thomas G.,   A CAD/CAM World?", Barrons December 22, 1980.

[10]   Douds, Charles F., The Effects of Work-Related Values on Communication Between
        R&D Groups, Doctoral Dissertation, Northwestern University 1970.

[11]   Duncan, W. Jack, Organizational Behavior, Boston: Houghton Mifflin Company,
        Second Edition, 1981.

[12] Emerson, R. E., "Power Dependence Relations," American Sociological Review, 27:
      31-41, 1962.

[13] Etienne, E. Celse, "Interactions Between Product R&D and Process Technology,"
      Research Management, January 1981, 22-27.

[14] Ettlie, J. E., "Technology Transfer from Innovators to Users;" Industrial Engineering,
      Vol. 5, No. 6, June 1973, 16-23.

[15] Ettlie, J. E. and Rubenstein, A. H., "Social Learning Theory and the Implementation
      of Production Innovation," Decision Sciences, Vol. 11, No. 4, October 1980, 648-668.

[16] Fortune Magazine, "Progress Report on the Moon Race," March 1964, 142-145.

[17] Geisler, E., An Empirical Study of a Proposed System for Monitoring Organizational
      Change in a Federal R&D Laboratory, Ph.D. dissertation, Northwestern University,
      1979.

[18] Gerstenfeld, Art, Effective Management of Research and Development, Reading,
      MA, Addison Wesley, 1970, 41-53.

[19] Gerwin, D., "Control and Evaluation in the Innovation Process: The Case of Flexible
      Manufacturing Systems," IEEE Transactions on Engineering Management, Vol. EM28,
      No. 3, August 1981, 62-70.

[20] Gerwin, Donald, "Do's and Don'ts of Computerized Manufacturing," Harvard Business
      Review, Vol. 60, No. 2, March-April 1982, 107-116.

[21] Ginn, Martin E., "A General Management Perspective," Chemical Times & Trends,
      April 1981, 33-34.

[22] Hage, J. and M. Aiken, Social Change in Complex Organizations, Random House,
      New York, 1970.

[23] Hage, Jerald, Theories of Organizations, New York, Wiley, 1980.

[24] Hickson, D. J., et al, "A Strategic Contingencies Theory of Interorganizational
      Power," Administrative Science Quarterly, 16, No. 2, June 1971, 216-222, 229.

[25] Hunger, J. D. and Stern, L. W., "An Assessment of the Functionality of the Super-
      ordinate Goal in Reducing Conflict," Academy of Management Journal, 19, No. 4,
      December 1976, 591-605.

[26] Huse, Edgar, F., Organization Development and Change, St. Paul, West Publishing
      Company, Second Edition, 1980.

[27] Johnson, Samuel C. and Jones, Conrad, "How to Organize for New Products," Harvard
      Business Review, 35 (3), 1957, 49-62.

[28] Kahn, R. L., "The Prediction of Productivity," Journal of Social Issues, 12, No. 2,
      1956, 41-49.

[29] Keller, R. and Holland, W., "Boundary Spanning Activity and R&D Management: A
      Comparative Study," IEEE Transactions on Engineering Management, November 1975.

[30] Lawrence, P. R. and Lorsch, J. W., "Differentiation and Integration in Complex
      Organizations," Administrative Science Quarterly, 12, 1967a, 1-47.

[31] Lawrence, P. R. and Lorsch, J. W., Managing Differentiation and Integration, Harvard University, Boston, 1967b).

[32] Leavitt, Harold J., Managerial Psychology, The University of Chicago Press, Chicago, Illinois, Third Edition, 1972.

[33] Levy, S. J. and G. Zaltman, Marketing. Society, and Conflict, Prentice-Hall, Inc., Englewood Cliffs, New Jersey, 1975.

[34] Longnecker, Justin G., Principles of Management and Organizational Behavior, Charles E. Merrill Publishing Company, Columbus, Ohio, Fourth Edition, 1977.

[35] Maidique, M. A., "Entrepreneurs, Champions, and Technological Innovation," Sloan Management Review, 21, No. 2, Winter 1980, 59-76.

[36] Matraj, J., "Models and Indicators of Organizational Growth, Changes and Transformations," in Sheldon and Moore: Social Indicator Models, Russell Sage Foundation, 1975, 301-318.

[37] Miller, Jeffrey G. and Graham, Margaret B. W., "Production/Operations Management: Agenda for the '80s," Decision Sciences, Vol. 12 No. 4, October 1981, 547-571.

[38] Miller, Richard B., Participative Management: Quality of Worklife and Job Enrichment, Noyes Data Corporation, Park Ridge, New Jersey, 1977.

[39] Mintzberg, Henry, Structure in Fives: Designing Effective Organizations, Prentice-Hall, Inc., Englewood Cliffs, New Jersey (1983).

[40] Newman, William H., Summer, Charles E., and Warren, E. Kirby, The Process of Management, Prentice-Hall, Inc., Englewood Cliffs, New Jersey, Second Ed., 1967.

[41] Nichols, J. B., "Developing New Products: The Role of Research," Mechanical Engineering, Vol. 98 (11), November 1976, 34.

[42] Quinn, James Brian and Mueller, James A., "Transferring Research Results to Operations," Harvard Business Review, 41(1) 1963, 49-66.

[43] Reitz, H. Joseph, Behavior in Organizations, Richard D. Irwin, Inc., Homewood, Illinois, 1981.

[44] Reve, Toger, Interorganizational Relations in Distribution Channels: An Empirical Study of Norwegian Distribution Channel Dyads, unpublished Doctoral Dissertation, Northwestern University, 1980.

[45] Roberts, G. W., "Quality Assurance in R&D," Mechanical Engineering, Vol. 100 (9), September 1978.

[46] Rogers, E. M., "Social Structure and Social Change," in Processes and Phenomena of Social Change, Gerald Zaltman, ed., Wiley Interscience, New York, 1973, 75-85.

[47] Rubenstein, A. H., "The Role of Imbedded Technology and the R&D/Innovation Process," Joint Economic Committee, Congress of the United States, Special Study on an Economic Change, Vol. 3, Research and Innovation: Developing a Dynamic Nation, December 29, 1980.

[48] Rubenstein, A. H., et al, "Factors Influencing Innovation Success at the Project Level," Research Management, May 1976, 15-20.

[49] Rubenstein, A. H. and Haberstroh, C. J., Some Theories of Organization, R. D. Irwin
      Inc., Homewood, IL, 1966.

[50] Sagal, M. W. "Effective Technology Transfer--From Laboratory to Production,"
      Mechanical Engineering, Vol. 100 (4), April 1978.

[51] Sapolsky, H. M., The Polaris System Development, Harvard University Press,
      Cambridge, MA, 1972.

[52] Sayles, Leonard R. and Strauss, George, Human Behavior in Organizations,
      Prentice-Hall, Inc., Englewood Cliffs, New Jersey, 1966.

[53] Schmidt, S. M. and Kochan, T. A., "Conflict: Toward Conceptual Clarity,"
      Administrative Science Quarterly, 17, No. 3, September 1972, 359-370.

[54] Souder, W. E. and Chakrabarti, A. K., "The R&D/Marketing Interface: Results
      from an Empirical Study of Innovation Projects," IEEE Transactions on Engineering
      Management, Vol. EM-25, No. 4, November 1978, 88-93.

[55] Stecke, K. E., "Linearized Nonlinear MIP Formulations for Loading Flexible
      Manufacturing Systems," working paper No. 278, Division of Research, Graduate
      School of Business Administration, University of Michigan, Ann Arbor, MI, Sept. 1981.

[56] Thomson, James D., Organizations in Action, Chicago, McGraw-Hill, 1967.

[57] Twiss, Brian, Managing Technological Innovation, London, Loggman, Second Edition,
      1980.

[58] Van de Ven, Andrew, et al., "Determination of Coordination Modes Within Organiza-
      tions," American Sociological Review, 1976, 41:322-338.

[60] Von Fange, Eugene K., Professional Creativity, Prentice-Hall, Inc., Englewood
      Cliffs, New Jersey, 1959.

Interim Citations to Work of Dissertation Students

(1)   Fischer, Bruce, "Factors Influencing Productivity in the Transfer of Process
      Innovations from R&D to Operations," related working paper, "Technology Transfer
      at the R&D/Production Interface," Paper presented at the 6th Annual Meeting and
      International Symposium of The Technology Transfer Society, Washington, D. C.
      June 14-17, 1982. (co-authors Albert H. Rubenstein, Martin E. Ginn, and Lakshmanan
      Prasad).

(2)   Ginn, Martin, E., Key Organizational and Performance Factors Relating to the R&D/
      Production Interface, (completed January 1983) related working paper, "Some Key
      Factors Affecting the R&D/Production Interface: Theoretical Considerations and
      Research Design," presented at ORSA/TIMS meeting, Houston, Texas, October 13,
      1981. (co-author: Albert H. Rubenstein).

(3)   Knapp, Connie M., Key Communicator Effectiveness in a Decentralized Industrial
      Corporation, (completed Fall 1983) related working paper, "Field Experiments with
      Key Communicators in R&D," paper prepared for presentation at IEEE Engineering
      Management Conference, Arlington, Virginia, November 1979 (co-authors: Albert H.
      Rubenstein and Kenneth Kirsch), and "Technology Networking in the Divisionalized
      Corporation," paper presented at the TIMS/ORSA meeting, San Diego, California,
      1982. (co-authors: Albert H. Rubenstein and Falguni K. Sen).

(4)   Prasad, Lakshmanan, "Inter-Organizational Coordination During New Product
         Introduction," related working paper, "Inter-Organizational Coordination During
         New Product Introduction," paper presented at the TIMS/ORSA meeting, Detroit,
         Michigan, April 18-21, 1982. (co-author: Albert H. Rubenstein).

(5)   Sen, Falguni K., The Role of R&D/Innovation Groups in the Acquisition and
         Implementation of New Technology, (completed Spring 1983) related working
         paper, "The Role of R&D/Innovation Groups in the Acquisition and Implementation
         of New Technology," paper presented at the ORSA/TIMS meeting in Detroit,
         Michigan, October 1982. (co-author: Albert H. Rubenstein).

Project Management: Methods and Studies
Burton V. Dean (editor)
© Elsevier Science Publishers B.V. (North-Holland), 1985   201

HOW TO DEVELOP IN-HOUSE CAPABILITY TO TRAIN PROJECT MANAGERS:
THE ALLEN-BRADLEY EXPERIENCE

Leslie Finkel

(formerly of)
The Allen-Bradley Company
Cleveland, Ohio
U.S.A.

This paper describes the implementation process of an in-house
training program in Project Management at the Allen-Bradley
Company, Systems Division. Four phases in the process are presented:
organizational needs assessment, program selection, pilot and in-house
implementation. Two major types of problems were encountered:
content-oriented and process-oriented. These problems and the
methods chosen to deal with them are described.

Evaluation of the first year of the program is presented. The results
indicate that participants not only rate the program favorably but
also are learning the techniques presented and are able to apply them
appropriately on their jobs. Additional data is needed before conclusions may be reached on "hard" criteria such as time to project
completion and change in Division revenues.

The paper concludes with some recommendations for companies considering similar programs. The value of an in-house Steering Committee,
of participative training tools and of on-going program evaluation is
emphasized.

Background

The Project Management Training Program currently in place at the Allen-Bradley Company,
Systems Division, focuses on the essential "how to" of the project management process:
project selection, planning, control, decision theory and conflict management. The implementation of the program required the use of current training technology to adapt project management concepts and techniques to a unique project environment. The training evolved from
a program piloted by an external consultant. The Division training staff and personnel from
other departments worked with the consultant to tailor the program for the Division. Training needs assessment, instructional design and program evaluation techniques were critical to
the in-house development of the program.

The Systems Division is a product division of the Allen-Bradley Company specializing in state-
of-the-art electronic control systems. Project work tends to be product-oriented. Products
range from individual modules to complete automated systems and vary in terms of development time, resource allocation and project team organization.

The Project Management Training Program evolved with a framework flexible enough to incorporate the variety and scope of Division projects. The Division itself was the primary
source of information on what such flexibility should entail.

Organizational Needs Assessment

The Division Marketing Department originally brought the need for project management training to the attention of the training staff. The staff then conducted assessment interviews
aimed at more specifically identifying Marketing and other departments' project management
training needs.

Training needs assessments are conducted based on the assumption that an accurate picture of "market" needs, in this case, training needs, will facilitate the development of a "product" which will meet those needs, in this case, the training program. The assessment may take the form of an interview and/or a questionnaire. The goal of the assessment is to define in specific, behavioral terms what the client department or organization wants to accomplish via training. This information aids the program developer in constructing an appropriate curriculum. Sometimes, training may not be the proper vehicle to meet the organization's needs and alternative solutions may be selected (i.e., employee counseling, manpower planning, attitude surveys, etc.). [3, 11]

Based on interviews conducted with a generous sample of Division directors and managers, the organizational need was summarized by the following statement: the need to complete project and individual tasks in a timely and cost-effective manner by implementing appropriate planning and control techniques to meet project objectives. The training staff and a small group of functional managers formed a Steering Committee which would review alternative training approaches and draft a recommendation.

Project Selection

Over a period of one month, the Steering Committee reviewed a number of training alternatives: in-house program development, courses at neighboring universities, and externally developed or "packaged" programs. The Committee decided to pursue a two-step program implementation format: (a) the purchase of an externally developed program and (b) the tailoring of the program for the Division, preferably with external consultant support. The program would then be conducted by in-house instructors.

The committee conducted an area search which resulted in the review of several programs. A prime consideration was the willingness of the program sponsor(s) to allow in-house modification and in-house instruction of the program. The committee believed that an externally developed program would require some changes in order to be relevant to the Division. Furthermore, in-house instructors would add to the relevance of the program by using "home grown" examples in their lectures which would be familiar and credible to the participants.

The committee selected a program flexible enough to be tailored to Division needs. The program developer (hereafter, to be referred to as the consultant) agreed to sell the program to the Division and to assist in in-house modification.

The Pilot

The consultant and the Steering Committee reviewed the results of the training needs assessment. The assessment pointed to certain content areas--planning and control techniques--but did not indicate specific techniques or the level of detail desired. The committee suggested that a Phase Two needs assessment be conducted by piloting a project management training program for department directors and managers. The program would offer a sampling of project management concepts and techniques. The participants would evaluate the program based on a consideration of Division needs. Their evaluation would serve as the basis for in-house modification of the program.

The consultant agreed to conduct the pilot program. The program was held off-site in a series of six, four-hour sessions. Table 1 shows the outline of the pilot program.

The program was evaluated using questionnaires and a follow-up meeting with the participants. Participants supported the basic content of the program, including the Tower Construction Game which they felt gave them the opportunity to practice the project management techniques they had learned. They did suggest that the program offer more examples relevant to the Systems Division. They also suggested that the program offer less detail on management theory and network analysis and more detail on Gantt and Milestone charts, project control, available computer software, and conflict management. There was less consensus on how the program should be used at the Systems Division. Should the program be used for general educational purposes or for specific, technique-oriented training? How should the training be integrated into the existing organizational structure? The participants decided to set up a committee to address these issues. In the meantime, they agreed to permit in-house program development to proceed based on the content evaluation obtained from the pilot program.

Table 1. Outline of the Pilot Project Management Training Program

I. PRINCIPLES OF MANAGEMENT

- Objectives of Project Management
- Project/Product Life Cycle
- Management Process and Functions
- Systems Management
- Organizational Structures
- Shared Project Responsibility

II. PROJECT ORGANIZATION AND STAFFING

- Project Definition
- Project Proposal
- Project Manager
- Project Team/Staffing
- Performance Appraisal

III. PROJECT SELECTION AND PLANNING

- Decision Tables
- Decision Trees
- Project Planning
- Gantt and Milestone Charts
- Work Breakdown Structure
- Work Packages
- Program Plan

IV. ACTIVITY NETWORK ANALYSIS

- Network Construction
- Critical Path Method (CPM)
- Program Evaluation and Review Technique (PERT)
- Time/Cost Tradeoffs

V. PROJECT SCHEDULING AND CONTROL

- Operating Cycle
- The Management Cost and Control System
- Variance Analysis
- Rescheduling and Reporting

VI. TOWER CONSTRUCTION GAME

- Introduction and Description
- Formulating Goals and Objectives
- Organization Staffing
- Design Evaluation
- Material Purchasing
- Redesign and Replan
- Construction
- Oral and Written Communication

In-House Implementation

Following the pilot program, the consultant met with a group of in-house instructors over a
period of two weeks to assist in program modification. The instructors had been chosen prior
to the pilot program. A number of Steering Committee members, including members of the
training staff, were selected based on their knowledge of project management. By the time
of the pilot program, there were ten instructors representing the Training, Engineering,
Marketing and Operations departments. All instructors attended the pilot program.

The instructor meeting served two main purposes: (a) to modify the program for Division use,
and (b) to train the instructors in classroom techniques. The instructor group reviewed the
pilot program evaluations and incorporated the suggested content changes into the program.
The group developed Systems Division case studies and contributed documentation to illustrate
portions of current Division project work. The group condensed the material on general management and combined it with the module on organization and staffing. They condensed the
information on network analysis and combined it with the decision theory segment of the
selection and planning module. They added information on Gantt and Milestone charts, control
system requirements, and computer software available at the Division. Finally, they added a
module on conflict management. The group decided to maintain the six, four-hour module
format.

The training staff conducted sessions on classroom techniques. The sessions focused on facilitating group discussion, handling participant questions and using platform skills such as voice
projection and gestures. Each instructor gave a practice presentation.

Heavy emphasis was placed on group facilitation as opposed to lecture. The lecture form of
instruction is instructor-oriented, allowing for minimal exchange of ideas among participants
and bestowing upon the instructor the sole role of "expert." Examples provided tend to be
more relevant to the instructor's field of vision than to the participants'. Given the expected
level of experience of program participants in engineering project work, the facilitative instruction style was recommended. This style is more participant-oriented, taking the burden
of expert off the shoulders of the instructor and allowing the participants to assert their own
areas of expertise. The instructor follows a program content guide, but there is time "built in"
for discussion of the key content areas and other areas of interest to the participants. There
is a higher level of exchange of ideas among participants. There is also substantial evidence
that learning is enhanced by the facilitative rather than the lecture style of instruction. [3,10]

The instructor group made tentative plans for the in-house introduction of the program. They
decided on a class size of 12 to 15, a size conducive to group discussion. They also decided
that each instructor would teach only one module per program. Time constraints prevented
an instructor from assuming responsibility for the total program.

In the meantime, a newly established project team requested that they attend the program as
soon as possible. Given the business need, the training staff scheduled the session. The project team response was enthusiastic. They made immediate use of many techniques introduced including objectives design, Gantt charts and Work Breakdown Structure.

The program's success gained the attention of the committee which had been set up to consider the program's ongoing use. Members of the committee met with representatives of management who were aware of the program but not included in the original pilot session. This
management group then requested that a condensed version of the program be held for them.

Following the executive session of the program, the management group agreed that the program should be implemented. They felt that the techniques introduced would positively affect product development times and eventually result in a cost-savings for the Division. They
asked that the Steering Committee monitor the progress of the program and issue status reports on a quarterly basis.

The program was implemented on a bi-monthly basis. As of this writing, 7 programs have been held with over 100 employees trained. These programs were conducted for intact project groups. However, certain "unaffiliated" individuals were permitted to attend based on expressed need by department managers. Table 2 shows the final outline of the in-house program. As was mentioned earlier, the six, four-hour session format was retained.

Table 2.   Outline of the In-House Project Management Training Program

I.   DEFINITIONS, ORGANIZATION, AND STAFFING -

· Definition of Project Management
· Objective of Project Management
· Project/Product Life Cycles
· Organizational Structures
· Shared Project Responsibility
· Project Staffing
· Pitfalls in Project Management: Communication and Time Management

II.   PROJECT SELECTION AND PLANNING

· Project Definition
· Project Proposal
· Project Planning
· Gantt and Milestone Charts +
· Work Breakdown Structure
· Work Packages
· Work Plan

III.   DECISION THEORY AND NETWORK ANALYSIS

· Decision Tables
· Decision Trees
· Network Analysis (CPM/PERT)
· In-House Computer Software +

IV.   CONFLICT MANAGEMENT +

· Introduction to Conflict Management
· Exploration of Conflict Management Styles
· Escalation/De-escalation of Conflict
· Practice in Conflict Management
· Conflict: A Process to be Managed

V.   PROJECT SCHEDULING AND CONTROL

· Operating Cycle
· Design requirements of a Control System +
· The Management Cost and Control System
· Variance Analysis
· Rescheduling and Reporting

VI.   TOWER CONSTRUCTION GAME

· Introduction and Description
· Formulating Goals and Objectives
· Organization Staffing
· Design Evaluation
· Material Purchasing
· Redesign and Replan
· Construction
· Oral and Written Communication

- Material condensed from pilot program content.
+ Material added to pilot program content.

Implementation Problems: Content-Oriented

Two major content-oriented problems occurred during the implementation of the Project Management Training Program. The first problem stemmed from semantic confusion over the terms "project management" and "matrix management." The second problem arose in the establishment of a central, unifying theme for the program.

The terms project management and matrix management are often used synonymously to refer to a type of organizational structure. This structure has both functional and project departments which form a communications and responsibility matrix. The term project management also refers to the planning, organizing, leading and controlling of scarce resources required to meet project objectives. [5, 6] Project management techniques do not require, but are often associated with, a matrix structure.

Concern arose among Division management that training in project management techniques might spill over into the matrix issue by association. They recognized that the training program was potentially an impetus for reorganization, but felt that any such change should be closely monitored and congruent with overall organizational objectives. They felt that the primary role of the program should be training in project management techniques.

In response to these concerns, the instructor group which developed the in-house program separated the organizational structure issues from the project management techniques. The program includes a section on organizational structures--traditional, product and matrix. However, advantages and disadvantages of each structure are discussed so that no one structure is inadvertently advocated. The Steering Committee agreed to submit quarterly reports focusing on participant reaction to the program and any organizational impact issues. Should the reorganization issue arise, Division management would be aware of it, via the reports, and could then recommend follow-up. To date, the reorganization issue has not surfaced.

A second problem stemmed from the technique orientation of the program. Since the program focuses on an array of project management techniques, there was a risk that it might be disjointed, lack essential continuity. The use of different instructors during the program further complicated the problem. In order to deal with the problem, the instructor group attempted to build in continuity by focusing group discussion and certain group exercises on projects on which the participants were currently working. In this manner, the program material would not only be more relevant to the participants but also would be less disjointed because of the central focus on on-the-job projects. The disjointed effect, however, was not completely handled by this strategy as will be discussed in a later section.

Implementation Problems: Process-Oriented

Two major process issues were encountered during the implementation of the Project Management Training Program. The first issue was originally identified by the pilot group: the posture of the program as training versus education. The second issue involved the selection of appropriate evaluation criteria for the program.

The pilot group was undecided as to whether the program should be used for general educational purposes or for technique-oriented training geared to the specific jobs of employees. The resolution of this issue required the consideration of two questions: What was the program meant to accomplish? and Who would participate in the program? Based on the original needs assessment and the pilot evaluations, the instructor group compiled a list of program objectives. These objectives are listed in Table 3.

Table 3. In-House Project Management Training Objectives

Provide techniques and methods to:
· Complete project and individual tasks in a timely and cost-effective manner
· Identify project characteristics
· Identify roles in a project group
· Implement appropriate planning techniques as individuals and groups
· Implement appropriate control techniques
· Manage conflicts to ensure that individual/group resources are effectively utilized.

The instructor group also developed a strategy for participant selection. Priority would be given to project teams who would most immediately and directly benefit from the training. After these team needs were met, employees who had responsibility for individual and/or informal group projects would be considered. Supervisory and management consent would be mandatory for all enrollment.

Based on the objectives of the program and the selection of participants, a balance between training and education was adopted. The program provides general exposure to management principles, project terminology and some basic project management theory. However, the program also focuses on critical project management techniques (see Table 2), in enough detail to permit the employee to apply them appropriately on the job.

Once program objectives and content were established, the issue of how to measure program effectiveness was addressed. The training staff explored appropriate criteria which would not be contaminated by non-relevant factors. The criteria selected and first-year results are discussed in the following section.

Program Evaluation: The First Year

The criteria for program evaluation are participant reaction, learning, behavior and organizational impact. [8] These criteria were measured and compiled over the first year of the program.

The reaction measure is taken from evaluation forms which are given to participants at the conclusion of each module and, again, at the conclusion of the program. The evaluation form asks the participants to rate the instructors and the program content and to describe how the program would help them to perform their jobs more effectively. To date, on the average, the program received a 5.5 rating out of 7 on a scale from poor to excellent. Participants typically expressed favorable comments regarding the instructors and the content of the program. They felt that the planning, decision theory and conflict management techniques would be particularly useful to them on their jobs. As noted earlier, the instructors focused group discussion on participants' on-the-job projects. In light of the evaluations, a new procedure was recently set up. The group instructing a program now meets prior to that program to establish a plan for transitioning between modules. The plan includes having each instructor report to the others on content covered during a module so as to reduce redundancy and allow for smoother transition. Preliminary evaluation suggests that this approach has been effective.

The learning measure is based on the performance of participants on the Tower Construction Game. The game allows participants to apply their acquired project management skills--such as Work Breakdown Structure, Gantt and conflict management--to a simulated project: the construction of a tower. Participants divide into teams which work on the game at the same time. At the conclusion of the game, each team reports its results and how they were achieved. [4] Participants reported that they have a better understanding of the techniques once they have applied them during the game. Informal assessments of participant behavior indicated that participants were able to apply project management techniques appropriately to the simulated project. This type of learning measure is less threatening than a formal test and serves as an adequate indicator of how well participants have learned.

The behavior measures focus on changes in participants' behavior on the job following their participation in the program. Two measures are used: the participant action plan and pre- and post-program interviews with participants' immediate supervisors/managers.

The action plan is a behaviorally-based set of goals which the participants define based on what they have learned in the program. Three months following the program, a member of the training staff follows up with each participant to track progress on the action plan. Action plans were found to focus on the following areas: definition of measureable objectives, implementation/documentation of planning and control techniques, and effective use of conflict management techniques. Follow-up with participants indicated that action plans were implemented. One project team, for example, designed a project manual emphasizing clear objective-setting, Work Breakdown Structure and network planning techniques. Reports from the project team indicated that milestones were achieved on time and that the definitions of objectives and general flow of the project were excellent.

In pre-program interviews, participants' supervisors indicated that emphasis should be placed on the following areas: writing measurable objectives, understanding why planning is important, using Gantt cha. ts and other planning tools, implementing project control and meeting deadlines. These areas were very similar to those targeted in participants' action plans. Follow-up with the supervisors after the program indicated that participants implemented planning and control techniques on their jobs/projects and did gain an understanding of the importance of project planning. While there were preliminary indications that participants were meeting more deadlines, additional time must elapse before these indications are strong enough to be clearly interpreted.

The desired organizational impact of Project Management training would be the more efficient use of financial and non-financial resources to achieve Division goals. The bottom line, here, would be an increase in Division revenues. This measure not only requires time to mature but also is contaminated by a host of factors unrelated to the training. Realistically, the training program would take from 2 to 5 years to impact revenues once a sufficient percentage of Division personnel were trained. Furthermore, the process of partialing out the effects of unrelated factors would be highly speculative. At present, therefore, this measure has not been investigated.

In a "field" environment, as opposed to a laboratory, opportunities to control the environment are very limited. "Treatment" effects, in this case, the effects of a training program, are difficult to measure because of uncontrollable extraneous factors in the work environment. Assessment of effects also tends to be more anecdotal than statistical. The training staff at the Systems Division attempted to evaluate the effectiveness of Project Management training using available resources. The first year results indicate that participants reacted favorably towards the program, learned the techniques presented and applied these techniques appropriately on their jobs. The long-range effects of the program will require more time to mature before they can be measured. Division revenues may not be a feasible measure. However, other measures such as project completion times may be considered.

Conclusion

The implementation of Project Management training at the Systems Division represents a realistic example of the training process from needs assessment through program evaluation. Some of the pitfalls encountered in the process have been described in detail. With gratitude for the value of hindsight, a number of recommendations may be made for other companies considering Project Management training.

First, the importance of a representative Steering Committee in the selection and implementation of Project Management training is paramount if the training is to successfully meet organizational needs, satisfy organizational objectives and gain the personal support of key managers. Members should represent functional departments and several levels of management, including top management. Since the program is targeted at organizational change-- from specific uses of control techniques to more far-reaching modes of strategic planning-- it is critical that it be managed on all levels, but most critically, beginning with top management. This waterfall approach helps not only to ensure that the training material itself will target the needs of the organization but also that the program has credibility within the organization, having been backed by top management. At the Systems Division, the Steering Committee facilitated the selection of an appropriate program and its subsequent acceptance.

Secondly, a general strategy for implementing a program, including the selection and order of participants, should be identified before in-house training begins. If a strategy had existed prior to the pilot of the Project Management program, the participants in that program would have been less concerned with implementation process issues.

A third point involves the selection of a Project Management program. The group selecting the program should consider how much tailoring of the program will be necessary to make it fit their organization's needs. In-house development may be an option if adequate resources exist. If an outside program is purchased, then permission should be obtained to make content adjustments, use in-house instructors if desired, etc. In the case of the Systems Division, certainly the use of Division cases and examples by in-house instructors contributed to the program's relevance and enhanced its acceptability to participants.

Fourthly, the choice of instructional techniques is equally critical to training outcomes as the choice of the program itself. These techniques not only include style of instruction, but also include audio-visual material, in-class projects, management games; in short, the instructional tools which make up the training. The training literature suggests that adult learners are able to retain and utilize information better when they actively participate in training. [3, 10] The implications for training design are that facilitative instruction style is preferable to lecture and that participative instructional techniques, such as in-class projects and games, should be built into a program.

At the Systems Division, instructors were encouraged to use a facilitative style. The program content included various in-class projects focusing on Division cases and the Tower Construction Game. The Tower Game exemplifies the participative approach because it allows the participants, within certain guidelines, to actively design a project--not simply think about its design. [4] Evaluation measures indicate that participants enjoy the training program, especially the in-class projects and the Tower Game. These measures indicate, further, that participants are learning the program material and are able to apply it on the job. These results suggest that companies considering Project Management training should pay heed to the instructional techniques as well as the content offered by a program.

Finally, the program's effectiveness should be evaluated using available criteria. Timely evaluation allows the instructors to make in-course or permanent changes to the program where the need arises. Long-range, it keeps the program current with dynamic organizational issues.

REFERENCES

[1] Argyris, C., Understanding Organizational Behavior, Dorsey Press, Homewood, Illinois, 1960.

[2] Bass, B. M. and Vaugh, J. A., Training in Industry: The Management of Learning, Wadsworth Publishing, Belmont, California, 1966.

[3] Craig, R. L., ed., Training and Development Handbook: A Guide to Human Resource Development, McGraw-Hill, New York, 1976.

[4] Dean, B. V., "Project Management Game: Implementation and Evaluation," Bulletin of TIMS/ORSA Joint National Meeting, Chicago, Illinois, April 25-27, 1983.

[5] Galbraith, J., Designing Complex Organizations, Addison-Wesley, Reading, Mass., 1977.

[6] Huse, E. F., Organization Development and Change, West Publishing Company, New York, 1980.

[7] Kerzner, H., Project Management: A Systems Approach to Planning, Scheduling and Controlling, Van Nostrand Reinhold, New York, 1979.

[8] Kirkpatrick, D., Evaluating Training Programs, American Society for Training and Development, Madison, Wisconsin, 1975.

[9] _____, Practical Guide for Supervisory Training and Development, Addison-Wesley, Reading, Mass., 1971.

[10] Knowles, M., The Adult Learner: A Neglected Species, Gulf Publishing Company, Houston, Texas, 1973.

[11] Lawrie and Boringer, "Training Needs Assessment and Training Program Evaluation," Training and Development Journal, November 1971.

[12] Likert, R. and Likert, J. G., New Ways of Managing Conflict, McGraw-Hill, New York, 1976.

[13] Mager, R. F., Preparing Instructional Objectives, Fearon Publishers, Inc., Belmont, California, 1962.

[14] Mesics, E. A., Education and Training for Effective Manpower Utilization: An Annotated Bibliography on Education and Training in Work Organizations, Cornell University, Ithaca, NY, 1969.

[15] Thomas, K., "Conflict and Conflict Management," in Dunnette, M., ed., Handbook of Industrial and Organizational Psychology, Rand McNally, Chicago, 1976.

[16] Tracey, W. R., "Evaluating Training and Development Systems," American Management Association, New York, 1968.

[17] U. S. Office of Personnel Management, Assessing Changes in Job Behavior due to Training: A Guide to the Participant Action Plan Approach, Washington, D. C., February 1980.

[18] Zimbardo, P., Ebbeson, E., and Maslach, C., Influencing Attitudes and Changing Behavior, Addison-Wesley, Reading, Mass., 1977.

Part IV
APPLICATIONS AND STUDIES

Project Management: Methods and Studies
Burton V. Dean (editor)
© Elsevier Science Publishers B.V. (North-Holland), 1985

PROJECT MANAGEMENT AND INNOVATIVE START-UP FIRMS[1]

Burton V. Dean

Case Western Reserve University
Cleveland, Ohio
U.S.A.

Entrepreneurship is having a major impact on this country's economy
in terms of both job creation and capital appreciation. Published
studies have demonstrated that there are several features common
to the start-up of technology-based entrepreneurally oriented organizations. However, there is no evidence in the published literature
on the subject of a network planning method being developed and
applied to manage such ventures. This is in significant contrast to
the widespread use of such planning methods in other areas of
management to schedule and control complex projects. Based on
the use of a systems approach, a project management method is
developed and applied to the management of an entrepreneurially
oriented innovative start-up company.

INTRODUCTION

Background

Associated with an innovative start-up is one or more entrepreneurs. The practice of being
an entrepreneur in a technology-based environment has been characterized as follows:

> Entrepreneurship clearly refers to the capacity for innovation,
> investment, and activist expansion in new markets, products and
> techniques. As such, entrepreneurship may reflect superior information
> and, perhaps more importantly, imagination, which subjectively reduces
> the risks and uncertainties of new opportunities which are ignored or
> rejected by other investors. Alternatively, the entrepreneur has special
> aptitudes for bearing risks and uncertainty, which permit him to act as
> promoter and catalytic agent who seizes new investment and production
> opportunities. These traits, in effect, shift the opportunity set, and
> increase the probability that a new project will in fact be implemented.
> [14]

Baty has defined the entrepreneur as achieving a specific goal with

> "The entrepreneur shall have won when he succeeds in bringing his firm
> to a position where, in order to continue the growth of sales and earnings,
> the substantial infusion of new capital is required." [1]

He then goes on to state that success is achieved when

> "The business has been born, has survived the period of infancy, and has
> been set upon a projectory of profitable, sustainable growth." [1]

The focal point of this study is the investigation of the managerial problems of the entrepreneur or the CEO, who is attempting to achieve an exponential growth by exploiting some

new technological or marketing advantage with the possibility of achieving an extremely high return on capital investment.

This study has as its major concern those management problems associated with the <u>high technology</u> start-up situations. Vesper has analyzed the differences between (1) the conventional manufacturing start-ups as investigated by Collins and Moore and (2) those in more recent high technology companies.

> The life histories and educational levels of entrepreneurs in (1) and (2) were different. The fields in which they gained their work experience, production versus engineering, were different. The kinds of business strategies with which they began their companies, simply adding more manufacturing capacity versus beginning with product breakthroughs, were different. The kinds of resources with which they began, personal savings of the entrepreneurs and partners versus use of investor capital, were different. A common factor seems to have been that virtually all the entrepreneurs in both categories knew the business well from a technical standpoint on the basis of successful work experience in the companies of others before starting on their own. In the Collins and Moore cases this technical knowhow appears to have been an ability to solve production problems and get the work out faster, better, and cheaper. In the technology start-ups it was in how to design a next-generation product. [29, p. 95; 5]

This study is not concerned explicitly with the activities leading up to starting an innovative technology based firm. In this study, the emphasis is on managing the key elements that are <u>different</u> in the start-up phase of the firm, as compared to the growth stages of the firm. Following the incorporation of the firm, we may represent the stages of the enterprise as being – start-up, rapid growth, and continued growth. We note that the best descriptor of the various stages would be the number of employees in the firm, as indicated in Figure 1.

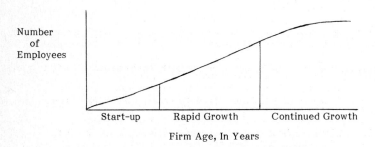

Figure 1: Development States of the Technology Based Firm

The stage of interest in this study is the period from the start of the firm to approximately 50-100 employees where the break-even point may have been achieved. Rapid changes over this period may be anticipated. A flexible and adaptive approach is needed to meet what may become catastrophic situations.

A financial flow diagram for the technology based firm is presented in Figure 2, where the horizontal scale is firm age, in years, and the vertical scale is cash flow. The start-up period will be where the cash flow becomes increasingly negative, turns around, and ultimately reaches a break-even point, followed by a positive cash flow.

The break-even point is the major firm goal investigated in this study, as this is a necessary condition for the ultimate surviveability of the firm. A technology based firm is not successful until, as a minimum, it is able to reach a sufficient size (as measured by number of employees) to achieve a break-even stage of operations.

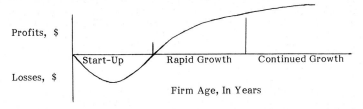

Figure 2: Profitability Growth of the Technology Based Firm

Problems

Although there are numerous decisions facing technology based firms, a relatively small number of problems occur in such firms, as follows:

Financial Problems

1. Obtaining Venture and Working Capital
2. Obtaining Capital Equipment

Personnel Problems

3. Providing Competitive Salaries and Benefits
4. Attracting and Keeping Personnel

R&D Related Problem Areas

5. Maintaining Adequate R&D Levels
6. Making the Transition from Research and Development to Marketing
7. Undertaking High-Risk R&D Projects

Table 1 presents the magnitude of these problems as obtained in the 1981 NSF sample survey of 1,232 firms.

Table 1: Problem Areas of Major Concern to Small High Technology Firms

Problem Area	Percentage of Firms Considering it a Major Problem
1. The ability to provide competitive salaries and benefits to key personnel	69%
2. The ability to maintain an adequate level of R&D activity	68%
3. Obtaining venture and working capital	66%
4. Attracting and keeping personnel	63%
5. Ability to obtain capital equipment as needed	62%
6. Marketing a product once it has been successfully developed	60%
7. Undertaking high-risk R&D projects	60%

Source: National Science Foundation, *Problems of Small, High Technology Firms*, December 1981.

Assumptions

This study is not concerned with the qualitative factors affecting the Management of an Innovative Start-up (MIS). A considerable literature exists on this subject (see references). Rather, this study is concerned with the quantitative aspects in the MIS.

The key assumption in this study is to formulate the management problem as a project to be managed, incorporating the following stages that exist in all projects: planning, budgeting, organizing, scheduling, and controlling.

The following reasons call for utilizing a systematic planning method in the MIS.

1. a large number of tasks/activities to be performed,
2. a number of key events and milestones that must be achieved for the MIS to be successful,
3. the existence of complex interactions and precedence relations among activities,
4. the need for frequent updating of status and plans,
5. the occurrence of stochastic elements in the MIS, where

    · some activities may not be completed or successful as planned,
    · some activities may exceed duration and cost expectations, and
    · some activities may need to be performed several times until a successful result is achieved, and

6. the need for contingency planning to be incorporated in the start-up plan and schedule.

Vesper [29] has identified a set of events that characterize the creation or start of a new venture –

1. When the desire for entrepreneurship is recognized.
2. When the idea for what the new venture is to be occurs.
3. When the break is made with former employment.
4. When contracts are made with a potential partner, lawyer, banker, accountant, or other outside advisor,
5. When the legal papers for partnership or incorporation or business licenses are filed,
6. When the first dollars are invested in the new venture,
7. When the firm becomes ready to accept orders,
8. When its logo is first displayed,
9. When the first order arrived,
10. When the first delivery or performance is done,
11. When the company first breaks even,
12. When the first profitable year has been accomplished.

From the point of view of this study, we have taken event 5 as the initial event and event 11 as an objective to be realized, subsequent to the start-up of the firm. [29]

SYSTEMS APPROACH

System Characteristics

The essential structure of this approach is the fact that strategic and operational planning will be based on the concept of an innovative start-up as a system to be managed. For the purpose of this study, we consider that a system is characterized by the following five elements:

1. the total system <u>objectives</u>: or the <u>performance measures</u> of the entire system;
2. the system's <u>environment</u>: the fixed constraints;
3. the <u>resources</u> of the system;
4. the <u>components</u> of the system: their activities, goals, and measures of performance; and
5. the <u>management</u> of the system.

Associated with the above five characteristics of a system, we may view MIS characteristics as follows:

1. performance measures of the entire system

    · sales revenues to be maximized
    · total costs to be minimized
    · profit maximization
    · conservation of working capital
    · survival of the firm

An interim goal necessary to achieve each of the above in the long run is the ability to reach the <u>break-evven point</u>. This objective is considered to be the primary objective for MIS as investigated in this study.

2. The environment of an innovative start-up consists of the following:

    · high technology impact and availability
    · competition from other firms in the market
    · financing need and availability
    · networking with support services and close personal and business contacts
    · close working relationships with suppliers
    · potential sales derived from a relatively small number of customers
    · need to conform to a multitude of federal/state/city/governmental regulations

3. Resources of primary interest in the innovative start-up are the following:

    · personnel
    · management
    · financial
    · production
    · marketing
    · technology

4. The essential components of the system are those tasks (mission oriented), activities (work to be performed), precedence relations of the activities, stochastic/chance elements, and decision events. These components need to be carefully delineated, planned, organized, budgeted, scheduled, and controlled.

5. Associated with the management of the system, as well as subsystems, would be an overall perspective of the firm as a whole. To avoid suboptimization of subsystems, it is necessary to achieve business planning, setting task goals, allocation of resources to tasks, and a methodology for controlling system performance. This chapter will demonstrate the essential role that business planning plays in managing all innovative start-ups.

<u>Study Methodology</u>

The underlying structure of the study is a consideration of MIS as a system, utilizing a systems approach. Eight subsystems of an MIS, consisting of the major tasks to be performed in the MIS, are developed.

This chapter is concerned with the development, test, and evaluation of a general network-based method for use in the management of innovative start-ups. The major tasks accomplished in each start-up, including organizational, legal and financial, R&D, market research, manufacturing, and marketing were identified. For each major task, the significant activities, precedence relations, decision nodes, alternative choices of action, and feedback loops were identified. Activity durations and probabilities of successful accomplishment are also determined.

Although it is generally realized that no single network is applicable to all cases of MIS, the basic assumption of this chapter is that a network-based planning method can be utilized in each case of MIS.

Information and data have been collected on a small number of innovative start-up, and discussions have been held with several venture capital funds. In addition, published literature on innovative start-ups, venture capital funds, and entrepreneurs have been reviewed. This process has resulted in considerable experimentation with the network-based planning method for MIS.

The Q-GERT approach is used to model the management process, as this method provides the means to model situations involving probabilistic elements, decision processes and choices, and the variety of cycles occuring in an innovative start-up. A computer program for Q-GERT simulation has been developed and applied to analyze different scenarios. The program is currently being used to validate the durations and probability distributions based on preliminary sample data. In addition, computer outputs are obtained of such parameters as the critical path, the criticality index of each start-up task, the distribution times of each event, and the probability of reaching each end-state.

The CPM/PERT approach is used to obtain the necessary information from innovative start-ups, and to process this information in a systematic way. The GANTT Chart is utilized to present management reports and to carry out the monitoring and control function of the chief executive officer. The Job Report is used to report on the status of individual activities and associated precedence relations to provide the means for detailed control at the activity level of the firm.

SYSTEM DECOMPOSITION AND SUBSYSTEMS

The Role of the Entrepreneur as the CEO

The focal point of this study are the problems of the entrepreneur or the CEO, who is attempting to achieve an exponential growth by exploiting some new technological or marketing advantage with the possibility of achieving an extremely high return on capital investment.

Accordingly, we model the problem of MIS from the point of view of the entrepreneur/CEO, and we are therefore concerned with overall system optimization. Accordingly, we require that the entrepreneur/CEO establish overall goals of the organization, strategically plan its activities, assign/organize its work elements, and allocate resources to specific tasks/activities, monitor specific tasks, and replan depending on the performance of individual subsystems.

The Subsystems

Based on an analysis of several innovative start-up firms, it is possible to classify (decompose) all activities that are being performed into a set of eight specific subsystems (tasks). Table 2 presents a list of tasks that occur in an innovative start-up.

Table 2: Basic Tasks in an Innovative Start-Up Firm

1. R and D and Engineering
2. Finance and Venture Capital
3. Market Research
4. Organization and Personnel
5. Legal and Accounting
6. Manufacturing
7. Marketing
8. Business Planning

Model Construction

For the (MIS) system, S, we may represent S as

$$S = (S_1, S_2, ..., S_8) \qquad (1)$$

where S_i is a subsystem of S.

Each subsystem, S_i, is a major task to be performed in accomplishing S. S may be considered to be a <u>union</u> of subsystem tasks,

$$S = S_1 \; u \; S_2 \; u \; ... \; u \; S_8 \qquad (2)$$

We may further represent or decompose a subsystem task, S_i, as

$$S_i = S_{i1}, S_{i2}, ..., S_{in_i} \qquad (3)$$

where each subsystem task S_i may also be represented as a <u>union</u> of specific activities,

$$S_i = S_{i1} \; u \; S_{i2} \; u \; ... \; u \; S_{in_i} \qquad (4)$$

We note that S_{ij} is the jth activity in task S_i and

n_i = total number of activities in task S_i.

We say that a <u>precedence relationship</u> exists between two activities in S_i, if

$$S_{ij} < S_{ik} \qquad (5)$$

A precedence relation exists if the initiation of S_{ik} requires the completion of S_{ij}.

We may wish to have several activities interrelated, extending (5) to the case where activities are required to be completed prior to the initiation of another.

Application of the Systems Approach

We apply the Systems Approach given in the previous section to the MIS problem in three stages, as follows:

Stage 1

Classify all activities in the MIS as being elements in a subsystem (task) of the start-up. Note that each subsystem of the start-up will also be considered to be a major task to be performed, such as engineering, manufacturing, marketing, and finance.

Stage 2

Establish precedence relations for activities in each subsystem, as indicated in relationship (5) above. Precedence relations between activities in different tasks are also to be established, as indicated in the following section.

Stage 3

Apply the five elements of the Systems Approach including establishing objectives (measures), determining environmental conditions, allocating resources, defining components, and establishing management procedures for each subsystem (task).

As will be demonstrated subsequently, we utilize Task 8, Business Planning, as a coordinating task in MIS to plan, schedule, and control all tasks/activities.

Furthermore, we relate the tasks/activities to financial and manpower planning, thus tieing together the actual work that is being performed as encompassed in Tasks 1-8, with the elements that appear in the Business Plan.

The Role of Business Planning

This study utilizes the business planning function of the firm as an essential element in MIS. The general approach in planning is to "prepare and work from a written plan that delineates who in the total organization is to do what, by when." [2]

"A business plan is most usefully thought of as an internal, operating document, not a showpiece for raising money or satisfying attorneys. A sound businessman can be an important contributor to the success whenever one, two, three, or more peole wish to organize and synchronize a purposeful business effort over time in order to achieve specific results." [2, p.22]

"After preparing a business plan, the entrepreneurial management team involved should have before it an agreed program for action and results to which it will willingly commit itself. After reading a business plan, a director, potential investor, or other interested party should know precisely what those involved intend to do, by when, with the human and financial resources called for in the plan." [2, pp.22-23]

The seven basic tasks appearing in Table 2 are coordinated by means of Task 8, Business Planning. In addition to the precedence relations that occur among the activities in the individual tasks, there are precedence relations between the activities that are performed in the seven individual tasks and Task 8 (Business Planning). This may be shown as in the following Figure 3.

Figure 3: The Central Role of Business Planning in MIS

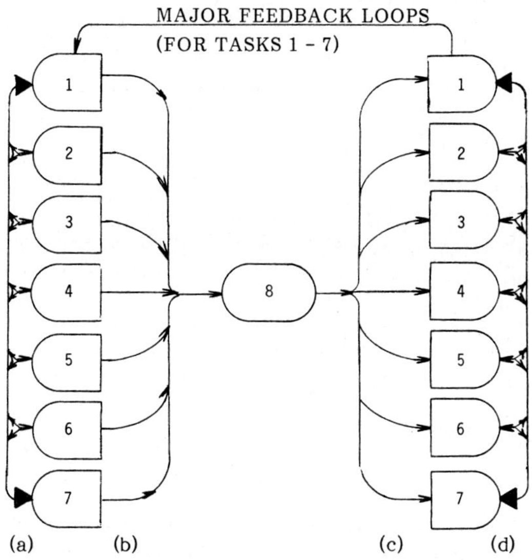

For examples of (a), (b), (c), and (d), see Table 5.

PROJECT MANAGEMENT

Network-Based Planning Approach

In this study, a network-based planning approach is utilized in MIS. We have the following definitions.

An activity is any portion of a start-up that requires time or resources to perform. A task is considered to be an integrated set of activities. An activity will be represented by an arrow in the network diagram.

An event is an instantaneous point of time that represents the start or completion of an activity. An event is represented as a node in the network diagram.

Precedence relations among activities are such that the ending event of a predecessor activity may occur before the starting event of another activity. A precedence relation is represented in a network as two activities in series separated by a node (event). Every activity that emanates from the node has each activity incident to the node as a precedence activity.

A network is a collection of arrows and nodes that represent the start-up, including decision nodes and decision trees.

Table 3 presents the lists of activities for each of the eight tasks listed in Table 2. These lists should be considered as typical of the activities that need to be accomplished in a successful high technology case of MIS.

Table 3: Tasks and Activities in the MIS

Task 1:   Research & Development and Engineering

Activity Number	Activity Description
1.1	Establish R&D Objectives
1.2	Define R&D Problem
1.3	Develop Solution Alternatives
1.4	Evaluate Alternatives
1.5	Redefine Problem if Solutions are Applicable
1.6	Continue Solution(s) Development
1.7	Develop Prototype of Selected Alternative
1.8	Test and Evaluate Prototype
1.9	Unsuccessful Prototype Test
1.10	Successful Prototype Test
1.11	Conduct Patent Search
1.12	Begin Patent and License Procedure
1.13	Redevelop Prototype if Previous Effort is Unsuccessful
1.14	Identify Next Alternative
1.15	Select Next Alternative to be Developed
1.16	Discontinue Start-up if all Alternatives are Unsuccessful

Task 2:   Finance and Venture Capital

Activity Number	Activity Description
2.1	Identify Immediately Available Personal Resources
2.2	Identify all Capital Needs
2.3	Perform Initial Sales Projections, Cost Estimates, and Cash Flow Analysis
2.4	Construct Pro-Forma Income Statement, Breakeven Analysis, and Balance Sheet, Budget
2.5	Formulate Initial Business Plan
2.6	Identify Alternative Sources of Financing/Expand List of Sources
2.7	Identify Sources of Working Capital
2.8	Identify Venture Capital Sources
2.9	Seek Venture Capital
2.10	Capital Funds Obtained and Applied
2.11	Identify Alternative Capital Needs if Funds are Insufficient
2.12	Update Cash Flow Analysis
2.13	Update Pro-Forma Income Statement and Balance Sheet
2.14	Determine Business Plan Effects

Task 3:   Market Research

Activity Number	Activity Description
3.1	Define Start-up Product Concept
3.2	Conduct Market Survey
3.3	Describe Potential Market (General)
3.4	Compile Sales and Acceptance Information on Similar Competitor Products/Services
3.5	Identify Market Segments by Composition and Sales Volume
3.6	Identify Specific Types of Customers
3.7	Define Start-up Sales Objectives (Size and Sectors)
3.8	Identify Government Short Term Influences

3.9	Conduct Economic Analysis of the Industry
3.10	Analysis of Competition: Product Performance Prices, Sales Volume
3.11	Determine Market Entry and Growth Obstacles
3.12	Describe Future Economic Conditions and Prepare Sales Forecasts

Task 4: Organization and Personnel

Activity Number	Activity Description
4.1	Analyze Entrepreneur's Strengths and Weaknesses
4.2	Evaluate Organizational Structures
4.3	Choose an Organizational Structure
4.4	Incorporate
4.5	Define Job Positions/Job Descriptions/ Expectations, Rewards (Short & Long Range)
4.6	Select Board Members/Advisory Board Members/ Consultants
4.7	Define Key Employee Positions & Agreements
4.8	Establish Personnel Salary, Wage, Benefits and Equity Ownership Policies
4.9	Define Training and Development Needs
4.10	Establish Timetable of Personnel Needs
4.11	Announce Available Positions and Interview
4.12	Seek Additional Information
4.13	Define Government Regulations Concerning Personnel
4.14	Evaluate Interviewees
4.15	Select Staff
4.16	Update Personnel Timetable
4.17	Prepare Final Organization Manual

Task 5: Legal and Accounting

Activity Number	Activity Description
5.1	Select Law Firm
5.2	Select Patent Lawyer
5.3	Select Accountant
5.4	Establish Budget
5.5	Design Initial Control System
5.6	Set Timetable for Reports (Quarterly, Annual, Monthly, etc.)
5.7	Select Auditor

Task 6: Production Methods

Activity Number	Activity Description
6.1	Specification/Drafting of Components and Process
6.2	MRP/Product Costing for Each Component
6.3	Production Doctrine Study (Buy, Rent, etc.)
6.4	Production Process Planning for Manufactured Items
6.5	Define Quality Control Standards
6.6	Review Government Safety Regulations
6.7	Distributor Evaluation
6.8	Vendor Evaluation
6.9	Site Study (Facility Requirements)

6.10	Evaluation of Site Study
6.11	Define Inventory Policies (Procurement, Work-in-Process, and Finished Goods)
6.12	Selection of Site, Vendors, and Distributors
6.13	Site Preparation (Build, Remodel, etc.)
6.14	Define Specific Equipment Requirements and Purchase
6.15	Install Equipment
6.16	Indentify Initial Test and Production Schedule
6.17	Check Design and Material Specifications
6.18	Run Schedule Identified in 6.16 or 6.20
6.19	Evaluate Quality of Manufacturing Process
6.20	Make Production Run Schedule Adjustments
6.21	Set Standard Production Run Schedule

Task 7:   Marketing and Distribution

Activity Number	Activity Description
7.1	Set Marketing Goals
7.2	Develop Sales Projections
7.3	Define Start-Up Image (Logo, etc.)
7.4	Define Service Policies
7.5	Define Promotion Plans and Contingency Plans for Competitor Reaction
7.6	Conduct a Test Market
7.7	Evaluate Test Market Results
7.8	Redo Promotion Plans if 7.7 is Unfavorable
7.9	Adjust Plans, Projections, and Policies
7.10	Obtain Sales
7.11	Compare Actual Sales Results with Projected Sales
7.12	Breakeven Cash Flow Position Achieved
7.13	Breakeven Cash Flow Position not Achieved
7.14	Continue Sales Promotion
7.15	Consider Contingency Plans if Actual Sales
7.16	Adjust Marketing Goals, Contingency Plans, etc.
7.17	Continue Sales Promotion to Obtain Additional Sales

Task 8:   Business Planning

Activity Number	Activity Description
8.1	Define Current and Future Market (Sales Volume, Sales Revenues, Market Share)
8.2	Identify Key Personnel Needs
8.3	Develop Cost Estimates (COGS, Fixed)
8.4	Economic Environment Analysis (Technical)
8.5	Identify Competitors
8.6	Establish Cash Flow; Pro-Forma Balance Sheet and P&L
8.7	Determine Financial Needs
8.8	Financing Alternatives
8.9	Capital Structure (Current and Future)
8.10	Review and Modify Current Business Plan

Precedence Relations

The following table for Task 1, R&D and Engineering, is typical of the precedence relations associated with major tasks that are performed in an innovative start-up. (Table 4)

For each major task, a list of activities involved in the accomplishment of the task is presented in a table. The identification of the specific activities has been performed as a result of analysis of published literature and discussions with individuals involved in innovative start-ups.

Precedence relations associated with the individual activities are also presented in the tables. The precedence relations have been obtained in the same manner as the specific activities that are associated with each task. In all cases, the activities associated with each task are interdependent and involve feedback loops, or cycles.

The associated networks for each task are constructed. In each case, the task networks have the following properties:

1. Some activities have multiple predecessors and/or multiple successors,
2. Some activities may require that previous activities be performed a number of times, and
3. Each task involves a number of cycles.

The R&D and Engineering task network is illustrated in Figure 4.

Table 4

Task 1 – Research & Development and Engineering Activity Characteristics

ACTIVITY NUMBER	ACTIVITY DESCRIPTION	PRECEDENCE RELATIONSHIPS	MEAN TIME	PROBABILITY
1.1	ESTABLISH R&D OBJECTIVES	1.1 < 1.2	2	
1.2	DEFINE R&D PROBLEM	1.2 < 1.3	1	
1.3	DEVELOP SOLUTION ALTERNATIVES TO 1.2	1.3 < 1.4	4	
1.4	EVALUATE ALTERNATIVES IN 1.3	1.4 < 1.5, 1.4 < 1.6, 1.4 < 1.7	2	
1.5	REDEFINE PROBLEM IF 1.4 YIELDS NON-APPLICABLE SOLUTIONS	1.5 < 1.2	1	0.25
1.6	CONTINUE SOLUTION(S) DEVELOPMENT IF 1.4 YIELDS NON-APPLICABLE SOLUTIONS	1.6 < 1.3	2	0.50
1.7	DEVELOP PROTOTYPE OF SELECTED ALTERNATIVE in 1.4 or 1.13	1.7 < 1.8	8	0.25
1.8	TEST AND EVALUATE PROTOTYPE	1.8 < 1.9, 1.8 < 1.10	4	
1.9	UNSUCCESSFUL PROTOTYPE TEST	1.9 < 1.11, 1.9 < 1.12	0	0.50
1.10	SUCCESSFUL PROTOTYPE TEST	1.10 < 1.10A	0	0.50
1.10A	CONDUCT PATENT SEARCH	SINK	4	
1.11	REDEVELOP PTOTOTYPE IF 1.8 UNSUCCESSFUL	1.11 < 1.8	8	0.75
1.12	IDENTIFY NEXT ALTERNATIVE	1.12 < 1.13, 1.12 < 1.14	0	0.25
1.13	SELECT NEXT ALTERNATIVE TO BE DEVELOPED	1.13 < 1.5, 1.13 < 1.6, 1.13 < 1.7	1	0.50
1.14	DISCONTINUE START-UP IF 1.12 IDENTIFIES NO MORE ALTERNATIVES	SINK	0	0.50

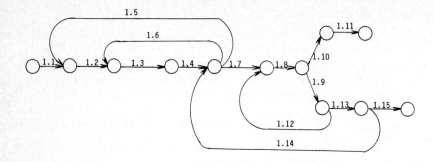

Figure 4: Task 1 - Research & Development and Engineering Network

Interrelationships Among Activities in Different Tasks

A significant number of interrelationships exist in an innovative start-up firm, as in the case of ongoing firms. Table 5 presents the interrelationships that occur between activities in Task 1, R&D and Engineering and other tasks.

Table 5: Interrelationships Between R&D and Engineering and Other Tasks

COLUMN (a) of Figure 3:
    2.2 Identify All Capital Needs
        PRECEDES
    1.3 Develop Solution Alternatives;

    3.1 Define Start-Up Product Concept
        PRECEDES
    1.1 Establish R&D Objectives;

    3.7 Define Start-Up Sales Objectives
        PRECEDES
    1.7 Develop Prototype of Selected Alternative;

    4.5 Define Job Positions . . . Rewards
        PRECEDES
    1.3 Develop Solution Alternatives;

    4.7 Define Key Employee Positions & Agreements
        PRECEDES
    1.7 Develop Prototype of Selected Alternatives;

COLUMN (b) of Figure 3:
    1.7 Develop Prototype of Selected Alternative
        PRECEDES
    8.3 Develop Cost Estimates (COGS, Fixed);

COLUMN (c) of Figure 3:
    8.10 Review and Modify Current Business Plan
        PRECEDES
    1.8 Test and Evaluate Prototype;

COLUMN (d) of Figure 3:
    2.10 Capital Funds Obtained and Applied
    PRECEDES
    1.8 Test and Evaluate Prototype;

    4.5 Select Staff
    PRECEDES
    1.8 Test and Evaluate Prototype;

    5.2 Select Patent Lawyer
    PRECEDES
    1.11 Conduct Patent Search

Information Collection

Basic network information on the following was collected from a variety of sources:

1. Lists of activities.
2. Lists of decision events and alternatives,
3. Precedence relations among activities and decision events,
4. Estimates of durations and probabilities of success of each activity,
5. Feedback loops and cycles.

The methodology used in the information collection process was as follows:

1. Surveys of existing literature on innovative start-ups, with particular reference to high technology ventures,
2. Selected interviews of CEO's involved in MIS on a small scale basis, and
3. Review and analysis of information collected, as required.

As an example of (3), empirical studies have shown that approximately 80% of the high technology ventures survive for a period of 5 years or more. In addition, empirical studies also show that several rounds of venture capital financing are required prior to and subsequent to a breakeven point being reached.

NETWORK ANALYSIS

Q-GERT Program

The Q-GERT approach to innovative management has involved five key steps as follows:

1. The innovative management process is analyzed and described in terms of its significant tasks and associated activities, considering both choice and chance elements,
2. Precedence relations are established for each of the activities, as well as the tasks, based on (1),
3. A network model as a graphical picture of the innovative management process is developed, utilizing (2),
4. For each element in (1), associated durations and probabilities are estimated, and
5. The performance of the innovative management process is assessed using computer simulations of (3) and (4).

The computer simulation process is accomplished by means of Q-GERT, the Queue Graphical and Review Technique. This technique has been utilized in many project planning applications.

The Q-GERT computer program is written in Standard ANSI FORTRAN IV on the Case Western Reserve University DEC-20 computer. Summary statistics are generated as reports on the following variables:

1. Average (mean) time and standard deviation of occurrence of each event,
2. Cumulative probability distribution of occurrence times of each event, and
3. Probability of occurrence of each activity in the network.

Analysis of Results

Each task in the innovative start-up was analyzed using a sample of 40 simulated runs of the
Q-GERT network. Summary statistics for the R&D and Engineering Task are presented in
the following table. (Table 6)

It may be noted that the R&D and Engineering Task may be accomplished if successful, within 22 to 90 weeks after inception of the task. On the average, this task is completed in
almost one year (49.4 + 3.7 weeks). This agrees with the case of Convergent Technologies,
Inc., a 1979 start-up that had its first product in the market in 14 months. The large standard deviation (20.5 weeks) is due to the fact that some activities had to be repeated. In
25% of the successful cases, the task is completed within 31 weeks.

The unsuccessful completion of the R&D and Engineering Task occurs on the average after
64.2 + 9.9 weeks. Approximately 25% of the unsuccessful cases have failed within the first
nine months (38 weeks). A histogram displays graphically the frequency with which the values of the time to reach each event in the R&D and Engineering Task is accomplished. It
is also possible to develop a curve representing this histogram, utilizing a computer program
called AID. [18, p. 484]

In addition to the individual task networks, an integrated innovative start-up process network
has been developed. In this case, the seven basic tasks are described in inter-dependent
terms, where specific activities in a task are required to be completed prior to the initiation
of other activities in another task.

Table 6: Summary Statistics – R&D and Engineering Task

Number of Activities   12

Number of Probablistic Activities   7

Duration, in Weeks

    · Successful (75%)

       · Mean 49.4
       · Standard Deviation 20.5
       · Standard Deviation of Mean 3.7
       · Range 22-90
       · Quartiles . . . . (31,43,68)

    · Unsuccessful (25%)

       · Mean 64.2
       · Standard Deviation 31.5
       · Standard Deviation of Mean 9.9
       · Range 22-122
       · Quartiles . . . .(38,59,75)

    · All (100%)

       · Mean 52.1
       · Standard Deviation 24.2
       · Standard Deviation of Mean 3.8
       · Range 22-122
       · Quartiles . . . .(31,49,68)

The PERT/CPM Approach

In addition to the general Q-GERT approach for MIS, the PERT/CPM approach may be considered for early stage application in MIS.

For the first six months of the company's operation, the PERT chart is recommended. [22] The PERT chart relates the key tasks (products, equipment, plant, and people) to both time and costs. An example of a PERT chart is given for an education company. [22] Furthermore, the PERT chart is related to the Business Plan (see Exhibits 3.1 - 3.11). [22]

Recently, this study has applied the PERT/CPM approach to provide frequent reports on the status of the innovative start-up firm. Figure 5 presents computer printouts of the network-based method applied in the start-up.

The Job Report presents a status report of each activity, in the form of early start, early finish, late start, and late finish. The predecessors are identifed. The critical path is identified as those activities which have no slack.

The second report presents the GANTT Chart, where each activity is identifed as to its criticality, its start, and its completion date.

The Visi Schedule computer program was utilized on the IBM/PC to provide frequent reports, as required by management.

Specifically, Figure 5 presents a typical output of the Visi Schedule computer program as applied to a new medical instrumentation firm. Figure 5 also presents the GANTT Chart for the same reporting period. The Job Report presents each identified activity in which the firm is engaged. Both figures are updated approximately monthly to provide timely and accurate information on the current status and plans of the firm.

Computer Programs

Computer programs have been developed, tested, and applied utilizing (1) the Case Western Reserve University DEC-20 computer facilities for the Q-GERT application and (2) the Weatherhead School of Management's Computer Laboratory for the CPM/PERT applications. As a result of significant application and testing with an MIS firm, we have found the following situations to be applicable:

- Q-GERT is most applicable for use in the case of large, complex cyclic, decision event networks
- CPM/PERT is most applicable for use in the case of acyclic networks, where all activities are performed as planned
- GANTT Chart and Job Report computer printouts are extremely useful for managerial monitoring, reports, and control

Currently, applications are underway with five small high technology firms, with primary emphasis on early stage MIS situations. In two of the cases, corporate ventures are also involved.

The following table presents a comparative analysis of the PERT/CPM and Q-GERT methodologies in the case of MIS.

Figure 5: GANTT Chart and Job Report for the MIS

```
                     May       Jun       Ju GANTT Chart  Sep       Oct       Nov       Dec       Jan
Job Description      4 11 18 25 1 8 15 22 29 6 13 22 27 3 12 17 24 31 7 14 21 28 5 12 19 26 2 9 16 23 30 7 14 21 28 4
                     0  1  2  3 4 5 6  7  8 9 10 11 12 13 14 1516 17 18 19 20 21 22 23 24 25 26 27 2829 30 31 32 33 34
 1 2/ Idea           # . . . . . . . . . . . . . . . . . . . . . . . . . . . . . . . . . . .
 2 3/Cognitive Prototype# . . . . . . . . . . . . . . . . . . . . . . . . . . . . . . . . . .
 3 4/Define In-Output # . . . . . . . . . . . . . . . . . . . . . . . . . . . . . . . . . . .
 4 5/Cognize Software # . . . . . . . . . . . . . . . . . . . . . . . . . . . . . . . . . . .
 5 6/Define Software  # . . . . . . . . . . . . . . . . . . . . . . . . . . . . . . . . . . .

 6 7/Define Visual Input# . . . . . . . . . . . . . . . . . . . . . . . . . . . . . . . . . .
 7 8/Define Alarms    # . . . . . . . . . . . . . . . . . . . . . . . . . . . . . . . . . . .
 8 9/Define Display   # . . . . . . . . . . . . . . . . . . . . . . . . . . . . . . . . . . .
 9 Dummy Operation    # . . . . . . . . . . . . . . . . . . . . . . . . . . . . . . . . . . .
10 12/Define Feasible # . . . . . . . . . . . . . . . . . . . . . . . . . . . . . . . . . . .
    Software

IIIIIII/Write Oper. Man.  # . . . . . . . . . . . . . . . . . . . . . . . . ) . . . . . . . .
12 12/FDA 510(k) Form  # . . . . . . . . . . . . . . . . . . . . . . . . . . . )
13 13/Patent          ) - - - - ) . . . . . . . . . . . . . . . . . . . . . . )
14 14/Cognize Hardware # . . . . . . . . . . . . . . . . . . . . . . . . . . . . . . . . . . .
15 15/Define Hardware  # . . . . . . . . . . . . . . . . . . . . . . . . . . . . . . . . . . .

16 16/Def. Enrgy. Srce. # . . . . . . . . . . . . . . . . . . . . . . . . . . . . . . . . . . .
17 17/Def. Pow.Spp.Bttry# . . . . . . . . . . . . . . . . . . . . . . . . . . . . . . . . . .
18 18/Def. Vacation Pac # . . . . . . . . . . . . . . . . . . . . . . . . . . . . . . . . . . .
19 19/Def. Mem. Bttry.  # . . . . . . . . . . . . . . . . . . . . . . . . . . . . . . . . . . .
20 20/Def. Syringe      # . . . . . . . . . . . . . . . . . . . . . . . . . . . . . . . . . . .

21 21/Def. Infusion Set # . . . . . . . . . . . . . . . . . . . . . . . . . . . . . . . . . . .
22 22/Define Motor      # . . . . . . . . . . . . . . . . . . . . . . . . . . . . . . . . . . .
23 DUMMY               # . . . . . . . . . . . . . . . . . . . . . . . . . . . . . . . . . . .
24 DUMMY               # . . . . . . . . . . . . . . . . . . . . . . . . . . . . . . . . . . .
25 23/Brdbrd. for Funct.# . . . . . . . . . . . . . . . . . . . . . . . . . . . . . . . . . . .
26 24/Obtain Ener. Srce # . . . . . . . . . . . . . . . . . ) . . . . . . . . . . . . . . . . .
27 25/Obtain Syringe    ) - - - - ) . . . . . . . . . . . . ) . . . . . . . . . . . . . . . . .
28 26/Obtain Inf. Set   # . . . . . . . . . . . . . . . . . ) . . . . . . . . . . . . . . . . .
29 27/ Obtain Motor     ) - - - - - - - - ) . . . . . . . . ) . . . . . . . . . . . . . . . . .
30 DUMMY               . . . . # . . . . . . . . . ) . . . . . . . . . . . . . . . . . . . . .

31 32/Sec. Prdctn. Fac. ) = = = = = = = = = ) . . . . . . . . . . . . . . . . . . . . . . . . .
32 31/Staff (Prod,GA,QC). . . . . ) = = = = = = = = = = = = = ) . . . . . . . . . . . . . . . .
33 31/Des. Bld,Test,Tool . . . . # . . . . . . . . . . . . . . . )
34 28/Des.Cryng. Case    . . . . ) = = = = ) . . . . . . . . )
35 29/Des.Labels/Boxng   . . . . . . ) = = = ) . . . . . . . )

36 31/dummy             . . . . . . # . . . . . . . . . )
37 32/Instructions      . . . . . . . . ) = = ) . . . . . . . . . )
38 33/Syringe           . . . . . . . . . . . . ) = = )
39 34/Energy Sources    . . . . . . . . . . . . ) = = )
40 35/Infusion Set      . . . . . . . . . . . . ) = = )

41 dummy                . . . . . . . . . # . . . . . . . . )
42 36/First Prod. Run   . . . . . . . . . ) = = = = = = = = = = = )
43 37/Qual.Control Test . . . . . . . . . . . . . . . . . . . . ) = )
44 38/G.K.P. Compliance . . . . . . . . . . . . . . . . . . . . . . . ) = = = = = = = = )
45 38/dummy             . . # . . . . . . . . . . . . . . . . . . . . . . . . . . . . . )

46 39/Inv. Build-up(1000). . . . . . . . . . . . . . . . . . . . . . . . . . . . ) = = = = = = = = = = = = = = = = = = = = = = = = )
47 40/Market            . . . . . . . . . . . . . . . . . . . . . . . . . . . . . . . . . . . #
48 netclosed           . . . . . . . . . . . . . . . . . . . . . . . . . . . . . . . . . . . X
                     May       Jun       Jul       Aug       Sep       Oct       Nov       Dec       Jan
Job Description      4 11 18 25 1 8 15 22 29 6 13 20 27 3 10 17 24 31 7 14 21 28 5 12 19 26 2 9 16 23 30 7 14 21 28 4
                     0  1  2  3 4 5 6  7  8 9 10 11 12 13 14 15 16 17 18 19 20 21 22 23 24 25 26 27 28 29 30 31 32 33
```

Job Report

JOB	NAME	DERA TION	WORK DONE	EARLY START	EARLY FINISH	LATE START	LATE FINISH	SLACK TOT	SLACK FREE	PREREQUISITE 1	2	3
1	2/Idea	0	0	5/ 4/84	5/ 4/84	5/ 4/84	5/ 4/84	0	0			
2	3/Cognitive Prototype	0	0	5/ 4/84	5/ 4/84	5/ 4/84	5/ 4/84	0	0	1		
3	4/Define Input and Output	0	0	5/ 4/84	5/ 4/84	5/ 4/84	5/ 4/84	0	0	2		
4	5/Cognize the Software	0	0	5/ 4/84	5/ 4/84	5/ 4/84	5/ 4/84	0	0	3		
5	6/Define the Software	0	0	5/ 4/84	5/ 4/84	5/ 4/84	5/ 4/84	0	0	4		
6	7/Define the Visual Input	0	0	5/ 4/84	5/ 4/84	5/ 4/84	5/ 4/84	0	0	5		
7	8/Define the Alarms	0	0	5/ 4/84	5/ 4/84	5/ 4/84	5/ 4/84	0	0	5		
8	9/Define the Display	0	0	5/ 4/84	5/ 4/84	5/ 4/84	5/ 4/84	0	0	5		
9	Dummy Operation	0	0	5/ 4/84	5/ 4/84	5/ 4/84	5/ 4/84	0	0	6	7	8
10	10/Define Feasible Software	0	0	5/ 4/84	5/ 4/84	5/ 4/84	5/ 4/84	0	0	9		
11	11/Write the Operations Manual	0	0	5/ 4/84	5/ 4/84	9/28/84	9/28/84	21	0	10		
12	12/FDA 510(k) Form	0	0	5/ 4/84	5/ 4/84	10/12/84	10/12/84	23	2	11		
13	13/Patent	2	0	5/ 4/84	5/18/84	9/28/84	10/12/84	21	0	11		
14	14/Cognize the Hardware	0	0	5/ 4/84	5/ 4/84	5/ 4/84	5/ 4/84	0	0	10		
15	15/Define Hardware	0	0	5/ 4/84	5/ 4/84	5/ 4/84	5/ 4/84	0	0	14		
16	16/Define Energy Source	0	0	5/ 4/84	5/ 4/84	5/ 4/84	5/ 4/84	0	0	15		
17	17/Define Pow. Supp. Battery	0	0	5/ 4/84	5/ 4/84	5/ 4/84	5/ 4/84	0	0	16		
18	18/Define Vacation Pac	0	0	5/ 4/84	5/ 4/84	5/ 4/84	5/ 4/84	0	0	16	17	
19	19/Define Memory Battery	0	0	5/ 4/84	5/ 4/84	5/ 4/84	5/ 4/84	0	0	16		
20	20/Define the Syringe	0	0	5/ 4/84	5/ 4/84	5/ 4/84	5/ 4/84	0	0	15		
21	21/Define Infusion Set	0	0	5/ 4/84	5/ 4/84	5/ 4/84	5/ 4/84	0	0	15		
22	22/Define the Motor	0	0	5/ 4/84	5/ 4/84	5/ 4/84	5/ 4/84	0	0	15		
23	DUMMY	0	0	5/ 4/84	5/ 4/84	5/ 4/84	5/ 4/84	0	0	18	19	20
24	DUMMY	0	0	5/ 4/84	5/ 4/84	5/ 4/84	5/ 4/84	0	0	21	22	
25	23/Breadboard for Function.	0	0	5/ 4/84	5/ 4/84	5/ 4/84	5/ 4/84	0	0	23	24	
26	24/Obtain Energy Source	0	0	5/ 4/84	5/ 4/84	7/ 6/84	7/ 6/84	9	4	25		
27	25/Obtain Syringe	2	0	5/ 4/84	5/18/84	6/22/84	7/ 6/84	7	2	25		
28	26/Obtain Infusion Set	0	0	5/ 4/84	5/ 4/84	7/ 6/84	7/ 6/84	9	4	25		
29	27/Obtain Motor	4	0	5/ 4/84	6/ 1/84	6/ 8/84	7/ 6/84	5	0	25		
30	DUMMY	0	0	6/ 1/84	6/ 1/84	7/ 6/84	7/ 6/84	5	0	26	27	28
31	30/Secure Facililty for Prod	5	0	5/ 4/84	6/ 8/84	5/ 4/84	6/ 8/84	0	0	25		
32	31/Staff(Prod.,GA/QC.Marketg	7)	0	6/ 8/84	7/27/84	6/ 8/84	7/27/84	0	0	31		
33	31/Design, Build,Test,Tool	0	0	6/ 1/84	6/ 1/84	7/27/84	7/27/84	8	8	30		
34	28/Design Carrying Case (pouch)	2	0	6/ 1/84	6/15/84	7/ 6/84	7/20/84	5	0	30		
35	29/Design Labels and Boxin	1	0	6/15/84	6/22/84	7/20/84	7/27/84	5	0	34		
36	31/DUMMY	0	0	6/22/84	6/22/84	7/27/84	7/27/84	5	5	35		
37	32/Instructions	1	0	6/22/84	6/29/84	7/27/84	8/ 3/84	5	5	35		
38	33/Syringe	1	0	7/27/84	8/ 3/84	7/27/84	8/ 3/84	0	0	32	33	38
39	34/Energy Source	1	0	7/27/84	8/ 3/84	7/27/84	8/ 3/84	0	0	32	33	38
40	35/Infusion Set	1	0	7/27/84	8/ 3/84	7/27/84	8/ 3/84	0	0	32	33	38
41	DUMMY	0	0	8/ 3/84	8/ 3/84	8/ 3/84	8/ 3/84	0	0	37	38	39
42	35/First Productn Run	5	0	8/ 3/84	9/ 7/84	8/ 3/84	9/ 7/84	0	0	41		
43	37/Quality Control Test	1	0	9/ 7/84	9/14/84	9/ 7/84	9/14/84	0	0	42		
44	38/G.M.P. Compliance	4	0	9/14/84	10/12/84	9/14/84	10/12/84	0	0	43		
45	38/DUMMY	0	0	5/18/84	5/18/84	10/12/84	10/12/84	21	21	12	13	
46	39/Inventory Build-up (1000)	12	0	10/12/84	1/ 4/85	10/12/84	1/ 4/85	0	0	44	45	
47	40/Market	0	0	1/ 4/85	1/ 4/85	1/ 4/85	1/ 4/85	0	0	46		
48	netclosed	0	0	1/ 4/85	1/ 4/85	1/ 4/85	1/ 4/85	0	0	47		

Table 7: Comparison of PERT/CPM and GERT Methods

Advantages of PERT/CPM Networks

1. Clarity of presentation to management
2. Ease of understanding
3. Cost savings in preparation
4. Critical path clearly identified
5. Time and control of project easy to accomplish

Disadvantages of PERT/CPM Networks

1. No cycles allowed
2. No consideration of activity failure
3. No capability of queueing activities
4. No consideration that actual activity performance may result in changes and timing of other activities
5. All activities are required to be performed exactly once
6. No probability considerations in the performance of activities are permitted
7. Underlying assumptions concerning activity durations are specified, in advance.

SUMMARY AND CONCLUSIONS

This chapter is concerned with the development, test, and evaluation of a generic network-based method for use in the management of innovative start-up firms. The major tasks accomplished in each start-up, including R&D and engineering, market research, organization and personnel, legal and accounting, finance and investment, manufacturing, marketing, and business planning, were identified. For each major task, the significant activities, precedence relations, decision nodes, alternative choices of action, feedback loops, and durations, were identified.

Information and data has been collected on a small number of innovative start-up firms, and several discussions have been held with entrepreneurs and venture capital funds. In addition, published literatures on innovative start-ups, venture capital funds, and entrepreneurs have been reviewed.

The Q-GERT approach is used to model the management process, as this method provides the means to model situations involving probabilistic elements, decision processes and choices, and the variety of cycles occurring in an innovative start-up. CPM/PERT networks are utilized for an individual firm, incorporating the basic features of Q-GERT, and considering that decisions that are indicated in Q-GERT are in fact made as desired. GANTT Charts are used for management monitoring and reporting purposes.

Computer programs for simulation have been developed and applied to analyze different scenarios. The programs are currently being used to validate the durations and probability distributions based on preliminary sample data. In addition, computer outputs are obtained of such parameters as the critical path, the criticality index of each start-up task, the distribution times of each event, and the probability of reaching each end-state. In general, start-up firms use GANTT Charts for the monitoring, control, and reporting of activities associated with the start-up.

In conclusion, it is demonstrated that the MIS may be enhanced by utilizing the systems approach and a network-based planning method. The MIS is viewed as a project to be managed. Business planning is considered to be the coordinating and control task, where the other seven tasks are interrelated with this task. At the present time, five start-up firms are utilizing this methodology.

FOOTNOTES

[1] Revision of manuscript appearing in Proceedings, Engineering Management Conference, International Congress on Technology and Technology Exchange, Pittsburgh, PA, October 8-10, 1984.

REFERENCES

[1]   Baty, G. B., Entrepreneurship for the Eighties, Reston, VA: Reston Publishing Company, 1981.

[2]   Brandt, S., Entrepreneuring, Addison-Wellesley, 1982.

[3]   Buskirk, R. H., P. J. Vaughn, Managing New Enterprises, St. Paul, MN: West Publishing, 1978.

[4]   Balinsky, G., The Innovation Millionaires, New York: Scribners, 1976.

[5]   Collins, I., D. G. Moore, The Organization Makers, New York: Appleton-Century Crofts, 1979.

[6]   Cooper, A. C., The Founding of Technologically Based Firms, Milwaukee, MN: Center for Venture Management, 1971.

[7]   _____, J. L. Komives, Technical Entrepreneurship, A Symposium. Center for Venture Management. Milwaukee, WI: 1972.

[8]   Cossman, E. J. Entrepreneurial Flow Charts, Palm Springs, CA: Cossman International, 1975.

[9]   Dean, B. V., "A Network Method in the Management of Innovative Start-Ups," Entrepreneurial Research Conference Proceedings, Wellesley, MA, 1983.

[10] Dible, D. M., Business Start-Up Basics, Santa Clara, CA: Entrepreneur Press, 1978.

[11] Ellis, L. W., The Financial Side of Industrial Research Management, New York: John Wiley & Sons, Inc., 1984.

[12] Hanan, M., Venture Management, New York: McGraw-Hill, 1976.

[13] Kent, C. A., D. L. Sexton, K. H. Vesper, Encyclopedia of Entrepreneurship, Englewood Cliffs, NJ: Prentice-Hall, 1982.

[14] Leff, N. H., "Entrepreneurship and Development: The Problem Revisited," Journal of Economic Literature, March 1979, p. 47.

[15] Liles, P. R., New Business Ventures and the Entrepreneur, Homewood, IL: Irwin, 1974.

[16] Martino, J. P., Technological Forecasting for Decision Making, Second Edition, New York: Elsevier Science, 1983.

[17] "New High Technology Firms Post 80% Success Record," Industrial Research, November 1970.

[18] Pritsker, A. B., C. E. Segal, Management Decision Making, Englewood Cliffs, NJ: Prentice-Hall, 1983.

[19] Roberts, E. B., "How to Succeed in a New Technology Enterprise," Technology Review, 73, No. 2, December 1970.

[20] Rogers, E. N., <u>Diffusion of Innovations</u>, Third Edition, New York: The Free Press, 1983.

[21] Schumpter, J. A., <u>The Theory of Economic Development</u>, Cambridge, MA: Harvard University Press, 1934.

[22] Silver, A. D., <u>The Entrepreneurial Life</u>, New York: John Wiley & Sons, Inc., 1983.

[23] Smith, W. N., E. G. Meyer, A. R. Hirsig, <u>Industrial R&D Management – The Modern Issues</u>, New York: Marcel Dekker, Inc., 1982.

[24] Stanford, M. J., <u>New Enterprise Management</u>, Reston, VA: Reston Publishing Company, 1982.

[25] Swayne, C., W. Tucker, <u>The Effective Entrepreneur</u>, Morristown, NJ: General Learning Press, 1973.

[26] Timmons, J. A., L. E. Smollen, A. L. Dingee, Jr., <u>New Venture Creation</u>, Homewood, IL: Irwin, 1977.

[27] Vesper, K. H., <u>Entrepreneurship Education: A Bicentennial Compendium</u>, Milwaukee, WI: Center for Venture Management. 1976.

[28] _____, "Venture Idea Sources," <u>Proceedings, Annual Meeting of the American Institute for Decision Sciences</u>, St. Louis, MO, 1978.

[29] _____, <u>New Venture Strategies</u>, Englewood Cliffs, NJ: Prentice-Hall, Inc., 1980.

[30] Webster, F., "A Model for New Venture Initiation," <u>Academy of Management Review</u>, Vol. 1, No. 1, January 1976.

[31] "Big Business Tries to Imitate the Entrepreneurial Spirit," <u>Business Week</u>, McGraw-Hill, April 13, 1983.

Project Management: Methods and Studies
Burton V. Dean (editor)
© Elsevier Science Publishers B.V. (North-Holland), 1985

THE APPLICATION OF GERT TO AIR FORCE SYSTEMS [1] DEVELOPMENT PLANNING

John C. Papageorgiou

University of Massachusetts
Boston, Massachusetts
U.S.A.

A number of command, control, communications and intelligence systems are currently being developed by the U. S. Air Force and Gantt charting is being used for establishing milestones and controlling the progress of their development. Given their complexity and the inherent uncertainty regarding the outcome of the different stages of the process of their development, PERT, or one of its variations, could not be suggested as an appropriate approach for their systematic planning and control. Instead, the simulation approach GERT was chosen and in this paper it is described how it was applied to the planning of one of these systems as a demonstration. The system selected was the Assault Breaker Program, a joint project between the Air Force and the Army.

The system acquisition process is described and the objectives of the study are discussed. The advantages of GERT over PERT are briefly reviewed, the process of constructing the GERT network is described and the results of the simulation are discussed.

As a result of this demonstration, the project manager and his staff improved their perceptions of the structure of the project and the interrelationships among the activities. The GERT network was subsequently used by them in time-phasing the activities of the project. A number of other benefits that could be derived from the implementation of GERT in system development and R & D throughout the Air Force, Army and Navy are discussed. It is pointed out that introduction of GERT would significantly contribute to improving the planning and control of what is considered by the people involved to be 'unplannable.'

INTRODUCTION

The Electronic Systems Division, U. S. Air Force Systems Command, has as a mission to plan, acquire, manage and conduct technological development (research, exploratory, advanced and engineering) for command, control, communications and intelligence systems. One of its deputies is the Deputy for Development Plans which is responsible for system development planning. The developmental process is quite long, some systems taking fifteen to twenty years. During that period frequent revisions of the conceptual and mechanical configuration of the planned systems take place. Furthermore, there is a great deal of uncertainty associated with the different activities involved in terms of both their realization and their outcome. As a result, the planning process becomes very complex.

At the present time Gantt charting is being used for establishing milestones and controlling the progress of the projects. The objective of this study was to demonstrate the benefits to be gained from the application of GERT (Graphical Evaluation and Review Technique) to the planning of these Air Force systems. This paper describes the system acquisition process followed by the Air Force, the suitability of GERT to the Air Force system development planning, the project which was selected as a case study to demonstrate the application of GERT and the actual application of the method.

The Assault Breaker Program, which is a joint project between the Air Force and the Army, was used as a demonstration. A GERT network was developed and estimates were made of the input data required for demonstration purposes. The network was simulated and different kinds of statistics were collected for a number of nodes. Although the statistics derived were based on approximate estimates of the input data, they were adequate to demonstrate to the managers of the different projects the usefulness of the GERT approach.

A number of benefits were derived from this demonstration. During the construction of the GERT network the people involved were required to organize their perceptions of the structure of the project and the interrelationships among the activities. Using the statistics derived from the simulation, it was demonstrated how to set realistic goals and evaluate the changes of completing the projects and project milestones within certain time limits. As a result, additional resources could be secured or existing ones could be reallocated through proposals documented on the basis of the GERT approach simulation results.

Due to the nature of these projects, there is a great deal of uncertainty involved with respect to the structure of the network and the data. It is suggested that such situations be analyzed by means of sensitivity analysis. Different perceptions of the network should be considered and their effect upon the plans should be determined. Also, the input data could be varied so that ranges of values of the statistics could be derived. Finally, as the project progresses, perceptions about the project change and the value of the data can be estimated more accurately. Thus, the GERT approach, as a dynamic tool, can prove to be valuable in planning complex projects.

The System Acquisition Process

The system acquisition process, which aims at the satisfaction of identified mission needs, is divided into four major phases demarcated by respective major decision points called milestones. They are as follows:

Milestone 0 - Program Initiation. A mission need is determined to be essential, it is reconciled with other Department of Defense capabilities, and it is approved by the Secretary of Defense. Following this approval, technological solutions are proposed and developed; technological, military and economic bases for acquisition are established; a program manager is designated; and competing contractor efforts are started and brought to the point when approval is required for a hardware and software demonstration and validation of both technological and economic considerations of one or more proposed system concepts.

Milestone I - Demonstration and Validation. The recommendations developed in the previous phase are reviewed by the Defense System Acquisition Review Council, and the Secretary of Defense approves one or more selected alternatives for competitive demonstration and validation. Following this approval, the approved concepts are developed into hardware and software for testing; field demonstrations take place; and studies are carried out toward improving and advancing the system performance definition and cost/schedule data.

Milestone II - Full-scale Engineering and Development. The recommendations for full scale engineering development, based on the outcome of the demonstration and validation phase, are reviewed by the Defense System Acquisition Review Council. The Secretary of Defense will then approve the full-scale engineering development of one of the alternative systems. This approval will include procurement of long lead production items and also limited production for operational test and evaluation. The task of the Deputy for Development Plans, Electronic Systems Division, ends at this point with the recommendation for production and deployment of the system.

<u>Milestone III - Production and Deployment</u>. The recommendation for production at a certain rate and deployment to the using agency, based on the outcome of the operational test is reviewed by the Defense System Acquisition Review Council and approved by the Secretary of Defense.

Objectives of the Study

The Deputy for Development Plans is currently involved with the development planning of a number of programs ranging from programs that are just being conceived to programs that are going through their full scale engineering development stage. Each of these programs consists of hundreds of activities that have to be completed with a certain precedence relationship among them. Because of the nature of the planned systems, there is some uncertainty associated with the different activities regarding their realization and their outcome if they are performed. Frequent revisions of the conceptual and mechanical configuration of the planned systems cause revisions of the number and type of activities, as well as their precedence relationships. As a result, the planning process becomes very complex. At the same time, however, good planning is absolutely necessary, given the fact that technology advances exponentially, the world changes very fast, and that a delay in the production of a system may render it outdated by the time it reaches the user.

A systematic and scientific planning approach is therefore necessary to help the managers of these programs with their planning task. At the present time Gantt charting is used for establishing milestones and controlling the progress of the different projects. Time estimates for the different parts of a project used in drawing the Gantt charts are usually made on the basis of intuition and without a systematic approach. The program director has no way of systematically evaluating the chances of reaching the different milestones on time or the time necessary to complete a certain part of the project. If through a systematic approach the program director could evaluate the risk of certain delays, then he would be in a better position to call attention to this fact and to better support his demands for additional resources. As a result, the overall time span needed to deliver a system to the user could be shortened significantly.

Network modeling techniques like PERT/CPM have facilitated the planning and control of large projects and they have become well known and popular in their use. However, due to some disadvantages they present in the modeling of complex R & D projects [11,32,41], more flexible network techniques have been developed during the last few years. GERT is such a powerful and flexible technique and the objective of this project was to demonstrate its usefulness to the planning process of Air Force systems development. This study demonstrated the usefulness of the GERT approach and the way it can be applied and implemented.

The program that was selected for this demonstration was the Assault Breaker Program [26]. It is a joint project between the Air Force and the Army and aims at the fulfillment of the goal of developing systems that could detect, locate, and strike enemy armor at ranges well beyond the forward edge of the battle area. The Assault Breaker Program is an accelerated program and the different subsystems have not followed the normal planning and development processes. For example, some subsystems will meet their first official milestone at milestone II without having gone through the approval decisions at milestones 0 and I.

Another consideration is the inter-agency character of the program which requires integration, coordination and monitoring of its different aspects with all the activities of the participating agencies. For example, subsystems to be developed by the Army have to be successfully completed before the program can continue. Such a subsystem is a surface-to-surface missile developed by the Army which is interoperable with an airborne moving target indicator and synthetic aperature radar developed by the Air Force. Data Processing Communications Systems have also to be developed independently and then integrated with the other subsystems of the project. There are several other subsystems which have to be developed independently and then integrated which, given the uncertainties in their development, make the coordination and planning of the overall project very complex.

The GERT Network

Application of network methods to the planning and control of large projects has been limited for a number of years to PERT and its variations. Although PERT has been applied extensively, it has a number of limitations that render it inflexible in modeling complex projects such as R & D projects. To overcome PERT's limitations, GERT was developed which has the following characteristics:

(a)   An activity has associated with it a probability that it will be selected, ranging from zero to one. The nodes are, therefore, constructed differently to denote their nature as deterministic or probabilistic.

(b)   The realization of a node may be specified to occur upon the realization of one or more of the activities leading to it; it may be realized one or more times; and the first time it is realized the number of activities to be completed may be different from subsequent repeats.

(c)   Looping in simple or complex forms is allowed.

(d)   The network can have more than one source node and/or sink node (success, failure, postponement, etc.).

(e)   Modifications of the network, which take place upon the completion of a certain activity for each modification, can be incorporated.

(f)   Several types of probability distributions can be used to represent activity times.

(g)   Cost can be assigned to each activity in terms of a fixed and a variable per unit time component.

(h)   Statistics can be collected for the sink as well as other designated nodes on time, cost, and activity counts for specified activities.

Due to the above characteristics, it was judged that GERT is an ideal method for dealing with the complexity and stochastic aspects of Air Force systems development.

As in any other case of network modeling, one of the major benefits derived from the application of GERT is the fact that the people involved are required to organize their perceptions of the structure of the project and the interrelationships among the activities in a systematic way. This was particularly true in the case of the Assault Breaker Project. Although at the beginning the detailed structure of the project was nebulous in the minds of the people involved, they were forced through the networking process to think about it, clarify their perceptions, cross-verify them, and arrive at some kind of consensus. As a result, the original draft of the network went through a number of revisions with each one of them approaching closer the modeled reality. The final draft of the network includes approximately five hundred activities and three hundred nodes, making it impossible to present here or to discuss in detail.

Three kinds of data had to be estimated for each activity in order to simulate the network: probability that it will be performed, time required, and cost. It would be impossible within the two-month time limitations of this study to systematically derive the most suitable probability distribution for each activity and estimate with relative precision its parameters. Approximate estimates of activity probabilities and durations were therefore judged adequate at this stage of the analysis in demonstrating the usefulness of the approach. The Beta distribution fitted to three parameters (as in the case of PERT) was used to represent the time distribution for each activity. In cases where duration was not subject to variation a constant was used instead of a distribution. The parameters of the distribution, or the constants, together with the selection probability for each activity were estimated. As parts of the network had already been completed or contracted for completion with a promised delivery date, a constant time was assigned to that part of the network equal to the time still remaining until the completion deadline. Sample of the input data is presented in Appendix I. Cost data were not employed and they are equal to zero in the respective columns; it was felt by the program director that cost estimates would not be of much interest at this stage of the analysis.

Simulation Results

In order to simulate the network we used the prewritten software package GERT IIIZ supplied by Pritsker & Associates, Inc. after some modifications so that it would accomodate the particular size of our network. A newer version of the package called Q-GERT was not available to us at the time of the simulation. We simulated the network 500 times on the MITRE Corporation IBM 370 Computer and it took 4.8 minutes CPU time.

Sample of the statistics collected are given in Appendix II; it consists of two parts: in the first part, summary statistics are given for the nodes for which statistics were collected. If a node was never realized, the message "no values recorded" is given. The same message is given for the row in which cost data should be reported for each node. The information provided includes probability of realization of a node; mean, standard deviation, and minimum and maximum values for duration; number of observations; and type of statistics collected. The count statistics refer to activity completions with a specific counter type with respect to releases of the particular node for which the specific statistics are collected; they include all the above measures.

As an example take the summary statistics for Node 186 (Program approved for full-scale engineering development). There is a .532 chance that the program will be approved for full scale engineering development. As an average it will take 91.14 months, with standard deviation of 18.22 months. The minimum observed completion time out of the 266 observations was 70.34 months and the maximum was 205.49 months. With respect to releases of Node 186, the average number of activity completions with counter type I (Activities 276, 283, 290, and 304 according to the activity description data of Appendix I; is not shown) is .44 with standard deviation .80, a minimum number of 0 and a maximum of 3. Analogous is the interpretation of statistics for the other counter types.

The second part of Appendix II gives the relative frequency and cumulative relative frequency distributions of duration for two of the nodes together with their respective histograms. Thus, for example, the realization of Event 190 (cancellation of the Surface to Surface Missile Program) could occur with a chance of .052 (according to the summary statistics). If this happens, there is a .192 chance that this will take place before the 40th month, a .500 chance that it will occur before the 44th month, and a .385 chance that it will happen after the 50th month (according to the time distribution). This information could be used by the program director in assessing the risk involved regarding the whole or any part of the program. As a result, action could be taken at an earlier stage to decrease risk and alleviate the consequences of cancellation of that part of the program.

As another example take the interval statistics for the part of the network between noded 144 and 251 (Preparation of Specifications for Contractor Review). This set of activities would be performed with a chance of .668 at an average time of 14.75 months with standard deviation of 1.62 months (summary statistics). There is a .156 chance that it will take up to 13 months and a .144 chance that it will take more than 16.5 months (time distribution).

Discussion

As it was indicated above, the objective of the study was to demonstrate the usefulness of the GERT approach in planning complex R & D projects which many regard as unplannable. Also, due to limited time, approximate estimates of the input data were used which, however, were adequate for demonstration purposes. Thus, for example, the Beta distribution or a constant were used in representing activity times. It is obvious that if GERT was to be adopted for actual planning, more careful and precise estimates should be made of the input data. In such a case, the appropriate input distribution should be used for each activity. Of course, there would be no practical way of systematically studying each activity and deriving the most representative type of distribution for its duration. It would be possible, however, through further analysis to come up with certain generalizations. For example, as there are many activities in the network representing tests of particular components or subsystems, we could find that the normal, say, distribution would be most appropriate for such activities. Similarly, we could generalize about other types of activities and find that the lognormal would be most appropriate for another type of activity and so on.

Given the size and nature of this kind of project, the input data cannot be estimated with a high degree of precision. The best practical approach would be to carry out sensitivity analysis to determine the sensitivity of the results to the accuracy of the input data. Through such analysis, ranges of the statistics could be established within which the program director would base his actual planning of the project. It is also possible, given the complexity and unclear structure of this kind of projects, to carry out sensitivity analysis with respect to alternative versions of the network and determine the impact of these different perceptions of the structure of the project upon the plans.

As it is true with many other approaches, decisions will not be made by means of the approach per se, but more information will be provided to the decision maker to make better decisions. With this understanding, the kind of information provided by the GERT approach would be extremely valuable for the program director of a project that involves so much uncertainty and is so different from, say, a construction project which involves a more clear cut set of activities and less risk. Setting milestones for such programs without a systematic analysis carries the risk of setting unrealistic goals and thus disrupting the whole defense planning process. But if GERT is used and the simulation and sensitivity analysis, as discussed above, show that a major program has a small chance to be completed within a specified time, several actions can be taken to secure additional resources or reallocate resources so that the goal is achieved within the required time limits.

The information provided to the program director by the GERT approach is not only useful at the stage of initial planning but also at any other later stage. Having drawn the first GERT network which represents the first conception of the structure of the project, it is easier at a later stage to check the current conception of its structure and modify the network. Simulation of the new network will provide more concise estimates of the consequences of earlier planning errors and a basis for updating the plans, making up for lost time, and taking action to decrease the impact of these errors.

CONCLUSION: SUMMARY AND EXTENSIONS

GERT was applied as a demonstration in the planning of the Assault Breaker project, a cooperative effort between the Air Force and the Army, directed by the Air Force. The network model was developed and, on the basis of approximate estimates of the relevant parameters, it was simulated using a prewritten software package. Although the objective of the analysis was only to demonstrate the approach and its advantages, certain benefits were derived from this demonstration. The network development process itself helped the people involved with the project gain a better understanding of its structure and of the interfacing of its component parts. To use the words of the Technical Director of the Deputy for Development Plans, ". . . the study contributed greatly to the understanding of the program planning management concept." The network was subsequently used by the program director and his staff in time-phasing the activities of the program. It could also be used for briefings on the project of new staff of any people, such as outside contractors, that have an involvement with the project.

The simulation showed the value of the derived output that can prove extremely helpful to the program director in planning the future course of the program, estimating the possibility of meeting deadlines, and systematically documenting proposed plans. Given the difficulties involved in estimating the values of the input parameters, sensitivity analysis can be carried out to test the sensitivity of the results to the accuracy of the data. Also, given the uncertainty that surrounds such programs, experimentation can be carried out by modifying the network and observing the effect of the modifications upon the plans. All this information would significantly contribute to improving the planning for what is considered to be 'unplannable.'

The GERT approach should not be viewed as a static tool used at the beginning of the planning process only, but as a dynamic one used frequently as the project progresses, new information is added, and perceptions about the project change. By modifying the network and/or the data, the plans can be updated, the possibility of meeting schedules can be reevaluated and appropriate corrective actions may be taken. It should be emphasized that it will still be the program director who will be making plans and decisions, but this method of analysis will help him do this in a systematic way and on the basis of analysis rather than on educated guessing. GERT has subsequently been further improved into a more powerful version called Q-GERT [39,41].

In view of the above usefulness of the GERT Approach, it should be adopted as a regular approach throughout the Air Force, the Army and the Navy, in planning major systems and R & D projects generally. It was recommended that the Deputy for Development Plans further refine the Assault Breaker program GERT network and the estimates of the relevant input parameters and use the results to evaluate the feasibility of already established schedules. It should then use the approach in programs that are at their conceptual stage to prove its equal usefulness as an initial planning device. The general adoption of the approach as a planning device throughout the Deputy for Development Plans should be preceded by a proper training of the staff on the approach itself, its capabilities and the use of the results in planning and decision making. In spite of the fact that expert advice should be used during the implementation of the approach it is necessary that the particular people involved are completely familiar with the approach.

Similar steps can be taken to introduce the approach throughout similar agencies in the Air Force, Army and Navy. The world has become so competitive and changeable, and technology advances at such an exponential rate that systematic analytical management techniques would prove very useful. The Air Force, therefore, as well as the other agencies, should consider introducing such approaches to a larger extent than it has been done so far. A number of reasons could be responsible for the fact that such planning techniques have not been introduced yet in system development and R & D projects. These reasons would be similar to those that are responsible for the fact that in private industry as well they have not been introduced. Lack of familiarity with the techniques and their potential in facilitating the planning and control process would be one of the most important reasons. Furthermore, the size of the agencies, budgetary and other system structure constraints, and unwillingness to change on behalf of personnel with technical rather than managerial education and background, could be given as additional reasons. It is hoped that these obstacles will gradually be eliminated and that more sophisticated approaches will eventually be introduced in systems development in the Air Force and the other agencies.

ACKNOWLEDGEMENTS

I would like to thank the Air Force Systems Command, the Air Force Office of Scientific Research, and the Southeastern Center for Electrical Engineering Education for providing me with the opportunity to carry out this research project. I am at least as thankful to the Deputy for Development Plans, Electronics Systems Division, for their hospitality and help in actually carrying out my research. In particular I would like to mention Dr. Donald E. Brick, Scientific Director, Col. Ernest L. Hatchell, Jr., Head of the Deputy, Col. Anthony Napoli, Director of Tactical Planning, and Lt. Col. Charles T. Jaglinski, Assault Breaker Program Director, without whose cooperation I would not have been able to accomplish my goal. I would like also to thank in particular Mr. Albert E. Ward of MITRE Corporation who collaborated with me and provided me with all the information to carry out my research project. Finally, my thanks go to the reviewers of the paper for their contribution through their useful comments.

FOOTNOTES

[1]Research sponsored by the Air Force Office of Scientific Research/AFSC, United States Air Force, under Contract F49620-79-C-0038. The United States Government is authorized to reproduce and distribute reprints for governmental purposes notwithstanding any copyright notation hereon.

REFERENCES

[1]   Arisawa, S., and S. E. Elmaghraby, "Optimal Time-Cost Trade-Offs in GERT Networks," Management Science, Vol. 18, No. 11, July 1972, pp. 589-599.

[2]   Auterio, V. J., "Q-GERT Simulation of Air Terminal Cargo Facilities," Proc. PittsburghModeling and Simulation Conference, Vol. 5, 1977, pp. 1181-1186.

[3]   Auterio, V. J., and S. D. Draper, "Aerial Refueling Military Airlift Forces: An Economic Analysis Based on Q-GERT Simulation," Material Airlift Command Chicago ORSA Conference, 1974.

[4]   Bandy, D. B., and S. D. Duket, "Q-GERT Model of a Midwest Crude Supply System," Milwaukee ORSA/TIMS Joint National Meeting, October 1979.

[5]   Bellas, C. J. and A. C. Samli, "Improving New Product Planning with GERT Simulation," California Management Review, Vol. 15, No. 4, Summer 1973, pp. 14-21.

[6]   Bird, M. M., E. R. Clayton, and L. J. Moore, "Industrial Buying: A Method of Planning for Contract Negotiations," Journal of Economics and Business, Vol. 26, 1974, pp. 209-213.

[7]   Bonham, T. W., E. R. Clayton and L. J. Moore, "A GERT Model to Meet Future Organizational Manpower Needs," Journal of Personnel, Vol. 54, 1975, pp. 402-406.

[8]   Burgess, R. R., "GERTS Models of a University," M.S. thesis, Virginia Polytechnic Institute and State University, 1970.

[9]   Byers, J. K., "Application of GERT to Reliability Analysis," Ph.D. dissertation, University of Arkansas, 1970.

[10]   Case, K. E., and K. R. Morrison, "A Simulation of System Reliability Using GERTS III," Virginia Academy of Science Meeting, May 14, 1971.

[11]   Clayton, E. R., and L. J. Moore, "GERT vs. PERT," Journal of Systems Management, Vol. 22, No. 2, 1972, pp. 11-19.

[12]   Cobb, H. C., Jr., "A Q-GERT Model and Analysis of the Communications in a Mechanized Brigade Covering Force," Masters' thesis, Naval Postgraduate School, Monterey, CA, March 1979.

[13]   Dabaghian, L. Y. Akiba, and W. W. Happ, "Simulation and Modeling Techniques Using GERTS IIIQ: An Introductory Account for Prospective Users," Seventh Asilomar Conference on Circuits, Systems and Computers, Monterey, CA, November 27-29,1973.

[14]   Dean, B. V., "Q-GERT for Project Management Applied to Start-ups," Proceedings of the Conference on Research and Entrepreneurship, Babson College, Wellesley, MA, 1983.

[15]   Dean, B. V., and A. K. Chaudhuri, "Project Scheduling: A Critical Review," TIMS Studies in the Management Sciences, Vol. 15, 1980, pp. 215-233.

[16]   Devor, R. E., G. L. Hogg, and M. Handwerker, "Analysis of Criminal Justice Systems
       with GERTS IIIQ: A Case Study," Proc. Pittsburgh Modeling and Simulation Conference,
       Vol. 5, 1974, pp. 1193-1199.

[17]   Duket, S., and D. Wortman, "Q-GERT Model of the Dover Air Force Base Port Cargo
       Facilities," MACRO Task Force, Material Airlift Command Scott Air Force Base,
       IL, 1976.

[18]   Enlow, R. A., "An Application of GERT Network Techniques to the Selection and
       Management of Research and Development Projects," Ph.D. dissertation, Arizona
       State University, 1970.

[19]   Faurie, B. R., "A Q-GERT Approach to a Requisition Processing Simulation at Naval
       Supply Center San Diego," Masters' thesis, Naval Postgraduate School, Monterey,
       CA, September 1980.

[20]   Grant, F. H., III, and A. A. B. Pritsker, "GERT Network Model of Burglary
       Resistance," NSF Grant No. GI34978, Purdue University, December 1973.

[21]   Hebert, J. E., III, "Critical Path Analysis and a Simulation Program for Resource-
       Constrained Activity Scheduling in GERT Project Networks," Ph.D. dissertation,
       Purdue University, 1975.

[22]   Hogg, G. L., et al., "GERTS QR: A Model of Multi-resource Constrained Queueing
       Systems, Part I: Concepts, Notations, and Examples," AIIE Transactions, Vol. 7,
       No. 2, 1975, pp. 89-99.

[23]   Hogg, G. L., et al., "GERTS QR: A Model of Multi-resource Constrained Queueing
       Systems, Part II: An Analysis of Parallel Channel, Dual Constrained Queueing
       Systems with Homogeneous Resources," AIIE Transactions, Vol. 7, No. 2, 1975,
       pp. 100-109.

[24]   Huang, P. Y., E. R. Clayton, and L. J. Moore, "Analysis of Material and Capacity
       Requirements with Q-GERT," International Journal of Production Research, Vol. 20,
       No. 6, 1982, pp. 701-713.

[25]   Iwersen, A., Jr., R. R. Berry, and J. E. Brawner, Jr., "A Cost Analysis of the KT-73
       Inertial Measurement Unit Repair Process Using GERT Simulation," Masters' thesis,
       Air Force Institute of Technology, Wright-Patterson Air Force Base, January 1975.

[26]   Jaglinski, T., Program Management Plan for Ground Target Attack Control System
       Assault Breaker (3rd draft). Unpublished document, HQ Electronics Systems Division,
       Hanscom Air Force Base, Bedford, MA, April 1980.

[27]   Lawrence, K. D., and C. E. Sigal, "A Work Flow Simulation of a Regional Service
       Office of a Property and Casualty Insurance Company with Q-GERT," Proc. Pittsburgh
       Modeling and Simulation Conference, Vol. 5, 1974, pp. 1187-1192.

[28]   Maggard, M. J., W. G. Lesso, et al., "GERTS IIIQR: A Multiple Resource Constrained
       Network Simulation Model," Management Datamatics, Vol. 5, No. 1, 1976, pp. 5-14.

[29]   Maggard, M. J., W. G. Lesso, et al, "Network Analysis with GERTS IIIQR,"
       Industrial Engineering, Vol. 6, No. 5, May 1974, pp. 24-29.

[30]   Mentzer, J. T., and S. C. Cosmas, "The Application of GERT Modeling and Simulation
       to Logistics," International Journal of Physical Distribution and Materials Management,
       Vol. 10, No. 1, 1979, pp. 35-50.

[31] Moder, J., R. A. Clark, and R. S. Gomez, "Applications of a GERT Simulator to a
      Repetitive Hardware Development Type Project," AIIE Transactions, Vol. 3, No. 4,
      1971, pp. 271–280.

[32] Moore, L. J., and E. R. Clayton, Introduction to Systems Analysis with GERT Modeling
      and Simulation, New York: Petrocelli Books, 1976.

[33] Moore, L. J., and B. W. Taylor III, "Multiteam, Multiproject Research and Development
      Planning with GERT," Management Science, Vol. 24, No. 4, December 1977, pp. 401–410.

[34] Mortenson, R. E., "R, M, and Logistics Simulations Using Q-GERT," 1980 Proceedings
      Annual Reliability and Maintainability Symposium, pp. 1–5.

[35] Ohta, H., "GERT Analysis of a Single Conveyor System," International Journal of
      Production Research, Vol. 17, No. 4, 1979, pp. 405–410.

[36] Phillips, D. T., and A. A. B. Pritsker, "GERT Network Analysis of Complex Production
      Systems," International Journal of Production Research, Vol. 13, No. 3, 1975, pp. 223–
      237.

[37] Phillips, D. T. and R. F. Slovick, "A GERTS IIIQ Application to a Production Line,"
      Proc. 1974 AIIE National Conference, pp. 307–318.

[38] Pritsker, A. A. B., "GERT: Graphical Evaluation and Review Technique," The RAND
      Corporation, RM-4973-NASA, Santa Monica, CA, April 1966.

[39] Pritsker, A. A. B., Modeling and Analysis Using Q-GERT Networks, 2nd ed., New
      York: Halsted Press, 1979.

[40] Pritsker, A. A. B., and C. E. Sigal, Management Decision Making: A Network Simula-
      tion Approach, Prentice-Hall, 1983.

[41] Pritsker, A. A. B., and C. E. Sigal, The GERT IIIZ User's Manual. West Lafayette,
      IN: Pritsker & Associates, 1974.

[42] Raju, G. V. S., "Sensitivity Analysis of GERT Networks," AIIE Transactions, Vol. 3,
      No. 2, 1971, pp. 133–141.

[43] Randolph, P. H., and R. D. Ringeisen, "A Network Learning Model with GERT Analysis,"
      Journal of Mathematical Psychology, Vol. 2, No. 1, 1974, pp. 59–70.

[44] Richard, J. H., "Q-GERT Model of Planned Product Distribution Network," Proc. 1981
      Winter Simulation Conference, Atlanta, GA, December 1981.

[45] Sabuda, J., "A Study of Q-GERT Modeling and Analysis Using Interactive Computer
      Graphics," M.S. thesis, Purdue University, December 1977.

[46] Samli, A. C., and C. Bellas, "The Use of GERT in the Planning and Control of
      Marketing Research," Journal of Marketing Research, Vol. 8, August 1971, pp. 335–339.

[47] Sigal, C. E., S. Duket, and A. A. B. Pritsker, New Additions to Q-GERT, West Lafayette
      IN: Pritsker & Associates, Inc., 1976.

[48] Taylor, B. W., III, and K. R. Davis, "Evaluating Time/Cost Factors of Implementation
      via GERT Simulation," OMEGA, Vol. 6, 1978, pp. 257–266.

[49] Taylor, B. W., III, and A. V. Keown, "A Network Analysis of an Inpatient/Outpatient
      Department," Journal of the Operational Research Society, Vol. 31, 1980, pp. 169–179.

[50] Taylor, B. W., III, and L. J. Moore, "Analysis of a Ph.D. Program Via GERT Modeling and Simulation," Decision Sciences, Vol. 9, No. 4, 1978, pp. 725-737.

[51] Taylor, B. W., III, and L. J. Moore, "R & D Project Planning with Q-GERT Network Modeling and Simulation," Management Science, Vol. 26, No. 1, 1980, pp. 44-59.

[52] Taylor, B. W., III, L. J. Moore, and R. D. Hammesfahr, "Global Analysis of a Multi-product, Multi-line Production System Using Q-GERT Modeling and Simulation," AIIE Transactions, June 1980, pp. 145-155.

[53] Taylor, B. W., III, and R. S. Russell, "A Simulation Approach for Adapting a Production Line Balancing Procedure to a Probabilistic Environment," International Journal of Production Research, Vol. 20, No. 6, 1982, pp. 787-801.

[54] Townsend, T., "GERT Networks with Item Differentiation Capabilities," Masters' thesis, Purdue University, 1973.

[55] Turban, E. and N. P. Loomba, Readings in Management Science, Business Publications, 1976.

[56] Velenzuela, C. A., and G. E. Whitehouse, "The Application of Q-GERT to Materials Handling Problems in Open Pit Mining," Proc. Ninth Annual Pittsburgh Conference, April 27-28, 1978, pp. 273-278.

[57] Whitehouse, G. E., "GERT, A Useful Technique for Analyzing Reliability Problems," Technometrics, February 1970.

[58] Whitehouse, G. E., and E. C. Hsuan, "The Application of GERT to Quality Control: A Feasibility Study," (NASA Contract NAS-12-2079) Department of Industrial Engineering, Lehigh University.

[59] Wiest, J. D., "Project Network Models Past, Present, and Future," Project Management Quarterly, Vol. 8, No. 4, December 1977, pp. 27-36.

[60] Wortman, D. B., and C. E. Sigal, Project Planning and Control Using GERT, West Lafayette, IN: Pritsker & Associates, Inc., October 1978.

APPENDIX I

SIMULATION INPUT (PARTIAL)

Part 1: Activity Description

START NODE	END NODE	PARAMETER NUMBER	DISTRIBUTION TYPE	COUNT TYPE	ACTIVI- TY NO.	PROBA- BILITY	SETUP COST	VAR- IABLE COST
.	.	.	.	.	.	.	.	.
.	.	.	.	.	.	.	.	.
.	.	.	.	.	.	.	.	.
31	35	5	9	0	58	0.5000	0.0	0.0
32	33	7	9	0	54	1.0000	0.0	0.0
33	32	8	9	0	55	0.7000	0.0	0.0
33	35	5	9	0	59	0.3000	0.0	0.0
34	32	8	9	0	56	0.5000	0.0	0.0
34	35	5	9	0	60	0.5000	0.0	0.0
35	36	1	9	0	61	1.0000	0.0	0.0
36	37	9	9	0	62	1.0000	0.0	0.0
37	36	10	9	0	63	0.7000	0.0	0.0
37	56	11	9	0	93	0.3000	0.0	0.0
38	36	10	9	0	64	0.5000	0.0	0.0
38	56	11	9	0	94	0.5000	0.0	0.0
39	40	2	10	0	65	1.0000	0.0	0.0
39	43	0	10	0	66	1.0000	0.0	0.0
39	46	0	10	0	67	1.0000	0.0	0.0
39	49	0	10	0	68	1.0000	0.0	0.0
.	.	.	.	.	.	.	.	.
.	.	.	.	.	.	.	.	.
.	.	.	.	.	.	.	.	.

Part 2: Activity Parameters (for BETA distribution)

PARAMETER NUMBER	MOST LIKELY TIME	OPTIMISTIC TIME	PESSIMISTIC TIME
1	2.0000	1.0000	4.0000
2	1.0000	0.5000	2.0000
3	1.2000	1.0000	2.0000
4	1.2000	1.0000	2.0000
5	0.5000	0.2000	1.0000
6	2.0000	1.0000	4.0000
7	1.0000	0.5000	2.0000
8	1.5000	1.0000	3.0000
9	1.0000	0.5000	2.0000
10	1.5000	1.0000	3.0000
11	0.5000	0.2000	1.0000
.	.	.	.
.	.	.	.
.	.	.	.

APPENDIX II
SIMULATION OUTPUT (PARTIAL)

Part 1: Summary Statistics

NODE	PROB.	COUNT TYPE	MEAN	ST. DEV.	NO. OF OBS.	MIN	MAX	TYPE	(EXPLANATION)
.	.	.	.	.	.	.	.	.	
.	.	.	.	.	.	.	.	.	
190	0.0520		46.2589	7.9264	26	29.6007	60.1873	F	(Realization of Node 190)
		(Cost)	No values recorded						
		1	0.0385	0.1961	26	0.0	1.0000		
		2	0.0		26	0.0	0.0		
		3	0.1923	0.4019	26	0.0	1.0000		
		.	.	.	.	.	.		
		.	.	.	.	.	.		
		.	.	.	.	.	.		
251	0.6680		14.7499	1.6183	334	9.7069	19.2786	I	(Realization of part of network between Node 144 and Node 251)
		(Cost)	No values recorded						
		1	0.0479	0.2139	334	0.0	1.0000		
		2	0.0	0.0	334	0.0	0.0		
		3	0.0180	0.1330	334	0.0	1.0000		
		.	.	.	.	.	.		
		.	.	.	.	.	.		

186	0.5320		91.1450	18.2222	266	70.3394	205.4856	F (Realization of Node 186)
		(Cost)	No values recorded					
		1	0.4398	0.7951	266	0.0	3.0000	
		2	1.4173	0.7076	266	1.0000	4.0000	
		3	0.6090	0.8180	266	0.0	6.0000	
		.	.	.	.	.	.	
		.	.	.	.	.	.	
		.	.	.	.	.	.	
...	...	...	...	...	...	...	...	

Part 2: Detailed Frequency Distributions and Histograms
(In following pages for Nodes 190 and 251).

TIME STAT HISTOGRAM FOR NODE 190 (REALIZATION OF EVENT 190)

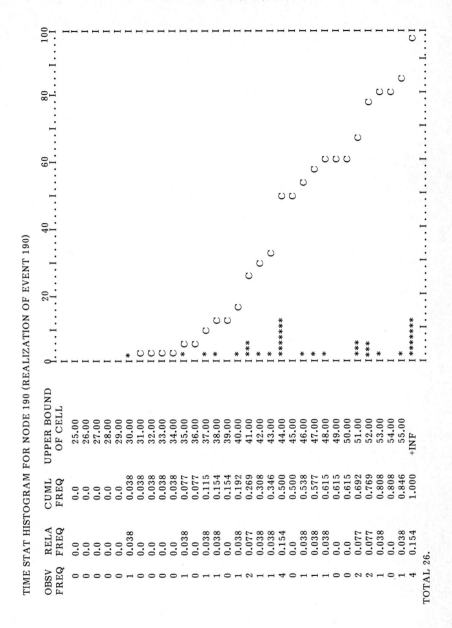

OBSV FREQ	RELA FREQ	CUML FREQ	UPPER BOUND OF CELL
0	0.0	0.0	25.00
0	0.0	0.0	26.00
0	0.0	0.0	27.00
0	0.0	0.0	28.00
0	0.0	0.0	29.00
1	0.038	0.038	30.00
0	0.0	0.038	31.00
0	0.0	0.038	32.00
0	0.0	0.038	33.00
0	0.0	0.038	34.00
1	0.038	0.077	35.00
0	0.0	0.077	36.00
1	0.038	0.115	37.00
1	0.038	0.154	38.00
0	0.0	0.154	39.00
1	0.038	0.192	40.00
2	0.077	0.269	41.00
1	0.038	0.308	42.00
1	0.038	0.346	43.00
4	0.154	0.500	44.00
0	0.0	0.500	45.00
1	0.038	0.538	46.00
1	0.038	0.577	47.00
1	0.038	0.615	48.00
0	0.0	0.615	49.00
0	0.0	0.615	50.00
2	0.077	0.692	51.00
2	0.077	0.769	52.00
1	0.038	0.808	53.00
0	0.0	0.808	54.00
1	0.038	0.846	55.00
4	0.154	1.000	+INF

TOTAL 26.

TIME STAT HISTOGRAM FOR NODE 251 (PART OF THE NETWORK BETWEEN NODES 144 and 251)

OBSV FREQ	RELA FREQ	CUML FREQ	UPPER BOUND OF CELL
0	0.0	0.0	8.00
0	0.0	0.0	8.50
0	0.0	0.0	9.00
0	0.0	0.0	9.50
1	0.003	0.003	10.00
1	0.003	0.006	10.50
4	0.012	0.018	11.00
2	0.006	0.024	11.50
11	0.033	0.057	12.00
12	0.036	0.093	12.50
21	0.063	0.156	13.00
20	0.060	0.216	13.50
26	0.078	0.293	14.00
37	0.111	0.404	14.50
53	0.159	0.563	15.00
40	0.120	0.683	15.50
32	0.096	0.778	16.00
26	0.078	0.856	16.50
24	0.072	0.928	17.00
12	0.036	0.964	17.50
6	0.018	0.982	18.00
3	0.009	0.991	18.50
2	0.006	0.997	19.00
1	0.003	1.000	19.50
0	0.0	1.000	20.00
0	0.0	1.000	20.50
0	0.0	1.000	21.00
0	0.0	1.000	21.50
0	0.0	1.000	22.00
0	0.0	1.000	22.50
0	0.0	1.000	23.00
0	0.0	1.000	+INF

TOTAL 334.

Project Management: Methods and Studies
Burton V. Dean (editor)
© Elsevier Science Publishers B.V. (North-Holland), 1985

MULTI-PROJECT MANAGEMENT: A CASE STUDY ON A VOICE-ACTIVATED DECISION SUPPORT SYSTEM

George J. Titus

Temple University
Philadelphia, Pennsylvania
U.S.A.

Matthew J. Liberatore

Villanova University
Villanova, Pennsylvania
U.S.A.

This case study examines a multi-billion dollar aircraft company's efforts to develop and implement a multi-project monitoring and control system for the Chief Engineer of Research and Technology. This decision support system utilizes advances in electronics and computer technology, and is driven by an automatic speech recognition (ASR) system for access and command execution. The case describes the organizational background and approach, the origins of the voice-activated project management system (VAPMS), the Chief Engineer's decision-making environment, the ASR technology, VAPMS development and uses, its future, and the lessons learned. The data for this study were collected through a series of extensive, on-site interviews with personnel responsible for the origin, design, development, testing and use of this system. For effective design and use of project management systems, management scientists and project managers should place additional emphasis on the user's requirements and organizational level and the advances in dialog systems (hardware/software).

INTRODUCTION

The typical Research, Development and Engineering (R,D&E) organization manages projects with the assistance of scheduling and control techniques developed about three decades ago. These techniques were designed for detailed project management and are appropriate for first and second level supervision. A review of the literature revealed that no project management system exploiting the recent advances in electronics and computer technology has been designed for middle to upper-level R, D&E managers. These advances appear especially suitable for assisting project-related decision making at higher levels in the organization. This case study reports on the Lockheed-Georgia Company's efforts to develop and implement a multi-project monitoring and control system for senior management based on Decision Support System (DSS) concepts. Driven by an automatic speech recognition (ASR) system for access and output command execution, the system supports the multi-project tracking and monitoring activities of the Chief Engineer of Research and Technology, one of the original respondents of our study on R&D project management techniques [3]. As suggested in our study [3], more situation-specific case studies discussing the use of project management techniques or systems are in order. In what follows, we describe several aspects of the Voice Activated Project Management System (VAPMS), including its origins, choice of technology, development process, advantages and disadvantages, and planned future developments.

COMPANY BACKGROUND AND ORGANIZATION

The Lockheed-Georgia company is a multi-billion dollar technology-driven aircraft firm which conducts research on aeronautical systems and designs, develops and manufactures aircraft and ancillary electronic systems. This acknowledged industrial leader manufactures and sells these high technology products and markets related services to the U. S. Government, foreign governments and to commercial customers. The company is organized in the matrix management structure in which the functional vice presidents and program vice presidents report to the president. Project management is conducted by corresponding program organizations and functionally by the Advanced Programs and Engineering Organization. Because programs represent the sum of all activities directed toward the development and production of a specific aircraft system, particular project activities run the spectrum from new technology through design, testing, and ongoing technical and production support.

L. W. (Bill) Lassiter, Jr., the Chief Engineer responsible for managing the Research and Technology (R&T) activities of Lockheed-Georgia, reports to the director of engineering. He, in turn, reports to the Vice President of Advanced Programs and Engineering. R&T is functionally organized by scientific and engineering disciplines. There are about 600 people with varying scientific and technical skills reporting to the Chief Engineer, and working on about 200 active R&D projects totalling $50 to $60 million annually.

The Chief Engineer's organization has three primary responsibilities: 1) it provides engineering support for all proposed, developing and ongoing aircraft programs; 2) it conducts applied research and engineering to support aircraft technologies and to coordinate all research activities in the company not related to specific programs called Independent Research and Development (IRAD); and 3) it conducts and controls all contract research and development. The hard copy reports available to the Chief Engineer provide detailed information for each project under his direction. Although all of his project management data are available to him through a CRT, there is limited flexibility for aggregating the data to suit his needs. The Chief Engineer also felt that even with improved software, it would still be time consuming to access and report the data. This prompted him to incorporate developments from an ongoing R&T project into the design of an innovative, "personalized" project management and information system. In this context, it is necessary to understand and describe the origin of VAPMS and the Chief Engineer's decision-making environment.

THE ORIGINS OF VOICE-ACTIVATED PROJECT MANAGEMENT SYSTEM (VAPMS)

Mr. R. B. Ormsby, Jr., President of the Lockheed Corporation's Aeronautical Systems Group is committed to pushing the frontiers of technology to improve managerial and technical productivity at all levels of the corporation. The Chief Engineer's original motivation for investigating voice-activated technology was to encourage his engineers to learn how this new technology could be applied to a flight station. Much of the data the flight crew receives is non-critical and distracting, requiring numerous manual adjustments with dials and knobs which can divert attention from the crew's field of view, especially during take-off and landing. Since speech is one of the fastest and easiest communication media to streamline time and motion in manual tests, voice-activated input-output seemed more natural to obtain and transfer data/information in a cockpit. Meanwhile, the Chief Engineer's R&D personnel recognized an analogy between the information processing needs of flight crews and those of upper level managers. The cost, schedule and manpower data at the project or task level are often non-critical and distracting relative to multi-project control activities at the Chief Engineer's level. In both environments, methods are needed to process large quantities of data with ease of access into formats suitable for pilots or for managers to make vital decisions. Although response time is more critical in a cockpit environment than in a manager's office, higher level executives can increase managerial productivity by reducing data search time. The development of VAPMS began as a prototype to demonstrate the feasibility of voice technology. It was conceived that the experience gained from VAPMS would be applied to information transfer and control in a cockpit. To understand the complexities of the Chief Engineer's project management activities, an explanation of his decision making environment and style is necessary.

The Chief Engineer's Decision Making Environment

The project management techniques and tools that were available to the Chief Engineer were inadequate for his position in the organization and his personal decision making style. For example, Lockheed-Georgia has a management decision support system (MIDS) which contains an extensive set of color graphic displays which can be accessed only by a few top executives. The information about the Advanced Programs and Engineering Organization on this system is much too aggregated for management control at the Chief Engineer's level. On the other hand, the conventional project management techniques and systems provide voluminous detail which is used by the Chief Engineer only as an ancillary decision making aid. From the Chief Engineer's perspective, "the volume of information that is available is immense and more than you can cope with in written communication formats." The Chief Engineer preferred a DSS with voice input (as opposed to keyboard control) for the following reasons: (1) the Chief Engineer does not like to type; (2) voice input is faster; (3) fewer instructions and commands need to be remembered, and (4) voice imprint matching provides increased security for system access.

The Chief Engineer approaches his project management responsibilities initially from the point of view of exercising budget control over the major accounts related to the divisions reporting to him. He prefers (1) to review budgeting variances at a division level, and (2) to conduct funding reallocations at the project level[1]. The management of the Chief Engineer's accounts is a dynamic process which must be adjusted to accommodate changes in program priorities. Whenever needed, he has access to a series of computer printouts which provide "absolute detail" on every specific project. He calls for face-to-face meetings with his managers to communicate critical program changes or exchange information concerning problems relating to specific projects. Thus, the Chief Engineer wanted a compatible match between the level of information needed and the level of management control required for effective multi-project management.

Technology of Automatic Speech Recognition (ASR)

Speech is the most natural, familiar, convenient and spontaneous form of human communication. Voice input to computers requires minimal user training and provides the highest capacity output communication channel. However, the problem of speech recognition is very complex from the point of view of someone (or something such as a computer) who is unfamiliar with idiomatic or highly individualistic characteristics of natural language-human speaker combinations [2]. Our speech patterns, like our fingerprints, are unique. This very quality is a major obstacle to a universal or speaker independent speech recognition system.

ASR systems are categorized as either continuous (connected) or isolated (discrete) speech systems. Continuous-speech systems can extract information from strings of words as would occur in natural speech, whereas isolated-speech systems such as VAPMS, require a short pause before and after utterances or words [4]. The basic operation of the ASR can be explained briefly. The spoken word or utterance is converted into an electrical signal by means of a microphone. This electrical signal is processed to extract its identifying features. These features are then digitized by an analog-to-digital converter creating a template for each spoken word of utterance. A collection of templates stored in the system constitutes the "vocabulary" of the ASR. When a voice-input is made, its template is compared to the templates forming the vocabulary of the ASR and the computer selects the closest match. The voice-template selected activates software routines to generate the desired displays on the video display terminal (VDT). Figure 1 is a schematic diagram of the operation of an ASR [1].

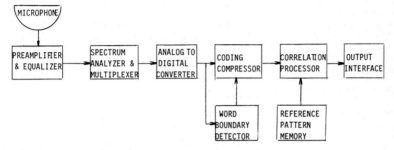

Figure 1. A Schematic Diagram of the Operation of an ASR.

Most ASR applications are used for source data entry, such as inventory control or sales or order entries [2], [4], [5]. In these applications, the additional hardware and software costs associated with ASR must be cost justified on the basis of increased productivity, reduced labor force, or reduced training costs. As applied to executive information and decision support systems, the direct and indirect cost-benefits of ASR are much more difficult to measure. Important benefits include: minimal user training, flexibility to personalize system access and command execution, improved system security, rapid introduction and acceptance among users, reduced paper files, and less search time for critical information. Principal disadvantages of current ASR technology include the limited vocabulary, variation in recognition accuracy, and increased costs due to the lack of system integration between the computer hardware and ASR. Recognition accuracy can be improved significantly by selecting vocabulary words which are not easily confused. The remaining shortcomings of ASR systems are not major obstacles to successfully implementing an executive information system. In future years, technology advancements should lessen them considerably.

Development and Uses of VAPMS

Since the use of voice-activated systems for executive information was not widespread in the late 1970's, electronics specialists at Lockheed-Georgia studied speech input and determined that the accuracy of speech input is comparable to manual data entry via a computer terminal. These results prompted the Chief Engineer to develop VAPMS with a small project engineering team. It is interesting to note that concurrent with VAPMS, the Chief Engineer and his staff participated in the development of a company-wide management information and decision support system (MIDS) for executives above the level of the Chief Engineer.

Most micro-computers can support automatic speech recognition. The developers of VAPMS selected a relatively low cost micro-computer with a color CRT and a dual disk drive (See Figure 2).

Early in software development, important topics--overhead, research and technology expenditures, fixed assets and manpower needs--were selected for tracking by the system. Data from the mainframe computers on these and other topics are summarized and made available on the ASR system. The completed system monitors more than 200 projects with an annual budget in excess of $50 million through voice commands. Detailed tracking of purchase orders, labor hours per work order, and other items is done on larger business computers.

Before the Chief Engineer can use his system, he has to "train" the machine to recognize particular voice patterns. Each key word is spoken into the microphone three times. The voice recognition unit averages the three utterances and stores them in a digitized form called a template. Administrators update the information contained on VAPMS using an identical configuration without the voice-control capability. The information is updated whenever there is a change so the Chief Engineer has the most current information. The software is structured so that changing a single line in the BASIC program allows keyboard control rather than voice. The keyboard on the Chief Engineer's terminal is locked out to prevent unauthorized access to the information contained on this system. Words or commands used in VAPMS are summarized in Table 1.

Figure 2.

Table 1.

WORDS USED IN VAPMS

NO.	WORD	MODE	NO.	WORD	MODE
1	PASSWORD	any	28	SUPPLIES	overhead
2	COMMANDS	any	29	TOOLS	overhead
3	MENU	any	30	FURNITURE	overhead
4	BLANK	any	31	RENTAL	overhead
5	OVERHEAD	any	32	MEMBERSHIPS	overhead
6	NEXT	any	33	SERVICES	overhead
7	HEADCOUNT	any	34	TRAVEL	overhead
8	IRAD	any	35	R & M	overhead
9	–		36	M & DC	overhead
10	–		37	PROGRAMMING	overhead
11	RESEARCH	irad	38	PROCESSING	overhead
12	DEVELOPMENT	irad	39	DESIGN	overhead
13	BID	irad	40	PREMIUM	overhead
14	–		41	DOUBLE-D	overhead
15	–		42	02*	overhead/headcount
16	BRANCH TRAVEL	irad	43	03	overhead/headcount
17	DOLLARS	irad	44	06	overhead/headcount
18	TECHNOLOGY	irad	45	11	overhead/headcount
19	ASSETS	irad	46	14	overhead/headcount
20	RATIOS	irad	47	18	overhead/headcount
21	SIGNUPS	irad	48	22	overhead/headcount
22	–		49	24	overhead/headcount
23	–		50	83	overhead/headcount
24	ENGINEERING	overhead	51	85	overhead/headcount
25	HOURLY	overhead	52	90	overhead/headcount
26	SALARY	overhead	53	DIVISIONS	headcount
27	TRAINING	overhead	54	–	

*Each two-digit code represents a specific division reporting to the Chief Engineer, such as Flight Sciences, Structures, etc.

Note that there are seven commands that can be accessed anytime (in any mode). Three of these (IRAD, overhead and headcount) allow access to a specific set of voice-activated commands. For example, the headcount mode allows access to staffing information in any of the Chief Engineer's divisions or in total.

The Chief Engineer uses the system to monitor projects in different ways. For example, when the Chief Engineer wants to view the overhead budget of division 03 and its spending to date against budget, he may find a positive variance (underspending); concurrently, he may recollect that the same division manager had requested additional staff. This apparent contradiction would prompt the Chief Engineer to look at each of the projects under division 03 in absolute detail. If the project details he requested did not answer or resolve his inquiry satisfactorily, he could call for a face to face meeting with the manager of division 03 to discuss details and obtain relevant information. The Chief Engineer then would give approval for that change and make proper adjustments in the division's budget. As a second example, the Chief Engineer often must consider requests for higher budget allocation from a division manager. The Chief Engineer then can obtain information on the budget status of all projects in that division or any other division under him before he calls for a meeting among the concerned managers, to resolve budget reallocations.

Future of VAPMS

Lockheed-Georgia plans to develop and improve this voice system. A major time-saving step will be to tie the system on-line with the administrative computer which contains all of the raw data, thus eliminating the administrative task of hand-loading the data into the computer. In the very near future, the range and variety of available management data will increase, and the number of summary tracking charts will be greatly expanded. Implementation of an ASR system which accesses an established management information system (MIDS) in the company is underway.

After observing the Chief Engineer's satisfaction with the performance of the prototype voice-activated model, the Engineering Management Systems Department developed a similar system for the Director of Engineering to manage the activities of the entire Engineering Branch. This system differs from the one discussed earlier in that it is not a stand-along system. The Director of Engineering can access any one of approximately 500 displays contained in two management information systems that reside in a host computer. The problem of a limited vocabulary was eliminated by using more than one vocabulary, i.e., multiple sets of 100 words. One of the MIS systems contains information on the internal operation of the Engineering Branch; the other is the MIDS system used by senior executives [1]. The system is being further refined to be of use to lower level project managers.

Lessons Learned

The company President's goal to have all programs managed with timely and accurate information provided the impetus to develop better controls over schedules and costs. The ideas for developing such management systems arose from the technology impetus of the company to integrate the most advanced computer technology into its product design and manufacture, and management systems. The Chief Engineer's R&T organization with its keen interest in research and technological leadership in the industry was the locus for these developmental activities.

The matrix structure of the organization simplified the collection of data in various departments by programs and projects. The existence of a central data center, the Engineering Management Control Center, facilitated the VAPMS implementation process for data collection, update and dissemination. Because the administrator of this center was familiar with the manner in which management requested data, the process of systematizing the necessary computer data was simplified.

Although the initiative for a project control information system originated with the President, there was no mandate to adopt his or any other system. The success, ease of operation, and the quality of information that came out of the system for management purposes led many middle managers to experiment with the system and adopt it to their needs.

Some implications can be drawn for management scientists and others involved in the development of project management systems. First, management scientists should place more emphasis on relating project management models to the needs of the users at various levels in the organization. For example, at upper management levels, descriptive models must be considered along with the normative and heuristic models often used in project management. Second, designers of project management systems should utilize the advances in computer technology whenever appropriate. Specifically, project management dialog systems, including input and output devices and selection of effective modes of data presentation (for e.g., graphical versus tabular displays) must be given more emphasis during the design phase.

ACKNOWLEDGMENTS

The authors are grateful to Lockheed-Georgia Company and specifically Mr. Lassiter, Chief Engineer - Research and Technology, and his managers, whose participation and patient cooperation made this study possible. They also wish to thank the many unnamed contributors and anonymous referees for their helpful suggestions to improve the quality of this case. The research was partially supported by grant-in-aid funds provided by Temple University.

FOOTNOTES

[1]An alternative modeling approach for resource (as opposed to overall funding)
reallocation in a multi-project environment is described by Leachman and Boysen in
Chapter 5.

REFERENCES

[1]   Dixon, P. W., and R. W. Daniel, "Converting a Menu Driven Management Information
        System to a Voice Activated System,: in Proceedings of Nineteenth Annual Meeting
        of the Institute of Management Sciences, September 1983, pp. 736-744.

[2]   Lea, A. W., "Speech Recognition: Past, Present and Future," in Trends in Speech
        Recognition, Wayne A. Lea (ed.), Prentice Hall, Inc., Englewood Cliffs, NJ, 1980.

[3]   Liberatore, M. J. and G. J. Titus, "The Practice of Management Science in R&D
        Project Management," Management Science, Vol. 20, No. 8, 1983, pp. 962-974.

[4]   Martin, T. B., and J. R. Welch, "Practical Speech Recognizers and Some Performance
        Effectiveness Parameters," in Trends in Speech Recognition, Wayne A. Lea (ed.),
        Prentice-Hall, Inc., Englewood Cliffs, NJ, 1980.

[5]   Nye, M. J., "The Expanding Market for Commercial Speech Recognizers," in
        Trends in Speech Recognition, Wayne A. Lea (ed.), Prentice Hall, Inc., Englewood
        Cliffs, NJ, 1980.

Project Management: Methods and Studies
Burton V. Dean (editor)
© Elsevier Science Publishers B.V. (North-Holland), 1985

AN APPROACH TO THE MEASUREMENT OF PROBABILITY
USING PAIRWISE COMPARISONS

Geoff Lockett   Tony Gear

Manchester Business School   Trent Polytechnic
Manchester, England   Nottingham, England

An approach to the assessment of discrete probabilities is presented
which is based on a procedure developed by Saaty for analysing
hierarchies. The results of two experimental trials in research and
development situations are presented. One involves a replication
over an extended time period, and the other uses a series of subjects
undertaking the same evaluation separately. Preliminary results
indicate the potential of the method for deriving subjective probability
estimates in practice.

INTRODUCTION

Much has been written about models for R&D and their development is continuing (e.g. see
Souder (1978)). However, the success rate is questionable, and there is little substantive
evidence that it has been worth the effort. This is not peculiar to R&D, and the problem of
implementation of OR/MS models is a topical issue (Schultz (1975), Polding (1981)). In the
past most of the models were based in the tactical arena using "real data" on problems where
things could be measured. Today the movement is increasingly towards the more strategic
problems, where measurement is more difficult, i.e. using "fuzzy data." R&D modeling has
had this problem since the beginning, and in most instances we are dealing with subjective
estimates on which to base decisions.

This paper describes an approach to the assessment of discrete probabilities by means of an
interactive procedure using a ratio scale. Although rarely discussed, such discrete probabilities are normally the ones requested by models of decision analysis. They are also non-repe-
titive, i.e. they are "one-offs," and the creative element in forecasting possible outcomes is
at least as important as the subjective probabilities themselves. The applications presented
in this paper are from Research and Development where subjects are intermittently requested for subjective data. Some cases are presented where the uncertain events are systematically compared using a ratio scale of judgments, and the resulting data analyzed using an
adaptation of the analytic hierarchy method developed by Saaty (1977). The method lends
itself to the production of pooled estimates from a group of experts, e.g. Lockett (1981),
which has also been approached by other researchers, e.g., Mancini (1981), Jensen (1982).
Details of the technique are described in the Appendix.

In the following sections the literature which strongly overlaps with this paper is briefly
reviewed, and we have chosen to divide it into papers on Multiple Criteria Decision Making
(MCDM), R&D applications and Probability Assessment. Two case studies are then presented
and the results discussed in detail.

Multiple Criteria Decision Making

MCDM models are pouring out at a vase rate, e.g. see Despontin et al (1980), but most of
these lack real-life data or spend no time discussing this issue. The recent proceedings of
the IVth International Conference on MCDM are no exception (Morse (1981)). Although con-
taining over 30 interesting and stimulating papers, little space is devoted to the problem of

obtaining subjective data. One interesting paper by Schoemaker (1981) tries to redress the balance, and after discussing the psychological literature on the subject he concludes that "the premises underlying the normative methodology are much in need of empirical verification," and points to "the substantial evidence that exists to doubt man's ability as an intuitive statistician."

Similarly, Fischer (1979) reviews recent developments in multi-attribute utility (MAU) theory. After reviewing the large body of psychological research, he concludes that "simple MAU models have been able to provide excellent approximations to human preferences in virtually every context studied by psychologists." But he notes their limited use so far, and states that "only through application can the ultimate usefulness of MAU-based evaluation procedures be determined." On a related topic Park and Boland (1979) have experimented on the role of data in the problem formulation process. Although considering information systems, they do highlight the problem of the effect of data on the model for which it is being collected. An attempt to compare methods for weighting decision criteria was made by Nutt (1981), and of the methods considered the ARS (anchored rating scale) using a continuous scale was found to have the greatest consistency. It took the least time to carry out, and the more complex methods were not perceived to have a greater accuracy by the participants.

In a recent edition of Decision Sciences (1982, Vol. 12, No. 4) a number of specialists in Decision Theory discussed the future of the subject. While pointing to successes they highlight major difficulties that still exist - "The literature concerning the elicitation of both probabilities and preferences remains unsatisfactory," Hogarth (1982). One is left with a feeling of unease about the appicability of some of the ideas in real life situations.

Using a quite different approach, Saaty (1977), (1981) has proposed a method of obtaining subjective data using pairwise comparisons, and calculating the weights from eigenvectors of the resulting matrices. Lockett (1981), Gear (1982) describe an application in detail when used on a group decision making problem, and a simple example outlining the procedure can be found in Gear (1982).

The overall picture is one of increasing competition between methods with limited application to date. Of the attempts at implementation in managerial environments, most of the effort has been in modelling, rather than addressing the problem of obtaining subjective data.

R&D Applications

A review of an empirical investigation of the quality of subjective probabilities of technical success in R&D has been reported by Schroder (1975) who concludes that ". . . considerable improvements of their (probability assessments)[1] quality might be expected from the employment of a variety of measures suitable to reduce unintentional errors and conscious biases." Rubenstein and Schroder (1977) reported on their research into how different levels of management assessed probabilities. Although only tentative conclusions could be drawn, their research shows that some biasing of subjective estimates of the probability of technical success does occur, and that such estimates are negatively correlated with the assessor's hierarchical position in the organization. Balthasar et al (1978) describe some cases where the collection of subjective probabilities over time has   proved of great benefit to an organization in forecasting future potential successes. However, such articles are rare, and most of the attention is given to applying the models, where the data is assumed to be available, e.g. Bonson et al (1982), Boschi (1982), Stahl and Zimmerer (1983). Little is said about the problem of obtaining subjective probabilities, or to their usefulness. But this does not apply to R&D alone, and in other fields researchers are grappling with similar problems (e.g. in accounting see Belkauoi (1982) and in forecasting Sjoberg (1982)).

Probability Assessment

Reviews of procedures for assessing probabilities have been provided by Spetzler (1975), Hampton (1973), Moore (1975), and more recently by Heurion (1980). Unlike MCDM, the major part of this work has been undertaken from a psychological perspective, and tends to appear in a different segment of the literature.

In their extended review article Slovic and Lichtenstein (1971) compare several hundred studies on "the rather narrowly-defined topic of information utilization in judgment decision making." One of their findings is "that judges have a very difficult time weighting and combining information, be it probablistic or deterministic in nature." In a broad review of methods for quantifying subjective probabilities Huber (1974) comes to no simple conclusion, and states that "Admittedly much more research needs to be done, especially in organizational settings, but it seems safe to say that in the meantime more decision scientists should consider using alternative methods of obtaining SP's or single attribute utilities." He also points out "A related and important fact is that the accidental neglect of a creative alternative can also be much more serious than inaccuracies in the Subjective Probability Distribution or Multi-Attribute Utility Models. The generation of creative alternatives is a step easily neglected and must be consciously guarded against. It is our experience that this area cannot be over-emphasized."

However, most of the literature has concentrated on the problem of calibration of probabilities: Lichtenstein et al (1977), Schmitt and Levine (1977), Schmitt (1978), Ferrell and McGoey (1980), Lichtenstein and Fischhoff (1980). The results, although impressive, are mainly derived from using students or academics in artificial settings. They have shown that people's calibration is usually poor, and that training does help to improve people's capabilities. Nevertheless, there is still a lot of research to be done and very little real field work has been attempted, as is illustrated by the last sentence in the latest review by Heurion (1980); "It is apparent that current methods for the assessment of probabilities are by no means established beyond challenge; decision analysis might be unwise to be complacent about their reliance upon them."

A number of attempts have been made to compare methods of obtaining subjective probabilities. The research on the seven methods from the psychological literature compared by Cook and Stewart (1975) led to the surprising result: "All methods performed equally as well." When comparing methods for aggregating forecasts Fischer (1981) made two strong comments: "First, subjective probability forecasts can be substantially improved by aggregating the opinions of groups of experts rather than relying on a single expert. Second, from a practical standpoint, there is no evidence to suggest that the method to aggregate opinions will have a substantial impact on the quality of the resulting forecast."

Recently Wallsten and Budescu (1983) reviewed the empirical literature on Subjective probability encoding from a psychological and psychometric perspective. Their excellent paper gives a very detailed account of all the research that has been done on reliability, i.e. a probability encoding is said to be reliable if it is relatively free of random error, and validity, i.e. an encoding is valid if it accurately represents the opinion of the person from whom it was elicited. Most of the research is done when there is "relatively little interaction between the encoder and the experimenter." Also there has been little work done on business applitions, and the majority of the literature concentrates on meteorology and medicine - two areas where there are a large number of similar types of events occurring. Nearly all the methods used have an underlying theory of additivity which makes the forecasters obey certain strict axioms. This may cause problems as pointed out by Wallsten and Budescu, "It becomes very important to determine whether forcing additive coherence distorts judgement, and whether decision makers should be appraised of the degree of vagueness of an expert's probabilities, as well as what those probabilities are."

It is to some of these problems that this paper is addressed. We are using real situations for analysis. The methodology does not require many of the stringent constraints that are commonly found, and does give limited feedback on consistency of data. In the following sections two case studies are reported in detail, which use an adaptation of the pairwise comparison procedure developed by Saaty (1977).

Case A

This study was carried out with the help of the research laboratory on the International Wool Secretariat (IWS). Two research projects were discussed, taking about a half-day in each case.

The outcome was a decision-tree diagram of the early decision and chance stages in the life of each project over the coming 12 month period.

The first chance node in time on each decision-tree was made the subject of the pilot study. Considerable care was taken to identify the chance outcomes at this node in a detailed verbal statement, and for each of the projects under study, a discrete, exclusive and exhaustive set of chance outcomes was attempted.

At this stage the Section Leader was asked to attach subjective probabilities to each outcome by direct assessment, correcting his values to add to unity. He was also asked to provide a rank ordering of the desirability of outcomes in terms of his preferences. The pairwise comparison method was then employed, modifying the Saaty scale definitions, (see Appendix for details).

A terminal was used to call for the input comparisons and display the results, including a measure of consistency, to the Section Leader so that he was able to provide new sets of pairwise entries until satisfied with his inputs. A record of all the repeat runs was kept.

The pairwise procedure was subsequently repeated for the same chance node on each project at points in time 5 months and 3 months after obtaining the initial set of data from the Section Leader. The results from this longitudinal follow-up were used as a basis for discussion of progress on the projects.

Results: Project 1

This project was aimed at developing processes to pre-heat wool in order to make it like a polyester in the sense of being easy to print on colours and patterns. At the time of the initial interview, a major chance milestone was envisaged in eight months. The planned research activities involved two parallel sub-projects, each feeding data and information to the other.

A set of 5 chance situations was defined for the node. These are:

(1) no new compounds or solvents developed
(2) reacts chemically, new compound(s) developed which are water soluble
(3) does not react chemically, new compound(s) developed which are water soluble
(4) reacts chemically, new compound(s) developed which are non-soluble
(5) does not react chemically, new compound(s) developed which are non-soluble.

The Section Leader assessed directly the probabilities of each of these chance outcomes as shown in Exhibit 1. It should be noted that the initial 30% assessment on outcome 2 was modified to 25% after a check was made to see if estimates summed to 100%. The ratings in terms of desirability of the outcomes were ranked A (highest) to E (lowest) by the Section Leader (Exhibit 1).

He then used the pairwise comparison procedure to produce 'probabilities', and he decided to repeat the exercise five times. The input matrices are shown in Exhibit 2[2], and the sets of calculated subjective probabilities, associated eigen-values, and the direct assessments of probability are presented in Exhibit 3.

chance states of the world	direct assessment of probabilities (DA)	outcome desirability rankings (OD)
1. no new compound(s), or solvents developed	5%	C
2. reacts chemically, new compound(s) and aqueous	(30)→25%	A
3. does not react chemcially, new compound(s) and aqueous	5%	D
4. reacts chemically, new compound(s) and non-aqueous	60%	B
5. does not react chemically, new compound(s) and non-aqueous	5%	E

Exhibit 1. Direct Assessment for Project 1

Chance States

		1	2	3	4	5
	1	1	9-7-7 / -5-5	-232 / 22	9-9-9 / -9-9	112 / 34
	2		1	-257 / 77	9-7-5 / -5-5	-255 / 77
Chance States	3			1	9-5-5 / -9-9	211 / 11
	4				1	-299 / 99
	5					1

Key   1 2 3   (numbers 1 to 5 correspond in position to
       4 5   the pairwise inputs for successive runs 1 to 5 respectively)

Exhibit 2. The Data for the 5 Trials for Project 1

		1	2	3	4	5	D/A
				Run Number			
	1	35.2	6.5	6.6	7.3	7.9	5
	2	12.1	22.4	26.1	24.3	24.3	25 (30)
Outcome	3	32.4	5.2	5.2	4.1	4.1	5
	4	3.5	61.2	57.6	60.3	60.9	60
	5	16.8	5.0	4.6	3.9	3.8	5

Eigenvalue	5.93	5.66	5.46	5.30	5.37
Consistency	81%	87%	91%	94%	93%

Exhibit 3. Computed Probabilities for Project 1

Results: Project 2

This project was aimed at finding a chemical product and process suitable for dyeing wool while also acting as a shrink resisting agent. The methods by which a successful outcome could be achieved were defined by the Section Leader at the time of the interview. It was planned to spend a year working on a solution for knitwear before working on yarn. Major milestones are shown in Exhibit 4.

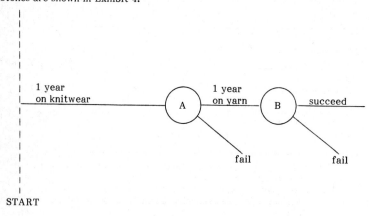

Exhibit 4. Major Milestone for Project 1

For the purposes of the trial application, attention was focused on chance node A. The Section Leader defined 5 methods by which a successful outcome could be achieved at node A (and B) as follows:

(1) alter resin presently used
(2) alter the chemical used as an "exhaustion aid"
(3) alter both the resin and the aid
(4) add a restraining agent to the system when the resin starts to exhaust
(5) add resin slowly at a controlled rate

The sixth possible outcome was failure by any method.

The direct assessment of subjective probabilities is shown in Exhibit 5 together with the subjective rankings of the 6 outcomes. The Section Leader provided 5 successive sets of input comparisons as shown in Exhibit 6 and an analysis of these runs provided 5 sets of subjective probabilities as shown in Exhibit 7 where the final set of direct assessments is displayed for comparison.

<u>Exhibit 5. Direct Assessment for Project 2</u>

Chance states of the world	Direct assessment of probabilities (1)			Outcome Desirability Rankings (2)
	1	2	3	
1. Success by changing the resin used	60	30	30	D/E
2. Success by changing the exhaustion aid used	30	15	15	A/B
3. Success by changing both the resin and the aid used	70	35	35	D/E
4. Success by adding a restraining agent	10	5	7	A/B
5. Success by adding Lankrolan slowly	20	10	10	C
6. Failure by any method	5	2	3	F

Notes: (1)   The three sets of numbers shown for the direct assessment recorded how the decision-taker finalised his assessment (attempt 3) by this procedure, after checking and finding that attempts 1 and 2 did not normalise to 100%

(2)   Rankings of desirability count 'A' as highest

G. Lockett, T. Gear

Exhibit 6. Data for the 5 Trials for Project 2

Chance States

	1	2	3	4	5	6
1	1	555 / 55	-3-2-2 / -2-2	355 / 56	146 / 44	777 / 87
2		1	-5-5-6 / -6-6	111 / 11	-3-2-2 / -2-2	333 / 22
3			1	554 / 66	556 / 66	777 / 88
4				1	1-2-2 / -2-2	522 / 32
5					1	444 / 44
6						1

Chance States

key

1	2	3
4	5	

the numbers 1 to 5 indicate the positions of data inputs for runs 1 to 5

Exhibit 7. Computed Probabilities for Project 2

Run Number

		1	2	3	4	5	D/A
	1	21.5	30.7	31.7	30.3	30.7	30
	2	6.9	7.2	6.6	6.2	6.2	15
Outcome	3	44.7	40.8	42.7	42.6	42.6	35
	4	9.9	6.6	6.0	6.8	6.1	7
	5	13.8	11.1	9.7	10.8	10.8	10
	6	3.2	3.6	3.3	3.3	3.6	3

Eigenvalue	6.37	6.19	6.26	6.14	6.12
Consistency	93.9%	96.9%	96.0%	97.6%	97.9%

Analysis of Initial Results

After a short learning period, the Section Leader became thoroughly used to the comparative questioning procedure applied to assessing probabilities of a set of outcomes, and the measure of consistency used tended to increase, that is, improve in value on successive runs.

A study of Exhibit 2 and 5 reveals that the major changes of input data occur between the first and second trials. After that there are smaller adjustments in both directions. Although non integer values are allowed, in all cases the decision maker did not choose to use a finer scale.

For project 1, a comparison of the derived probabilities of run 5 with those of direct assessment in table 3 shows an exceptionally close agreement. The same applies to project 2 results in Exhibit 7. Although there are marked differences for outcomes 2 and 3, (6.2% compared with 15%, and 42.6% compared with 35% respectively).

As the relationship of the output to the input is mathematically complex, these results could not easily be "engineered," although this possibility cannot be excluded at this stage of testing.

Follow-Up Study

Both projects were analyzed again after a few months interval, and in this instance the data was collected on the same day. The revised probability data is shown in Exhibit 8 and 9 together with the previous final results. In both cases there are significant changes in the values.

Exhibit 8. Revised Computed Probabilities for Project 1

		Run Number			
		5	6	7	DA	OD
	1	7.9	43.6	52.8	5	C
	2	24.3	20.0	14.7	25 (30)	A
Outcome	3	4.1	4.4	4.3	5	D
	4	60.9	26.2	24.0	60	B
	5	3.8	5.8	4.2	5	E

Eigenvalue	5.37	5.35	5.32
Consistency	93%	93%	93.5%

Run 5   : Initial data

Runs 6, 7   : New data

Exhibit 9. Revised Computed Probabilities for Project 2

		Run Number			
		5	6	DA	OD
	1	30.7	24.9	20	D/E
	2	6.2	8.1	10	A/B
Outcome	3	42.6	37.9	20	D/E
	4	6.1	5.2	10	A/B
	5	10.8	21.3	40	C
	6	3.6	2.6	0	F

Eigenvalue	6.37	6.53
Consistency	93.9%	91.2%

For project 1, outcomes 2 and 4 become less likely, and outcome 1 more likely. The Section Leader stated that the project activities were unchanged, and that the revisions simply reflected his changing feelings in the light of five months of experience on the projects. As the highly ranked (A and B) outcomes 2 and 4 have gone down in probability, while outcome 1 (ranked C) has become more probable, the project has grown less promising over time.

The revised analysis of project 2 shows some changes in probability with respect to the earlier analysis (Exhibit 9). The Section Leader stated that in this case the outputs from the first analysis caused him to re-think through his project plan. He was particularly concerned that the chance of outcome numbered 5 was low. This resulted in a deliberate shift of emphasis within the activities in order to increase the effort on activities associated with outcome 3. The changes appear to be reflected in the revised figures. An approximate analysis of the expected monetary value of incremental wool demand resulting from the project increased by 17% as a result of the alterations introduced by the Section Leader in response to the information fed back from the initial analysis.

Comments

We have presented a study of two R and D projects that were carried out over a period of months. The method sometimes gives different results to the normal direct assessment procedure, and the decision maker himself thought that the results were "better." One interesting outcome was the way in which our original data caused him to change the way the research was being carried out, and he altered the probabilities by manipulating his resources. The interactive method used in this experiment encourages people to have more than one attempt. However, the fact that the subject believed the results were better is not an adequate test of the method.

Case B

This case is taken from a completely separate and different organization. For the purposes of initial evaluation of the method, the application was concerned with a defined and new chemical engineering process. A specific sub-problem of heat recovery was also isolated for attention in terms of forecasting an actual loss of thermal efficiency as compared with a theoretical optimum. It was thought that the loss due to heat recovery problems could range between 0 and 9%. This range was divided up into defined steps of 0, 0-3%, 3-6% and 6-9% for the purpose of making the pairwise comparisons.

The Method

The sub-problem was assessed by three engineers, each of them independently providing sets of pairwise inputs. Prior to making the comparisons, they also provided direct assessments of the subjective probabilities for the loss of efficiency falling in one of the above defined bands. Results were fed back to each researcher individually and were subsequently compared and discussed as a group.

The Results

Subject 1 provided 4 sets of pairwise comparisons before being happy with his input, subject 2 had 3 runs, and the third engineer had only a single run. The results are shown in Exhibit 10.

Exhibit 10. Results for the 3 Engineers

% Heat Loss	Subject 1						Subject 2				Subject 3	
	D.A.	Run 1	Run 2	Run 3	Run 4	D.A.	Run 1	Run 2	Run 3	D.A.	Run 1
0	30	25.6	31	48.2	21.6	10	11.8	10.8	11.4	20	12.8
0 – 3	60	54.7	53.4	30.3	56.7	40	32.2	44.5	34.5	40	53.5
3 – 6	10	15.1	11.3	17.1	17.2	40	45.8	35.0	43.9	30	27.5
6 – 9	0	4.5	4.3	4.5	4.5	10	10.2	9.8	10.2	10	6.3
Consistency		91%	91%	83%	93%		98%	99%	99.5%		93%

Comparison and Comments

Exhibit 10 clearly shows that there are differences of opinion between each of the researchers and no consensus emerges. These differences are not explained by inconsistency as this
was always satisfactorily high, and the technique is clearly detecting this. During group discussion, all the participants were pleased with their own results and although they did not
agree with each other, the technique was praised. In all it took about one hour to perform
the experiment, and was seen to be extremely efficient. The results were taken further but
for commercial reasons cannot be reported here.

Interpretation of the Derived Eigenvector

When making probability assessments we are concerned with values on the standardized scale
from zero to unity. The ratio scale used in this paper with its semantic definitions contains
a degree of indeterminancy. One method of resolving this problem would be to compare the
unknown probabilities with a set of events with "known" probability, using the same ratio
scale.

At this stage we report some preliminary experiments which have been carried out with the
subjects of the experimental trials in order to assess how closely the subjects were able to
replicate a set of given input probabilities. The subject used in Case A was given two hypothetical research projects, the first experiment involving 5 chance routes from a node with
given probabilities shown in Exhibit 11, and the second experiment involving 6 chance routes
as shown in Exhibit 12.

Exhibit 11. Results from Experiment 1

	Input Probs.	Run 1	Run 2
Event 1	12	10.8	11.2
2	20	23.9	22.2
3	05	4.0	4.0
4	60	58.3	59.7
5	03	3.0	2.9
Consistency		87%	88%

Exhibit 12. Results from Experiment 2

	Input Probs.	Run 1	Run 2
Event 1	31	31.2	24.6
2	06	5.0	5.6
3	43	44.2	48.2
4	05	4.1	4.5
5	11	11.8	13.3
6	04	3.7	3.8
Consistency		97%	96%

These results must be used with caution as a basis for drawing conclusions at this stage. They were obtained from the subject via the telephone after the experimental trails described in this paper were completed. The results for run 1 were not fed back to the subject before run 2 inputs were also provided.

A similar type of experiment was also carried out with the 3 subjects of Case B. They were presented with a hypothetical chance branching node with defined probabilities rounded to the nearest 5% age point to be similar to derived values from the actual situation already described.

Exhibit 13 shows the results for each of the 3 subjects. A study of this table shows, as in Case A, a close correlation for each subject, between given values and values derived from the ratio scale.

Exhibit 13. Results from Experiment 3

Subject 1		Subject 2		Subject 3	
Input Values	Output Values	Input Values	Output Values	Input Values	Output Values
20	20.8	10	8.0	10	8.2
60	61.3	35	30.9	55	55.2
15	12.8	45	51.7	30	31.3
5	5.1	10	9.4	5	5.4
Eigenvalue 4.19		4.03		4.05	
Consistency 95.3%		99.1%		98.7%	

Discussion

Some cases have been presented showing the detailed application of a technique for discrete probability assessment. Although the examples are only small in number, the outcomes have some interesting results. In each instance the subjects were pleased to take part, found the technique easy to use, and used the derived probabilities, i.e. they took some action on them. The technique has also given us some insights into probability assessment, particularly the importance to management of data changes over time. The ease of use is a very important factor which clearly quickly overcomes the major problem of "a willingness to try, then, an understanding of, and finally confidence in, the method among the R and D line managers" [Balthasar (1978)]. Its very simplicity is one of its major assets, allowing alterations to be made with little effort. However, we are still left with the question of whether or not the subjects are manipulating the data to get the "right answer." This possibility exists with the proposed method – as well as for all methods known to the authors and little research has been done in this area. Our own feeling is that our subjects did not consciously manipulate, but it is possible in practice.

An attempt has been made to "validate" the procedure using some hypothetical cases (see Exhibit 14). In Experiment 2, comparison between the input probabilities and the generated sets of numbers shows close agreement. This strengthens the hypothesis that the numbers generated in Experiment 1 relate closely to the required and unknown probabilities.

The results are encouraging but not conclusive, and we feel that the methodology has potential. Validation is still a problem, but the experiments go as far towards validation as other experiments. As pointed out by Wallsten and Bandescu (1983), there has been little work done on this in business applications where one-off events are the norm. Of more importance is the problem of how subjective probabilities are used and when should they be updated? The group results clearly show that agreement is often unobtainable – but decisions have to be reached. Methods that help people to attempt quantification should be encouraged. Clearly, this is one of them and it could be a powerful research tool in applied settings.

G. Lockett, T. Gear

Exhibit 14. Validation Method

Experiment 1

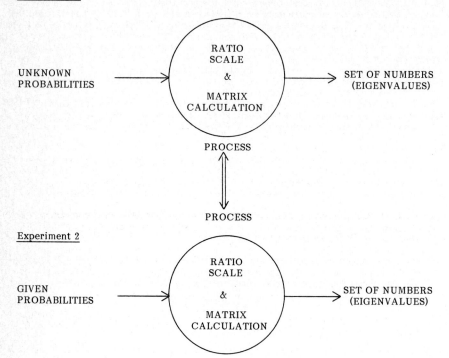

Experiment 2

FOOTNOTES

[1] authors' insert

[2] For convenience, the computer package uses a negative sign to denote reciprocal, and this conventition has been kept in all subsequent tables, i.e. -7 should be taken as 1/7 etc.

REFERENCES

[1] Balthasar, H. U., Boschi, R. A., Menle, M. M., "Calling the Shots in R&D," Harvard Business Review, May-June 1978, pp. 151-160.

[2] Belkauoi, A. "Judgment Related Issues in Performance Evaluation," Journal of Business Finance and Accounting, Vol. 19, No. 4, 1982, pp. 484-500.

[3] Bonson, A. B. Judd, B. R., Morris, P. A., Sussman, S. S., "Applying Analytic Methods to R&D Planning: Two Case Studies," Research Management, No. 1982, pp. 17-25.

[4] Boschi, R. A. A., "Modelling Exploratory Research," E.J.O.R., Vol. 10, 1982, pp. 250-259.

[5] Cook, R. L., Steard, T. R., "A Comparison of Seven Methods of Obtaining Subjective Descriptions of Judgmental Policy," Organizational Behavior and Human Performance, Vol. 13, 1975, pp. 31-45.

[6] Despontin, M., Moscarola, J., Spronk, J. "A User-oriented Listing of Multiple Criteria Decision Methods", Report CSOOTW/152, Free University of Brussels, V.U.B. Center for Statistics and Operations Research, Pleinlann 2, B-1050 Brussels (1980).

[7] Ferrell, W. R., McGoey, P. J., "A Model of Calibration for Subjective Probabilities," Organizational Behaviour and Human Performance, Vol. 26, 1980, pp. 32-53.

[8] Fischer, G. W., "Utility Models for Multiple Objective Decisions: Do They Accurately Represent Human References," Decision Sciences, Vol. 10, 1979, pp. 451-479.

[9] Fischer, G. W., "When Oracles Fail - A Comparison of Four Procedures for Aggregating Subjective Probability Forecasts," Organizational Behaviour and Human Performance, Vol. 28, 1981, pp. 96-110.

[10] Gear, A. E., Lockett, A. G. Muhlemann, A. P., "A United Approach to the Acquisition of Subjective Data in R&D," IEEE Trans. Eng. Man., Vol. EM-29, No. 1, pp. 11-18, 1982.

[11] Hampton, J., Moore, P., Thomas, H., "Subjective Probability and its Measurement," Journal of the Royal Statistical Society, Series A, 1973, pp.

[12] Heurion, M., "Assessing Probabilities: A Review", Dept. of Eng. & Public Policy, Carnegie-Mellon University, Pittsburgh, 1980.

[13] Hogarth, R. M., "From Romanticism to Precision to ...", Decision Sciences, Vol. 13, No. 4, Oct. 1982, pp. 543-546.

[14] Huber, G. P., "Methods for Quantifying Subjective Probabilities and Multi-Attribute Utilities," Decision Sciences, Vol. 5, 1974, pp. 431-458.

[15] Jensen, R. E., "Reporting of Management Forecasts: An Eigenvector Model for Elicitation and Review of Forecasts," Decision Sciences, Vol. 13, 1982, pp. 14-37.

[16] Lichtenstein, S., Fischhoff, B., Phillips, L. Ð., "Calibration of Probabilities: The State of the Art" in H. Hunderman and G. deZeeuw (Eds.), Decision Making and Change in Human Affairs, Dordrecht, Holland, P. Reidl, 1977.

[17] Lichtenstein, S., Fischhoff, B., "Training for Calibration," Organizational Behaviour and Human Performance, Vol. 26, 1980, pp. 149-171.

[18] Lockett, A. G., Muhlemann, A. P. Gear, A. E., "Group Decision Making and Multiple Criteria", A Documented Application in Morse (1981).

[19] Mancini, L., Meisner, J., Singer, E., "Assessing Uncertain Ventures Using Experts' Judgements in the Form of Subjective Probabilities," OMEGA, Vol. 9, No. 2, 1981, pp. 177-187.

[20] Moore, P. G., Thomas, H., "Measuring Uncertainty," OMEGA, Vol. 3, No. 6, 1975, pp. 657-672.

[21] Morse, J. N. (Ed), "Organizations: Multiple Agents with Multiple Criteria," Proceedings of the Fourth International Conference on MCDM, Newark, 1980, Springer-Verland, New York, 1981.

[22] Nutt, P. C., "Comparing Methods for Weighting Decision Criteria," OMEGA, Vol. 9, No. 2, 1981, pp. 163-172.

[23] Park, S. H., Boland, R. J., "Exploring the Role of Data in Problem Formulation," TIMS/ORSA Meeting, New Orleans, May 1979.

[24] Polding, E., Lockett, A. G., "Organizational Linkages and O.R. Projects," E.J.O.R., Vol. 7, 1981, pp. 14-21.

[25] Rubenstein, A. H., Schroder, H. H., "Managerial Differences in Assessing Probabilities of Technical Success for R&D Projects," Management Science, Vol. 24, No. 2, 1977, pp. 137-148.

[26] Saaty, T. L., "A Scaling Method for Priorities in Hierarchical Structures," Journal of Mathematical Psychology, Vol. 15, 1977, pp. 234-281.

[27] Saaty, T. L., "The Analytical Hierarchy Process," McGraw-Hill, New York, 1981.

[28] Schmitt, N., Levine, R. L., "Statistical and Subjective Weights: Some Problems and Proposals," Organizational Behaviour and Human Performance, Vol. 20, 1977, pp. 15-30.

[29] Schmitt, N., "Comparison of Subjective and Objective Weighting Strategies in Changing Task Situations," Organizational Behaviour and Human Performance, Vol. 12, 1978, pp. 171-188.

[30] Schoemaker, P.H.J., "Behavioral Issues in Multi-Attribute Utility Modelling and Decision Analysis", in Morse (1981).

[31] Schroder, H. H., "The Quality of Subjective Probabilities of Technical Success in R&D," R&D Management, Vol. 6, No. 1, 1975.

[32] Schultz, R. L., Slevin, D. P., "Implementing Operations Research/Management Science", New York, Elsevier, 1975.

[33] Sjoberg, L., "Aided Unaided Decision Making: Improving Intuitive Judgment," Journal of Forecasting, Vol. 1, No. 4, Oct-Dec, 1982, pp. 349-364.

[34] Slovic, P., Lichtenstein, S., "Comparison of Bayesian and Regression Approaches to the Study of Information Processing in Judgment," Journal of Organizational Behaviour and Human Performance, Vol. 6, 1971, pp. 649-744.

[35] Souder, W. E., "A System for Using R&D Project Evaluation Methods," Research Management, Sept. 1978, pp. 29-37.

[36] Spetzler, C. S., Holstein, S. Von., "Probability Encoding in Decision Analysis," Management Science, Vol. 22, 1975, pp. 340-358.

[37] Stahl, M. J., Zimmerer, T. W., "Modelling Product Development Decision Policies of Managers and Management Students: Differences Between Subjective and Relative Weights," IEEE Trans. Eng. Man., Vol. 30, No. 1, 1983, pp. 18-24.

[38] Wallsten, T. S., Budescu, D. V., "Encoding Subjective Probabilities: A Psychological and Psychometric Review," Management Science, Vol. 24, 1983, pp. 151-173.

APPENDIX

The Pairwise Technique

The approach is based on simple pairwise comparisons of the chance routes according to their relative likelihood or probability of occurring. The method utilizes a semantic ratio scale originally derived and tested by Saaty (1977) for deriving the relative weights of a group of items.

The method of pairwise comparisons used to estimate probabilities is explained with the aid of the chance branching node shown below:

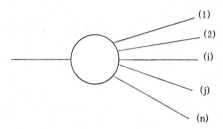

A set of pairwise comparisons is made which can be represented by the matrix of entries as follows:

$$
A = \begin{array}{c|cccc}
 & (1) & (2) & \cdots & (n) \\
\hline
(1) & 1 & A(12) & \cdots & A(1n) \\
(2) & & 1 & \cdots & A(2n) \\
\cdot & & & & \cdot \\
\cdot & & & & \cdot \\
\cdot & & & & \cdot \\
\cdot & & & & \cdot \\
(n) & & & & 1
\end{array}
$$

where: A(ij) is defined as likelihood/probability of event (i): likelihood/probability of event (j).

For each comparison, the subject is asked to compare the relative likelihood of one outcome with another outcome. In answering these comparative questions, the subject selects a value from a continuous ratio scale of values with semantically defined points as follows:

1 : equally likely/probable
3 : weakly more likely/probable
5 : strongly more likely/probable
7 : demonstrably more likely/probable
9 : absolutely more likely/probable

Intermediate entries, e.g. 2.5, represent a compromise between the points 1 and 3, etc. Each entry provides a response to the question: when the element of the left-hand side of the matrix is compared with the element on the top, how much more (or less) likely/probable is the one compared with the other? If the top element entry is more likely/probable than the left-hand element, then a reciprocal entry is selected from the 1-9 scale. For example, 1/3 of the top element is weakly more probable than the left-hand element. For convenience, the computer package developed for this purpose accepts a negative value (in this case -3) rather than a reciprocal. Values are entered above the leading diagonal and the programme computes values below the diagonal assuming consistent replies to the same comparisons when made in reverse order.

There is a degree of internal checking built into the procedure. For example, if the subject is entirely consistent with his entries, A(12) A(23) = A(13) and so on.

For the consistent case it can easily be shown that $A\lambda = n\lambda$ where n is the size of the consistent square matrix A. In this case the A(ij)'s are simply the ratios $\lambda(i)/\lambda(j)$.

In the more general case a degree of inconsistency is only to be expected amongst the entries, even though the matrix is forced to be reciprocal by only carrying out the comparisons above the diagonal. Let an inconsistent set of entries be labelled as a matrix A^1. From the pairwise comparisons, A^1 represents an approximation to A. In this case the problem $A^1 \lambda^1 = n_{max}\lambda^1$ is solved where λ^1 is the largest eigenvector of A^1, and n_{max} the associated eigenvalue. The derived values of the elements of λ^1 are used as estimates of the values of $\lambda(i)$. The derived value of n_{max} as compared with n, the size of the matrix, is used as a measure of consistency. An analysis of the effects of perturbations of A^1 and a discussion of the uniqueness of the associated eigenvector and eigenvalue are given in Saaty (1977, 1981).

To summarize, the method assumes that solution of $A^1 \lambda^1 = n_{max}\lambda^1$ provides a normalized eigenvector, λ^1, the elements of which will represent relative likelihoods. The value, $\lambda(i)$, is further assumed to closely resemble the subjective probability for outcome i. The measure of consistency adopted in this paper is simply $1 - (n_{max}-n)/n$, expressed as a percentage. For a discussion of alternative measures of consistency, see Saaty (1981).

In the cases reported in this paper we have used a 1-9 scale, and this results in very small and very large probabilities being unobtainable. If it was necessary the scale could be changed to a 1-99 (say) which could overcome this problem. However, in the situations under consideration this was not an obstacle, and the difficulty was theoretical rather than practical.

Project Management: Methods and Studies
Burton V. Dean (editor)
© Elsevier Science Publishers B.V. (North-Holland), 1985

"PATIENTS TAKE PRIORITY" - A CASE STUDY
OF SCHEDULING IN HEALTH CARE OPERATIONS

George M. Marko

Gilbane Building Company
Cleveland, Ohio
U.S.A.

Project scheduling, whether concerned with human or machine
activities, requires both a scientific methodology and an intuitive
"feel" approach. The former has produced a number of well-defined
structured methods from PERT, CPM, and GERT to other heuristic
models like SDR/CPM. The latter, intuitive approach, often derives
from an analysis of the various methodologies and a tailoring of
their attributes to meet the respective project needs. As the level
of human interaction increases on a project, the impact of an
intuitive approach on the project schedule expands accordingly.

This was the case the Gilbane Building Company was presented
by the Cleveland Clinic Foundation in determining a schedule for the
construction and subsequent occupancy of new facilities. The scheduling task appeared to be relatively uncomplicated, however, when
informed that patient services could not be disrupted, the task became
increasingly complex. Gilbane conducted a thorough evaluation of the
available scheduling techniques based on both user and client needs.
After numerous client contacts and identification of program objectives
and goals, PDM (Precedence Diagramming Method) was selected.

PDM, as this case study shows, offers a high degree of flexibility while
maintaining a strong degree of simplicity in understanding and communication. Because it can be presented in an almost Gantt Chart-like
format, it can be quickly assimilated by most viewers. PDM's main
advantage though can be seen in the various precedence relationships
that can be drawn. Apart from the traditional "finish-to-start" relationship, PDM adds "finish-to-finish," "start-to-start," and "start-to-
finish" relationships. This larger set of precedence relationships provides
increased flexibility for the project network, and although this increases
the computational complexity, it permits a basic reduction of the network
complexity in terms of understanding and interpretation.

Scheduling of projects addresses what is perhaps the highest priority,
from a management perspective - time. The old adage - "time is
money" - is no more evident than in construction operations, as in this
case, but, is typical of most business operations. As managers are
confronted with increased levels of computerization and other technological advances, gains in efficiency and productivity are expected.
Through real case situations presented, a small picture of the many
and diverse management opportunities that exist are shown. While
many of the techniques employed in Project Management require a
specialized knowledge or synthesis of management and engineering
approaches, the basic foundations for the decision making process
can be traced to general management and scientific principles. Lastly,
the major unifying theme is communication. All successful management
knows not only its message, but how to convey it.

In most construction projects, the main emphasis is on time, cost, and quality. These have, typically, been addressed by construction management firms through well-established scheduling, cost, and quality control programs. The challenge, in many of these projects, is with early/beneficial occupancy, as in typical office buildings, or with on-line operations, as in manufacturing facilities.

But what approach should be used, given the constraint "Patients take priority!"? This constraint framed the main program objective, "Build and move-in with minimum disruption," given to the Gilbane Building Company by the Cleveland Clinic Foundation for the construction and subsequent occupancy program for the new clinic facilities. This case study centers on the choice of a scheduling method for the occupancy program, and the development of the occupancy schedule to meet the Cleveland Clinic Foundation's program goals and objectives.

In choosing an appropriate planning methodology, the Gilbane Building Company had to consider an approach that would do the following:

(1) Address the program's needs.
(2) Provide flexibility in execution.
(3) Be readily understood by the larger cohort with whom Gilbane would be dealing; namely, doctors and other medical care professionals.

After a careful evaluation of the various techniques employed on previous company projects (Gantt Charts, Arrow Diagram CPM's, and Precedence Diagrams), a choice was determined through a process of elimination, judged against program criteria. Gantt Charts, while easily understood, could not address the many and varied complex interrelationships involved in the program; such as, owner installed equipment, department transfers, and even the stocking of supplies. The Arrow Diagram CPM's, while having full logic capabilities to integrate most constraints, suffered from what Moder and Crandall have called "its networking complexity." [2] As such, its effectiveness for communication at management levels becomes mired in lengthy computer printouts and, oft-times, confusing logic sequences. This left the Precedence Diagram Method, which was ultimately selected for its ease of understanding (similar to Gantt Charts), high level of constraint identification through lead-lag time predecessor/successor relationships, and a close resemblance to the actual thought process of typical planning methodologies.

Following the choice of PDM, Gilbane put the client and its representatives through a process it refers to as the "Gilbane Card Trick." The card trick helps to identify all tasks that must be accomplished to meet project objectives. While the main objective was defined, the plan to achieve it remained vague and spread across various responsibilities. Through the efforts of Gilbane, the Cleveland Clinic Foundation and its concerned parties (i.e. suppliers, technical contractors, etc.) these tasks were identified, along with the interrelationship between them. The "card trick"-generated schedule requires that:

(1) All tasks must be monitorable with defined end results.
(2) All tasks must have some level of accountability assigned to them, with ownership of the task given to a person or organization.

The key to any successful schedule development is cooperation. By viewing this process as a team function and stressing ownership of tasks in its development, a successful end product will result.

As shown on the simple card (see Diagram 1), estimates of time (duration) and resource usage (manpower) are identified. These data items contribute to the overall effectiveness of the schedule. The cards are placed on a time scale (in months) and the resultant collage of cards form the backbone of the PDM schedule. The format of the cards is, in fact, closely allied to the PDM concept utilizing predecessor and successor events. This permits a relatively easy transition from the meeting format to document production.

Preceding   Succeeding
Activities   Activities

1.   1.

2.   2.

3.   3.

_____

Activity Description

Manpower   Duration
Needed   Work
_____ People   Days _____

Diagram 1.

Apart from straight tasks contributing to the Clinic Occupancy Schedule, other "natural/ physical" configurations of the building helped determine the schedule. The ziggurat form of the building reflects both its function and departmental size. (See Diagram 2) The first four above-ground floors provide the foundation of the Clinic's work in terms of service (i.e. Patient Accounts, Radiology Labs, etc.) and its larger departments of Radiology, Opthamology, and Orthopedics. These areas, coupled with the records areas in the basement levels, are paramount to clinic operations. As the building rises, the "foot print" becomes smaller due to the size and special nature of departments and services. As a result, the building tiers contributed to "natural" dividers for schedule work segments.

This was further reflected through the atrium spaces that occured at two floor intervals from level four up. These "naturally" occuring divisions in building form lent a sensible approach to the project schedule. The final building configuration that gave the schedule direction was the bifurcated floors, averaging two departments per floor.

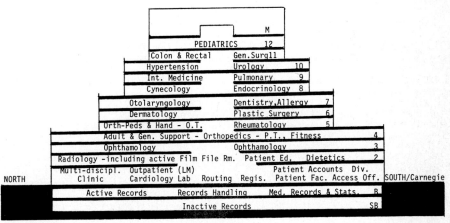

SECTION FACING EAST

Diagram 2.

Taking this information and the Clinic's objectives of a three month move time with minimum disruptions, an initial schedule was developed. Looking at a time frame of three months (13-14 weeks) and a fourteen usable-floor building, the most evident approach appeared to be one floor per week. Constraint information on equipment support systems, stocking of supplies, and personnel moves from existing facilities became parameters for predecessor events. This leads to a phased and sequential occupancy schedule of the building from the core floors (subbasement - Floor 3) up to Floor 12, one floor at a time.

The resulting occupancy schedule was developed through the use of Primavera, a state of the art project scheduling system that operates on a PC with at least 496K storage capability. This software includes features previously available only through large mainframe systems. Its features extend to schedule graphics and examples shown in diagrams 3 and 4 are products of the system.

The Occupancy Schedule for the Cleveland Clinic Foundation used PDM because it provided the best features of the available scheduling techniques for the program requirements. It provided both a comprehensive and flexible approach to scheduling the project. Although from a logic standpoint PDM is different from ADM only in notational concept and execution, it presents a clearer, more concise format for presentation purposes. This facilitates an ease of understanding not only among practitioners, but also among laymen, resulting in a greater understanding of the important concepts that address management concerns. This increased management awareness optimizes the typical time constraints confronting most managers in the decision-making process and, as such, is a most valuable tool.

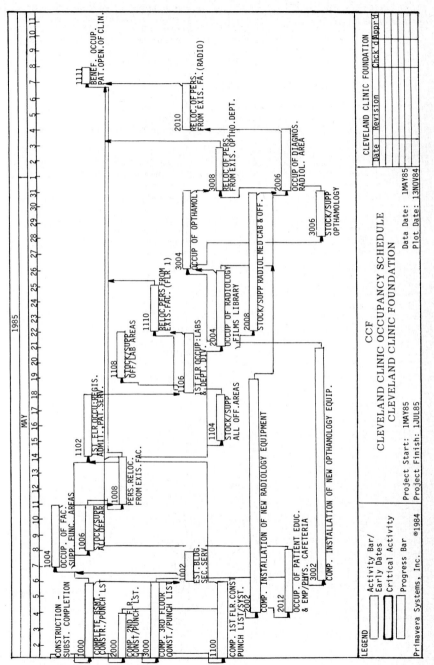

Diagram 3.

CCF   PRIMAVERA PROJECT PLANNER   CLEVELAND CLINIC OCCUPANCY SCHEDULE
REPORT DATE 7NOV84 RUN NO. 3   CLEVELAND CLINIC FOUNDATION   START DATE 1MAY85 FIN DATE 1AUG85
CCF - OCCUPANCY PREDECESSORS & SUCCESSORS   DATA DATE 1MAY85 PAGE NO. 1

ACTIVITY NUMBER	ORIG DUR	REM DUR	PCT	CODE	ACTIVITY DESCRIPTION	EARLY START	EARLY FINISH	LATE START	LATE FINISH	TOTAL FLOAT
1	0	0	100	SUCC ACT.NOS	CONSTRUCTION - SUBSTANTIAL COMPLETION * 1000,* 1100,* 2000,* 3000	1MAY85	1MAY85A			
1000	5	5	0	PREC ACT.NOS SUCC ACT.NOS	COMPLETE BSMT CONSTRUCTION & PUNCH LIST * 1, 1002, 1004,	1MAY85	5MAY85	25JUN85	29JUN85	54
2000	3	3	0	PREC ACT.NOS SUCC ACT.NOS	COMPLETE 2ND FLOOR CONSTRUCTION & PUNCH LIST * 1, 2002,* 2012,	1MAY85	3MAY85	7JUL85	9JUL85	65
3000	5	5	0	PREC ACT.NOS SUCC ACT.NOS	COMPLETE 3RD FLOOR CONST. & PUNCH LIST * 1, 3002,	1MAY85	5MAY85	5JUL85	9JUL85	63
1002	2	2	0	PREC ACT.NOS SUCC ACT.NOS	ESTABLISH BUILDING SECURITY SERVICES 1000, 1004,	6MAY85	7MAY85	30JUN85	1JUL85	54
1004	4	4	0	PREC ACT.NOS SUCC ACT.NOS	OCCUPANCY OF FACILITY SUPPORT FUNCTION AREAS 1000, 1002, 1006,* 1008,* 1102,	7MAY85	10MAY85	1JUL85	5JUL85	54
1006	3	3	0	PREC ACT.NOS SUCC ACT.NOS	STOCK & SUPPLY ALL OFFICE AREAS 1004, 1008,	8MAY85	10MAY85	26JUL85	28JUL85	77
1008	3	3	0	PREC ACT.NOS SUCC ACT.NOS	PERSONNEL RELOCATION FROM EXIST. FACILITIES 1004,* 1006, 1111,	11MAY85	13MAY85	29JUL85	31JUL85	77
1102	4	4	0	PREC ACT.NOS SUCC ACT.NOS	1ST FLR OCCUPANCY:REGIS.., ADMIT.,PATIENT SERV. 1004, 1100, 1104,* 1106,* 2004,	14MAY85	17MAY85	9JUL85	12JUL85	54
1111	1	1	0	PREC ACT.NOS PREC ACT.NOS	BENEFICIAL OCCUPANCY - PATIENT OPENING OF CLINIC 1008, 1100, 2012,* 2010 3008,	7JUN85	7JUN85	1AUG85	1AUG85	54
1100	5	5	0	PREC ACT.NOS SUCC ACT.NOS	COMPLETE 1ST FLOOR CONST, PUNCH LIST & SYSTEMS * 1, 1102,	1MAY85	5MAY85	3JUL85	8JUL85	62

Diagram 4.

CCF
PRIMAVERA PROJECT PLANNER
REPORT DATE 7NOV84   RUN NO. 3
CLEVELAND CLINIC FOUNDATION
CCF - OCCUPANCY PREDECESSORS & SUCCESSORS

CLEVELAND CLINIC OCCUPANCY SCHEDULE
START DATE 1MAY85 FIN DATE 1AUG85
DATA DATE 1MAY85 PAGE NO. 2

ACTIVITY NUMBER	ORIG DUR	REM DUR	PCT	CODE	ACTIVITY DESCRIPTION	START	FINISH	START	FINISH	TOTAL FLOAT
1108	3	3	0		STOCK & SUPPLY OFFICE AND LAB AREAS	19MAY85	21MAY85	26JUL85	28JUL85	66
				PREC ACT.NOS	1106,					
				SUCC ACT.NOS	1110,					
2002	15	15	0		COMPLETE INSTALLATION OF NEW RADIOLOGY EQUIPMENT	4MAY85	18MAY85	10JUL85	24JUL85	65
				PREC ACT.NOS	2000,					
				SUCC ACT.NOS	2006,					
2012	4	4	0		OCCUPANCY OF PATIENT EDUC. & EMP/PHYS. CAFETERIA	4MAY85	7MAY85	28JUL85	31JUL85	83
				PREC ACT.NOS	2000,					
				SUCC ACT.NOS	1111,					
2006	4	4	0		OCCUPANCY OF DIAGNOSTIC RADIOLOGY AREA	31MAY85	3JUN85	25JUL85	28JUL85	54
				PREC ACT.NOS	2004, 2002,* 2008,					
				SUCC ACT.NOS	2010,					
2008	8	8	0		STOCK & AUPPLY RADIOLOGY MED. CABINETS & OFFICES	22MAY85	30MAY85	17JUL85	24JUL85	54
				PREC ACT.NOS	2004,					
				SUCC ACT.NOS	2006,					
3004	4	4	0		OCCUPANCY OF OPTHOMOLOGY	26MAY85	30MAY85	25JUL85	28JUL85	58
				PREC ACT.NOS	2004, 3002,					
				SUCC ACT.NOS	3006,* 3008,					
2010	3	3	0		RELOCATION OF PERSONNEL FROM EXIST FAC. (RADIO)	4JUN85	6JUN85	29JUL85	31JUL85	54
				PREC ACT.NOS	2006,					
				SUCC ACT.NOS	1111,					
3002	15	15	0		COMPLETE INSTALLATION OF NEW OPTHAMOLOGY EQUIP.	6MAY85	20MAY85	10JUL85	24JUL85	63
				PREC ACT.NOS	3000,					
				SUCC ACT.NOS	3004,					
3006	3	3	0		STOCK & SUPPLY OPTHAMOLOGY	28MAY85	30MAY85	26JUL85	28JUL85	58
				PREC ACT.NOS	3004,					
				SUCC ACT.NOS	3008,					
3008	3	3	0		RELOCATION OF PERSONNEL FROM EXIST OPTHO. DEPT.	31MAY85	2JUN85	29JUL85	31JUL85	58
				PREC ACT.NOS	3004,* 3006,					
				SUCC ACT.NOS	1111,					

PRIMAVERA PROJECT PLANNER
CLEVELAND CLINIC FOUNDATION

CCF
REPORT DATE 7NOV84 RUN NO. 2
CLEVELAND CLINIC FOUNDATION OCCUPANCY PROGRAM

CLEVELAND CLINIC OCCUPANCY SCHEDULE
START DATE 1MAY85   FIN DATE 1AUG85
DATA DATE 1MAY85   PAGE NO. 1

ACTIVITY NUMBER	ORIG DUR	REM DUR	PCT	CODE	ACTIVITY DESCRIPTION	EARLY START	EARLY FINISH	LATE START	LATE FINISH	TOTAL FLOAT
1	0	0	100		CONSTRUCTION - SUBSTANTIAL COMPLETION	1MAY85A	1MAY85A			
1000	5	5	0		COMPLETE BSMT CONSTRUCTION & PUNCH LIST	1MAY85	5MAY85	25JUN85	29JUN85	54
2000	3	3	0		COMPLETE 2ND FLOOR CONSTRUCTION & PUNCH LIST	1MAY85	3MAY85	7JUL85	9JUL85	65
3000	5	5	0		COMPLETE 3RD FLOOR CONST. & PUNCH LIST	1MAY85	5MAY85	5JUL85	9JUL85	63
1002	2	2	0		ESTABLISH BUILDING SECURITY SERVICES	6MAY85	7MAY85	30JUN85	1JUL85	54
1004	4	4	0		OCCUPANCY OF FACILITY SUPPORT FUNCTION AREAS	7MAY85	10MAY85	1JUL85	5JUL85	54
1006	3	3	0		STOCK & SUPPLY ALL OFFICE AREAS	8MAY85	10MAY85	26JUL85	28JUL85	77
1008	3	3	0		PERSONNEL RELOCATION FROM EXIST. FACILITIES	11MAY85	13MAY85	29JUL85	31JUL85	77
1102	4	4	0		1ST FLR OCCUPANCY REGIS., ADMT., PATIENT SERV.	14MAY85	17MAY85	9JUL85	12JUL85	54
1111	1	1	0		BENEFICIAL OCCUPANCY - PATIENT OPENING OF CLINIC	7JUN85	7JUN85	1AUG85	1AUG85	54
1100	5	5	0		COMPLETE 1ST FLOOR CONSTR, PUNCH LIST & SYSTEMS	1MAY85	5MAY85	3JUL85	8JUL85	62
1104	3	3	0		STOCK & SUPPLY ALL OFFICE AREAS	15MAY85	17MAY85	26JUL85	28JUL85	70
1106	4	4	0		1ST FLOOR OCCUPANCY: LABS & DEPT DIVISIONS	18MAY85	21MAY85	25JUL85	28JUL85	66
2004	5	5	0		OCCUPANCY OF RADIOLOGY FILMS LIBRARY	21MAY85	25MAY85	16JUL85	20JUL85	54
1110	3	3	0		RELOCATE PERSONNEL FROM EXIST FACILITIES (FLR 1)	22MAY85	24MAY85	29JUL85	31JUL85	66
1108	3	3	0		STOCK & SUPPLY OFFICE AND LAB AREAS	19MAY85	21MAY85	26JUL85	28JUL85	66
2002	15	15	0		COMPLETE INSTALLATION OF NEW RADIOLOGY EQUIPMENT	4MAY85	18MAY85	10JUL85	24JUL85	65
2012	4	4	0		OCCUPANCY OF PATIENT EDUC. & EMP/PHYS. CAFETERIA	4MAY85	7MAY85	28JUL85	31JUL85	83
2006	4	4	0		OCCUPANCY OF DIAGNOSTIC RADIOLOGY AREA	31MAY85	3JUN85	25JUL85	28JUL85	54
2008	8	8	0		STOCK & SUPPLY RADIOLOGY MED. CABINETS & OFFICES	22MAY85	30MAY85	17JUL85	24JUL85	54
3004	4	4	0		OCCUPANCY OF OPTHOMOLOGY	26MAY85	30MAY85	25JUL85	28JUL85	58
2010	3	3	0		RELOCATION OF PERSONNEL FROM EXIST FAC. (RADIO)	4JUN85	6JUN85	29JUL85	31JUL85	54
3002	15	15	0		COMPLETE INSTALLATION OF NEW OPTHAMOLOGY EQUIP.	6MAY85	20MAY85	10JUL85	31JUL85	63
3006	3	3	0		STOCK & SUPPLY OPTHAMOLOGY	28MAY85	30MAY85	26JUL85	28JUL85	58
3008	3	3	0		RELOCATION OF PERSONNEL FROM EXIST OPTHO. DEPT.	31MAY85	2JUN85	29JUL85	31JUL85	58

REFERENCES

[1]   Burman, P. J., <u>Precedence Networks for Project Planning and Control</u>, McGraw-Hill, New York, 1972.

[2]   Crandall, K. C. and J. J. Moder, "Precedence Diagramming: Time Computations, Anomalies and Remedies," North-Holland Publishing Co., New York, 1984.

[3]   Gray, C. F., <u>Essentials of Project Management</u>, Petrocelli Books, Corvalis, Oregon, 1981.

[4]   Harris, R. B., <u>Precedence and Arrow Networking Techniques for Construction</u>, John Wiley & Sons, New York, 1978.

[5]   Moder, J. J., and C. R. Phillips, <u>Project Management with CPM & PERT</u>, Van Nostrand Reinhold Company, New York, 1970.

Project Management: Methods and Studies
Burton V. Dean (editor)
© Elsevier Science Publishers B.V. (North-Holland), 1985

A STATE OF THE ART SURVEY OF RESEARCH ON PROJECT MANAGEMENT
(1976-1983)

Sushil K. Gupta

Florida International University
Miami, Florida
U.S.A.

Larry R. Taube

University of North Carolina
Greensboro, North Carolina
U.S.A.

The objective of this paper is to present a guided tour of the recent developments in the area of project management. The time horizon for the literature search spans from 1976 to 1983. The articles have been classified into four sections which include: selection and evaluation, planning and scheduling, control, and human resources management. The articles reviewed have been synthesized to present a comprehensive view of the contemporary approaches dealing with various aspects within each category. Some of the important findings and observations are as follows.

Project selection is influenced by various qualitative and quantitative factors. These factors are to be combined according to a specific scheme so that a single valued measure may be obtained to rank the projects. Most of the papers discussed in this section attempt to provide such schemes. The selection of an appropriate scheme is, however, affected by numerous organizational and environmental factors. Several authors have taken note of this fact and have tried to portray project selection as a process rather than as a model. The selection process thus considers the human, organizational, and environmental constraints for the problem/project under consideration and then proceeds towards identifying the best alternative for project selection. Some of the papers have used real life situations to illustrate the applications of the proposed concepts.

The thrust of the writings on planning and scheduling is more theoretical and on model building. This section has been discussed under three subsections which include: project activities and planned accomplishments, scheduling, and resource allocation/budgeting. The first subsection contains papers in which several authors have written about various difficulties, and proposed solutions, that occur in the planning stage. These deal mainly with shortcomings present in precedence networks caused by uncertainty or other complexities. Although most solutions consist of modification to the precedence network, several alternatives to PERT such as Precedence Diagramming Method, Monte Carlo simulation, Bayesian PERT, and GERT have also been suggested. The literature in the subsection on scheduling has concentrated on multi-project and/or multi-resource constrained scheduling. The proposed approaches include zero-one integer programming, branch and bound, heuristic algorithms, simulation models and a combination of CPM/MRP. The focus of the last subsection is on allocation or budgeting of scarce resources. The literature deals with groups of both unlimited and limited, and renewable and non-renewable resources. The suggested approaches include simulation models, linear and dynamic programming and network theory. The research also investigates a situation concerning limited resources and activities which cannot be interrupted. Several heuristics and theoretically optimal methods are compared for this particular situation. There is a need for reporting on the results in using these techniques in real life situations.

The subject matter of project control is discussed under the following three subcategories: implementation, progress measurement and reporting, and analysis of delays/cost overruns. Most of the papers under implementation have discussed problems and successes in implementing real life Operations Research Projects. One of the papers discusses GERT simulation for evaluating the time/cost factor of implementation of management systems. There is a need for reporting on the experiences in implementing R&D, construction, engineering and MIS projects. Different approaches to measuring progress in a project are presented in the second subsection. Each has been designed to circumvent a particular limitation of existing reporting measures. The third subsection presents the causes for delays and cost overruns in projects. Some of the papers are based on surveys of project managers. Simulation models have also been used in analyzing cost overruns and delays.

The section on human resources management discusses those papers which are concerned with organizational structure, selection of a project manager, leadership and motivation, conflict management and communication in a project environment. Several articles present the pros and cons of matrix organizations, centralized versus decentralized decision-making, and the value of, and procedure for, finding the appropriate individual for project manager. Several studies and surveys have been performed to determine the best managerial style and/or organization for different situations such as the military, academia, and R&D environments. The literature abounds with specific communication approaches to project management and attempts to increase the quality and quantity of information flows.

This survey reveals that project management is not merely a technique, rather it is a philosophy which can be used in the management of any organization, at any level, and for any function. It is expected that this paper will provide useful resource material for both practitioners and researchers in the area of project management.

INTRODUCTION

This paper presents a survey of the literature on project management from 1976 to 1983. This period is chosen because of a need for synthesizing the literature of the recent past. The two most recent papers which have consolidated project management literature include Dyer & Paulson [38] and Cook et al [25]. For the period under consideration, we found an enormous wealth of information and knowledge in the form of journal articles, doctoral dissertations, reports, books, and conference proceedings. The focus of this survey is on journal articles because of space limitations, which should not undermine the importance of the rest of the published literature. Further, the articles that are related but not directly concerned with project management are also excluded: for example, theoretical developments in network theory, in behavioral science or in investment analysis. Even after using these "rules of thumb" for exclusion, we were confronted with reviewing more than 400 articles.

These articles represent a big diversity in the project levels which spanned from development projects at the national level to departmental level projects like developing and installing a new system. The papers are concerned with different industries such as construction, health, pharmaceutical, energy, recreation and mining; with different functional areas such as R&D and information systems; and with different aspects of project management such as benefit/cost analysis, evaluation, selection, financing, planning, scheduling, monitoring, control, organizational structure and human aspects. Most of these papers are reviewed in Gupta and Taube [50].

In the present paper we have reviewed only those articles which in our opinion made substantial contributions towards new research or application under the following categories: selection and evaluation, planning and scheduling, control, and human resources management.

PROJECT SELECTION AND EVALUATION

Project selection and evaluation is invariably based on economic as well as social benefit/cost analysis. This involves the consideration of both quantitative and qualitative factors. The papers discussed here essentially provide schemes for the measurement and aggregation of these factors so that a ranking of projects may be obtained.

Souder [103] critically reviews and appraises eight different models for project evaluation and proposes a system for using various models within different organizational settings. The eight models are index models, portfolio models, decision theory models, risk analysis models, frontier models, scoring models, profile models, and checklists. He argues that these management science models reflect only the analytical aspects of project evaluation, whereas the real world decisions are often profoundly influenced by a number of organizational and human behavioral factors. Souder describes a structured process called Q-Sort/Nominal Interacting (QS/NI), a method which combines the uses of psychometric methods and controlled group interactions. He suggests that a consensus set of goals must be established first using the QS/NI process for project evaluation. Then, depending on the type of project or problem under consideration, a specific model for project selection may be used. Schwartz & Vertinsky [94] are concerned with another component of the selection process: the formulation of individual preferences among R&D investment opportunities. Executives make tradeoffs among three classes of attributes: commitment of resources, expected payoffs, and risks. This paper gives special attention to the relationship between the characteristics of the executives, such as position and function, the attributes of the organization, and the tradeoffs that they are willing to make in forming judgments. Cook & Seiford [24] discuss practical approaches to the R&D project selection process that incorporate some of these tradeoffs. In a similar paper, Rubenstein & Schroeder [90] study the effects of personal, organizational, and situational variables in assessing probabilities of technical success for R&D projects and find that both the assessor's specific relations towards the project to be evaluated and his organizational rank affect the assessment.

The Project Appraisal Methodology (PAM) proposed by Silverman [98] is based on scoring and economic approaches of project evaluation. PAM is in fact a concept and not a model, and therefore, it has to be adapted to each new situation. PAM was applied to the Division of Fossil Fuel Utilization, Department of Energy, to assess relative merits of sixteen advanced fossil fuel utilization technologies receiving federal R&D support. Economic and scoring criteria were energy benefits (energy/cost ratio), consumer savings (consumer/cost ratio), and societal factors (effects and impact score). PAM was used to rank order the sixteen projects for three different funding levels: minimum, current, and enhanced. A sensitivity analysis was also carried out for the various factors.

Cooper [26], Merrifield [72], Paolini & Glaser [79], and Plebani & Jain [84] have identified different sets of factors that affect project selection and have given schemes for rating, scoring and aggregating these factors so as to obtain a single-valued measure of evaluation for each project. Balachandra & Raelin [7] have suggested the use of discriminant analysis to distinguish between the projects that should be continued and those that should be terminated. In a related article, Bedell [9] considers the problem of prematurely-terminated projects. Glazebrook's work [45,46] provides a method for ranking "alternative research projects." Alternative research projects represent a collection of projects with the property that success in research occurred at the first successful completion of one of the projects from the collection. Jackson [59,60] summarizes the various decision methods for evaluating and selecting R&D projects.

Tang et al [111] give a quantitative approach for appraising the industrial projects from the broader socio-economic context in a developing country. The evaluation model uses social benefit-cost analysis for appraisal of economic factors and preference theory techniques for evaluating subjective factors and establishing an overall measure of contribution by each alternative project. Sensitivity analysis may also be performed which will help the policy-makers of developing countries in investment decisions.

Martel & d'Avignon [67] consider the problem of evaluating a project according to a set of m criteria. The objective is to select the "best" projects from a set of A of n projects. Each project P(i) of A is evaluated by a set of K(i) experts. For each criterion j, there is a scale E(j) signifying the performance level. Each expert evaluating a project assigns a value on that scale for the jth criterion. The assigned performance level may be different for different experts, which produces a distribution of anticipated performance of each project with respect to each criterion. This paper develops a method for ranking the projects in such situations. A case study is presented, consisting of development projects in the health service area.

The projects whose expected benefits are in monetary terms require the determination of the magnitude and timing of the cash flows and the uncertainty surrounding thses cash flows. Net present value (also called discounted cash flow) is a generally accepted criterion for analyzing the magnitude and timing of cash flows. The treatment of risk is done by both deterministic as well as probabilistic approaches. Some of the papers which have discussed specific techniques for risk measurement include: Bhattacharya [11], Constantinides [22], De et al. [33], Gitman [44], Hoskins [57], Lucken & Stuhr [66], Park & Thuesen [80], and Zinn et al. [136].

One of the important contributions in economic analysis of interdependent projects is due to Goldwerger & Paroush [47]. The activity analysis approach suggested by them requires the formulation of an integer programming model in which the basic decision variables are not projects but rather combinations of projects called activities. The decision maker's utility function is not defined over activities but rather over characteristics of activities. The two main advantages claimed for this approach include: (a) the separation between objective and subjective information available to the decision maker, thereby distinguishing between efficient and optimal choice of projects, and (b) handling interrelationships among projects, which result from efficiency considerations and not only from feasibility restrictions. Erlenkotter & Rogers [41] develop a procedure for finding the sequencing of a finite set of capacity expansion projects that minimizes total discounted operating and investment costs. Variable operating costs are specified in a general continuous time function that requires projects to be competitive in a certain sense. This definition of operating costs shows the use of an optimization submodel, such as a multilocation distribution problem, to determine operating decisions. Several refinements to the basic solution approach are presented.

Ginzberg [43] presents benefits of various measurement practices and suggests some possible improvements for selection of information systems projects. Carter [18] performs a similar analysis for commercial projects.

PLANNING AND SCHEDULING

The literature devoted to this topic has been divided into the following categories: (1) project activities and planned accomplishments, (2) scheduling, and (3) resource allocation/budgeting.

    Project Activities and Planned Accomplishments. The project must be subdivided into a number of manageable activities, each with its own tangible end product. These activities are interrelated using precedence relationships, and are combined with all other activities to form a network diagram for the overall project. A final requirement of this planning stage is the need for various estimates of the project's resource needs.

Smeda [10] discusses precedence constraints and the problem of determining whether or not a set of such constraints is consistent. The author describes several different approaches to the problem, yielding a survey of existing algorithms for each approach. An efficient algorithm, designed especially for checking the consistency of activity networks, is developed through the combination of recently developed graph algorithms. Rhodes & Yuncheng [88] discuss a modification to Smeds approach which combines a cycle checking procedure with forward time calculations. The user is provided with certain diagnostic information about the activities involved in the cycles.

Three articles discuss the complexities of precedence networking. Elmaghraby & Herroelen [39] consider the following three objectives: (a) determine the critical path assuming deterministic time estimates; (b) determine the probability distribution function of project completion time assuming random durations of activites; and (c) determine the optimal schedule for a limited availability of a single resource. The paper proposes the form in which the complexity of a network can be measured for each objective and explicitly exhibits the form of the measure relative to the first objective based on a sample of 116 networks. Such estimates of complexity are needed to estimate the computing requirements and/or to validate the comparison to alternative heuristic procedures. Haag [51] develops an alternative to precedence networking called the two step method. Haag also lists and defines four rules which must be applied when using the method, but he states that the method can easily be adopted to fit personal needs and can greatly reduce the time needed to produce project networks. Willis [129] examines the problem of creating an activity-on-arrow network diagram from activity precedence data. A heuristic is developed which incorporates a computer program that can tackle problems of a practical size. Some computational experience is reported in the article.

Wiest [128] develops an alternative to PERT called the Precedence Diagramming Method (PDM). This method uses activity-on-node networks with additional precedence relationships to offer an easier and more flexible approach to modeling large projects than conventional PERT/CPM. However, the new relationships (start to start and finish to finish constraints) can change some of the basic notions of critical path methodology, including the concept of a critical path itself. Calculations of early and late job start times are affected, along with total slack. Traditional methods of shortening a project by crashing jobs on the critical path can occasionally have anomalous effects. These little-known characteristics of PDM are discussed, along with their implications for project managers, analysts, and other users of network methodology.

Monte Carlo simulation has often been suggested as an alternative means of analyzing PERT networks but simulating a network of real world proportions is often assumed to be prohibitively expensive. Cook & Jennings [23] measure the accuracy and cost of using standard PERT and simulation methods in real world sized problems. In addition, several computational heuristics are described and tested that indicate that simulation is a viable alternative. The results indicate that intelligent simulation of PERT networks is considerably more accurate than standard PERT analysis and is definitely not cost prohibitive. Two articles by Britney [14,15] explore the possibility of using Bayesian point estimation for PERT scheduling. He develops an alternative scheduling procedure called Bayesian PERT, or BPERT, which employs an activity-based estimation loss structure and a cost minimization criterion. The Bayesian point estimates are formulated for beta-distributed activity duration times minimizing the potential losses of misestimation. These time estimates are then aggregated to yield a single project completion time. Crashing is introduced, and its implications for BPERT are examined. An illustrative example contrasts PERT and BPERT.

A more well-known alternative to PERT is GERT. The GERT modeling technique is described and differentiated from PERT and CPM by Taylor & Moore [113,114], Taylor & Moore [114] describe a simulation study of two cases of research and development planning. The first case is for a series of R&D projects analyzed sequentially by a single R&D team, while the second case is for a series of R&D projects analyzed sequentially and concurrently by two teams. Q-GERT was employed for the modeling and simulation effort. This technique includes numerous network modeling capabilities which make it more applicable to R&D project planning than traditional network techniques such as CPM and PERT.

Kapur [61] details the design of a computer-based, multilevel network system. The system permits development of independent but related networks at the different levels of a project hierarchy. The level of detail of the activites and the time estimates can be specified by the project personnel at different levels. The system requires inputs only at the most detailed (lowest) levels but produces various control reports at all the hierarchical levels. The methods for performing time calculations and aggregating progress data are briefly explained. Kapur envisions that the system would find wide applications in cases where the flow of information is complex or where the projects are very complex and require elaborate organizations for their execution. He has successfully applied the model for monitoring multi-purpose river valley projects. One of the major limitations is that it permits explosion of only one activity at a time, but Kapur feels that the limitation can be removed by redefining the scope of activities.

Hindelang & Muth [54] propose a dynamic programming algorithm for Decision CPM (DCPM) networks. DCPM is a natural, powerful and general way of handling the discrete-time/cost tradeoff problem. The algorithm exhibits only a linear growth in the solution times based on the number of connections between nodes. In addition, the structure of the algorithm is such that it simultaneously determines the optimal solution for any desired number of project due dates with only a slight increase in computer time. This feature provides valuable information in performing a sensitivity analysis for the project and in preparing for negotiations about the project due date.

Scheduling

This section deals with the technical aspects and details of activity scheduling, such as project status points, recovery time and resources, and many scheduling techniques such as "back scheduling" and "forward scheduling" and multiple parallel assignments, etc. Morton [76] discusses many of these tools and techniques. Although some of these topics may also be considered as planning activities, their major impact is on the project schedule and/or evaluating the amount of that schedule accomplished.

Some of the quantitative approaches for handling varying or random activity times in a project schedule include Wolfe et al. [132], Moore & Taylor [73], Robbilard & Trahan [89], and Leifman [64]. Wolfe et al. [132] discuss a simulation approach. CPM/PERT techniques have not been adequate in the cases where activity durations need to be modified to reflect improvement curve trends, storage limitations are significant, or disruption costs are to be evaluated. Limitations such as these are of particular concern when planning the construction of large projects such as ships, aircraft and turbines. The authors describe a system developed to incorporate these considerations and other aspects of real life operations into a more comprehensive network planning and control system. Moore & Taylor [73] report on a simulation study of multiple R&D projects that are worked on concurrently and sequentially by more than one research team. The GERT results included statistical data on individual project duration and cost as well as overall network time and cost. These results were employed to provide management with an evaluation of different model configurations, prepare overall time and cost estimates as inputs to contract negotiations and to plan and schedule manpower, equipment and capital investment. Sensitivity analysis was employed to determine key stages in the R&D process where changes in success-failure probabilities might reduce network time and cost. Implementation experiences validated the model as satisfactory with minor problems. Robillard & Trahan [89] consider the total duration time of a project from a statistical point of view. Their paper is concerned with a technical improvement in PERT methodology by introducing a new approach to approximating, in a computationally efficient way, the total duration distribution function of a program. It is assumed that the activity durations are independent random variables and have a finite range. The first part of the paper considers PERT networks and deals with the lower bound approximation to the total duration distribution function. Then the authors use the approximation and CPM to propose bounds for the different moments of the function. The authors also adapt their results to PERT decision networks. Leifman [64] presents optimization procedures in outline form to find two kinds of estimates for any resource: pointwise (i.e. for single time units) and interval (for large time spans).

Lee et al. [63] develop an approach which may be used to estimate resource requirements, in an economical manner, for multiple projects that must be serviced by multiple resource types. Past information of resource usage and projected workloads are used to determine low cost levels of resource utilization. Special attention is given to the effects that the usage of high cost equipment has on the estimated low cost levels of the manpower resources, since those resources are not subject to cutbacks during low utilization periods.

Several heuristic approaches have also been investigated. Cooper [27] considers the project scheduling problem with multiple constrained resources. Two classes of heuristic procedure making use of priority rules are discussed: the parallel method, generating one schedule; and the sampling method, generating a set of schedules using probabilistic techniques and selecting the best schedule from the sample. An experimental investigation is described which attempts to assess the effects of the method, the project characteristics, and the priority rule. Holloway et al.[56] evaluate a heuristic procedure for solving the resource constrained project scheduling problem. Two approaches are used to resolve unfeasible project schedules. The indirect method uses resource leveling procedures to improve the schedule. Formulating the problem with explicit resource constraints is another, more direct, way to accommodate limited capacities. The procedure evaluated here is representative of a class of multi-pass procedures based on problem decomposition. Comparisons were made between this procedure and others, with the results suggesting that the method and procedure used may provide an effective means of computing schedules for resource-constrained projects. Kurtulus & Davis [62] have examined various heuristic scheduling rules based on their performance relative to total resource requirements and rate of utilization of resources. They propose a new rule which performs significantly better on most categories of projects, and a possible scheme for categorizing the performance in a multi-project environment.

Thesen [119,120] extends the field of heuristic algorithms for resource constrained scheduling problems in three important areas. First, an algorithm is introduced where the role of the heuristic scheduling urgency factor is expanded to determine the combination of activities to be scheduled at a given instant as well as the order of the activities. Second, a new hybrid scheduling urgency factor is introduced which exploits the fact that this algorithm is sensitive to the absolute value rather than the relative sequence of urgency factors. Finally, a systematic approach to the evaluation of such algorithms is introduced. Dar-El & Tur [30] describe a heuristic for scheduling a multi-resource project where the objective is to minimize the project cost for any project duration between some specified time range. Input conditions are realistic and include alternative resource combinations (ARC) for each activity, resource cost functions, and hiring and dismissal costs for changes in resource quantities. The algorithm selects the combination of activity ARCs that gives the minimum cost solution for any feasible project duration, and eventually generates the Variable Cost-Time tradeoff relationship from which the minimum cost conditions for the project can be found.

Aquilano & Smith [4] introduce a hybrid model which combines the critical path method with material requirements planning (CPM/MRP). They feel that the technique provides an integrated approach to project scheduling as it incorporates project activities and technological relationships with resource requirements and inventory records. CPM/MRP is not yet capable of handling a set of constrained resource heuristics and has yet to be applied to a multi-project example. The article by Digman & Green [35] compares various scheduling techniques on the basis of the following criteria: project phase applicability, parametric focus, preparation requirements, data base, system operating cost, comprehensiveness, flexibility, ease of update, and focus reporting. The authors compare PERT/CPM with PERT/COST, LOB, GERT, and VERT. They also present a framework for modular integration of network techniques for management needs during a product's life cycle.

A final set of scheduling articles deal with optimization approaches, such as zero-one and branch-and-bound. Talobt & Patterson [109] describe an integer programming algorithm for allocating limited resources to competing activities, such that the completion time of the project is the minimum. An artifice called a network cut removes from consideration the evaluation of job finish times that cannot lead to a reduced project completion time. This procedure is applicable in instances when computer primary storage is limited. Talbot [108] also introduces an algorithm that solves a general class of nonpreemptive resource constrained project scheduling problems in which the duration of each job is a function of the resources committed to it. The algorithm has the potential to be a useful scheduling tool for organizations having small computer systems. Elmaghraby & Pulat [40] present an optimal algorithm for dealing with project compression due to time constraints imposed on a project by due dated events. Weglarz [127] deals with a class of project scheduling problems concerning the allocation of continuously divisible resources under conditions in which both total usage at every moment and total consumption over the period of project duration are constrained. Possible generalizations of the presented results are indicated.

Trypia [121] addresses a similar problem: find the total durations of all the projects, which are carried out simultaneously, so that the sum of their total costs is minimized and the availability of the critical resource is never exceeded in any time period. The total project cost consists of the direct performance cost and the indirect cost which refers to overheads, penalties, etc. The basic form of a 0-1 integer programming model has been presented to solve the problem. Patterson & Roth [81] develop an algorithm which takes special advantage of the structure of the 0-1 formulation and solves the project scheduling problem with a significant decrease in the amount of computation time required to solve a multi-resource problem. A description of the computer program for implementing the procedures is provided. Furthermore, extensions of their approach are applicable to the machine sequencing problem. Doersch & Patterson [36] develop a zero-one integer programming formulation of the project scheduling problem which maximizes the discounted value of cash flows in a project when progress payments and cash outflows are made upon the completion of certain activities.

Two articles use the branch-and-bound technique to schedule activites. Willis & Hastings [130] consider the problem of minimizing the overall duration of a project subject to constraints on the availability of resources. A new resource-based bound, new dominance rules and an innovative network breakdown technique which preserves optimality are reported, along with computational experience and comparisons with schedules obtained by decision rule methods. Stinson et al. [104] focus upon the problem of assigning feasible start times to a set of activities making up a project, static job shop, or static flowshop type schedules under two constraint sets: (1) no activity may be started until all activities technologically established as its predecessor set have been completed, and (2) the total resource requirements of all activities in process at any time in the schedule must not exceed the level of availability for each of the multiple resource classes. The resulting schedules are optimized with an objective of minimizing the completion time of the entire set of activities.

Resource Allocation/Budgeting

This section deals with articles that have a primary focus on the allocation or budgeting of scarce resources. Although some of these articles could also be classified in earlier sections, they are discussed here because their main impact is on resource allocation.

Burt [17] and Slowinski [99,100] perform comparative studies on resource allocation techniques. Burt [17] addresses the problem of planning and controlling projects under conditions of uncertainty through resource allocation decisions. Particular attention is given to the dynamic reallocation of resources over the duration of projects as information about actual activity times becomes known. For a set of project networks of relatively simple structure, the efficacy of several heuristic decision rules is tested via simulation. The results of these simulation studies indicate some general concepts that should be applicable to the management of larger, more realistic, projects. Slowinski [99,100] deals with a class of problems of resource allocation among project activities, where the resource requirements of each activity concern various resource units from given finite sets of particular resource types. Time and cost criteria are considered for project performance evaluation. In solving these problems, two general approaches using linear programming in specific ways are described. An extensive comparison of both approaches is shown, characterizing the state of the art across the problems and pointing out desirable directions for further research. Tufekci [122] develops another algorithm that performs well when dealing with the time-cost tradeoff. Mehrez & Sinuany-Stern [71] deal with the problem of resource allocation to indivisible projects with uncertain outcomes. They outline an overall procedure for structuring the model and use a branch-and-bound algorithm.

Three articles develop modifications to resource allocation algorithms. Dar-el & Tur [31] describe an algorithm for resource allocation of multi-resource projects which assumes the availability of unlimited resources. Optimality is defined by the minimal schedule deviation, which measures the squares of weighted deviation between future resource loads and currently assigned resource levels. The algorithm simplifies both scheduling and project control, since the next period's allocation depend only on the current schedule status. Appropriate changes in levels for all resources over the project duration are consistent with the needs of project managers in practice. Dar-el et al. [32] present the development of a multi-project scheduling model called SCREAM, which meets the requirements of an effective computer model. The objective function of the model was viewed in terms of resource usage, activity splitting, overtime work, and project tardiness. Project tardiness is a variable which can be controlled through the concept of critical slack. The program is interactive, allowing the schedules to control various resource allocations. SCREAM was found to be effective for moderately sized projects, but not yet ready for industrial use. Reeves & Sweigart [87] consider a multiperiod resource allocation model with variable technological coefficients, resulting in a heuristic procedure that is intuitively appealing. The model was formulated as a nonlinear programming problem, and obtains excellent feasible results when compared to fixed technology solutions.

Talobt & Patterson [110] deal with the problem of obtaining optimal schedules under two sets of constraints: limited resources and noninterruptable activites. The impact of limited resources, which produces scheduling conflicts, and the limitations of PERT and CPM are discussed. Heuristic and theoretical optimal methods are compared and contrasted. In addition the authors have compared their approach with Stinson's [104] optimal procedure.

Taylor et al. [115] develop a nonlinear goal programming model to handle the difficulties present in allocating manpower to alternative R&D projects. The model selects projects and allocates researchers such that a prioritized goal structure is most satisfactorily achieved.

Two papers discuss the time/cost tradeoff problem explicitly. Esogbue & Marks [42] develop two essentially equivalent dynamic programming formulations of the resource allocation variety by minimizing either the project cost or the completion time. For nonserial precedence relationships, this problem cannot be solved by routine invocation of conventional dynamic programming formulations. The intent of the paper is to show that efficient nonserial dynamic programming formulations can be developed for complex nonserial CPM/COST problem situations. Phillips & Dessouky [83] introduce a solution procedure for solving the project time/cost tradeoff problem of reducing a project duration at a minimum cost. The solution to the time/cost problem is achieved by locating a minimal cut in a flow network derived from the original project network. This minimal cut is then utilized to identify the project activities which should experience a duration modification in order to achieve the total project reduction. The paper documents the cut-based procedure and provides a practical application to a project situation.

In an application of time/cost tradeoffs to technology transfer projects, Teece [116] postulates and tests for a time/cost tradeoff during the establishment of manufacturing plants abroad; the plants are based on U. S. technology. Data on twenty international projects are used to estimate negatively sloped tradeoff functions for which time/cost elasticities are then analyzed and shown to bear some similarities with the determinants of time/cost tradeoffs in technological innovation. The elasticity measurements were higher for projects where the technology had not been previously commercialized, for large scale projects, and for projects carried out by the larger firms.

PROJECT CONTROL

The papers concerned with project control are discussed under the following categories: (1) implementation, (2) progress measurement and reporting, and (3) analysis of delays/ cost overruns.

Liberatore & Titus [65] present the results of a survey of practicing managers in R&D projects. The survey found increased use of Gantt charts for project control, and formalized systems for budgeting and cost reporting.

   Implementation.   Taylor & Davis [112] use GERT simulation in evaluating time/cost factors of implementation of management systems. The authors state that time and cost are often overlooked factors in such situations. Because of potential failure during implementation, managers often focus attention on achieving implementation with little regard for the price of success. The purpose of this paper is to describe a generalized GERT simulation model of an implementation process. The model provides statistical data on the time and cost of implementation. Such a model enables the planning of the implementation process so that excessive disruptions in the work environment (budget, scheduling, etc.) can be avoided.

The papers by Anderson & Narasimhan [3], Dane et al. [29], Wedley & Ferrie [126], and Wilson [131] are related to the implementation of Operations Research (OR) projects. Anderson & Narasimhan [3] propose a methodology to assess project risk so that strategies may be developed which can increase the chances of successful implementation of the project. The methodology uses a discriminant function to (a) identify high, marginal, or low risk implementation situations, and (b) point out particular "risk factors" that reduce the chances of successful implementation. The methodology is illustrated by developing a discriminant function based on case study data. Wilson [131] has examined the reasons for successful application of computer simulation projects in health care. Dane et al. [29] have identified nine factors which affect the successful application of PERT/CPM systems in a governmental organization. Wedley and Ferrie [126], after analyzing forty-nine projects in different areas have established that greater participation of managers increases the probability that findings of an OR/MS study will be implemented. Houlden [58] also discusses the applications of project management concepts in managing OR projects.

   Progress Measurement and Reporting.   Gupta and Buddhdeo [49] give a method to measure the progress in different phases of engineering projects. The system proposed in this paper yields awards based on progress achieved at the completion of job steps/milestones which are physically measurable. The approach implicitly takes into account the efficiency of the people involved in the system under consideration.

Pollock [85] reviews the earned value technique for its relevance to engineering efforts. The technique was developed by the Department of Defense to control the costs and schedules of R&D efforts by measuring performance. To do so, it is necessary to define the work to be performed, to establish a realistic work package plan, to agree on a method of measurement, and then to develop an objective estimate to use to compare the actual cost against the plan. A reexamination of the estimate leads to the calculation of three variances every month. Unfavorable trends are noted by an analysis of these variances and corrective actions are specified. Turf [123] proposes an alternative to the work package technique for obtaining performance measurement data; he terms it "No Work Package" and lists its advantages and the conditions under which it can be implemented.

For engineering projects, Martin [68] provides a checklist for work progress to be reported consistently and at a detailed level. This can help in identifying problems for early correction. Aharonian [2] describes Accomplishment Value Procedure (AVP) for tracking the status of an information systems development project. AVP leads to a project visibility chart for a particular project or a summary visibility chart for a group of projects. Changes in resources or time are also summarized in relation to these charts. The measurement and improvement of productivity in construction proejcts have been discussed by Hohns & Murray [55].

The focus of the paper by Sotthemes & Lewis [102] is on the analysis and use of the information provided by an information system on the overall progress of the project. They suggest a method to calculate a measure of "project urgency", defined as the "actual project status" divided by the "planned project status." The method can be used to indicate where corrective actions are needed to resolve deviations from the original plan. Caspe [20] describes the development of a Management Support System which can help in reporting and monitoring progress, in addition to design and construction, resource allocation and trend analysis.

Analysis of Delays/Cost Overruns. Sharad [96] has presented a list of questions which involve cost and schedule control. The causes of overruns, which should be continually monitored, are listed and defined along with suggested corrective actions. Bhargava and Gupta [10] have analyzed the causes of delays and cost overruns in various phases of engineering projects in India. The methodology adopted is an opinion survey of practicing managers using a structured questionnaire. Depending on the ratings obtained, the causes fall into three categories: fatal (requiring the most managerial attention), hurting, and annoying. Schonberger [93] uses simulation to show that deterministic critical path analysis understates the likely project duration which can partially explain the phenomenon of projects "always" being late. Certain generalizations based on network simulation are also offered for improving project management. Simulation has also been used by Ward et al. [125] to study the problems of overruns on due dates and on costs for organizations which have to deal with variable workloads of project-like activities.

Pekar and Burack [82] present the "project planning continuum" to meet cost and schedule estimates. The two major elements of this tool are the Uncertainty and Complexity Model (U/C) and a series of models called Resource Appraisal Models (RAM). Ruth [91] shows how lateness can be quantified and dealt with for data processing projects, and Wall [124] discusses important steps in project control.

HUMAN RESOURCES MANAGEMENT

The management of human resources is one of the important functions of a project manager because a project is managed both as a technical and as a behavioral system. Baker & Wileman [6] and Murdick & Schuster [78] have provided comprehensive reviews of research writings concerning human elements in project management. Aspects considered in this section include: organizational structure, selection of the project manager, leadership and motivation, conflict management, and communication. Caspe [19], Cleland [21], McCarney [69], Stuckenbruck [107], and Youker [134,135] have reviewed the reasons for using matrix organizations, its advantages and disadvantages, specific problems in its implementation and their solutions.

Adam & Barndt [1] have studied 10 R&D projects and have concluded that there is considerable variability in internal organizational environments over the life cycle of a project. The difference seems to be highly consistent across projects for a given life cycle phase. A set of propositions has been made concerning how projects change over their life cycles and possible management actions that should be considered in anticipation of these changes. Similar observations are reported by Barndt et al. [8]. A conceptually new approach for the process of optimal delegation of authority in a project environment for capital budgeting decisions has been introduced by Sharon [97]. The tradeoff lies between the cost of centralized (i.e. duplicate) review, and the opportunity cost and risk of having (otherwise) "unacceptable" projects. The paper discusses two explicit limits to optimal decentralization that help headquarters identify decision making problems.

Several authors have discussed the qualities of a good project manager and the steps involved in selecting the right individual. Some of these include Atkins [5], Buck [16], Morris [75], Mueller [77], Stuckenbruck [105,106], and Wolff [133]. A good project manager should induce in project staff self-fulfillment, self interest and recognition, responsibility, confidence, participation, team spirit, and enthusiasm, as observed by Buck [16]. Effective project leadership is, however, dependent on a number of factors. Thamhain & Wileman [117] have conducted a survey involving 68 project managers and 33 of their superiors to find the effective leadership styles of project managers under different work environments. The characteristics of work environment include: organizational climate, task complexity, and the position power of the project manager. They found that "leader-oriented" style is more effective in a poor organizational climate while "team-oriented" style is more effective in a good organizational climate.

Dunne et al. [37] have studied the perceptions of project staff in a military matrix organization regarding the sources of influence of both project managers and functional managers. The findings indicate that the perceptions of project staff and project managers were the same about the project manager's sources of influence. Project staff perceived differences in strength and ranking of project and functional managers' influence sources. However, expertise/professional challenge and position/responsibility were rated as important influence sources of both type of managers. The position/responsibility of the project manager was identified as distinct from formal authority by project staff. One of the major findings of the study is that, for both types of managers, the three influence sources mentioned above are very important and are positively associated with project staff work attitudes. Potts [86] presents similar observations. In a study by Birnbaum [12] of interdisciplinary research projects in academic institutions, it was found that large stable projects with highly educated staff performed best.

A project manager needs to be aware of conflict environment at all times in the project. Resolution of conflict is an important function of the project manager. Sears [95] presents four strategies for managing conflict which are based on conflicts inherent in interpersonal and personal relationships in the project team. These strategies include: (a) be clear about goals and objectives, (b) stay in a problem solving mode, (c) allow genuine participation, and (d) confront problems, not people. The paper also provides some sample questions and responses to be used in dealing with the project manager-team relationship. Thamhain & Wileman [118] also deal with key problems faced by project managers in managing complex tasks. The emphasis is on the focal position of the project manager--how he or she develops support from functional specialists and handles the ever-present conflict situations in managing projects, and how these activities influence management performance. The research study concerns the project managers in high technology organizations. A situational approach to project management effectiveness is developed and specific guidelines are provided to help project managers become more efficient. Hill [53] has stated that of all the types of conflict common to project teams as they work through the phases of their project life cycles, personality conflicts remain the most constant. He has studied project teams at a large oil company. In his study, he distinguishes between the coping responses of high producing managers of project teams and lower producing ones. His isolation of those characteristics in managerial style that result in effective conflict management is important for all managers called upon to conciliate and make peace.

Moravec [74] describes how Organizational Development can help in project team development, project client interfaces, human engineering goals and increasing productivity. Dailey [28] has analyzed the relationship between task and team properties, collaborative problem solving and team productivity in R&D environments. It was found that team cohesiveness and task certainty were robust predictors of collaborative problem solving and productivity. This problem solving-productivity relationship was found to be sensitive to high and low levels of task certainty, task interdependence, team size and team cohesiveness. These findings have implications for a manager in structuring the team and its task. Gunz & Pearson [48] consider the problem of deciding which decisions belong at the project level and which belong at the organizational level in project-based (R&D projects) technical organizations. A model is presented which clarifies the multi-level nature of this decision-making and defines the areas of ambiguity.

Borcherding [13] and Head [52] discuss the problem of improving communication in construction projects and operations improvement projects, respectively. Borcherding [13] attempts to integrate communication research and construction through a discussion of the communication system elements as they are applied to a construction project. He considers both tangible and intangible information as communication messages. Head [52] states that ineffective communication between the project analysts and accountant creates problems for identifying relevant costs in operations improvement projects. Lack of control over information and lack of education of accounting personnel as to managerial needs are two additional problems in these projects. DeBrabander & Edstrom [34] propose a specific theory for predicting the effect of user-specialist interaction on the success of information system projects and discuss a management tool for establishing effective patterns of such interactions.

CONCLUSIONS AND RECOMMENDATIONS

This paper has reviewed the literature on project management for the period 1976-1983. A brief summary is provided in the abstract at the beginning of the paper. This review makes it clear that project management is not merely a technique (often confused with PERT, CPM or GERT); rather, it is an idea, a concept and a philosophy. Project management has its roots in the form of a new idea. The cherished idea is nurtured by some one until it presents itself in the form of a sprout. The ideas may appear in the form of a mushroom growth also, in which case the appropriate idea to be pursued is identified and selected. Once this is done, the idea needs to be given a shape and needs to be concretized. This requires organization for resources, planning, scheduling, control activities and a committed work force. Through the efforts of a dedicated team and under the leadership of a project manager, the little sapling grows into a full tree. Of course, it is not a smooth process. Numerous human, organizational, financial, and technical problems give a roller coaster ride to the project manager. The end result, in the form of a new product or process or system or plant, etc., is handed over to its ultimate user; the project team withdraws and disassociates itself to give shape to new ideas and thoughts. This concept of project management can be used in any organization, at any level, and for any activity or function. However, each situation is unique in terms of objectives, constraints, impinging variables and the general management. Therefore, a unique approach is needed for managing each project.

There are several papers which report successful application of project management concepts. This is an encouraging trend because, if the literature is heavy on the theoretical side as compared to the applied side, then the theoretical developments are merely 'cries in the wilderness.' Ryan [92] supports this statement by discussing the reasons for the gap that exists between theory and practice, using PERT as one of his examples. He suggests several ways to improve the utility of research.

However, it may be pointed out that project management as a philosophy depends and draws heavily upon the developments in other fields including operations research, statistics, behavioral sciences, finance, computers, and production. The specific developments in these fields and the findings may not be transplanted to a project management environment without adequate precaution. This fact has been mentioned by some authors and it points to the need of more theoretical developments in the project management environment.

The growing interest in the field of project management is illustrated by the number of articles, the number of professional journals in which project related articles can be found and, more importantly, the number of authors who have contributed to this field. Table 1 gives a list of major topics in project management and the references in which each topic is discussed.

TABLE 1

CONTROL
 ANALYSIS OF DELAYS/COST OVERRUNS: 10,82,91,93,96,124,125
 IMPLEMENTATION: 3,29,58,65,92,112,126,131
 PROGRESS MEASUREMENT AND REPORTING: 2,20,49,55,68,85,102,123

HUMAN ASPECTS
 COMMUNICATION: 13,34,52
 CONFLICT MANAGEMENT: 48,53,74,95,118
 LEADERSHIP AND MOTIVATION: 6,12,28,37,78,117,133
 ORGANIZATIONAL STRUCTURE: 1,8,19,21,69,97,107,134,135
 SELECTION OF PROJECT MANAGER: 5,16,75,77,86,105,106

PLANNING AND SCHEDULING
 PROJECT ACTIVITIES AND PLANNED ACCOMPLISHMENTS: 14,15,23,35,39,51,
  54,61,88,101,113,114,128,129
 SCHEDULING: 4,27,30,36,40,56,62,63,64,70,73,76,81,89,104,108,109,119,120,121,
  127,130,132
 RESOURCE ALLOCATION/BUDGETING: 17,31,32,42,71,83,87,99,100,110,115,116,122

SELECTION AND EVALUATION: 7,9,11,18,22,24,26,33,41,43,44,45,46,47,57,59,60,66,67,
  72,79,80,84,90,94,98,103,111,136

SURVEY PAPERS: 25,38,50

REFERENCES

[1] Adams & Barndt, "Organizational Life Cycle Implications for Major Projects," Project Mgmt. Quarterly, 9, 32-39, 1978.

[2] Aharonian, "Project Management Through the Accomplishment Value Procedure," Project Mgmt. Quarterly, 11, 13-21, 1980.

[3] Anderson & Narasimhan, "Assessing Project Implementation Risk: A Methodological Approach," Mgmt. Sci., 25, June 1979.

[4] Aquilano & Smith, "A Formal Set of Algorithms for Project Scheduling with Critical Path Scheduling/Material Requirements Planning," J. Op. Mgmt., 1, 57-68, 1980.

[5] Atkins, "Selecting a Project Manager," J. Syst. Mgmt., 31, 34-35, 1980.

[6] Baker & Wilemon, "A Summary of Major Research Findings Regarding the Human Element in Project Management," Project Mgmt. Quarterly, 8, 34-40, 1977.

[7] Balachandra & Raelin, "How to Decide When to Abandon a Project," Res. Mgmt., 23, 24-29, July 1980.

[8] Barndt, et al., "Organizational Climate Changes in the Project Life Cycle," Res. Mgmt., 20, 33-36, Sept. 1977.

[9] Bedell, "Terminating R&D Projects Prematurely," Res. Mgmt., 26, 32-35, July 1983.

[10] Bhargava & Gupta, "Analysis of Delays and Cost Overruns in Engineering Projects," Proj. Mgmt., 4, 1-8, December 1981.

[11] Bhattacharya, "Project Valuation with Mean-Reverting Cash Flow Streams," J. Fin., 33, 1317-1331, December 1978.

[12] Birnbaum, "Assessment of Alternative Management Forms in Academic Interdisciplinary Research Projects," Mgmt. Sci., 24, 272-279, 1977.

[13] Borcherding, "Improving Construction Communications," Project Mgmt. Quarterly, 9, 50-56, 1978.

[14] Britney, "Bayesian Point Estimation and the PERT Scheduling of Stochastic Activities," Mgmt. Sci., 22, 938, May 1976.

[15] Britney, "Project Management in Costly Environments," Project Mgmt. Quarterly, 9, 31-42, 1978.

[16] Buck, "Managing the Most Valuable Resource: People," Project Mgmt. Quarterly, 8, 41-44, 1977.

[17] Burt, "Planning and Dynamic Control of Projects Under Uncertainty," Mgmt. Sci., 24, 249-258, Nov. 1977.

[18] Carter, "Evaluating Commercial Projects," Res. Mgmt., 25, 26-30, Nov. 1982.

[19] Caspe, "A Breakthrough in Matrix Communication," Project Mgmt. Quarterly, 11, 29-34, 1980.

[20] _____, "Developing a Management Support System, Project Mgmt. Quarterly, 8, 41-51, 1977.

[21]   Cleland, "Cultural Ambience of the Matrix Organization," Mgmt. Rev., 70, 24-28, Nov. 1981.

[22]   Constantinides, "Market Risk Adjustment in Project Valuation," J. Fin., 33, 603-616, May 1978.

[23]   Cook & Jennings, "Estimating a Project's Completion Time Distribution Using Intelligent Simulation Method," J. Op. Res. Soc., 30, 1103-1108, 1979.

[24]   Cook & Seiford, "R&D Project Selection in a Multidimensional Environment: A Practical Approach," J. Op. Res. Soc., 33, 397-406, May 1982.

[25]   Cook et al. "The Basic Project Management Reference Library," Project Mgmt. Quarterly, 7, 13-16, 1976.

[26]   Cooper, "Evaluation System for Project Selection," Res. Mgmt., 21, 29-33, July 1978.

[27]   _____, "Heuristics for Scheduling Resource-Constrained Projects: An Experimental Investigation," Mgmt. Sci., 22, 1186-1194, July 1976.

[28]   Dailey, "Role of Team and Task Characteristics in R&D Team Collaborative Problem Solving and Productivity," Mgmt. Sci., 24, 1579-1588, Nov. 1978.

[29]   Dane, et al., "Factors Affecting the Successful Application of PERT/CPM Systems in a Government Organization," Interfaces, 9, 94-98, Nov. 1979.

[30]   Dar-El & Tur, "A Multi-Resource Project Scheduling Algorithm," AIIE Trans., 9, 44-52, March 1977.

[31]   _____, "Resource Allocation of a Multi-Resource Project for Variable Resource Availabilities," AIIE Trans., 10, 299-300, Sept. 1978.

[32]   Dar-El, et al., "SCREAM – Scarce Resource Allocation to Multi-Projects," Project Mgmt. Quarterly, 9, 19-24, 1978.

[33]   De, et al. "Estimation of Mean and Variance of Net Present Value With Certain and Uncertain Project Life: A Multiperiod CAPM Approach," Eur. J. Op. Res., 8, 363-368, Dec. 1981.

[34]   DeBrabander & Edstrom, "Successful Information System Development Projects," Mgmt. Sci., 24, 191-199, Oct. 1977.

[35]   Digman & Green, "Framework for Evaluating Network Planning and Control Techniques," Res. Mgmt., 24, 10-17, Jan. 1981.

[36]   Doersch & Patterson, "Scheduling a Project to Maximize Its Present Value: A Zero-One Programming Approach," Mgmt. Sci., 23, 882-889, April 1977.

[37]   Dunne, et al. "Influence Sources of Project and Functional Managers in Matrix Organizations," Acad. Mgmt. J., 21, 135-140, March 1978.

[38]   Dyer & Paulson, "Project Management: An Annotated Bibliography," Cornell Industrial and Labor Relations Bibliography Series No. 13, 1976.

[39]   Elmaghraby & Herroelen, "On the Measurement of Complexity in Activity Networks," Eur. J. Op. Res., 5, 223-234, 1980.

[40]   Elmaghraby & Pulat, "Optimal Project Compression with Due-Dated Events," Nav. Res. Log. Qty., 26, 331-348, June 1979.

[41] Erlenkotter & Scott, "Sequencing Competitive Expansion Projects," Op. Res., 25, 937-951, Nov.-Dec. 1977.

[42] Esogbue & Marks, "Dynamic Programming Models of the Nonserial Critical Path Cost Problems," Mgmt. Sci., 24, 22-29, Oct. 1977.

[43] Ginzberg, "Improving MIS Project Selection," Omega, 7, No. 6, 527-537, 1979.

[44] Gitman, "Capturing Risk Exposure in the Evaluation of Capital Budgeting Projects," Eng. Econ., 22, 261-276, Sum. 1977.

[45] Glazebrook, "A Profitability Index for Alternative Research Projects," Omega, 4, No. 1, 79-83, 1976.

[46] _____, "Some Ranking Formulae for Alternative Research Projects," Omega, 6, 193-194, 1978.

[47] Goldwerger & Paroush, "Capital Budgeting of Interdependent Projects: Activity Analysis Approach," Mgmt. Sci., 23, 1242-1246, July 1977.

[48] Gunz & Pearson, "How to Manage Control Conflicts in Project Based Organizations," Res. Mgmt., 22, 23-29, March 1979.

[49] Gupta & Buddhdeo, "Progress Measurement During Project Execution," Eng. Mgmt. Int., 1, 281-285, 1983.

[50] Gupta & Taube, "A State of the Art Survey on Project Management Literature (1976-1981)," UNC-G Working Paper Series Number 830201, 1983.

[51] Haag, "The Two Step Method," Project Mgmt. Quarterly, 7, 16-18, 1976.

[52] Head, "Costing of Operations Improvement Projects," Project Mgmt. Quarterly, 7, 17-20, 1976.

[53] Hill, "Managing Interpersonal Conflicts in Project Teams," Sloan Mgmt. Rev., 18, 45-61, Winter 1977.

[54] Hindelang & Muth, "Dynamic Programming Algorithm for Decision CPM Networks," Op. Res., 27, 225-241, March 1979.

[55] Hohns & Murray, "Effects of Management on Productivity in Construction," Project Mgmt. Quarterly, 11, 20-30, 1980.

[56] Holloway, et al. "Comparison of a Multi-Pass Heuristic Decomposition Procedure with Other Resource-Constrained Project Scheduling Procedures," Mgmt. Sci., 25, 862-872, Sept. 1979.

[57] Hoskins, "Capital Budgeting Decision Rules for Risky Projects Derived From a Capital Market Model Based on Semivariance," Eng. Econ., 23, 211-222, Sum. 1978.

[58] Houlden, "Some Aspects of Managing OR Projects," J. Op. Res. Soc., 30, 681-690, Aug. 1979.

[59] Jackson, "Decision Methods for Evaluating R&D Projects," Res. Mgmt., 26, 16-22, July 1983.

[60] _____, "Decision Methods for Selecting a Portfolio of R&D Projects," Res. Mgmt., 26, 21-26, Sept. 1983.

[61] Kapur, "Designing a Multi-Level Network System," J. Op. Res. Soc., 29, 1121-1125, 1978.

[62] Kurtulus & Davis, "Multi-Project Scheduling," Mgmt. Sci., 28, 161-172, Feb. 1982.

[63] Lee, et al. "Resource Planning for Multiple Projects," Decision Sciences, 9, 49-57, 1978.

[64] Leifman, "Estimation of Resource Requirements in Optimization Problems in Network Planning," Eur. J. Op. Res., 2, 265-272, 1978.

[65] Liberatore & Titus, "Management Science Practice in R&D Project Management," Mgmt. Sci., 29, 962-974, Aug. 1983.

[66] Lucken & Stuhr, "Decision Trees and Risky Projects," Eng. Econ., 24, 75-86, Winter 1979.

[67] Martel & d'Avignon, "Projects Ordering with Multicriteria Analysis," Eur. J. Op. Res., 10, 56-69, May 1982.

[68] Martin, "The Goal: To Improve Credibility in the Reporting of Engineering Progress," Project Mgmt. Quarterly, 11, 14-22, 1980.

[69] McCarney, "Implementing Matrix Management in a Research and Development Environment," Project Mgmt. Quarterly, 11, 41-42, 1980.

[70] McGinnis & Nuttle, "Project Coordinator's Problem," Omega, 6, No. 4, 325-330, 1978.

[71] Mehrez & Sinuany-Stern, "Resource Allocation to Interrelated Risky Projects," Mgmt. Sci., 29, 430-439, April 1983.

[72] Merrifield, "Selecting Projects for Commercial Success," Res. Mgmt., 24, 13-18, Nov. 1981.

[73] Moore & Taylor, "Multiteam Multiproject Research and Development Planning with GERT," Mgmt. Sci., 24, 401-410, Dec. 1977.

[74] Moravec, "How Organization Development Can Help and Hinder Project Managers," Project Mgmt. Quarterly, 10, 17-20, 1979.

[75] Morris, "Interface Management - An Organization Theory Approach to Project Management," Project Mgmt. Quarterly, 10, 27-37, 1979.

[76] Morton, "A Practical Approach to Project Planning," Project Mgmt. Quarterly, 8, 35-40, 1977.

[77] Mueller, "Education for Project Management," Project Mgmt. Quarterly, 10, 33-35, 1979.

[78] Murdick & Schuster, "Managing Human Resources in Project Management," Project Mgmt. Quarterly, 7, 21-25, 1976.

[79] Paolini & Glaser, "Project Selection Methods That Pick Winners," Res. Mgmt., 20, 26-29, May 1977.

[80] Park & Thuesen, "Combining the Concepts of Uncertainty Resolution and Project Balance for Capital Allocation Decisions," Eng. Econ., 24, 109-131, Winter 1979.

[81] Patterson & Roth, "Scheduling a Project Under Multiple Resource Constraints: A
      Zero-One Programming Approach," <u>AIIE Trans.</u>, 8, 449-455, Dec. 1976.

[82] Pekar & Burack, "New Directions for Management Control of Project Plans,"
      <u>Project Mgmt. Quarterly</u>, 7, 23-30, 1976.

[83] Phillips & Dessouky, "Solving the Project Time/Cost Tradeoff Problem Using the
      Minimal Cut Concept," <u>Mgmt. Sci.</u>, 24, 393-400, Dec. 1977.

[84] Plebani & Jain, "Evaluating Research Proposals with Group Techniques,"
      <u>Res. Mgmt.</u>, 24, 34-38, Nov. 1981.

[85] Pollock, "R&D Engineers Face Up to Earned Value," <u>Project Mgmt. Quarterly</u>, 8,
      43-45, 1977.

[86] Potts, "Project Manager: Technician or Administrator.", <u>J. Syst. Mgmt.</u>, 33,
      36-38, Jan. 1982.

[87] Reeves & Sweigart, "Multiperiod Resource Allocation with Variable Technology,"
      <u>Mgmt. Sci.</u>, 28, 1441-1449, Dec. 1982.

[88] Rhodes & Yungcheng, "Combining Cycle Determination with Forward Time
      Calculations in Determining Activity Networks," <u>AIIE Trans.</u>, 13, 206-211, Sept. 1981.

[89] Robbilard & Trahan, "Completion Time of PERT Networks," <u>Op. Res.</u>, 25, 15-29,
      Jan. 1977.

[90] Rubenstein & Schroeder,"Managerial Differences in Assessing Probabilities of
      Technical Success for R&D Projects," <u>Mgmt. Sci.</u>, 24, 137-148, Oct. 1977.

[91] Ruth, "Those Late Projects: New Approaches to an Old Problem," <u>Data Mgmt.</u>, 14,
      29-31, Sept. 1976; also in <u>Mgmt. Rev.</u>, 66, 48-51, Jan. 1977.

[92] Ryan, "Management Practice and Research - Poles Apart," <u>Bus. Horizons</u>, 20,
      23-29, June 1977.

[93] Schonberger, "Why Projects are Always Late: A Rationale Based on Simulation
      of a PERT/CPM Network," <u>Interfaces</u>, 11, 66-70, Oct. 1981.

[94] Schwartz & Vertinsky, "Multi-Attribute Decisions: A Study of R&D Project
      Selection," <u>Mgmt. Sci.</u>, 23, 285-291, Nov. 1977.

[95] Sears, "Conflict Management Strategies for Project Managers," <u>Project Mgmt.
      Quarterly</u>, 11, 10-12, 1980.

[96] Sharad, "About Delays, Overruns, and Corrective Action," <u>Project Mgmt. Quarterly</u>,
      7, 7-16, 1976.

[97] Sharon, "Decentralization of the Capital Budgeting Authority," <u>Mgmt. Sci.</u>, 25-34,
      Jan. 1979.

[98] Silverman, "Project Appraisal Methodology: A Multidimensional R&D Benefit/Cost
      Assessment Tool," <u>Mgmt. Sci</u>, 27, 802-821, July 1981.

[99] Slowinski, "Multiobjective Network Scheduling with Efficient Use of Renewable and
      Nonrenewable Resources," <u>Eur. J. Op. Res.</u>, 7, 265-273, July 1981.

[100] _____, "Two Approaches to Problems of Resource Allocation Among Project
       Activities - A Comparative Study," <u>J. Op. Res. Soc.</u>, 31, 711-723, 1980.

[101] Smeds, "Method for Checking the Consistency of Precedence Constraints," AIIE Trans., 12, 170–178, June 1980.

[102] Sotthewes & Lewis, "Project Urgency," Project Mgmt. Quarterly, 9, 12–14, 1978.

[103] Souder, "System for Using R&D Project Evaluation Methods," Res. Mgmt., 21, 29–37, Sept. 1978.

[104] Stinson, et al. "Multiple Resource-Constrained Scheduling Using Branch and Bound," AIIE Trans., 10, 252–259, Sept. 1978.

[105] Stuckenbruck, "Project Manager – The Systems Integrator," Project Mgmt. Quarterly, 9, 31–38, 1978.

[106] _____, "The Effective Project Manager," Project Mgmt. Quarterly, 7, 26–27, 1976.

[107] _____, "The Matrix Organization," Project Mgmt. Quarterly, 10, 21–33, 1979.

[108] Talbot, "Resource-Constrained Project Scheduling with Time/Cost Tradeoffs," Mgmt. Sci., 28, 1197–1210, Oct. 1982.

[109] Talbot & Patterson, "An Efficient Integer Programming Algorithm with Network Cuts for Solving Resource-Constrained Scheduling Problems," Mgmt. Sci., 24, 1163–1172, July 1978.

[110] _____, "Optimal Methods for Scheduling Projects Under Resource Constraints," Project Mgmt. Quarterly, 10, 26–33, 1979.

[111] Tang, et al. "Appraisal of Industrial Projects in a Developing Country – A Quantitative Approach," Omega, 8, No. 3, 388–392, 1980.

[112] Taylor & Davis, "Evaluating Time/Cost Factors of Implementation via GERT Simulation," Omega, 6, No. 3, 257–266, 1978.

[113] Taylor & Moore, "Project Management Using GERT Analysis," Project Mgmt. Quarterly, 9, 15–20, 1978.

[114] _____, "Project Planning with Q-GERT Network Modeling and Simulation," Mgmt. Sci., 26, 44–59, Jan. 1980.

[115] Taylor et al, "R&D Project Selection and Manpower Allocation with Integer Nonlinear Goal Programming," Mgmt. Sci., 28, 1149–1158, Oct. 1982.

[116] Teece, "Time-Cost Tradeoffs: Elasticity Estimates and Determinants for International Technology Transfer Projects," Mgmt. Sci., 23, 830–837, April 1977.

[117] Thamhain & Wilemon, "Leadership Effectiveness in Program Management," Project Mgmt. Quarterly, 8, 25–31, 1977.

[118] _____, "Leadership, Conflict, and Program Management Effectiveness," Sloan Mgmt. Rev., 19, 69–89, Fall 1977.

[119] Thesen, "Heuristic Project Scheduling, Project Mgmt. Quarterly, 9, 23–29, 1978.

[120] _____, "Heuristic Scheduling of Activities Under Resource and Precedence Restrictions," Mgmt. Sci., 23, 412–422, Dec. 1976.

[121]   Trypia, "Cost Minimization of m Simultaneous Projects that Require the
        Same Scarce Resource," Eur. J. Op. Res., 5, 235-238, 1980.

[122]   Tufekci, "A Flow Preserving Algorithm for the Time-Cost Tradeoff Problem,"
        AIIE Trans., 14, 109-113, June 1982.

[123]   Turf, "Cost/Schedule Performance Measurement Without Work Packages,"
        Project Mgmt. Quarterly, 10, 30-32, 1979.

[124]   Wall, "Ten Proverbs for Project Control," Res. Mgmt., 25, 26-29, Mar. 1982.

[125]   Ward et al. "Modeling the Flow of Projects Through an Architect's Office,"
        J. Op. Res. Soc., 29, 1147-1157, Dec. 1978.

[126]   Wedley & Ferrie, "Perceptual Differences and Effects of Managerial Participation
        on Project Implementation," J. Op. Res. Soc., 29, 199-204, March 1978.

[127]   Weglarz, "Project Scheduling with Continuously-Divisible Double Constrained
        Resources," Mgmt. Sci., 27, 1040-1053, Sept. 1981.

[128]   Wiest, "Precedence Diagramming Methods: Some Unusual Characteristics and
        Their Implications for Project Managers," J. Op. Mgmt., 1,121-130, 1981.

[129]   Willis, "A Note on the Generation of Project Network Diagrams," J. Op. Res. Soc.,
        32, 235-238, March 1981.

[130]   Willis & Hastings, "Project Scheduling with Resource Constraints Using Branch
        and Bound Methods," J. Op. Res. Soc., 27, No. 2, i, 341-349, 1976.

[131]   Wilson, "Implementation of Computer Simulation Projects in Health Care,"
        J. Op. Res. Soc., 32, 825-832, Sept. 1981.

[132]   Wolfe, et al "A GERT-Based Interactive Computer System for Analyzing Project Net-
        works Incorporating Improvement Curve Concepts," AIIE Trans., 12, 70-79, Mar. 1980.

[133]   Wolff, "When Projects Select You," Res. Mgmt., 26, 8-10, May 1983.

[134]   Youker, "Organization Alternatives for Project Management," Project Mgmt.
        Quarterly, 8, 18-24, 1977.

[135]   _____, "Organization Alternatives for Project Managers," Mgmt. Rev., 66,
        46-53, Nov. 1977.

[136]   Zinn et al, "A Probabilistic Approach to Risk Analysis in Capital Investment
        Projects," Eng. Econ., 22, 239-260, Summer 1977.

LIST OF REFEREES

The Editor is particularly grateful to the many individuals who acted as referees for the papers in this volume. In some cases, the referees were requested to (1) review several papers and (2) review papers in several stages of preparation and revision. The referees contributed significantly to the quality of the volume.

Thomas J. Allen

Sloan School of Management
Massachusetts Institute of Technology
Cambridge, Massachusetts 02139

Norman R. Baker

Department of Quantitative Analysis
School of Business Administration
University of Cincinnati
Cincinnati, Ohio 45221

R. Balachandra

Management Science Department
College of Business Administration
Northeastern University
Boston, Massachusetts 02115

H. U. Balthasar

Rheinhaldenstr / 105
CH 8200 Schaffhausen
Switzerland

Chiao-pin Bao

Department of Operations Research
Weatherhead School of Management
Case Western Reserve University
Cleveland, Ohio 44106

George S. Birrell

Department of Civil Engineering
School of Engineering
Case Institute of Technology
Cleveland, Ohio 44106

Alok Chakrabarti

Department of Management
Drexel University
Philadelphia, Pennsylvania 19104

Asok Chaudhuri

Chessie System Railroads
3800 Terminal Tower
Cleveland, Ohio 44113

Dale F. Cooper

Department of Accounting and Management
Economics
The University of Southhampton
Southhampton, England S09 5NH

Robert Cooper

Department of Marketing
Faculty of Business
McMaster University
Hamilton, Ontario, Canada L8S 4M4

Robert Culhan

Operations Research Department
McDermott, Inc.
Alliance, Ohio 44601

Edward W. Davis

Darden School of Business
University of Virginia
Charlottesville, Virginia 22906

Leslie Finkel

35265 Unit B
North Turtle Trail
Willoughby, Ohio 44094

Gregory W. Fischer

Department of Social Science
Carnegie-Mellon University
Pittsburgh, Pennsylvania 15213

William A. Fischer

School of Business Administration
University of North Carolina
Chapel Hill, North Carolina 27514

Ronald Fry

Department of Organizational Behavior
Weatherhead School of Management
Case Western Reserve University
Cleveland, Ohio 44106

Donald Gerwin

School of Business Administration
University of Wisconsin
Milwaukee, Wisconsin 53201

John Gilman

Amoco Research Center
P. O. Box 400
Naperville, Illinois 60566

Joel Goldhar

Stuart School of Business Administration
Illinois Institute of Technology
Chicago, Illinois 60616

John J. Graham

(Retired) Manager, Engineering Division
SOHIO
Midland Building
Cleveland, Ohio 44115

Sushil K. Gupta

Department of Decision Sciences
College of Business Administration
Florida International University
Miami, Florida 33199

Richard Kamien

College of Business Administration
Marquette University
Milwaukee, Wisconsin 53233

William R. King

Graduate School of Business
University of Pittsburgh
Pittsburgh, Pennsylvania 15260

Dundar F. Kocaoglu

Department of Industrial Engineering, Engineer-
ing Management and Operations Research
School of Engineering
University of Pittsburgh
Pittsburgh, Pennsylvania 15261

N. K. Kwak

Department of Management Science
School of Business and Administration
St. Louis University
St. Louis, Missouri 63108

Geoff Lockett

Manchester Business School
University of Manchester
Manchester, England M15 6PB

Gregory R. Madey

Goodyear Aerospace Corporation
Akron, Ohio 44315

Samuel J. Mantel

College of Business Administration
University of Cincinnati
Cincinnati, Ohio 45221

George M. Marko

Gilbane Building Company
2000 East Ninth Street
Cleveland, Ohio 44114

Joseph J. Moder

Department of Industrial Engineering and
 Systems Analysis
School of Engineering
University of Miami
Coral Gables, Florida 33124

Lawrence Moore

Department of Management Science
Virginia Polytechnic Institute and State
 University
Blacksburg, Virginia 24061

David C. Murphy

School of Management
Boston College
Chestnut Hill, Massachusetts 02167

Kenneth Musselman

Pritsker & Associates
P. O. Box 2413
West Lafayette, Indiana 47906

Thomas Naylor

Department of Economics
Duke University
Durham, North Carolina 27706

John Papageorgiou

College of Management
University of Massachusetts
Boston, Massachusetts 02125

Donald Pelz

Center for Research on Utilization of
 Scientific Knowledge
Institute for Social Research
University of Michigan
Ann Arbor, Michigan 48106

Alan Pritsker

Pritsker & Associates
P. O. Box 2413
West Lafayette, Indiana 47906

318

Bernard C. Reimann

Department of Management and Labor
College of Business Administration
Cleveland State University
Cleveland, Ohio 44115

Albert Rubenstein

Department of Industrial Engineering and
 Management Science
The Technology Institute
Northwestern University
Evanston, Illinois 60201

Thomas L. Saaty

Graduate School of Business
University of Pittsburgh
Pittsburgh, Pennsylvania 15261

Barry G. Silverman

Department of Engineering Administration
School of Engineering and Applied Science
George Washington University
Washington, D. C. 20052

William E. Souder

Department of Industrial Engineering
School of Engineering
University of Pittsburgh
Pittsburgh, Pennsylvania 15261

Arne Thesen

Department of Industrial Engineering
University of Wisconsin-Madison
Madison, Wisconsin 53706

Michael Tushman

Graduate School of Business
Columbia University
New York, New York 10027

Gary D. Whitehouse

Department of Industrial Engineering and
 Management Systems
University of Central Florida
Orlando, Florida 32816

Jerome D. Wiest

Department of Management
Graduate School of Business
University of Utah
Salt Lake City, Utah 84112

Stelios Zanakis

Department of Decision Sciences
College of Business Administration
Florida International University
Miami, Florida 33199